SPEAKING MEMORY

THE CULTURE OF CITIES
SERIES EDITORS: KIERAN BONNER AND WILL STRAW

Cities have long been a key focus of innovative work in the humanities and social sciences. In recent years, the city has assumed new importance for scholars working on cultural issues across a wide range of disciplines. Sociologists, anthropologists, media specialists, and scholars of literature, art, and cinema have come to emphasize the distinctly urban character of many of their objects of study. Those who study processes of globalization are drawn to analyzing cities as the places in which these processes are most deeply felt or where they are most strongly resisted.

The Culture of Cities series has its roots in an international research project of the same name, funded by the Social Sciences and Humanities Research Council of Canada during the period 2000–05. The series includes books based in the work of that project as well as other volumes that reflect the project's spirit of interdisciplinary inquiry. Case studies, comparative analyses, and theoretical accounts of city life offer tools and insights for understanding urban cultures as they confront the forces acting upon them in the contemporary world.

The Culture of Cities series is aimed at scholars and interested readers from a wide variety of backgrounds.

The Imaginative Structure of the City
Alan Blum

Urban Enigmas
Montreal, Toronto, and the Problem of Comparing Cities
Edited by Johanne Sloan

Circulation and the City
Essays on Urban Culture
Edited by Alexandra Boutros and Will Straw

Cartographies of Place
Navigating the Urban
Edited by Michael Darroch and Janine Marchessault

Speaking Memory
How Translation Shapes City Life
Edited by Sherry Simon

Speaking Memory

How Translation Shapes City Life

EDITED BY

Sherry Simon

McGill-Queen's University Press
Montreal & Kingston • London • Chicago

ISBN 978-0-7735-4788-9 (cloth)
ISBN 978-0-7735-4789-6 (paper)
ISBN 978-0-7735-4859-6 (ePDF)
ISBN 978-0-7735-4860-2 (ePUB)

Legal deposit fourth quarter 2016
Bibliothèque nationale du Québec

Printed in Canada on acid-free paper that is 100% ancient forest free (100% post-consumer recycled), processed chlorine free.

This book has been published with the help of a grant from the Canadian Federation for the Humanities and Social Sciences, through the Awards to Scholarly Publications Program, using funds provided by the Social Sciences and Humanities Research Council of Canada.

McGill-Queen's University Press acknowledges the support of the Canada Council for the Arts for our publishing program. We also acknowledge the financial support of the Government of Canada through the Canada Book Fund for our publishing activities.

Library and Archives Canada Cataloguing in Publication

Speaking memory : how translation shapes city life / edited by Sherry Simon.

(Culture of cities)
All the translated articles included in this volume were originally written in French.
Includes bibliographical references and index.
Issued also in electronic format.
ISBN 978-0-7735-4788-9 (cloth). – ISBN 978-0-7735-4789-6 (paper). – ISBN 978-0-7735-4859-6 (ePDF). – ISBN 978-0-7735-4860-2 (ePUB)

1. Urban dialects. 2. Languages in contact. 3. Translating and interpreting. 4. Cities and towns. 5. Sociolinguistics. I. Simon, Sherry, 1948–, author, editor II. Series: Culture of cities

P40.5.U73S64 2016 306.4409173'2 C2016-905448-9
C2016-905449-7

This book was typeset by True to Type in 10.5/13 Sabon

Contents

Acknowledgments

I would like to express my appreciation to Carmen Ruschiensky for her invaluable contribution to this volume; her dedication and enthusiasm greatly added to the pleasure of preparing this book. I am grateful to the Social Sciences and Humanities Research Council of Canada (Connections Program) and to the Office of the Vice-President, Research and Graduate Studies at Concordia University for the grants that allowed Concordia to host Cities in Translation, the stimulating international workshop at the origin of this volume. Thanks to Frances Pope for good-humoured editorial help. As always, it was an immense pleasure to work with Jonathan Crago and the staff at McGill-Queen's University Press.

Note: All the translated articles included in this volume were originally written in French.

SPEAKING MEMORY

Introduction

SHERRY SIMON

"One is always at home in one's past."

Vladimir Nabokov, *Speak, Memory*

Street photographs from the Central European city of Czernowitz in the early 1930s show men and women, alone or in groups, striding confidently down the main street. What language are they speaking as they move past the linguistic hodgepodge of store signs, shop names, placards, and advertising billboards – German, Romanian, Ukrainian, or Yiddish? (Hirsch and Spitzer 2010). Czernowitz was renowned for its exuberant mixture of languages, a polylingualism more pronounced even than that of neighbouring Habsburg cities. Tourist brochures made much of the multiplicity of languages, as did Yitzchak Peretz in his introduction to the celebrated conference on the future of the Yiddish language held in the city in 1908: "We stroll in the evening streets, and from different windows the tones of different languages waft out, all different kinds of folk music" (Weinrich in Olson 2010, 32).

But the passage of the city from Habsburg to Romanian rule, and then to a new Ukrainian identity after World War II, saw language choices gradually constricted. The Habsburg city of Czernowitz was replaced by the Romanian city of Cernăuţi, then after World War II by the Ukrainian city of Chernivtsi. Although the built environment of the city remained largely the same, the meaning and function of its urban spaces were transformed. The links that identified street names and street patterns as replicas of Viennese originals were severed. The main street once called the Herrengasse became the Strada Iancu

Flondor during the Romanian regime, and after World War II was renamed for the Ukrainian writer Olha Kobylianska. Statues were replaced (Schiller by Kobylianska) and buildings repurposed (synagogue into movie theatre). But the fact that returning visitors continue to refer to the city's street names in German underlines the fact that the city for them remains a mental construct, experienced and interpreted through the language of memory.

One city with three names? Three different versions of a city? Each Czernowitz is a variation on a theme: the multicultural Habsburg city, then the interwar Romanian city (the birthplace of Paul Celan and Aharon Appelfeld, and the literary milieu of Rose Ausländer), and finally the postwar Ukrainian Chernivtsi. Advancing through states of translation, the city is a movie with an ever-changing soundtrack. Each of its successive languages literally speaks memory.

Czernowitz is one version of the translational city that will be considered in the following pages. This is the city where translation takes the form of the sudden and forced suppression of languages and the imposition of others. Such transformations were frequent in Central European cities in the twentieth century, as a result of the territorial shifts of both world wars. Vilna-Wilno-Vilnius; Czernowitz-Cernăuţi-Chernivtsi; Lemberg-Lviv; Pressburg-Pozsony-Presporak-Bratislava; Danzig-Gdansk: these cities' successive names reflect the power of language to sponge out and remake the past. Fresh scripts declare a new version of the city. Writing as Prague underwent its transformation from German Habsburg to Czech city, the Bohemian historian Julius Lippert imagines the "old stones" ironically crying out: "Pilgrim, think of it: I am a Czech stone! Don't try to translate me!," knowing all the while that their "true" language is German. He clings to his version of the city, the memory of Prague before it was declared Czech (see Colombi, this volume, 64). Perhaps cities that have experienced language remakes are condemned to a perpetual state of dissonance, their surfaces forever troubled by spectral layers of memory.

The takeovers of regime change are one spectacular and highly visible way in which cities experience disputes over language as memory. But the interactions of competing languages are a feature of all urban life. The contributors to this volume argue that all cities, past and present, can be understood as fields of translational forces. In every city, the idioms of successive waves of migrants, traders, and governments enter into a conversation that is a continual reinvention of memory. In every city, connections across language communities write and rewrite history. From the nineteenth-century multilingual city to today's metropolis, language fractures and connections shape urban territory. Differing forms of transfer transform the ways in which the "foreign" and the "native" are defined, while creators devise cross-language "leaps" that cause deviations in language traffic. This volume makes these transactions more audible, foregrounding the translational nature of urban life.

The translational city, as the contributors to this volume describe it, is a space of heightened language awareness where exchange is accelerated or blocked, facilitated or forced, questioned and critiqued. The translational city is of course a multilingual city, but one viewed from the perspective of the movement and texture in urban language life. Multilingualism points to pure diversity, the number of languages spoken, but translation speaks to the relations of tension, interaction, rivalry, or convergence, among them as well as the particular spaces they occupy in the city. Translation tracks connections among variously entitled communities – those that have historic claims to the city's territory, as well as those that seek to establish claims as migrants, refugees, or exiles.

The interplay of languages within the city contributes to its distinctive feel, its particular sensibility, the ways in which knowledge in and of it is shaped. This may seem like a truism, but the abundant literature devoted to the city over the last decades, the many works of urban and cultural studies beginning with Walter Benjamin and extending through Richard Sennett, Edward Soja, Allan Blum, and many others, has largely neglected this linguistic and aural aspect in favour of the visual. The city has been seen, but not heard. Yet languages are not only part of the experiential feel of the city, they in turn become modes of representation of the city – poems and novels, essays and letters, paintings, engravings, photos, films, the biographies of people connected to the city. These texts contribute to the aura and mythology of the city, shaping and preserving it in the cultural memory.

To read a city in one language is to know one version of its text, one ensemble of materials. But for most cities, there are multiple and competing city texts, written either in the submerged languages of the past or in the rival languages of the present. And so those who live side by side may experience separate, even contradictory, versions of the urban imaginary. How is it different to read New York in English or Spanish? New Orleans in French or English? Johannesburg in English, Afrikaans, or Xhosa? Manila in Spanish or Tagalog? Barcelona in Castilian or Catalan? Montreal in French or English? Czernowitz in German, Yiddish, Romanian, or Ukrainian? Thessaloniki in Greek or Turkish? Each of these questions brings into being a different constellation of linguistic forces, shaped by moments of violence and conquest, patterns of immigration, diasporic networks, political jurisdictions, and emergent or declining cultural loyalties. These configurations put into play translational responses, and so bring these texts into dialogue and allow them to enter into new frames of interpretation. In cities where the major, tutelary language of the city is disputed, where more than one community lays claim to its territory, these language relationships occupy centre stage. The city becomes a crossroads of codes, a place of double entendres, where collective language insecurities nourish a culture of doubt, where memories meet at odd angles. This makes the space of the linguistically contested city a particularly modern space, where there is a heightened awareness of the plurality of meaning systems, of the testing of the limits of expression, where dissonance is understood as a productive force. Translation and translators play an especially important role as they move through the spaces of the city – a role that extends into the historiography of multilingual cities. Scholarly traditions that are restricted to one language can only provide very partial understandings of the city memory of, say, colonial Calcutta (Chattopadhyay) or Bratislava (van Duin). The border or translational city imposes on the scholar who studies it an obligation of translation.[1] In turn, polyglot readings cut across national narratives and provide a key for reconstructing local identities.

The contributors to this volume draw a variegated portrait of the translational city, historical and contemporary. Emblematic importance is given to the memory fractures of the Central European and the Habsburg city – cities that have experienced the trauma of passage from imperial to national urban centre. But the shaping power of language in relation to memory is foregrounded in each chapter. In today's global city, the migrant, the refugee, and the exile are recognized as figures who put pressure on the idea of translation as free circulation and flow across national borders and neighbourhoods. Communications technologies are crucial in shaping the translational activity in today's city, and these are examined in these pages, as well as the creative practices that take place at the intersection of languages. Architecture and planning, the creation of monuments, urban art, personal narratives – all these interventions identify the city as a place where memories are mapped, erased, layered, rearranged. Choosing what to remember is always a conflictual process, and particularly in cities with histories of internal strife – like Montreal, Belfast, Nicosia, Jerusalem, or Cape Town – heritage sites promote particular interpretations of the past. Acts of translation are a crucial part of this struggle.

While translation is the central theme of this volume, the contributors give it different interpretations and indeed different valuations. These challenges to the meaning and import of the term are an important part of this book. Translation has come to us through the humanist tradition as a "friendly" word, a process implying good will and harmonious outcomes. Yet as translation studies scholars have emphasized over the last years, translation rarely takes place among equal partners: the power and prestige of strong languages mean that cultural transfers are not chosen but imposed. What is more, translation is an activity integral to conflict and conquest – whether it be the work of interpreters in wartime, of missionaries in evangelical campaigns, or of migrants forced to self-translate. Translation is not only *implicated* in conditions of conflict – its very motivation and effects can be negative, that is, carried out in the service of inequality, disturbing ideologies, and violence. The wide-ranging effects of translation therefore include the negative outcomes of erasure and suppression.

As many contributors to this volume make clear (and as the story of Czernowitz corroborates), translation is driven by political forces – whether national conflicts or the violence and inequality intrinsic to global migration practices. Translation is a process organized and policed by technologies of communication and by differential rights – whether from the point of view of those who participate in language mediations, the communications technologies that shape them, or the political forces that use language as a medium of self-representation.

In this sense, some of the contributors express scepticism regarding successful translation in urban life – preferring to underline the more potent and active forces of nontranslation or the limitations of translation when it has purely symbolic functions. The idea of "presencing" as introduced by Michael Cronin complexifies our understanding of the varied physical and virtual ways through which languages today occupy urban space. Migrant experience in the city is increasingly dematerialized as it takes on more mobile, shifting, and improvised forms. Translation, however, is paradoxically more entrenched, though its outcomes are not those of a permanent bond. The contributors also underline the active role of translation in creating and reinforcing borders, as well as in unmaking them. As Sandro Mezzadra and Naoki Sakai (2014, 9) emphasize (and as Homi Bhabha notes through the idea of "the staging of difference," see Pizzi, this volume, 48), the notion of the border should be considered less an established fact than "a poietic act," an act of creation. The aligning of translation with the idea of bordering, of the active nature of language shifts and reconnections, is at the heart of the reflections here – which see the translational city as one that continuously seeks to create alliances across memories. Stretched beyond its usual confines, translation offers a fresh view of the interpretive practices that permeate urban experience.

LANGUAGE-SCAPES

It is surely more than a coincidence that Mikhail Bakhtin, the greatest philosopher of polyglossia, spent a good part of his childhood in the city of Vilno, today's Vilnius. As Liamis Briedis reminds us, "Bakhtin saw in polyglossia – the simultaneous presence of two or more linguistic terrains within a single narrative – an opportunity of entering a familiar landscape 'with another's eyes, from the point of view of a potentially different language,' and in the process unleashing the Galilean potentials of the place" (Bakhtin quoted in Briedis, this volume, 26). Years later another famous son of Vilnius, the poet and Nobel prize winner Czeslaw Miłosz (1992, 27), expressed a similar appreciation for the potential of languages to enhance the city when he wrote of the uneven, unfolding linguistic and ideological terrain surrounding Wilno making the city "eccentric," a homeland of "crazily commingled strata that overlapped each other, like Trieste or Czernowitz."

Each city shapes its own patterns of circulation and its translational dynamics, but as Miłosz emphasizes, certain cities of the Habsburg Empire and of Central Europe form a category of their own – with their "crazily commingled strata" of languages, their robust multilingualism. The contributors to the first part of the volume speak to this distinctiveness, addressing translation issues in Vilnius, Trieste, Prague, and Joseph Roth's Brody. In much of Central Europe the German language exercised cultural influence for several centuries and, especially in the Habsburg lands, acted as the undisputed idiom of cultural authority (Cornis-Pope and Neubauer 2002b, 29). The long era of German dominance came to an end following the defeat of Nazism. The perversions that Nazism inflicted on German culture and the scars it left behind should not, as Claudio Magris (1990) reminds us, entirely eliminate memory of the "great chapter in history" that the German presence brought about. "Its eclipse is a great tragedy, which Nazism cannot make us forget" (32). And for Cornis-Pope and Neubauer (2002b, 9), "A genuinely German transnational culture went up in smoke at Auschwitz. But it was alive from the Baltic Sea to the Danube delta, with centres in Prague, Lemberg, Budapest, Czernowitz, Vilnius, and elsewhere. That culture, epitomized for us by the names of Franz Kafka and Franz Werfel, Paul Celan and Rosa Ausländer, Elias Canetti, Joseph Roth and Karl Franzos, Sholem Aleichem, Rainer Maria Rilke, and Robert Musil, also included hundreds of newspapers, journals, theatres, and cultural societies. German, and especially German-Jewish, culture acted as a glue, an integrating force, among the various ethnic groups." The "nodal cities" of Central Europe participated in competing logics of translation related to their identity as "literary interfaces," the site of hybrid literary identity and cultural production. These "relays of literary modernization and pluralization" (Cornis-Pope and Neubauer 2006b, 9), whether provincial cities like Czernowitz and Bratislava or metropolitan centres like Prague or Budapest, participate in a plurality of language traditions and histories. In some ways prefiguring the multifaceted and decentred Western city of immigration, East-Central European literary representations offer "paradigms of plural societies that give insights into crucial questions of our time – questions concerning the preconditions for the fruitful interaction of peoples from different ethnic, religious, linguistic and cultural backgrounds as well as questions concerning the causes of violence and war in communities that had enjoyed peace for centuries" (11).[2]

It is not only the specific language combinations but also the separate histories of each city that account for their distinct translational dynamics. Vilnius was part of the Russian empire but long claimed by the Poles, and though inhabited by very few Lithuanians before World War II, became in 1945 a Lithuanian city. Trieste was for 400 years a city of Italian culture under Vienna's authority until Italy "redeemed" it in 1918. Prague was a majority German city until after 1850, when it became increasingly Czech. Brody was a small city within ten kilometres of the Russian border, with in 1910 a largely

Jewish and Yiddish-speaking population. In each case, political upheavals were accompanied by new language rearrangements and new landscapes of memory.

In chapter 1, Laimonas Briedis's distinction between horizontal and vertical translation is an evocative entry point into the troubled history of Vilnius. Along the horizontal axis, translation deploys an infinite series of Babelian narratives, an ever-receding horizon, challenging any single view of the city. Along the vertical axis, translation opens a descent into the violence of the separate, conflicting memories of the city's past. In Vilnius, names stand for languages and disputed memories, and translation is the story of one memory overtaken by another. Briedis's meditation on Vilnius tells the story of a Polish city, but also the capital of Yiddish-language modernism, translated by force into a Soviet city. This is a city of too many monuments, as memory is stuffed into the Procrustean bed of ideologies. Cemeteries are not final resting places but territory that can be framed within new parameters or covered over; the Soviet-Lithuanian victors postwar moved to eliminate traces of the "foreign" bodies that marked the city, flattening the original and ancient Jewish cemetery to make space for an Olympic-size swimming pool but maintaining the burial site of the Polish hero Piłsudski as a pilgrimage site. The actions of the Soviet government echoed in sinister ways the nefarious deeds of the Nazis toward their Jewish victims, whose bones were crushed to powder and dispersed. The struggle over spatial remains is also a struggle over vocabularies of memory.

In chapter 2, Katia Pizzi on Trieste responds to Briedis's Vilnius as a similarly fragmented city of disjunctions and contradictions. Pizzi focuses on the clash of competing modernisms, the parallel and mutually indifferent movements of cultural renewal that took place in Trieste and in its "affiliate" cultural spaces – Florence and Ljubljana. The story she tells is slightly different from that usually associated with the nineteenth century polyglot commercial emporium and port city of Trieste, habitually centred around its cultural icons – Italo Svevo, Umberto Saba, and James Joyce. Rather, Pizzi looks to the internationalization of modernism as it was envisaged by Scipio Slataper and the Stuparich brothers on the one hand and the Slovenian constructivist poet Srečko Kosovel on the other. Pizzi stresses the cosmopolitanism of Slataper and Giani Stuparich, both having looked outside of their own spheres, and notably to the Slav world, for cultural affiliations. But the Italian modernists do not see their allies "on the ground," as the Italian cultural world is drawn into ("hijacked by") the Fascism of postwar Italy and Kosovel in Ljubljana turns toward the influence of Russian constructivism. Though they emerged from the same multicultural crucible, these modernisms looked for different sorts of allies. Trieste's cultural configuration seems to provide the template of a "periphery where fissures, tensions and dissonances become particularly productive" (Pizzi, this volume, 46). This is not a harmonious but a vexed and entangled process of translation, where the doubly minoritized cultures fail to connect. By introducing the contrasting notions of Bhabha's staging of difference and Gramsci's *traducibilità* – in relation to the conditions following World War I but also today – Pizzi shows how the transnational aesthetics of the Stuparich brothers and of Slataper may have demonstrated their openness to the world but implicitly revealed their resistance to the Slavic difference next door. What connections would have been possible at the time? Was such translation unthinkable? To what extent were the writers aware of the alliance between ideology and their aesthetic strategies?

In chapter 3, Matteo Colombi on Prague presents in stark outlines the questions at the heart of this volume: How do the successive language memories of the city interact and through what media do they find expression? How do contradictory yet coexistent memories converse one with the other? During a period of some forty years, from 1880 to 1920, Prague was understood as German, or as Czech, or as German-Czech-Jewish. These separate narratives are generated not only through the historiography but also, as Colombi shows, through a variety of sources that name, caption, and contextualize the city – historical lore, postcards, travel guides, sporting events, novels, and the interpretations of individuals as they negotiate these narratives. Concentrating on the interwar period, one that saw a gradual transition to Czech hegemony, Colombi reminds us that, unlike other cities (Trieste, for instance), the German-speaking populations did not leave Prague en masse after World War I. As the imperial city was transformed into a national one, the three-city model persisted as an alternate version of the city – not a variation on the first two, but qualitatively different.

Sherry Simon concludes this subsection on the Habsburg city with chapter 4, focusing on the figure of the "edge of empire" as imagined by the novelist Joseph Roth. The border city takes on enhanced significance during the period leading up to and following the fall of the Romanov, Ottoman, and Habsburg empires at the end of World War I. This moment of fascination for the border city is of particular interest in the context of today's concern for the changing realities of borders – political, economic, and linguistic. Roth was an astute political observer and a renowned journalist – his novelist's eye is shaped by his prescient understanding of the upheavals to come. The border city, whose prototype is Roth's home city of Brody, is a place of both enchantment and danger, as shown especially in his novels *The Radetzky March* and *Weights and Measures*. Across the globe, Constantine Cavafy shared Roth's sensibility, revelling in polyglot and translational cities at the edge of his empire. Both Cavafy and Roth are alert to the geographical and cultural reach of their own tongues in conversation with the empire's outsiders.

COMMUNICATIONAL SPACES

The space of cities now ineluctably includes the space of the virtual, and as Cronin demonstrates in chapter 5, this hybrid communicational space has wide-ranging social consequences. In particular, the distinction between the foreign and the native has exploded in the face of the dramatic changes that affect the experience of migration in today's cities. Migration no longer implies the radical abandonment of one place for another, or of one language for another, and by the same token migrants and immigrants are no longer "translated" once and for all. In the place of this former model of transplantation, Cronin introduces the idea of presencing – that is, the varied forms of physical and immaterial ways in which migrants occupy space – i.e., "forms of presence that do not involve actual spatial or corporeal displacement but that bring someone or something into the field of attention of others at another point in space and/or time" and that introduce intermediate terms into the dichotomy home/away. Rather than being translated, migrants are translating, and participate in a processual form of being. How do these changes influence the city itself? Forms of translation have become dematerialized, as have the ethnic enclaves that were once the visible manifestation of migrant communities. In the digital age there is a new kind of linguistic trans-architecture where webs of virtual language connectivity envelop the physical spaces of the metropolis. The demands of disruptive and flexibilized labour markets have also created categories of repeat-migrants, who are obliged to follow the demands of volatile demands for employment.

While Cronin explores translation through the figure of the migrant, in chapter 6 Simon Harel chooses the perspective of the refugee – the traveller who has no status, who is an intruder, who is reduced to the role of formulating requests. The refugee's words are caught up in a circuit of international generosity but are not necessarily heard unless translated into the terms the host society requires. Here translation is not a connective process but a constraining one – one that must cross the *différend* of language in order to attain the desperately desired goal. Harel chooses the refugee as emblematic of the aporia of translation in the city, where the subaltern is an obstacle to fluent communication. The city as portrayed in Dave Eggers's *What Is the What* and in Rawi Hage's *Cockroach* is not the "festive" milieu of harmonious communication, but marked by radical inequality and violence. To translate effectively means to go beyond a repetition of the original "monolingual" language, the reductive confines of the mother tongue, to confront the incommensurate. What is translation when it is practiced in unfavourable conditions, not the comfortable universes of high-end nomadism and hybridity? Harel critiques conceptions of the city and of translation that are too easily shown to be convivial or reconciliatory. In both novels, the problem of translation is not necessarily resolved. In Eggers's account, the problem of translation has to do with the occlusion of the foreignness of the refugee's voice. The author becomes the "custodian" of the refugee's tale. In Hage's, it has to do with the power differential between the psychotherapist and the migrant. Successful translation must be a form of recognition – and not simply a reflection of an idealized image of the city as a factitious whole.

In dialogue with Cronin and Harel, Alexis Nouss in chapter 7 makes a connection between the city, patterns of integration, and patterns of communication. Nouss distinguishes between the city of exile, which exercises the appeal of assimilation, and the exilic city, where more actively ambivalent patterns may flourish. These distinctions are not labels to be applied to particular cities, but rather forces active in all cities – sometimes dominant, sometimes minor. In the city of exile, translation is an apparatus of authority and the perpetuation of order, and language flows only into the dominant language; in the exilic city, it plays a more disruptive and transformative role, and there is a dynamic of juxtaposition, of multiplicity, that disrupts the order of the city. These reflections tie into a historical and mythical link between the city and exile – the site founded by the exile Cain (Gen. 4, 17), or Rome founded by Remus and Romulus. The Hellenistic tradition also provides rich examples in the story of Cadmus founding the city of Thebes. Exile's relation to the city is one of contradiction and overlay, "like using a map of London to orient oneself in Paris," or like Joseph Brodsky seeing Saint Petersburg in the canals of Venice, or, on a broader scale, seeing the duplication of city names across continents – like Paris, Texas. Opposing Bourdieu's idea of "habitus" as simply reproducing ideas of monolithic identities, Nouss argues that the city allows for the creation of hybrid subjectivities. For Nouss, the force of translation resides, as for Cronin and Harel, in generating complex, problematic modes of communication – not translation once and for all, in the sense of "the foreigner adopting a dominant language," but a processual interaction with and among languages.

Communication technologies are the concern of the final chapters in this section – on the one hand the material technologies of print and broadcasting, which militate against language boundary crossings in the multilingual city, and on the other hand the reality anticipated by the media theories of Marshall McLuhan and Vilém Flusser in which translation plays a strong role.

In chapter 8, Will Straw introduces communications technologies as an obstacle to free language flows across the city – from the point of view of print and broadcasting. He shows how, in conventional media, the flow of language through social space is stopped. Far from reflecting the language practices of a city like Montreal, media "freezes" languages into place, creating artificial barriers that are maintained for political reasons. Practices of obligatory bilingualism are most often restricted to minor cultural forms and are absent at the centre of cultural life. Bilingual practices are to be found rather in the listening or reading habits of consumers, who cross linguistic barriers in search of preferred materials. In analyzing the discussions that led to the elimination of the one bilingual radio station in Montreal in the 1970s, Straw challenges the force of monolingual thinking in media – and shows the collusion between nationalistic conceptions of language exclusivity and media policy. His discussion is rooted in a rich debate about the fundamental nature of social relations in the city. Does the city encourage separations or encounters? These contradictory conceptions continue to characterize understanding of Montreal's language relations. In paying attention to everyday language uses, listening practices, and variations across age and institutions, Straw opens a relatively unexplored field of investigation: the connections between freely chosen individual language trajectories in the city and the enforced itineraries of communicational technologies.

In chapter 9, Michael Darroch introduces translation as a key element in the theories of communication of two key thinkers of our age, both of whom anticipated today's virtual reality and made translation an important element of their conception of this world (which neither lived to see). What did "translation" mean for McLuhan in theorizing the global village, and how does Flusser respond to these in his media theory? While McLuhan's notion of the global village is distinct from Flusser's concept of a posthistorical telematic society, each invokes understandings of translation – between languages, senses, codes, and media forms – as a metaphor for processes of communication deeply connected to urban life. Darroch's focus is on the multilingual Flusser, born in Europe and later living in Brazil, who sees cities as characterized by displacement, groundlessness, loss, migration, and unsettlement. His is a city of communicational structures, a network of information flows and patterns of intercultural communication. Flusser gradually expands the concept of translation beyond linguistic parameters to embrace notions of transference across media such as photography, film, and computing, and using metaphors of "bridges" and "leaps." While bridges offer the possibility of synthesis, ultimately only leaps from one situation or condition to another can guarantee that transference is achieved. This notion of the leap connects well with the idea of successful translation discussed elsewhere in this volume, not "simply" a contact but an intervention. The idea that translation, as mediation, always creates "noise" that accumulates as new information in the system is one that "translates" well into the language of contemporary translation theory – that insists on the effectiveness of the links created through mediation. Interestingly, Flusser developed his theories in his home city of São Paulo, a city that Roch Duval reveals to be intensely translational.

FLOWS, MIXTURES, CROSSINGS

The translational city is a privileged site of modernist literary practices. New Orleans, Montevideo, São Paolo, and Montreal are here explored for their potential to generate distinctive literary and aesthetic sensibilities. The conjunction of languages echoes the confrontations of value systems, showing received truth to be in dialogue with other possible truths. In chapter 10, Bill Marshall introduces the cities of the French Atlantic, a cluster of sites defined by the presence of the French language in dialogue with other colonial and indigenous languages, as well as a permanent relationship to metropolitan language authority. Invoking two of these cities, New Orleans and Montevideo, he traces out two different itineraries of translation – the first relating to the French heritage of New Orleans in translation, the second relating to the polyglot and translational origins of *Le chant de Maldoror* in Montevideo. Marshall challenges the idea of New Orleans as a city in translation, pointing rather to the repeated scenes of non-translation that maintained neglect of the French creole literary legacy – with the exception of rare individual acts of rediscovery of literary texts, those of George Washington Cable in the 1890s and of Langston Hughes in the 1970s. He sees New Orleans as a dual city, with distanced rather than bridged communities. Only in the 1990s did New Orleans begin to overcome these gaps and re-evaluate its past. The French connection in Montevideo is explored through Marshall's discussion of Isidore Ducasse, comte de Lautréamont, celebrated author of *Le chant de Maldoror* – identifying Ducasse as a translator of himself. Marshall returns to the Babel of Montevideo in the 1840s and 1850s and the many language influences Ducasse experienced. Dialoguing with previous criticism of *Le chant de Maldoror*, in particular with Julia Kristeva, Marshall shows how Ducasse's "contrary and simultaneous languages, dualizations and splittings" permitted "the juxtaposition of heterogeneities, and a concomitant defamiliarization of language and its relation to the real." The recontextualization of Ducasse's masterpiece in nineteenth-century Montevideo allows fresh understanding of this modernist work, as well as an appreciation of the generative powers of multilingual milieus.

In chapter 11, Duval traces out a similar appreciation of the modernist aesthetic. Writing on São Paulo, he describes two ways in which the major Brazilian writer Antônio de Alcântara Machado was a translator of his city – by developing a written urban language that corresponded to the rhythm of cinema, and by transcribing and making literary the mixed language of the Italians in São Paulo, once called *a cidade dos italianos*. *Brás, Bexiga e Barra Funda*, Machado's major work, is a visual and aural/oral description – acting as symbolic translation – of the continual interplay between Luso-Portuguese and Brazilian, as well as an endeavour to translate São Paulo in the sense of the broad modernist tradition of translating the rhythms and speed of the city: a writerly practice whose most eminent practitioner is perhaps the American John Dos Passos. Essentially, Machado attempted to capture the minutiae of daily life in 1920s São Paulo. The dialogue featured in his urban chronicles was mostly written in a literary style known as macaronic (i.e., Brazilian oral language interspersed with Italian words or grammar), which is characteristic of the ways Italian immigrants tried to speak Brazilian. This mixed language allowed Machado to break free from rigid European literary models. For Machado, the writer translates in order to create two expressions of the modernist impulse: the jerky, mobile, hectic phrases of the city understood as sequences of a movie, but also the actual code of the language, which is a mixture of Italian and Brazilian, not dismissed as an aberration but held up as a model of a new kind of hybrid urban speech.

The jazz-like works of modernist writers in the 1920s city could be compared to the interventions of activist urban artists today. Both use the devices of their craft to destabilize modes of representation, to highlight the disjunctions and "interstices" of urban life. In their collaborative chapter 12, Myriam Suchet and Sarah Mekdjian introduce practices of "artivism" (art and activism) as a way to challenge received ideas about the city and to show how meaning is created. Forms of artivism in the urban environment use translation, even as they challenge its meaning. In a style that foregrounds their very processes of research, highlighting the advantages of strategic, perhaps temporary alliances among disciplines, Suchet and Mekdjian test vocabularies one against the other, in a way performing the act of translation to create new modes of speech that undermine the limits of naturalized language. The interval, the "battements," are defined as disruptive events in space. Here there is an explicit displacement in the meaning of translation itself – introduced not for its potential to effect the transfer of ideas from one space to another, but rather to expose the spaces between languages, to expose the fictitious borders of language as such. The interval created by urban artivist translation becomes, in both its temporal and spatial dimensions, a disruptive event. By combining the sociological, urbanistic idea of the interstice with the stylistic, enunciative notion of the figural, Suchet and Mekdjian redefine translation as an interruption of discursive practices. It becomes a mode of critical thinking, with the goal of identifying urban practices that empower citizens to question their environment. Among the activities generated by this "translation hypothesis" is a project of city mapping described by Mekdjian, which attempts to account for the experience and angle of vision of the refugee. This portion of the chapter joins with Harel's reflections on the untranslatability of the refugee in the city. Map-making is a process that reflects the precarious status of the refugee in the city. "Counter-mapping" is a way to connect the experience of refugees with the right to urban citizenship.

In a manner similar to Suchet and Mekdjian, in chapter 13 Andre Furlani introduces a variety of literary practices that combine walking and cross-language experience – literary interventions with a modernist edge. This guide to pedestrian writing in Montreal proposes a sensibility derived from the situationists as a model for experiencing the city in a translational mode. Using examples that range from an innovative multilingual video game to sound walks that convey some of the sense of Montreal's language landscape, Furlani brings to life a genre, a type of practice, which is particularly effective in a city like Montreal – a city where struggles across languages are a prominent part of daily life. The web emerges as a space of circulation similar to the city itself, allowing for cross-language interaction, neighbourhood creoles, and personal idioms. Code-switching, implicit translation, the testing of one text against another – these are some of the devices that run through the Montreal pedestrian text, in its many forms. After Marshall, Duval, and Suchet and Mekdjian, but also following Pizzi, Furlani's deambulations further demonstrate that language interactions have a special role to play in critical modernism, and that cross-language practices open onto a radical cognitive and perceptual questioning.

The city does not exist outside of language, and access to its many worlds is a voyage across tongues. Translations bring into dialogue languages that are states of memory in the history of the city (layers in successive periods of conquest and reconquest) and languages that are vehicles of memory in the present that convey the contemporaneous, sometimes-competing narratives of long-standing inhabitants and newcomers alike. Translation points to the dissonance of city life, but also to the possibility of a generalized, public discourse, a space vital to urban citizenship – where the convergence of languages can be a source of new conversations.

NOTES

1 In his detailed historiography of social democracy in Bratislava, Van Duin emphasizes the fact that he consulted sources in half a dozen languages, including Slovak, Czech, German, English, and Hungarian. Scholars of Czernowitz are best off if they can read German, Romanian, Ukrainian, and Yiddish.

2 The tethering of German to imperial power (Austrian or German) is an incontrovertible fact, and indeed one might see the Mitteleuropean city as a variation on the colonial city. There has been a burgeoning field of reflection on the resemblances between imperial and colonial forms of language occupation (Feichtinger 2003) – and there is a resemblance in the ways that cities have been renamed and relanguaged in the wake of colonial liberation. Translation was often accompanied by the physical transfer or obliteration of newly designated "alien" or "illegitimate" language groups – whether through expulsion or mass murder.

PART ONE

Landscapes of Memory

1

Locating Vilnius on the Map of Translation

LAIMONAS BRIEDIS

TRANSLATION: MOVING FROM LANGUAGE TO MEMORY

While exploring the narrative possibilities of Wilno, Polish-Lithuanian-American poet Czesław Miłosz once remarked on the Sisyphean fate of a storyteller who seeks to bare the soul of a city that has no resonance among its more illustrious peers.[1] "I see injustice," declared Miłosz (1981, 54), a native of Wilno, for "a Parisian does not have to bring his city out of nothingness every time he wants to describe it." The image of Paris depends on a great wealth of allusions, as the French metropolis "exists in works of word, brush and chisel" and "even if it were to vanish from the face of the earth, one would be still be able to recreate it in the imagination" (54). By contrast, each time Wilno is placed on the map or is recalled in history, it is forced to take a new representational direction. Often, the new pathway comes into sight with the change of the city's name, each translation leading to a different territorial and linguistic location. In one of his earliest poems addressed to Wilno (written in California in the 1960s), Miłosz (1988, 184–8) underscores the metaphorical vagueness of the place by hailing it as "the city without a name," coming into mind from the shores of an uncharted continent like an outline of the invisible, "unexpressed, untold." The poem is composed in the likeness of a memorial, plotted out in a plethora of local topographical details and native personages, in compensation for the lack of their visibility.

Miłosz's desire to shed light on his native city without fully revealing its identity echoes the earliest known attempts to map the place. As the capital town of Lithuania, the city's geographical location and political importance has been known since at least the 1320s; yet not until the middle part of the Renaissance period did it appear on cartographical tables of Europe as a named, and hence identifiable, location. A city with no name presents few translation problems, for it escapes memory by coming into the picture as a faceless character. "We lived in this city," writes Miłosz (1988, 102) in one of his earlier poems composed in the aftermath of World War II, "without caring about its past. Its walls / Seemed to us eternal. Those who lived there before us / Were just a legend, undeciphered." In a similar vein, albeit with a possibility of being decoded, another native of the region, Yiddish writer Moshe Kulbak (1997, 17–19) compares Vilna to the "dream of a cabbalist" with a "thousand narrow doors into the universe." For Kulbak, who wrote his poem in 1926 as a personal farewell song to the city, Yiddish is the master key that opens "the gates, sacred and profane, into the city" (19). The memories of the place, however, "wander – stray," unfurling the cityscape back to its fabled beginnings (18).

The name Vilnius is of Lithuanian and pagan origin, but it resounds in various annals of history as Wilno (in Polish), Wilna or Wilda (in German), Vilna (in French), Vilno (in Russian), and Vilne but also Vilna (in Yiddish). This proliferation of names often sends translation astray, and produces a realm of narrative possibilities that works against the Cartesian cartography of the place. A map of Lithuania (*Lituania*), for instance, prepared by the Franciscan friar and cartographer Vicenzo Maria Coronelli and published in Venice as part of his illustrious world atlas *Atlante Veneto* (1690–1701), highlights the city with no less than six different names. Since all other place names on the chart are entered univocally, Coronelli uniquely demarcates Vilnius in the spirit of a Baroque cantata, as a composition of several diverging idioms rather than a foreign metaphrase of a native tongue. The genuine Lithuanian place name wavers too by denoting the meandering, rippling effect of the eponymous fast running local stream. But it also shares a root with the Lithuanian words *vėlė* and *velnias*, meaning the soul of a departed and/or a demon. Thus, indirectly, Vilnius implies a journey, a crossing into the otherworld. More specifically, the (original) Lithuanian name captures the mythopoeic nature of local topography: Vilnius is built in a valley at the confluence of two rivers in the hilliest part of Lithuania where, according to pagan cosmology, the netherworld opens up to the heavens (see Toporov 2000). The place name implies translation, both in the geographical – prosaic – sense as the site of the ford, and in the spiritual – poetic – sense as the location of mediation between the dead and the living; a vessel that carries a message. In the Renaissance, Vilnius chose as its symbol Saint Christopher, the patron saint of travellers and ferrymen; it could have easily opted for Orpheus, an ancient Greek father of songs, but who also, according to Strabo, was a trickster capable of leaving the netherworld alive only to return deep in grief.

Projected onto urban terrain, translation evokes both aural and visual changes, forming and shaping, in the words of Sherry Simon (2012), the intersection of language and memory. As a political act, translation weakens the mnemonic chord of Vilnius, and, with only one official name, the city finds it difficult to hear its other voices. On a more practical, linguistic level, each name serves as a point of departure, an initiation into a culturally specific topography. The same goes with almost every place name in and around the city, including the names of streets that have been routinely translated and/or changed following different national and ideological regimes. Hence, short of writing a polyphonic exposé of the city, I use here a variety of names following the original reference sources. While the multiplicity of names can make it difficult to establish the city's place in and passage through history, it nonetheless draws attention to the shortcomings of metaphrase. Behind every translation lies a shift in perspective, leaving empty spaces where there used to be well-plotted narration.

Miłosz, when pressed to be more precise, enters the city from the back door of history. In the language of a forensic report, the poet describes the Wilno of the interwar period as "around two hundred thousand inhabitants plus tons of memoranda, notes, and stenographs in the League of Nations archives" (Miłosz 1981, 55). On the other hand, Kulbak (2008, 17), who glosses over its statistical surface, finds the Yiddish-speaking Vilna of the same period to be "a dark amulet set in Lithuania. Old gray writing – mossy, peeling." In both instances, translating the place from an unknown, dreamed territory into historical reality is presented as dealing with relics. This takes lyrical imagination into the field of urban archaeology, rousing, to paraphrase Walter Benjamin, the memory of the unremembered and forgotten dead, those invisible figures from the past whose lives and deeds had never been taken too seriously (Gilloch 1996, 71). Finding the right phrases to flesh out the unrecognizable dead is less than epiphany, for, as Miłosz (1988, 488) says: "Just as it flickers, it vanishes. Innumerable lives / Unremembered. Cities on maps only, / Without the face in the window, on the first floor, by the market, / Without those two in the bushes near the gas plant."

From its ancient Roman shores, the word translation drifted into modern English idiom carrying several meanings. As Umberto Eco (2003, 74) reminds us, before indicating a "turning from one language into another," the Latin term *translatio* "first appeared in the sense of 'change,' even of address, 'transport,' banking operation, botanical craft, and metaphor." Translation involves a point of departure and arrival, connected by a potential loss and gain. Still, while translation is always a two-way street in ideal, that is, forward-looking circumstances, it also offers the possibility of reading, hearing, and seeing (if not always grasping) foreign language and culture as if they were an integral part of the familiar terrain. At the beginning of the nineteenth century, Wilhelm von Humboldt described translation as a step forward in the broadening of one's linguistic horizons (Ecco 2003, 108), and Mikhail Bakhtin (1996, 60), who spent a good part of his childhood growing up in tsarist-ruled Vilno, saw in polyglossia – the simultaneous presence of two or more linguistic terrains within a single narrative – an opportunity to enter a familiar landscape "with another's eyes, from the point of view of a potentially different language" and in the process unleash the Galilean potentials of the place.

Historically, many residents of Vilnius have been bilingual or multilingual, capable of entering different local linguistic territories without the need for translation. The noteworthy exception to this rule was the (visible and invisible) line separating the Jewish side of the town, as it was defined by the practice of Judaism and the usage of Yiddish (and, to a limited extent, Hebrew) from its non-Jewish counterpart. Even so, while Miłosz (1991, 35) points to the fact that in the interwar decades Jewish and non-Jewish Wilno led separate lives because each side spoke and wrote in different languages, Yiddish, in the words of Benjamin Harshav (1990, 80) (who grew up in the city during the same period as Miłosz), "was an *open language*, moving in and out of its component languages and absorbing more or less of their vocabularies, depending on the group of speakers, genre of discourse, and circumstances." In Vilna, as in many places around the world, those who spoke Yiddish, almost by definition, lived in a multilingual environment. Consequently, in the first part of the twentieth century when a good third of the city's population declared Yiddish to be the language of birth, "overstepping the boundaries into another language [was always] a viable option" (28). Crossing into another linguistic milieu, however, was primarily a necessity for the Yiddish speakers, because very few non-Jews needed or wanted to set foot in Jewish Vilna.

In addition to linguistic and mercantile meanings, the word translation denotes the exposure and/or uncovering of relics for the sake of moving them from one place to another. In many religious belief systems, relics are seen, read, and dealt with as the *pignora*, originally meaning "security deposits left by the saints upon their deaths as guarantees of their continuing interests in the earthly community" (Geary 1994, 202). In Christian theology, translating relics is a step toward a form of sanctity, usually reserved for objects of providential significance that contain human remains. In rare circumstances translation also signifies ascending to heaven without dying first. In the western and eastern parts of the religious divides, the city of Jerusalem stands as the focal point for such departures, but it is also a recurrent topos in poetry, especially after Dante's journey to paradise from the depths of hell. So while the act of translation in general expresses horizontal crossings, this association with transport into different spheres of existence – traversing the highs and lows of imagination, for example – offers the possibility of a vertical axis.

As a horizontal process, the exchange across spatial barriers is "defined by figures and trajectories that make translation possible" (Simon 2006, 17). In language, it tends to be an invisible act, a shift from one linguistic terrain into another, establishing and then enriching the arc of communication (Steiner 1998, 49). Translation inevitably leaves behind traces of the interchange, untied pieces of loose linguistic correlations, or scraps of misplaced meanings. Still, its goal is to present the exchange between languages as a smooth, almost effortless passage; and in the end, what has been lost in the process is usually kept out of sight. In contrast, in the realm of mystery, especially if it involves ascension to heaven and/or descent to hell, translation is validated by revelation. More often than not, in a vertical process, the arc of exposure is counted as epiphany, divine apparition, and enchantment. Still, the opposite of epiphany is blindness, for no revelation is possible without first acknowledging having lived through the eclipse. The same goes for urban memory, which calls for a certain degree of exposure in order to have long-lasting effect. A relic is not unlike a memorial marker, which "no matter how alien to its surrounding, is still perceived in the midst of its geography, in some relation to the other landmarks nearby" (Young 1993, 7).

The topographical location and monumental visibility of relics expose vertical potentials of translation, for "to change the geography of the other world and hence of the universe, to alter time in the afterlife and hence the link between earthly, historical and eschatological time, between the time of existence and the time of anticipation – to do those things was to bring about a gradual but nonetheless crucial intellectual revolution" (Le Goff 1986, 2). By bringing this eschatological notion of translation into the post-socialist landscape of Europe, anthropologist Katherine Verdery (1999, 28) reifies relics with additional representational characteristics. A buried relic is a recomposed citation, never standing "for one particular thing ... for among the most important properties of bodies, especially dead ones, is their ambiguity, mutivocality, or polysemy." In addition, dead bodies "have another great advantage as symbols: they don't talk much on their own (though they did once). Words can be put into their mouths – often quite ambiguous words" (29). As a result, exposing and then translating the dead is one of the most effective ways to stake political control of a place; but so is hiding, annihilating, or levelling them down. "By repositioning them, restoring them to honor, expelling them, or simply drawing attention to them, their exit from one grave and descent into another mark a change in social visibilities and values" (19).

Any conversion from one language into another proceeds as a recomposition of the original; but in the memorial undergoing of translation, it often follows decomposition. Hence, the obligatory presence of ruins in urban translation, since both aspects of exposure – decomposing and recomposing – "constitute the fundamental operations of any act of comprehension of the text as world, or rather, the world as textual palimpsest to be deciphered" (Hamon 1992, 58). My interpretation of translation in Vilnius in part relies on visualizing the local dead as part of the living, changing composition of the place. Historically, burial grounds in Vilnius captured the linguistic diversity of the city as each religious community was entitled to its own piece of God's acre. As a rule, remembers Miłosz (1981, 210), urban graveyards "are usually gloomy patches of stony space, but not in Wilno" where they mimic the city's undulating, layered landscape. As depositories of civic memory, the cemetery was nonetheless an intensely private affair with "a photograph of the departed, framed and protected from elements, attached to many a headstone" (McBride 1938, 117). Known in Yiddish as *dos heylike ort* (holy place) and in Hebrew as *bet olam* (house of eternity), the Jewish cemeteries in particular were considered to give the community monumental visibility. In the Jewish holy place, writes Israel Cohen (1992) in his chronicle of Vilna written in London during the darkest days of World War II, a "multitude of tombstones faces every direction. They are closely huddled together, with epitaphs in Hebrew, Yiddish, and Russian. Some are adorned with framed photographs" of the deceased (416).

By and large, Vilnius is a baroque city, not just in terms of its architectural heritage but also in terms of representational potentials. Baroque spatial imagination progresses as the interplay between light and darkness, visible and invisible, constantly changing perspective by altering the course of narration between "a *spiegare* (to explain, expound, unfold) and a *piegare* (to fold, wrap, crease)" in search of achieving the effect of "the *spiegamento* (the explication, the spread, the unfolding)" (Chambers 2001, 83). The unfolding makes cover-up an important part of the exposition, creating a memory terrain that is open to being unearthed. Locating this undulating narrative landscape on the Cartesian world map involves not so much tracing the passage from one language to another as unravelling the geological layers of memory. Hence, my reading of translation in Vilnius follows the baroque notion of illumination by exploring the helix-like character of local changes, starting with the horizontal – linguistic – perspective of the city during the interwar period, and then, moving to the vertical – memorial – notion of translation as it occurred after the war. At the junction of the two lies the changing relationship between the living and "departed communities" of the city. Moving from language to memory entails a shift in focus from the visible to the invisible elements of the local topography.

VILNIUS: BETWEEN JERUSALEM AND BABYLON

Vilnius, under the name of Vilna, entered the twentieth century as a politically Russian and culturally Polish town with a large Jewish population. In the first census of the Russian Empire of 1897, 40 per cent of 155,000 residents declared Yiddish to be their mother tongue, while 30 per cent reported Polish, 20 per cent Russian, 4 per cent Belarussian, and only 2 per cent Lithuanian (Jurginis 1968, 304). Age Meyer Benedictsen (1924, 174), a Danish ethnographer of Jewish background, depicted Vilna of the late tsarist period as a diorama presented in the form of an iconostasis. The official façade was undeniably Russian and Orthodox (in terms of Christian faith), but "if one looks beyond the uniform in the upper classes it is not difficult to discover that they are not all Russians." At times, especially, after two unsuccessful Polish-Lithuanian insurrections against the tsarist regime, it was prohibited to use Polish in public. As a result, the language retreated to the city's interior sanctum, inside its many Catholic churches and the drawing rooms of the old nobility, where "over the sofa may be seen the portrait of the Polish poet-king Adam Mickiewicz, in the bookcase are to be found all the great names in Polish literature, and in marble or plaster Kosciuszko looks down from his appointed place" (175). In every house where Polish was spoken "one could find the same sentiments and hope" (175). Nonetheless, the language of the agora was predominantly Yiddish, for "the busy crowds in Vilna who traded and throng the streets, who hurry and slave are the Jews, for Vilna more than anything else is the town of the Jews" (176). Finally, the "fourth people in Vilna, the Lithuanians themselves, are only met as the peasants en route, as the vadmal [cloak] garbed silent one at the market, and not often even there, for the White Russian [Belarussian] peasants have made their way right into Vilna, and have long ago ousted the Lithuanians from the land" (177). Lithuanian (urban) speech, notes Benedictsen, was "like the water mark in a gay coloured postage stamp. The name of the town is Lithuanian, the suburbs still have Lithuanian names" (177), but their original meanings had faded away over several centuries of translation.

A hundred years later, the picture could not have been more different: out of almost 600,000 inhabitants of Vilnius, close to 60 per cent declared themselves Lithuanian, with Russians and Poles counting about 15 per cent each. Less than 1 per cent of the city's population was Jewish, and among them, very few spoke or even knew Yiddish. Furthermore, all local place names had a distinct Lithuanian ring to them, even if they had been retranslated several times over. Raw data obscure the true nature of the transformation: in the decade during and after World War II, that is, in the 1940s, due to mass murder and population displacement, transfer, and exile, the city lost close to nine-tenths of its prewar population. Postwar Vilnius was an immigrant town, initially settled by mostly Russian-speaking workers, but steadily becoming more and more Lithuanian (see Weeks 2008). Once the city was fully transformed, everything that spoke the language of the past was erased or levelled. As a result, a narrative move from Wilno to Vilne, for instance, or the historical shift from Vilno to Wilna, has no resonance in the Lithuanian-language-dominated Vilnius.

Piles of documents (in most cases, typed in French) stamped with the name of Wilno-Vilnius-Vilna and stored at the archives of the League of Nations, hints Miłosz in his summary of the city, point to the failing language of international diplomacy. During the interwar period, no solution was ever reached to satisfy the two parties involved in the dispute – Poland and Lithuania – over possession of the city. For Lithuania, Vilnius was the constitutional capital of the country, the heart and soul of the nation, without whose presence its national history and territory made little sense. Lithuania also claimed to have an inborn right to Vilnius, as legend held the city to be the gravesite of the country's ancient rulers. For Poland, Wilno was a place of mounting cultural and geopolitical prominence, a location bridging the romantic idea of the national rebirth with its martial achievements. No symbolic gesture made this connection more apparent than the request of Marshal Piłsudski, the founder of modern Poland, to have his heart buried in Wilno together with the remains of his mother. On his deathbed, the marshal also commanded their joint tombstone to be made into a military-religious shrine, surrounding it with countless graves of his fallen fellow soldiers. Sentiments aside, statistics, counting both the dead and the living, were clearly on the Polish side. All in all, Wilno of the interwar period was predominately Polish and Catholic – about 60 per cent of the total population. On the other hand, Jewish Vilna, which counted about a third of the city's residents, was a centre of the Yiddish-language universe. Kulbak (2008, 17–19), following the notion of Vilna as the guardian of modern Yiddish identity, moulded the city into the image of "a psalm, spelled in clay and in iron," where "each stone a prayer" led up to a crescendo with "a hymn in every wall."

Walls are rarely listened to, and before the hermeneutical Kabbalist reading of local symbols Wilno had to be located on the linguistic map of modern Europe. In the early 1920s, when the German writer Alfred Döblin, in response to pogrom-like strife in Berlin, asked where he should go to find Jews, he was advised to visit Poland. After a brief stay in Warsaw, Döblin came to Wilno with the eye and ear of a sarcastic, nonchalant metropolitan traveller. Everything in and around the city – local identities, territorial affiliations, ideological stands – seemed to be in a state of flux, freshly demarcated, and raw. A threatening feeling of war movements and foreign invasion still permeated the cityscape. In response, Döblin fell prey to allegorical manoeuvring, calling Wilno a bridge without providing any clues about what it spanned. "I feel distressed," he laments over his own poor choice of words, while at the same time trying to breath new life into the senseless metaphor (Döblin 1991, 89).

Since Döblin did not speak "the language, or rather the languages of the country: Polish, Ukrainian, Byelorussian, Yiddish, Lithuanian" (31), placing the allegory of the bridge on Wilno's actual linguistic relief depended on the power of vision or *Tatsachenphantasie*, factual imagination. Hence, while curious about the city's contested geopolitical nature, Döblin, arriving in the middle of Sukkoth, nonetheless hoped to find the landscape of a traditional, static, and outmoded Eastern European Jewish shtetl. Within minutes, however, he came to see it as a world apart. The city's geography was polyglot, effervescent, but also hard to decipher. In the middle of the old town, reports Döblin, guarded by many churches, the main "street widens like a square" (85). Next to a movie theatre, "I notice that the posters come in two languages: there are Polish posters and Yiddish ones. The signs of many shops are likewise in the Hebrew alphabet, in Yiddish. I often encountered this in Warsaw, in the Nalewki [Jewish] district; but here, it's spread throughout the city. There seems to be a very large or very courageous Jewish population" (86). But, he remarks in surprise, "I don't see any Jews, and that's the second thing. Individual Jews must be standing around, even if it's a holiday. And now I notice that I do see them but don't notice them. They stand next to me outside the movie house, walk about in white caps, young men and girls, older ones slowly cross the bumpy square, conversing in their language." Among local Jews, "no one wears a caftan! I see no one in a black 'capote.' They all wear European clothes – and yet do not speak Polish" (86).

Despite being secular and modern, Wilno was Jewish, but if it was also a bridge, then crossing over it was certainly carrying Yiddish from speech onto map. In a city where fast-moving political and ideological changes outran the measured and calculated pace of cartography, every attempt to placate it ended in failure. "I have a map of Wilno from the Russian period and a more recent map. Nearly all the streets and squares have been renamed. In Warsaw, this renaming delighted me, elated me; strange: here," muses Döblin, "I don't really care for it. It seems to have been inflicted upon the city from above. It did not issue from within, as in Warsaw" (89). Being tongue-tied in all the local languages, the writer is fast to lose track until, strolling through German

Avenue, the main shopping artery in the old town, he comes across "the Jewish street. Here, I understand the language. Store by store, countless people, Jews, hauling, lugging, standing in groups. A rare caftan, usually European provincial garb. Very narrow side lanes, street peddlers all the way into the courtyards. The shops are open, often windowless, rows of meat and poultry stores cheek by jowl. Arches span a few streets. They mark the boundaries of the old ghetto" (98). In the thickness of all things traditionally Jewish, Döblin finally has a glimpse of the other side of the bridge. "This is an energetic life," sums up the visitor from Berlin, "here and ... on the water, where the [Polish] soldiers exercise" next to the old Jewish cemetery (98).

In the interwar period, the spoken language of the Christian side of the city, remembers Miłosz (1992, 26), was described as simply coming from "hereabouts." Being neither the language of education nor of the church, this "down-to-earth" tongue had much in common with the villagers' vernacular and defied all forms of forceful translation. Heavily influenced by the (official) Polish language, but also inflected with Russian words of the bygone century, it exhibited some idiosyncrasies of Lithuanian syntax and functioned as a language of translation. Hence, it mirrored the changing geographical and social patterns of Belarussian speech, but in a distinctly urbane – Wilno – way. Miłosz, for one, attributes his uncharacteristic Lithuanian-framed handling of poetic language to the organic interchange between the "hereabouts" of Wilno and the literary language of the Polish cultural elite. Coming of age in the city of approximations, he remembers, "was not the same as growing up in an ethnically homogenous area; our sense of language was different" (26–7). Even more so, concludes the poet, it made translation an exploration of the familiar territory, for "everything would be fine if language did not deceive us finding / different names for the same thing in different times and places" (Miłosz 1988, 258).

Still, for Lucy Dawidowicz, a New York native who spent the last year of peace in Europe doing research in Vilna, Yiddish never failed the city. From the fall of 1938, writes Dawidowicz (1989, 102) in her postwar memoirs, during the entire academic "year I worked and played almost exclusively in Yiddish, for I was, after all, in the Jerusalem of Lithuania, the capital of Yiddishland." Moreover, at the time it never occurred either to Dawidowicz or any of her local Jewish acquaintances "that there was anything anomalous about the near-universal presence of Yiddish" in town (102). As a result, Jewish Vilna dealt with the official linguistic and ideological changes by drawing up its own map of the place. "Indeed," reiterates cultural historian Cecile Kuznitz (1998, 67), "if Vilna had a specifically Jewish geography, it was largely created through the use of a distinct language." In Vilna, Yiddish place names were in abundance and because in modern times, the designation of local streets changed just as frequently as successive regimes, the Jewish ones were often older, more precise, and grounded in a local topographical consciousness that their official counterparts lacked. Yiddish place names neither required nor followed any rules of translation, and "while the city officially changed from Vilna to Wilno to Vilnius, Jews called the city *Yerushalayim d'lite* [the Jerusalem of Lithuania], a name that never appeared on any official map" (67).

According to legend, the title of Jerusalem was bestowed on the city by Napoleon, who in 1812 passed through Lithuania leading the ill-fated Grande Armée to Moscow. In truth, the nickname was an indirect invention of the writer Rashi Finn (Samuel Joseph Fuenn), who in 1859 published a Hebrew-language book titled *Kiryah Ne'emanah* (The faithful city), describing Vilna in biblical terms traditionally used for the city of Jerusalem. While Finn never used the nickname in his book, his illustrative parallel between biblical Jerusalem and contemporary Vilna prompted the expanding usage of the metaphor within the growing circle of various secular Jewish movements (Harshav 2002, xxxi). However, throughout the centuries, Vilnius, because of its linguistic and religious diversity, has been routinely taken for another biblical place: the city of Babylon.

The comparison is rarely meant to be a compliment, for the image of the tower of Babel was used to give the idea of the untranslatability of local linguistic "disorder." A seventeenth-century Jesuit pasquinade, for instance, satirized Vilnius for welcoming foreign Protestant ministers who, in an attempt to please the locals, preached in heretical "lingual spirits – in addition to the Greek [mixed with] Polish, Lithuanian, Ruthenian, Latin, German and a bit of Hebrew" in between (Frick 2013, 100). Several centuries later, in the attempt to untangle local language diversity, German military statisticians of the World War I period were no less sarcastic, and confirmed "the city view [to be] in many respects alien and disharmonious. Over half a thousand years the most different influences from Occident and Orient had brought forth a queer cultural mixture which matched the presently still-existing mess of nationalities" (quoted in Liulevicius

2000, 43). More responsive observers of the same era saw no need to transfer Wilna onto the familiar map of Europe, because everything in and around the city – "religions, languages, peoples, histories, and architectural styles" – worked in concert, proving every border drawn to keep West and East apart to be wrong (quoted in Albrecht 2006, 174). And just before the start of World War II, in the attempt to clarify local things to a foreign audience, the editors of the *National Geographic Magazine* (1938, 777) declared Wilno "a stepchild of the Polish frontier." Still, the monthly chose to illustrate the city's unresolved geographical location with a photograph of a local newsstand blanketed with publications in all kinds of different languages and scripts. The caption put down local rules of translation: "Wilno reads in many languages. Newspapers in Polish, Russian, Yiddish, Lithuanian and German" are read widely but "English and French journals are rare" (779).

Wilno, no doubt, was a crossroads, but the noticeable lack of the two "international languages" of the century – English and French – put the city, so to speak, on the backward-moving track of modernity. Dawidowicz (1989, 55), for instance, remembers Vilna being an undersized, parochial place, taking on the appearance of "an enchanted dream village" in winter. Still, by local standards, Jewish Vilna was a metropolis. Polish Wilno too, while never reaching the size of a well-known European capital or big port city, had an air of a cosmopolitan if somewhat slow-paced place, where things, according to Miłosz, including languages and local identities, did not "lend themselves to neat classifications" (Czarnecka and Fiut 1987, 47). In sum, the city was "an enclave: neither Poland nor non-Poland, neither Lithuania nor non-Lithuania, neither provincial town nor a capital, although it was more of a provincial town than anything else" (Miłosz 1992, 26–7). The uneven, unfolding linguistic and ideological terrain that surrounded Wilno made the city "eccentric," a homeland of "crazily commingled strata that overlapped each other, like Trieste or Cernowitz" (27). And levelling down local differences made the city's storyline even more confusing. In 1942, for instance, the Polish government-in-exile in London published a book reaffirming the city's national stand as a place firmly rooted in Poland, yet still exhibiting "some puzzling appearances" because "there seems to be some mystery about this city of Wilno, where sometimes everyone is Lithuanian and sometimes nobody is" (Polish Research Centre 1942, 2). The seeds for the city's downfall, as Döblin (1991, 103) prophesied, were "the changing, loosening forces" of linguistic character, for in Wilno, as anywhere else in Eastern Europe, "the emancipation of the masses is taking place within a national framework – indeed, the strongest accent is [always] on nationalism." Miłosz equates the segmentation of the cityscape based on the idea of nation-state to cloud splitting. For him, Wilno, in the lyrical form of translation, was the gathering of differences in the likeness of the celestial "architecture of clouds ... Baroque clouds" (Czarnecka and Fiut 1987, 54). They remind the living, insists the poet, that language as well as the city moves with "the passage of time, the melancholy of transience" (54).

TRANSLATIO: MEMORY ERASED

The corporeal (and memorial) translation of Wilno to Vilnius came on the heels of the German blitzkrieg against Poland. In September of 1939, following the signing of the Nazi-Soviet nonaggression pact and the beginning of war, the Red Army occupied Wilno. Six weeks later, Soviet authorities "returned" the city, now renamed Vilnius, to neutral Lithuania. Less than a year later, Lithuania together with its regained capital city was occupied by the Soviet Army, declared to be "a people's state," and incorporated into the Union of the Socialist Republics. Anna Louise Strong, an American journalist and labour activist visiting Vilnius in the summer of 1940 in expectation of localized revolutionary changes, nonetheless had a vision of the continent being carried away toward utopia. The story of the city, remarks Strong (1940, 31) in her book about the new – Soviet – prospects of the socialist Lithuania, is a litany of ethnic wrongdoings and linguistic transgressions, making its unsettling geography "a world example – there are many such in Europe – of the insolubility of the problem of national hates under capitalist rule." In the end, the burden of translation falls particularly hard on the city, for whoever "solves the problem of Vilna can [also] solve the problem of Europe" (31). Bringing her back to reality, an American diplomat stationed in Lithuania described the situation from a different angle, proposing a more radical and, at the time, seemingly no less likely solution. "The only thing to do with Vilna," the emissary nonchalantly remarked, "is to pick it up and take it a long way off and squeeze the people out into their respective nations and then put the town itself in a museum" (31).

The museum, according to Foucault's reading of urban geography, is the exemplary heterotopia. In general, heterotopia is characterized as having a capacity "of juxtaposing in a single real place several spaces," assuming an architectural carcass capable of holding "several sites that are in themselves incompatible" (Foucault 2012, 77). By encompassing different social meanings and functions, it operates through "a system of opening and closing" (78) that can be always found in graveyards. Cemeteries accumulate history by segmentation and compartmentalization of personalized "slices in time," such as individual gravesites, dated tombstones, and memorials. In the cemetery as in the heterotopia, remains either have a role to "create a space of illusion that exposes every real space," or else "to create space that is other, another real space, as perfect, as meticulous, as well arranged as ours is messy, ill constructed, and jumbled" (79). As a result, memory in the graveyard "unfolds between two extreme poles" of time: the eternity and the final break in life (79). In addition, conceived as being the entrance to the realm of the dead and, thus, governed by "chthonian and telluric forces, the depths and the heights" that point to the eschatological order of things, the cemetery literally outlives the city (Lefebvre 1991, 231). Indeed, there has been a long-standing tradition in Vilnius to visit a "holy place" to mark a time of sojourn, to either prepare for a departure or celebrate a homecoming.

The exact date of the founding of the first Jewish cemetery in Vilna is unknown, but a graveyard serving the growing Jewish community must have existed long before the completion of the Great Synagogue, around 1570 (Girininkienė 2004, 152–5). Situated on a flat terrain across the river from the city, the *bet olam* was one of the oldest burial grounds in town, with some tombstones featuring the elegaic sensibilities of the Baroque era. In time, as the local Jewish community grew in numbers, its territory expanded into surrounding fields and pastures. Still, located on the other side of the fast flowing river and cut off from the rest of the city, the cemetery stayed out of the frame of most maps of the place. Before the nineteenth century, Vilnius had no (known) public monuments, and Christian burial grounds were sites of a provisional nature. Belonging to individual parishes or monastic foundations, graveyards were essentially churchyards, and as there was never enough room to accommodate all the dead, the necropolis was a site of decomposition, a place of transience, where flesh turned into bones. Permanent graves were reserved for very few, and were mostly inside churches. In contrast, the Jewish cemetery, following the religious proscription against the desecration of graves, accumulated time by keeping relics in the ground in perpetuity.

Hence, with each passing century the Jewish necropolis became the antithesis to the official forgetfulness of the city. Deemed to be reaching the point of saturation, the ground was permanently closed down for burials by the tsarist administration in the 1830s. A fresh site, further afield and in a different direction from the city, was allocated for the new Jewish cemetery. Despite the closure, the *bet olam* remained, along with the main synagogue, the most treasured religious and historic site in Vilna.

In modern times, the old cemetery still had more than two hundred identifiable memorials covering "a very large area," but "looking for the most part like a deserted field, with grass growing wild; for the number of gravestones is comparatively small. There were only a few conventionally upright, most of them being merely shapeless stones or boulders, though there are some in the form of little Gothic structures with Hebrew inscriptions, on which the names have been painted over in yellow to facilitate identification" (Cohen 1992, 415). Döblin (1991, 111), who came to the cemetery on the last day of his visit, discovered it to be "a vast lawn with several trees" with many shards, headstone fragments, eroded grave marks, and heaps of memorial slabs crowding around. While showing signs of "terrible neglect" the graveyard nonetheless did not appear to be comatose: "Bits of bricks, small stones on many headstones. Straw under the small stones, also slips of paper with Hebrew writing" (111). The landscape built on relics and left to become a ruin had the spirit of a temple, with devout Jews travelling from far away "to pray at the graves of famous men, holy men" (111). The "deep and dark feeling" (111) of the decaying necropolis contrasted the ecstatic mood of the pilgrims, who looked at the hallowed ground as if they were approaching the gates of heaven. One way or another, notices Döblin, the arc connecting the transient with eternity has always been repaired, for the prayerful visitors "think, they feel the holy man is still by his grave, by his body, and they can approach him as their forebears did during his lifetime. The dead man is tied to his grave, his vanished soul to the corpse, and his soul can be evoked by prayer. And the pious man, the rebbe, the saints stand closer to God and can obtain more than a normal man from God, perhaps, by way of God" (111).

In the cemetery, ideological and geopolitical changes placed on the eschatological plane lose most of their (temporary) significance. Still, remembers Dawidowicz (1989, 48), the Jews of Vilna "knew their history not much from reading books as from visiting the two Jewish cemeteries, where their history was literally entombed." But if the old cemetery came next to being a place of messianic time, then the new cemetery situated on the hillside shouldering the old town was the secular ground made for the recomposition of the city's official narrative. Dawidowicz depicts this large nineteenth-century style urban graveyard as an open-air museum, with "long tree-lined walkways" and endless tombstones "crowded together, leaning against each other like infirm old people" (49). Among them, for instance, were "several mass sepulchers of Jewish political victims, one consisting of individual graves of fourteen Bundists [members of a socialist Jewish political party founded in Vilna] who died in the 1905 revolution, with an impressive tall stone monument at the center" (49). Other sculptures marked the graves of more recent pogroms (49). The coming together of separate sheets of civic memory made the cemetery less a temple than a memorial – *yizkor* – book, grounding Vilna's thousand voices on their native soil. The dirge coming from the Jewish cemetery, like the toll of church bells, added a distinct layer to the city's ever-changing soundscape, because "a stentorian voice could be heard every day offering up the prayer for the dead, and rending the air with heart-breaking grief in every note. Scarcely had the sound died away when," narrates the US-published 1944 guidebook to Jewish Vilna, "from an opposite quarter, the same moving, piercing chant rose again, uttered with even more poignant anguish of spirit, as though seeking to give expression to the infinite tragedy of the Jewish people" (Cohen 1992, 417–18).

A couple of months after the Nazis occupied Vilnius in the summer of 1941, the ghetto was set up to isolate the Jews from their Christian (mostly Polish and Lithuanian) neighbours. The establishment of the ghetto sealed the metamorphosis of the city, for even before a section of the old town was walled in, about half of the Jewish population had been massacred. Vilnius was one of the first cities in Europe where the mass killing of Jews proceeded as the way to translate the racial theory of *lebensraum* into a final spatial solution. By Christmas of the same year, the SS report declared most of Lithuania to be *Judenfrei*, "free of Jews" (Arad 1982, 170). The statement covered only a part of the truth, for in the Vilna ghetto alone there were about thirty thousand inmates.

During the German occupation, death was ever present in the city and its moribund population repeatedly compared life in the ghetto to being entombed alive. In the ghetto, according to the survivors, natural death was almost unheard of, and on those rare occasions when it occurred, Jewish mourners were never allowed to take the deceased beyond the ghetto gate to the cemetery. Left without caretakers, the Jewish graveyard was quickly profaned by its Christian neighbours. The Germans, however, ordered a written report on the "archeological condition" of both Jewish cemeteries, including maps of the territories, facsimiles of epigraphs, and biographical details of some of the relics. Herman Kruk, the head librarian of the ghetto, was ordered to compile the account, and went one afternoon to the new cemetery. The funerary landscape had been altered to make it more a part of the wartime city, with its surrounding fence taken apart, magnificent trees cut down for firewood, and better tombstones carried away. Farm animals roamed freely on the grounds, gradually turning the house of eternity into pastureland (Kruk 2002, 288). After the war, the Soviet administration of Vilnius used the same report to determine the "ideological value" and "historical importance" of the Jewish graveyards (Girininkienė 2004, 161). By that time, the new cemetery had already been shut down, and in Israel, Yiddish poet Abraham Sutzkever (1991, 368), a partisan of the Vilna ghetto, tried to envision the city without the memory of the Jewish gravedigger "who sowed half the graveyard with the sons of man," but "will bury no one anymore. Children, old people, all those born here, all entered the kingdom of the stars. At first – they became flaming branches. Bony winds, in tatters of shirts with Magen-Dovids, have scattered their sparks in a bloody crown over the skull of the earth. / They shamed his graveyard. / Shamed the tombstones. / So they sink with downcast heads, like offended in-laws when the bride disappears from the *Chupa*."

Vilna bled to death in the nearby forest of Ponar, situated across the city from both Jewish graveyards. Over the course of three years, approximately eighty to ninety thousand people – mostly Jews, but also some Poles, Soviet prisoners of war, and Lithuanians – were killed in the forest. The murder was commanded and supervised by the SS, but a battalion of Lithuanian volunteers made a brisk trade of it. A vast majority of the victims were buried in massive pits that were dug out before the war by the Soviet army for fuel storage. During shootings, some lasting for several days, the Lithuanian police secured the pits' perimeter; still, for most of time, the area was pretty much left open, unguarded. Locals, following the original industrial purpose of the fuel tanks, called the area (in Russian) the *baza*, meaning "distribution centre" or warehouse. In the fall of 1943, after the final liquidation of the ghetto, the Germans ordered all forensic evidence of the activities that took place at the *baza* to be destroyed. A number of pits were uncovered and ten thousands of human remains were translated and incinerated on the spot in huge pyres (Arad 1982, 445). The whole scheme was commanded and supervised by a special SS unit, but the bodies of the victims were recovered and set ablaze by a small team of Jewish prisoners. The Germans kept count of the relics, but under the threat of death forbade referring to them as human remains. The word *figuren* – pieces, characters, like those of puppet figurines in a play or a diagram – was used instead. By the time the city was retaken by the Red Army in the midsummer of 1944, Ponar was despoiled twice over. Burned to small pieces of bone and then reduced to dust, the remains of most of Vilna were scattered in the forest. Upon entering the city with Soviet forces, Sutzkever "went to Ponar, where more than a hundred thousand people are buried. My mother lies there, my child, my comrades. No! They are not there! Their bodies were burned on the execution pyres and their bones were crushed to powder, so that no trace of them remains" (quoted in Leftwich 1971, 128). On long summer evenings, the woody hills of Ponar possess the composure of Arcadia. The forest floor, however, has sunken into an abyss: "How beautiful the road! On the right the blue shimmering River Vilia. The pine-trees shine in the sunset glow. And there is the entrance to Hell! Is Hell beautiful?" (quoted in Leftwich 1971, 128).

Out of seventy thousand Jews who lived in the city before the Nazi occupation, only a few thousand survived. After the war, very few local Jews returned to Vilnius, with many leaving Lithuania within a year or two. Another native of Vilna, Yiddish writer Chaim Grade, returned to the city soon after it was taken back by the Red Army. The empty courtyards and alleyways of the Yiddish Vilna around the German Street engulfed him "like subterranean passages, like caves filled with ancient graves" (Grade 2004, 335). At the heart of the city, amidst the wreckage of the Great Synagogue, "lie buried – so they scream, in silence – here lie buried all the prayers that Jews have uttered for hundreds of years" (382). Indeed, "all of Vilna is a gravestone for its last Jews, and the Gentiles now sit in the Jews' stead, like owls amid the ruins" (382). In time, says Grade, this cemetery-city "will be razed and all that will remain of the Ghetto will be a space even smaller than a poor peasant's plot. Any small city park, a children's playground, will seem larger than the cleared space" (348) of Jewish history left in Vilnius. “But for me,” declares Grade, the memory of Vilna is “larger than that half of the world across which I wandered. Your emptiness says more to me than all the cities and countries I have seen” (348).

The first commemoration of Jewish victims in Vilnius was made of wood and stone soon after the Soviet troops returned. The monument was constructed with the help of survivors, and placed in Ponar; a part of the epitaph was written in Yiddish. Sutzkever was also instrumental in creating the Museum for Jewish Art and Culture on the city’s main street (Fishman 1998, 23–31). The exhibition of found documents and artifacts from the ghetto was initially arranged in the poet’s apartment, but was shut down by the KGB in 1949 (Ran 1974, 524). Soon the Ponar memorial lost its “approved status” as well, and following the anti-Zionist purges in the Soviet Union in the early 1950s, the memorial was dismantled by the orders of the Lithuanian Communist Party. A year or two later, a midsize granite obelisk with a star on top was erected on the site. The new monument spoke the standard Stalinist idiom with the commemorative inscription written in Russian and Lithuanian only, making the obligatory nod to the victims as “Soviet citizens.” Traces of the Vilna tragedy were few and far between in the Soviet-Lithuanian memorial jargon of Vilnius, and while the obelisk at Ponar was given the title of “a museum located at the site” of the Nazi death camp (see *Litovskaya SSR* 1974), it did little to form the Marxist narrative of the city. A Soviet-era travel guide, for instance, boasted that although the “war inflicted a number of grave wounds on the city none of them were fatal. With each year of peace Vilnius grows stronger, gathering strength like a river gathers spring water” (Metelsky 1959, 56). By 1960, the pastoral road “on the outskirts of the city” that witnessed countless marches of “death during the Nazi occupation” acquired a distinctly socialist, industrial outlook: “The dismal days of fascist brutality cannot be wiped out of the people’s memory although today there is nothing left to recall them. The buildings of the new factories and dwelling-houses erected along Paneriai [Ponar in Lithuanian] Street are a pleasure to behold” (60).

Vilnius had also no patience for Jewish relics, and as soon as about one hundred thousand Polish citizens of Wilno (most of them natives of the city) were “repatriated” to Poland after the war, any sign of nostalgia or even memory for the prewar city was declared ideologically indefensible (Stravinskienė 2011, 165; Weeks 2008, 526–30). The new Soviet-Lithuanian city left no room for “foreign” bodies and, based on that premise, in 1955 the old *bet olam* was flattened to make space for an Olympic-size swimming pool (Girininkienė 2004, 155). Two decades later, a Brutalist-style Palace of Sport was added to it. A decade later, the final axe fell on the new cemetery. A 1965 photograph of the vacant necropolis depicts a treeless terrain, stretching far into horizon, undulating but vast as a prairie, with a multitude of headstones sticking out like stumps in a forest clearing. By 1968, without any due historical or archeological process, the graveyard was razed, with many headstones taken away and used as building material on "socialist construction sites" (Girininkienė 2004, 166). One of them was the building of the national library, carrying the name of the sixteenth-century printer who published the first Lithuanian book; another was a new residential district that subsequently was awarded the Lenin Prize. A modern bridge built to connect the old city with the newly developed area north of the annihilated old cemetery was also rumoured to have foundations made in part from the new cemetery's crushed tombstones.

After Lithuania declared independence from the Soviet Union, Paneriai memorials proliferated in a number of small and big commemorative gestures, each reiterating a specific group of victims: Jews (two or three monuments in Hebrew, Russian, Yiddish, and English), Poles, Soviet citizens, Lithuanians, the unknown, etc. With very few Jewish sites left in town, the retranslation of Vilnius back to Vilna could never have been achieved without the uncovering of relics. Still, the place has never been recognized, at least not in official sources, as God's acre. The memorial landscape of the old cemetery keeps the burial ground in limbo, unable to find the right commemorative gesture that allows the translation of desecrated relics to become a meaningful history lesson. The new cemetery is still wasteland, although a small tribute to the unremembered graveyard was erected on the site in 2004. The monument, a sculptural wall built of headstones "found" in the cemetery, identifies the location as the protected area of "American Heritage Abroad," to remind the living, it seems, of the unbridgeable abyss that separates Vilna from Vilnius.

Miłosz (1990, 90), arriving in Vilnius a half a century after leaving Wilno, described the place as "a corpse of a city. The smallest heaps of rubble had been removed, lawns and flower beds were arranged, benches placed in newly delineated squares. Only there were no people. From time to time a couple of tourists would stop by the wall and slowly decipher letters on a memorial plaque." Much of the change in wartime and postwar Vilnius had occurred either under the sign of death or the force of exile, resulting in a scattering and erasure of its histories. So, while physically and, in many respects, architecturally, Vilnius has retained the appearance of its former self, its narrative landscape can no longer use the grammar of the past. The lack of readable (Jewish) relics in particular makes Vilnius a place of runaway translations. And Miłosz (2004, 8), coming to Vilnius-Wilno for the last time before his own death, calls it a second space (perhaps, Vilna?) that has no alternatives but to be mistranslated, for its "geography, says Swedenborg, cannot be transferred to maps. / For there, as one has been, so one sees. / And it is possible even there to make mistakes; for instance, / to wander about / Without realizing you are already on the other side."

NOTE

1 Research for this article was funded by the European Social Fund under the Global Grant Measure.

2

A Modernist City Resisting Translation? Trieste between Slovenia and Italy

KATIA PIZZI

In 1717 Charles VI designated Trieste, harbour city located on the upper Adriatic Sea, a free port and maritime hub of the Austro-Hungarian Empire. Situated within the broad Mediterranean region, which, from Fernand Braudel onward, has been regarded as an incubator of cultural convergences and interactions, Trieste's identity was predicated from the start upon a tension between Imperial and Mediterranean forces. This was a polyglot city whose commercial vocation went hand in hand with intellectual and cultural exchanges. Not a national capital but a cultural centre brimming with new modes of thinking and drawing in exiles, voyagers, and drifters, the city was a locus of literary and intellectual debate, as well as a site of rupture, tension, and conflict.

Issues of translation, translatability, internal colonialism, dissonance, multilingualism, and inequality loom large throughout Trieste's history, contributing to its uniquely "difficult" identity. Here, the vernacular and the standard, the assimilated and the nonassimilated, the regional and the national, the global and the local, the general and the particular collided and overlapped in particularly productive manners. In short, Trieste provides a cogent case study of both the productivity and the dissonance of cross-cultural intersections, of the tragedy and the (im)possibility of culture as translation.

In this chapter, I aim to highlight the productivity of cultural translation across the tectonics of history and memory in Trieste. In particular, I focus on the literary production of the minority Slovenes and the majority Italians in the early decades of the twentieth century – pointing to contrasting models of modernism and modes of translation. In the framework of globalized modernism, Trieste stands out as a peripheral city where "cultural action, the making and remaking of identities, takes place in the contact zones, along the political and transgressive intercultural frontiers of nations, peoples, locales" (Clifford 1997, 7) and where location is "an itinerary rather than a bounded site – a series of encounters and translations" (11).

The manner in which the culture of this peripheral region was particularly radical and dynamic in the early decades of the twentieth century highlights Trieste's genuinely modernist vocation. Entrenched and long-standing cultural and ideological protocols kept local cultures, languages, and communities both fiercely apart, yet entangled in symmetrical binary systems. These protocols and clichés tended to militate against the very notion of translation. Like distant galaxies hurtling toward the same point in time and space but never crossing paths, these separate frontier cultures more often than not failed to intersect and merge into zones of translation. Their trajectory within modernism was pursued independently in spite of comparable goals. These cultures were oblivious to cultural, linguistic, and ethnic "others," remaining fragmentary and competitive in their pursuits, as I elucidate below.

Trieste contributed substantially to consolidating the fortunes of Austria-Hungary as its major commercial port, both before and after the opening of the Suez Canal. The demise and dismemberment of the Austro-Hungarian Empire after 1918, however, jump-started a decline that eventually pushed this once-mighty port city to the margins of world history. Trieste and large portions of this multiethnic region, ancestral home to diverse language groups, were handed over to Italy in 1920 following the Treaty of Rapallo. The fierce competition of Italian harbours, many of which were of greater capacity than the Triestine port, contributed to the city's growing stagnation. Under the aggressive nationalizing and acculturating campaigns inaugurated by the Fascist state in the early 1920s, non-Italian cultures were persecuted with a view to eradication.

The dusk of Trieste's multiculturalism gave way to a growing enthusiasm for a belligerent and dynamic Italian nation that represented access not only to industrial modernity but also to a pre-eminent cultural and linguistic tradition. This enthusiasm was articulated, in particular, by the Italian-speaking middle classes of Trieste, who were socially and institutionally prominent given the city's commercial emphasis. Even under the Austro-Hungarian Empire, German had never prevailed in the linguistic fabric of the city, where business transactions were carried out in a pragmatic vernacular (*triestino* dialect) that, as is the case in the broader Veneto region, is the preferred vehicle of communication to this day.

Beginning in the mid-1920s, a Fascist nationalizing agenda aggressively quashed indigenous groups, both urban and rural, especially Slovenian and Croatian. Linguistic and cultural polarizations, bubbling below the surface since pre-Imperial times, received new impetus and visibility as part of the regime's modernizing and acculturating strategy. Institutional initiatives included forced nationalizations, bans on educational establishments and on spoken and written language in public, attacks on cultural institutions, and the Italianization of surnames. Monocultural Italian discourses, prevalent among the Italian middle classes before the war, were eventually hijacked by and subsumed under nationalistic banners. The regime imposed blanket normalization and standardization, "domesticating" non-Italian languages and cultures. Cultural translation cannot but break down where official Italianness is predicated entirely on anti-Slavness, as evidenced by violent attacks, such as the arson of Hotel Balkan on 13 July 1920, perpetrated by Fascist blackshirts. This particular attack carried a cultural as well as a coercive agenda, since the hotel was the site of Trieste's Slovenian House of Culture and included a library, theatre, and music hall.

Yet, the multilingual and multicultural make up of this region, its national and ethnic "fluidity," and its relative remoteness from canonical centres of culture such as Vienna, Florence, and increasingly Ljubljana, easily lent itself to thriving forms of eclectic experimentalism. The national, ethnic, and class polarizations that marred the social and political landscape frequently acted as a stimulus for radicalized, international, and pan-European cultural agendas. The very disconnects of a region fractured through history and memory were conducive to translation,[1] especially when seen within the overall framework of the fragmented, peripheral, decentred, and decentring experience of modernity itself. It seems now widely accepted that regions traditionally perceived as the geographical and cultural peripheries of global capitalism, such as this one, are best placed to capture experiences of the most authentic and generative modernity (see Parry forthcoming).

The enforced monoculturalism that prevailed in Trieste between the two world wars, largely predicated on the "colonial" domination of the Italian language and culture over competing Slavophone groups, may be looked at productively through two contrasting lenses: on the one hand Homi Bhabha's (1994) "staging of difference," and on the other hand Antonio Gramsci's (1992) "translatability."

Bhabha's notion points to the essentialization of cultural difference inherent in translational acts, which becomes, in turn, a platform for hegemonic discourses. The alterity inherent in all translational acts is also perceived as a value, as a prerogative of migrant cultures (Bhabha 1994, 339). Bhabha further asserts that it is necessary to "understand the part that emotions, affects, play in the construction of community politics" (213), an assertion that recalls Bakhtin, as well as Gramsci. In Gramsci's language theory, languages are fundamentally predisposed to interlingual and cultural translation. They are political vehicles of social communication and cohesion, redressing class inequalities through their inherently dialogical status. Reaching out beyond the absolutist ideology of monolingualism, Gramsci's notion of *traducibilità* (translatability) is infused with dialogical and communicative overtures toward an interlocutor no longer perceived as other, therefore ultimately eliding the "otherness" of the postcolonial subject.[2] Gramsci's idea of translatability refers to linguistic and cultural behaviours firmly embedded in historical and social praxis in a Marxist sense, rather than to historical languages as such. Translatability allows for networks of comprehension across different cultures on a nonhierarchical basis (see also Wagner 2012, 61).

Gramsci, in other words, underscores "the positive role of translation in overcoming linguistic barriers" (Carlucci 2013, 61). He rejects hierarchies, for example between language and dialect, predicated on the historical relativity of language codes, validating instead, if implicitly, a local-national bilingualism.[3] Both personal and political motivations, Carlucci argues, contributed to the development of his views. Gramsci's wife, Giulia Schucht, hailed from an elite, educated, multilingual family that engaged in populist linguistics, as was typical of the Russian intellectual class in the early twentieth century. To some extent, Gramsci follows Lenin's lead in his concern with national belonging of linguistic minorities and unity of language (104). Soviet national linguistic unification, designed to facilitate the use of the Russian lingua franca while promoting linguistic federalism within the Soviet state, also played a part in Gramsci's thinking, as is evidenced in Notebook 29 (130). Gramsci and Bhabha will provide useful insights here, especially as concerns the particular intellectual position of prominent Italian-speaking intellectuals in Trieste on the eve of World War I, namely Scipio Slataper (1888–1915) and Giani Stuparich (1891–1961). In particular, these contrasting models of translation account for the dissonant forces at work – at once resistance to translation between neighbours locked in increasing aggressive conflict under Fascism (Italians and Slovenes) and openness to translation inspired by modernism and cosmopolitan Socialism.

ITALIAN AND COSMOPOLITAN

Together with Giani's brother Carlo (1894–1916), these young Italian-speaking intellectuals played an instrumental role in inventing and constructing a literary culture in Italian in this region. Having defected from the Austrian conscript army in 1914, they sought shelter in mainland Italy. Since the early 1900s they had lived and studied in Florence, the traditional cradle of Italian language and civilization, attending university there rather than in nearby Imperial Vienna or Graz (Trieste, at this time, had no university of its own). Slataper and the Stuparich brothers revered and idealized Florence, regarding it as a stable centre of *italianità* (Italianness) against the multiple, unstable cultural and linguistic identity of Trieste – a paradigmatic platform, in Bhabha's words, for the "staging of a difference."

At the same time, Trieste's peripheral status provided them with the impetus to pursue broad intellectual and cultural experimentation, including *repêchages* of the most hackneyed literary canons (Dante and Petrarch in the Middle Ages, and also, seamlessly, Leopardi and D'Annunzio in the nineteenth century), amalgamating Romantic autobiographical leanings and modernist fragmentation. In short, Slataper and Giani Stuparich integrated disparate and heterogeneous cultural forms into what Ernestina Pellegrini (1980, 358) brands a "spiritual encyclopedism." Like their contemporaries James Joyce and Italo Svevo, two widely known modernists with strong ties to Trieste, Slataper and his Italian-speaking acolytes cultivated transnational references that renegotiated issues of language, imperialism, and national identity. As Mark Thompson (2008, 116) puts it, to his admirers Slataper "was a meteor in the skies above Trieste, alerting all Italy to the new ideas coursing through Europe." Slataper and Giani embraced a holistic pan-Europeanism, laced with Mazzini's *Risorgimento* liberalism and Austrian Marxism,[4] dipping into languages and cultures far removed from their own. Slataper (1916), for example, delved into Scandinavian literatures and wrote what is to this day one of the most celebrated monographs on Henrik Ibsen in the Italian language. Giani (1915) turned toward Bohemia, researching the history and cultural history of the Czech nation and also publishing a notable and enduring monograph. Significantly, however, both authors appear to gloss over translational, transcultural encounters with their Slovenian neighbours, interactions that would have made up much of their everyday experience back home, as I discuss below.

In a well-known "Triestine Letter," published in the influential Florentine periodical *La Voce* in 1909, Slataper berated complacent continental Italians for their foggy notions of the Adriatic region and its complex culture, inviting them to become better informed. It is worth noting at this juncture that Gramsci, by contrast, was familiar with the language issues and the cultural and political fragmentation of this region via the influence of his linguistics teacher Matteo Bartoli (1873–1946). Bartoli, who was born in Albona (now Labin in Croatia) in the north-eastern Adriatic, taught a course of historical linguistics at the University of Turin in the academic year 1912–13, attended by Gramsci, whose extensive notes are extant (Schirru 2011). Carlucci (2013, 148) notes that both Gramsci and Bartoli came from marginal areas, Sardinia and Istria respectively. It is therefore probable that Gramsci's attention to Slav populations originated from Bartoli (see a 1926 article where he argues that Slav peasants living in Istria could be organized politically given due consideration to the delicate national issues prevailing in those areas) (159).[5]

From *La Voce*, which he edited from 1910, Slataper advocated a pivotal role for Trieste, predicated on a productive tension between an elusive culture and the all-too-tangible matter of free market economics. His major work, and veritable *Ur-text* of Triestine literature, *Il mio carso* (My Karst, 1912) is a fragmentary, avant-garde lyrical prose poem that combines *Sturm und Drang* Romanticism with a rhetorical vitalism derived from Gabriele D'Annunzio's neoclassical rhetoric. Slataper's peppering of Slovene words into the narrative fabric of his Tuscan Italian is disjunctive. As in T.S. Eliot's *The Waste Land*, Slataper's insertions fail to serve as "bridges" between languages and cultures, pointing to unintelligibility and untranslatability.[6] His impermeable multilingualism largely highlights and endorses the modernity of Trieste as an urban centre, in contrast to the isolation of the rugged mountainous Karst area. The predominantly Slovenian Karst, from which Slataper's maternal family hailed, is evoked as a largely psychological and affective landscape, culturally backward when compared with Trieste's metropolitan dynamism. As his hybrid name suggests (his first name was Scipio), Slataper was of mixed ethnic background. Although he was a witness to the alterity inherent in translation, as well as to the transitivity and translatability of language, his approach suggests distrust of the pluralist and egalitarian potential encoded in linguistic exchange.

The sensory and emotional nature of the Karst landscape infuses Slataper's prose: touch, sound, smell, and sight influence, inscribe, and inflect his attachment to a space cherished nostalgically as the site of a remote childhood. One can perhaps evoke a kind of synesthetic nationalism here. The crucial role attributed to an affective landscape in *Il mio carso* points to the staging of a politics of difference, in Bhabha's terms.

Gramsci's translatability, on the other hand, stands behind Giani Stuparich's major novel *Ritorneranno* (1941). Set during a World War I contemplated through the medium of World War II, the novel focuses on a Triestine family loyal to Italy, save for one minor but key character: the Slovenian Berta. In his portrayal of Berta, a familiar figure of domestic labour in middle-class Triestine households, Stuparich deploys an arsenal of cultural and sociopolitical stereotypes that typify the interethnic relations between Italian and Slovenian communities. At the same time, however, Berta's complexity points to the author's genuine and serious effort to portray as faithfully and as objectively as possible the particularity of the Slovene situation. Stuparich's politics rely here on a subcategory of Marxist thinking, commonly known as Austrian Marxism, whose representatives include Otto Bauer and the Triestine Angelo Vivante. Stuparich was familiar with this *vulgata* via his forays into Czech national culture. In a context of entangled symmetries between Berta and her Italian antagonist, Angela, Austrian Marxism provides Stuparich with pertinent insights into Berta's growing national, cultural, and political consciousness – significantly portrayed here as progressive and reliant on language and acculturation. This is, of course, a process well known to Gramsci, who singles it out in his own linguistic and cultural translation theory.[7] As Carlucci (2013, 57) observes, Gramsci's approach to language education was "part of his generally open-minded attitude to linguistic plurality," honed in the translation work he undertook while still a student, communicating political issues in a language intelligible to the local peasants and working classes. "Gramsci attached great importance to the linguistic aspects of cultural and social differences and inequalities" (57), highlighting the instrumental role translation played in overcoming language barriers.

THE POLYGLOT AVANT-GARDE

Slataper and Stuparich were by no means alone as Triestines attracted to Italian culture and Florence. A group of young men and women, Italian speakers and fervent intellectuals, moved en masse from the Adriatic region to Florence in the years straddling World War I. This group included Gemma Harazim, Virgilio Giotti, Biagio Marin, Carlo Michelstaedter, and Alberto Spaini. Spaini, who admired Marinetti and the Florentine futurists, boasted special avant-garde credentials and connections as the only Italian national to have played a significant role in the Dada group at the Cabaret Voltaire since his move to Zurich in 1916. Spaini's early exposure to futurist soirées in Trieste and elsewhere in Italy influenced Dada's new style of declamation and even words-in-freedom printed on the walls of the *Meierei*. It was also through Spaini's familiarity with German, as well as Italian, that Tzara made contacts with prominent avant-garde figures in Italy, and had their work translated into German (Berghaus 2000, 287–9). Spaini and his heightened contacts and exchanges across the European avant-garde testify to the eminently translatable potential of Triestine culture at this time, uniquely poised to export successfully a model of hybridity and multilingualism. Even Gramsci lauded Marinetti and futurist experimentations, echoing the favourable opinion expressed by Lunacharsky who had saluted Marinetti as the one and only living "revolutionary intellectual" in Italy in the course of his speech at the Second Congress of the Communist International in Moscow in 1921, which prompted Gramsci's article "Marinetti the Revolutionary?," published in *L'Ordine Nuovo* of the same year. However, this dialogical potential remained episodic at best, and failed to result in a programmatic convergence.

These full immersions in the Florentine heart of canonical Italian culture were, to a large extent, paradoxically achieved at the cost of disengaging with the linguistic and cultural fabric of the nearer region. In a geopolitical area that experienced the disintegration of Imperialism, under the pressure of combusting national forces, Slataper and his group, as well as contemporary Slovenian intellectuals, pursued translational and transcultural dynamics within a broader European arena, but not closer to home. Ossified patterns of mutual incomprehension militated against Gramsci's cultural translation. One might be tempted to invoke here Gayatri Chakravorty Spivak's view of translation as a necessary pursuit, and, at the same time, a practice engulfed in impossibility.[8]

KOSOVEL AND CONSTRUCTIVISM

Firmly committed to pan-European identity and culture, Srečko Kosovel (1904–1926), to this day one of the major and best-loved Slovenian poets of all times, came to modernism via a different route. While Slataper and the Stuparich brothers endorsed Mazzini and, at their most radical, Bauer's Austrian brand of Marxism, Kosovel and his friends strode toward a constructivism rooted in a Marxist, Bolshevik, and Soviet matrix. Kosovel's intellectual and political militancy was also oriented toward a transnational goal: transcending the region and aiming for a progressive, liberal Europe, understood as a genuinely transcultural platform. This engagement was conveyed in the avant-garde *Kons* (short for *konstrukcije* or constructions), a lyrical form that echoed contemporary experimentations across Europe, especially Eastern Europe and the Soviet Union.

Kosovel's most significant and enduring work sits at the confluence of constructivism and central-European modernism. In the summer of 1925, he started writing the *Konses* (Constructions), consisting of words-in-freedom and typographic syntheses, following the Russian constructivist model. In polemics with Dadaism and unlikely to have turned toward Italian futurism, shortly to become compromised with the Fascist regime, Kosovel reoriented toward Soviet Russia, whose politics were attuned to his own project for Slovenia.[9] Among others, Kosovel became engaged in the rehabilitation of Vladimir Tatlin and his construction art, as testified by the Manifesto *Mehanikom* (To the mechanics; see Pahor 1993; Vrecko 2011). Kosovel's *Konses* were designed to propel Slovenian national and transnational identity, and advocated for the legitimization of the Slovene nation within the framework of a new Europe. The *Konses* became mouthpieces of Kosovel's pan-European and Socialist politics, offering a platform for Slovenian radical experimental poetry and avant-garde bolshevism.

The case of Kosovel highlights the glaring disjunction between the Italian-speaking intellectuals and their neighbours. Historical legacies constructed upon mutual diffidence, incomprehension, and oppression denied fruitful interactions between neighbouring intellectuals of comparable temperament. No evidence that Kosovel knew of Slataper's work exists. Yet though Kosovel was well versed in Italian language and literature, his intellectual interests were not aligned with those of the Italian-speaking Triestines who had defected to Italy before the war. Born in the small Karst village of Sezana, a part of the Austrian Littoral and in the very heart of that sensory landscape affectively revisited by Slataper, Kosovel grew up in Ljubljana in the 1920s. This bourgeoning and distinctive cultural centre, though physically close to Trieste, was distant enough to separate Kosovel from Triestine-Italian cultural developments. Rather, Kosovel's interest in Italian literature was mediated through the influential translations of the Slovene minister and scholar Ivan Trinko (1863–1954), who translated many Italian classics. His friend and fellow contributor of *Lepa Vida*, Mirijam (aka Fanica Obid), and especially his close friend, the Neapolitan Carlo Curcio, were also influential (see Pizzi 2005). A comparable binary of missed translatability is broadly at work in the activities of the Italian modernists, aided by widespread ignorance of Slavic languages. Without going as far as accusing Stuparich of paying attention to the Czech nation as a way to blissfully bypass the Slovenes closer to home, as Thompson implies, a lack of transitivity in linguistic acquisition and competence remains an anecdotal but nonetheless robust and painfully evident feature of intercultural exchanges even today.[10]

TRANSLATION THAT EXCLUDES

The experimentalism Kosovel and his Italian counterparts pursued followed parallel and nonintersecting tracks, despite obvious cultural, if not linguistic, overlaps. I believe this calls for a reassessment of the culture of the wider Triestine region in the light of comparative and translational methodologies. Gramsci's political and humanitarian translation framework would, I believe, help recompose the fractures of official history and memory between neighbouring linguistic and ethnic groups (see Wagner 2012, 64; Klabjan 2010; Foot 2009; Pizzi 2013). Gramsci "did not look at regional languages as symbols of identity by which boundaries might be erected, leading to the exclusion of those who do not share that particular identity" (Carlucci 2013, 149). His stress was on empathic response where the interlocutor is neither a mere listener nor a subaltern, nor a counterpart characterized by

Bhabha's "otherness" or alterity, but rather a social and cultural equal to engage with in paritarian exchanges. As Carlucci puts it, "Gramsci's experiences and reflections concerning linguistic diversity helped to make him aware of the importance of working towards unification through a careful consideration of diversity – not through its denigration or coercive elimination" (200).

Cultural translation must account for the hermeneutics of liminal spaces. Trieste in the early years of the twentieth century presents a strong model of the paradoxes such spaces can generate. In its very peripherality from the centres of global capitalism, Trieste and the wider Adriatic region absorbed European modernist trends, contributing significantly to them. On the other hand, the city's intellectual life entrenched national categories, remaining largely oblivious to the literary life of its *alter* neighbour.

Due to these fractures and disjunctions, this region could hardly be described as a melting pot, or a crucible of cultures. Rather, Trieste was more frequently a "crucible *manqué*," in the words of Elio Apih (1988), a peripheral area where diverse and conflicting cultures and subcultures held together within a splintered and entropic social fabric, without becoming homogenized.[11] Torn apart by centrifugal forces, this border invokes more frequently a rift than a cultural intersection. A region that was historically unsure of itself, and a city in search of a literary identity it could call its own, became all too prone to monocultural Italian discourses (see Pizzi 2001).

In entrenched border areas, identity is frequently predicated in the negative, in opposition to that of the culturally and linguistically alien "others." This is, in other words, a culture predicated largely on alterity, militating against *traducibilità*. Here, Bhabha's notion of cultural translation as a staging of difference may be a more pertinent hermeneutic tool than Gramsci's communicative, nonhierarchical, and empathic translatability.

Today the cultural scene in Trieste and the upper Adriatic region is composite, hybridized, and productive, despite the geopolitical marginality the region was consigned to after the Cold War. In a more recent context of globalized diasporas, the national question has subsided, following a sustained wave of migrations from South-East Asia, North Africa, and the Middle East. A new generation of translational authors, whose cultural and linguistic background does not match the essentialist, indigenous paradigm of Slovenia versus Italy, is emerging.

One prominent case is the novelist and translator Lily-Amber Laila Wadia, born in Mumbai in 1966 and a resident of Trieste since 1986. Wadia writes in Italian, her second language. Among other fictional and quasi-fictional works, in 2010 she published the exhilarating *Come diventare italiani in 24 ore: Diario di un'aspirante italiana* (How to become Italian in 24 hours: Diary of a would-be Italian). An ironic and tongue-in-cheek quasi-autobiography, this manual debunks received cultural notions in reconstituted national contexts. In interviews, Wadia frequently describes her abrasive use of irony as a "weapon of mass destruction." Bypassing the postcolonial paradigm and its legacies, including Bhabha's staging of difference, Wadia seems to turn upon its head the notion of the "subaltern interlocutor," achieving translation across cultures in dialogical and nonhierarchical fashion, as Gramsci recommends. Wadia's pertinent and successful productivity scrambles and resituates received paradigms, including the essentialist paradigm of the "untranslatability" of local culture. Alongside her parallel career as professional translator and language consultant for the University of Trieste, Wadia's popularity as a creative writer speaks volumes about the need to debunk canonical notions such as centre and periphery, national, regional and transnational, monocultural and multicultural. Her work shifts and explodes ossified local binaries, reconfiguring and translating them time and time again, and pointing convincingly to realistic and productive ways forward for the culture of Trieste and the wider Adriatic region.

NOTES

1 I borrow the term "fractured memories" from Foot (2009).

2 According to Boothman (2010), "traducibilità," clarified and made explicit in Notebook 11, though hardly at the core of Gramsci's preoccupations in the *Prison Notebooks*, is nonetheless key to Gramsci's conceptual network.

3 Carlucci discusses here a note from Gramsci's *Prison Notebooks*, Notebook 11. I am grateful to Dr Carlucci for his advice.

4 *Risorgimento* is the common denomination given to the national strife accompanying Italian unification in the 1860s and 1870s.

5 This information can be gleaned in Carlucci (2013), page 148 (Gramsci became aware of Istrian multilingualism via Bartoli) and 159 (Gramsci

advocating for Slav political organization). The quoted article can be found in Gramsci (1971, 106).

6 See also Taylor-Batty (2013, 30–2).

7 See also Galofaro (2012, 97–101). In particular, Galofaro provides a semiotic analysis of Stuparich's novel hinging on Greimas's analysis of passions. Further information on Austrian Marxism can be found in Apih (1988).

8 As well as famously translating Derrida's *Grammatology*, Spivak engages with translation in, among other writings, the 2000 essay "Translation as Culture." Here Spivak regards translation psychoanalytically as a continuum with the infant's struggle to translate the world. Spivak's positions appear close to Gramsci's political view of translatability of hegemonic discourses and ethnically bound systems of value.

9 Kosovel may well have been aware here of the founding principles of the Communist-futurist collective created in 1919 within the Russian Communist Party, better known as *Komfut*.

10 In particular, I cannot agree with Thompson's (2008, 95–105) overall view of Giani Stuparich as antidemocratic and anti-Slav.

11 See Apih (1988, 75): "Trieste fu frequentemente crogiolo mancato. Era città … caratterizzata da una forte esigenza di controllo sulla circolazione delle idee, esplicata non solo al livello generale del potere politico, ma ancor più nelle diverse culture e subculture che compongono … il disomogeneo tessuto sociale" ("Trieste was more frequently a crucible *manqué*. There was a powerful need to control the circulation of ideas in the city, not only at the political level, but even more frequently at the level of the cultures and subcultures making up the dishomogenous social fabric." My translation.).

3

(Ethni)city under Scrutiny: Or, Tell Me Which Prague You Like and I'll Tell You Which Nation You Are (Not)!

MATTEO COLOMBI

BETWEEN HRADČANY AND VYŠEHRAD, OR PRAGUE ON FIRE

The term *Dreivölkerstadt* (city of three peoples), which Hans Tramer used to define Prague in 1961, refers to the three ethnic groups that could claim a continuous presence in the city from the Middle Ages to the end of World War II: Czechs, Germans, and Jews. Other ethnic communities settled in Prague over the centuries, especially when it was the residence of the Holy Roman Emperor under Charles IV in the fourteenth century and Rudolf II from the sixteenth to the beginning of the seventeenth century. Until the first decades of the nineteenth century, Prague was not a national city, at least not in the modern sense of the term. It was rather a typical *ancien régime* and imperial centre: the Prague social system was based on a nonethnic and nonnational correspondence between social roles and their vehicular languages. Prague was in fact a bilingual city of the Habsburg Empire. German was the imperial language of politics, culture, and official administration, while Czech was, at least in the seventeenth and eighteenth centuries, mostly a vernacular language that people used in everyday life (Weger 2001, 134–7). Sebastian Willibald Schießler, author of a Prague city guide published in 1812, remarks that most of the Prague population around 1800 could easily switch from one idiom to the other (quoted in Weger 2001, 136–7). Jews spoke Yiddish at home until around 1800–50, but they also knew German and often spoke Czech as well (Demetz 1997, 283–4).

Prague's cultural setting, like that of many other multiethnic Habsburg cities, began to change with the growth of nationalisms in the nineteenth century (Csáky 2010). The ideal of ethnically homogeneous and monolingual nation-states led to increasing divisions in Czech and German politics and culture in Prague and shaped the tense atmosphere at the core of the city's representation by Franz Kafka and other, mostly Jewish, German-language Prague authors. The heaviness of Prague's national conflict was conveyed by the young Kafka in a famous line written to his friend Oskar Pollak in 1902: "We ought to set fire to it [Prague] at both ends, on the Vyšehrad and on the Hradčany, and maybe then it might be possible to escape" (quoted in Pawel 1982, 90).[1] This statement is (as always in Kafka) quite elusive, multilayered and multifaceted, yet it is possible to see in the Hradčany/Vyšehrad pairing an allusion to German and Czech culture. Hradčany (Hradschin in German), the ancient hill castle of Prague, had been the Habsburg family's – as well as their local governors' – residence since the sixteenth century and was therefore a symbol of the imperial power with which Prague Germans identified. The hill of Vyšehrad had been the seat of the first castle of the Přemyslids, the Czech royal dynasty from the Middle Ages, and has housed, since the 1860s, the Czech national cemetery where the great protagonists of the Czech cultural and political Renaissance from the nineteenth century onward are buried.[2]

Hradčany and Vyšehrad stand at both edges of old Prague, a space that is home not only to Czechs and Germans but also to the Prague Jews, who found themselves caught between the city's opposed nationalisms. Following Joseph II's Edict of Tolerance (1782), Jews gradually assimilated to the German language and culture only to find themselves some decades later in the midst of the rivalry between Germans and Czechs. Both ethnic groups alternately tried to win over, reject, or instrumentalize the Jews in their mutual fight for hegemony in Prague and Bohemia (Stölzl 1982). Hence, it is understandable that Kafka dreamt of setting fire both to Hradčany and Vyšehrad in order to escape Prague's conflicted national life.

Kafka's image of Prague as a city held in the grip of German and Czech antagonism can be read through Sherry Simon's (2012, 3) concept of the dual city, an urban space in which "two historically rooted language communities ... feel a sense of entitlement to the same territory ... Both communities are 'insiders' – original or longstanding presences." The Czech and German communities of Prague are – like those of other dual cities – "supported by institutions of similar authority – universities, writers' associations, publishing houses, governmental recognition ... Their separate institutions are wary of one another, aggressive in their need for self-protection, continually laying claim to areas of culture they consider vulnerable" (3). Simon also draws attention to the fact that "additional languages often play a significant intermediate role in addition to the two main languages" (3). These third languages participate in the double dynamism of the dual cities that try to support one main community or present themselves as a distinct, autonomous element, or both. Prague did not have a third language in Kafka's time, yet it had a third ethnic group, the Jews, who spoke German and/or Czech and contributed in many ways to the landscape of dual Prague.[3]

Simon considers dual cities as "translational" (3) in the broad cultural sense of the term. The very existence of two linguistic fields determines the presence of significant transfers between individuals and communities that perceive themselves as belonging to different cultures although they share the same place. We can call these translational transfers "mediation processes" if we intend the term not in its most usual sense of conciliation or compromise but in its broadest sense of emotional and intellectual exchanges through a common medium/space – exchanges that may not only produce "engagement and creative interference" but also rely on "indifference and negation" (3). Simon remarks that cultural mediation in dual cities normally oscillates between both poles of negative and positive transfer according to complex patterns of "distancing" on the one hand and "furthering" on the other hand. Distancing mediations "deepen a sense of otherness" (13) because they rely on the assumption that the subjects involved in the cultural transfer are basically different, with restricted possibilities for communication and interaction. This assumption can both lead to politics of cultural hegemony – if a group considers itself as the sole or superior culture and tries to assimilate (or annihilate) the other group or to hold it in a subaltern position – and to politics of moderate interculturality – if two groups accept to coexist next to each other but consider contact and transfer as not a norm but an exception. On the contrary, furthering mediations are committed to the "mutual becoming" of the dual cities' cultures (17) since they start out from the idea that the daily negotiation and even entanglement of cultural differences is not only possible but also normal and beneficial in a multicultural society.

In the following chapter, I present the ambivalent interplay of Prague's cultural duality through the analysis of three different ethnonational-oriented images of the Bohemian centre: (1) *Prag deutsche Kaiserstadt* (the German imperial city of Prague), a model that celebrates Prague's historical ties with German history; (2) *zlatá slovanská Praha* (golden Slavic Prague), a model that celebrates Prague as the centre of Czech culture; and (3) the *Prag Dreivölkerstadt*, a model that affirms the presence in Prague not only of Czechs and Germans but also of Jews. These three different models have been shaped in relation to – although not necessarily in support of – the growth and expansion of nationalisms between 1800 and 1918. Afterward, they continued to play an important role in several cultural discourses from the 1920s and 1930s (Masaryk's and Beneš's Czechoslovakia), during World War II (the Nazi Protectorate of Bohemia and Moravia), and in the second half of the twentieth century until today. I concentrate my analysis on the fin de siècle and the interwar period, and show which type of cultural mediation has been pursued by each of the three Prague representational models. Both narratives of Slavic and German Prague constitute patterns of distancing mediation based on the strong contraposition between an ethnonational "we-group" and an ethnonational "other group." In contrast, the *Prag Dreivölkerstadt* model reveals a cultural agenda based on furthering mediation among the different cultural components of the city.

The three different Prague representational models are analytically distinguishable, but they tend to be simultaneously present in many cultural practices and are also an aspect of individual agency, particularly in the literary field. I shall conclude with a clear example, focusing on how František Langer, a Czech-language author from an assimilated Jewish family, negotiated and mediated between Prague's different identities. Though Langer identified with a modern and democratic idea of *zlatá slovanská Praha* during the interwar period, he also sensed the *Prag deutsche Kaiserstadt* behind the Czechoslovak appearance of his city and had to face the peculiar Jewish form of *Prag Dreivölkerstadt* that his brother Jiří, also a writer, chose for himself.

PRAGUE POLITICS OF MULTIETHNICITY

Prague's multiethnicity must be seen in the context of the multiethnic structure of the whole Kingdom of Bohemia – the Habsburg crown land of which the city was part (and capital) until 1918. This territory was as multiethnic as Prague since it was populated by

Czechs, Germans, and Jews. The Habsburg census of 1910 reports for Bohemia that 4,241,918 citizens – around 63 per cent of the population – indicated Czech as their *Umgangssprache* (language of common use) while 2,467,724 – almost 38 per cent of the population – entered German (Urbanitsch 1980, 38–9). Furthermore, the Habsburg statistics count 85,826 people of Jewish religion – approximately 2 per cent of the Bohemian inhabitants – had German or Czech as their language of common use (Bihl 1980, 882).

Historians consider these numbers difficult to interpret since the meaning of *Umgangssprache* is quite ambiguous: it indicates the language spoken at home and/or at work, which in Bohemia might not necessarily coincide with the speaker's native language. Moreover, the census does not register native or learned bilingualism and forces people to make a linguistic choice that is often perceived as a national positioning (Koeltzsch 2010). Therefore, the superimposition of *Umgangssprache* and national identity leads to an oversimplification of the Bohemian identity landscape that is particularly evident in the case of the Jewish population.

The German inhabitants of Bohemia lived mainly all over the border region of the country and were (with some exceptions) much less numerous in inner Bohemia, the Prague countryside included. Immigration from the Czech rural areas to Prague during the nineteenth century resulted in rapid growth of the Czech population in the city. More than 400,000 Prague dwellers have Czech as *Umgangssprache* according to the Habsburg census of 1910, whereas only 32,332 of 442,017 Prague inhabitants (7 per cent of the population) considered German their language of common use – approximately 15,000 of them Jews (Cohen 2000, 76).[4] The rest of the Prague Jewish population, also around 15,000, opted for Czech so that Prague Jews were equally divided between both *Umgangssprache* of the city. However, in public opinion they were more closely associated with the German language and nation since they made up more than 40 per cent of the Prague German-speaking population, whereas Prague Czech Jews were a mere 4 per cent within the Prague Czech-speaking population. The situation was different in other parts of Bohemia, where Jews normally represented a small percentage not only of the Czech- but also of the German-speaking population.

The statistics did not change drastically after 1918. Czechoslovakia had in 1921 3,123,000 citizens who declared themselves linguistically

German (23 per cent of the state population).[5] Prague had about 30,000 citizens, or about 5 per cent of the urban population, who defined themselves as linguistically German. Unlike the Habsburg state, the Czechoslovak authorities recognized Jewish people as an autonomous group independent of the language they spoke, yet not all 30,000 Prague Jews registered their nationality as Jewish in 1921 (*Dějiny Zemí* 1993, 169; *Dějiny Prahy* 1998, 305–8).

In general, the legal framework of interwar Czechoslovakia overseeing the relationships among the different ethnic groups did not change very much from the late Habsburg period. The Austrian constitution of 1867 established equal rights for all ethnic groups and for those languages and cultures that were considered *landesüblich* (customary) for a certain territory (Stourzh 1980, 1011–49).[6] Czech and German both had a *landesüblich*-status in Habsburg Bohemia so that several institutions could exist in both languages (schools and universities, public offices, theatres, and so on) (Kořalka 1997, 100–1). After the fall of the empire, Czechoslovakia recognized the Germans as a state national minority and confirmed their right to maintain institutions in their language (109–12).[7] Jews were also granted national minority status.

The relatively permissive legislation that ruled ethnonational matters both in Habsburg Bohemia and in Czechoslovakia could not, however, prevent conflicts in politics, administration, and daily life (Alexander 1997). These concerned every aspect of the social coexistence of Czech and German culture, from the number and type of schools guaranteed in each language to the language train inspectors were required to use to the language in which letters and postcards should be addressed (Kučera 1999). The political history of the Czech-German struggle in Habsburg and Czechoslovak Prague is not the topic of this chapter, yet it constitutes the background against which the three representations of *Prag deutsche Kaiserstadt*, *zlatá slovanská Praha*, and *Prag Dreivölkerstadt* took shape. The clear ethnonational contraposition on which the two first images are founded relates to their location in a politically nationalist milieu. *Prag deutsche Kaiserstadt* and *zlatá slovanská Praha* constitute narratives largely used and partly created by politicians, whereas *Prag Dreivölkerstadt* seems to be the product of intellectuals and frequently expresses a polemical attitude toward nationalist politics.

IMPERIAL GERMAN PRAGUE

Tobias Weger sums up the features of the representation of Prague as *deutsche Kaiserstadt* in two main points. He claims that (1) Prague and Bohemia have been a constitutive part of the Holy Roman Empire and cradle of the German nation from the Middle Ages onward; and (2) defensive action is required to protect Prague German tradition against the Czechization of the city (Weger 2001, 139). The *deutsche Kaiserstadt* model focuses mainly on the two historical periods in which the city became the imperial residence of the Holy Roman Emperor under Charles IV and Rudolf II. Charles IV founded the Charles University of Prague in 1348, which, according to the *deutsche Kaiserstadt* narrative, has to be considered German although it was a typical "universalist" medieval cultural institution that hosted students from four main *nationes*: Bohemia, Bavaria, Saxony, and Poland (142). The German discourse on Prague stresses moreover that Rudolf II moved the emperor's residence from Vienna to Prague and invited many artists and craftspeople from all over Europe to embellish the city. This period of prosperity is presented as an achievement of German culture, although the Habsburgs hardly conceived of themselves as German rulers in the modern national(ist) sense. Finally, German art historians began in the nineteenth century to claim that Prague's baroque urban landscape was a German legacy since it was largely the result of a Bavarian architects' family, the Dientzenhofers, who moved to the city in the seventeenth century (Weger 2001, 141). The Bohemian German historian and politician Julius Lippert writes with regard to historical Prague: "Yet Old Prague remains also in this case a familiar place for a German. One can write it white on red[8] on every cornerstone: 'Pilgrim, think of it: I am a Czech stone! Don't try to translate me!' – But the old stones laugh at the writer and speak another language to the one who knows" (Lippert 1909, 348, my translation).[9]

Czechs are considered in the *deutsche Kaiserstadt* narrative as a people who are inferior in culture and political history to the Germans but have been shrewd enough to exploit their proximity to their highly civilized neighbour. Czechs are presumed to have benefited enormously from German education, which allowed them to gain social power in a city they did not really build. The emphasis on civilizational superiority is a crucial point in relation to the minority condition of Prague Germans. The discourse of the *deutsche Kaiserstadt* underlines the fact that most Prague Germans belong to the upper class and represent the economic and cultural power typical not of minorities' but of the majorities' elites in the major European cities and nation-states (Adam 2013, 113). This identification of Germanness with culture and progress – an essential component of German liberalism within the Habsburg Empire – allowed Prague's conspicuous German-speaking Jewish population to appropriate the *deutsche Kaiserstadt* discourse too. The Jews can in fact present their assimilation to the German language as a civilizational commitment to a culture that – even as the expression of a minority – combines a powerful tradition with a strong modern élan.

The *deutsche Kaiserstadt* image of Prague found diverse applications before and after 1900. Some of them were radically nationalist, others more moderate according to their willingness to acknowledge the Czech presence in Prague and to recognize the necessity of an open interethnic dialogue. Germans who moved from the Bohemian border territories to Prague often adopted a strong nationalist position. By contrast, Prague Germans – because many were Jewish – tended to be more conciliatory toward the Czechs.

A clear example of a radically nationalist representation of Prague as *deutsche Kaiserstadt* is the literary work of Karl Hans Strobl, a German writer from Southern Bohemia.[10] In his novels – among them *Die Vaclavbude* (Vaclav's digs, 1902) and *Das Wirtshaus "Zum König Przemysl"* ("King Przemysl's" inn, 1913) – he describes Prague as a battlefield in which Germans and Czechs fight for hegemony. Strobl's Prague literary image is extremely black and white: Germans play here the role of an ancient civilization forced to fight against the Czech barbarians. Moreover, the opposition between both groups is not only cultural but also racial. Strobl claims in *Das Wirtshaus "Zum König Przemysl"* that Czechs embody the Asian mongoloid character, yet he admits that some of them could take advantage of long proximity with the Germans to acquire a "germanoid" superior nature. These Czechs are worthy of assimilation to German culture (Strobl 1913; Vahoosthuyse 1996, 311–14).

An echo of Strobl's nationalism can be found also in some German Prague postcards from the turn of the century. They proudly show the old buildings of the city that are tied to German history and include sayings like "Prague – the German law ruled here once, and holy were here the German customs."[11] Other postcards reflect the national-liberal position of the Prague (Jewish) Germans and stress the achievements of German culture rather than the political power of the Germans.

These postcards depict among others the Deutsches Haus (German house), one of the most established Prague German cultural institutions.

The hard-core nationalist approach to *Prag deutsche Kaiserstadt* is a clear example of distancing cultural mediation in a dual city. It represents Germans and Czechs as two completely different groups divided by a clear hierarchical binarism (civilization/culture versus barbarism, law/customs versus social wilderness). This binarism can be explicitly stated as in Strobl's novels, or hinted at as in a postcard saying that there was – once upon a time – German order ruling in Prague. Soft-core German nationalism is different because it can also imply further moments of cultural exchange. This is the case of the travel city guide *Prag (Praha)* published in 1928 by the Prague German scholar Anton Michalitschke. The guide was mainly interested in presenting Prague from a German perspective, yet Michalitschke praised the lively building operations the Czechs conducted in Prague after 1918 (Thomsen 2010, 235). Nevertheless, his guide remains distancing at its core since it conveys the idea that the German and the Czech nations are two constitutively different entities. Both German hard- and soft-core nationalist discourses presuppose that being *Deutscher* or *Čech* is a much more fundamental identity marker than being a Prague dweller (whether *Prager* or *Pražan*).

MODERN CZECH PRAGUE

The Czech political and cultural Renaissance of the nineteenth century led to the representation of Prague as a Czech and more generally as a Slavic city. In the beginning, the Czech narrative resembled the German discourse on the historical *deutsche Kaiserstadt* Prague and highlighted the many achievements of the Czech people in Prague. The Czech historian František Palacký and the other organizers of the Slavic Congress that took place in 1848 in Prague invited the participants to *staroslawná slowanská Praha* (time-honoured Slavic Prague) – using this appellative to refer to the foundational myth of the city whose future greatness was first prophesied by the legendary Czech princess Libuše (Adam 2013, 104). Moreover, the idea of *staroslawná slowanská Praha* also implied a Czech perspective on the figure of Charles IV as the half-Czech son of Elizabeth of Bohemia, the last member of the Czech royal Přemyslid dynasty.[12] The third argument for the Czech historical legacy of Prague is its role as centre of Hussitism and its rebellion against the allegiance between the Catholic Church and the Holy Roman Empire – a late medieval/early Modern Age religious and political conflict that was simplistically interpreted in modern national terms as a Czech-German conflict (Demetz 1997, 138).

The Czech discourse on Prague clearly changed from the 1860s on, when Czechs became the majority in the city council (*Dějiny Prahy* 1998, 148–9). From then on, they made the city's modernization the main point of their political program. They supported the demolition and reconstruction of Josefov/Josephstadt, the neighbourhood of the old Prague ghetto, and they sponsored the construction of monumental public buildings like the National Theatre, one of the most visible symbols of Czech national power in fin de siècle Prague. The division of the university into a German and a Czech institution in 1882 also reflected Czechs' eagerness in presenting themselves and their capital as agents of progress and modernity (Schmitz and Udolph 2001, 84–6).[13] This was also the year in which the Czech mayor of Prague, Tomáš Černý, made the expression *zlatá slovanská Praha* popular. In his maiden speech, he clearly showed that Prague had not only a glorious Slavic and Czech history but also a prosperous present. Černý distinguished Prague as an intermediary between the German and the Slavic world, yet he also very confidently stated that this relationship was not based on the alleged superiority of German culture but on the fair competition of two equal nations (81).

Indeed, Černý's image of the golden Slavic city of Prague presents an aspect of furthering cultural mediation in the idea of a fair competition between Czechs and Germans. Nonetheless, his representational model is based on the same distancing principle of *Prag deutsche Kaiserstadt*. According to Černý, Czechness and Germanness constitute two unequivocally different entities whose encounter in Prague cannot help but become a "politically correct" race for hegemony. The distancing substructure of the *zlatá slovanská Praha* image became progressively stronger with the rise of Czech power in Bohemia and reached its peak in the interwar period after the foundation of Czechoslovakia. The distancing mediation pattern provided by this narrative can be observed – as in the case of the *deutsche Kaiserstadt* model – in different sectors of cultural public life, for example in literary criticism. In 1917, the Czech literary scholar Arne Novák published a very critical review of the Prague novel *Der Golem* (The golem, 1915), a bestseller by the German author Gustav Meyrink.[14] Novák's title already sounds inquisitive – *Pražský román?* (Prague novel?) – and he builds a strong opposition between (allegedly bad) German and (allegedly good) Czech novels on Prague. Novák claims that German writers are obsessed with the past and unable to perceive the lively atmosphere of modern Prague. They belong to and write about a decadent *plemeno* (race) "born to the pleasure of the spirit and the body, today tending its greedy hands toward all women and tomorrow swallowing in mystical dreams" (Novák 1922, 181).[15] Their novels, he says, present a nonexistent Prague preserved in a vicious circle of fantasies,[16] whereas Czech novels aspire "to become aware of the local social reality and to examine it," putting it "in a dramatic dialogue ... with the bygone ages" (182–3).[17]

The styling of *zlatá slovanská Praha* as a bridge between the past and present of Czech culture is also visible in Czech postcards from the city. They not only show ancient buildings like the Charles Bridge (Karlův most in Czech, Karlsbrücke in German), but also often reproduce symbols of Czech culture like the (Czech) National Theatre (Národní divadlo) or the roomy Wenceslas Square (Václavské Náměstí in Czech, Wenzelsplatz in German).[18] These postcards frequently celebrate Czech national events like the meeting of the national sport association *Sokol* (Hawk) (Jaworski 2010, 217–24).

The national praising of Czech Prague is also evident in Czech city guides – both the ones written in Czech for Czechs and the ones that Czechs published in German for German-speaking visitors and German Prague dwellers. These guides emphasize the history of Czech national buildings and describe the Czech-driven new architectural development of Prague in the twentieth century (Thomsen 2010, 236–8). They do mention the important role Germans played in old Prague's cultural history, yet they also try to relativize this German contribution. The Czech geographer Jiří Král remarks in his *Reiseführer durch die Čechoslowakische Republik* (Travel guide through the Czechoslovak Republic, 1928) that not only German but also French and Italian architects and artists worked in Prague for centuries. He also claims that "many Germanized families remained inwardly Czech" even in times of strong Germanization (Král 1928, 40–1, my translation).[19] In fact, the *zlatá slovanská Praha* image is clearly as ethnocentric as the *deutsche Kaiserstadt* discourse: it also considers national differences among Prague dwellers more important than their common belonging to the same place.

MAGICAL, POLEMICAL JEWISH PRAGUE

The image of *Prag Dreivölkerstadt* is an integrative one. It takes into account that the city's history as well as its present life has been shaped both by Czechs and Germans – and also by Jews. Like *Prag deutsche Kaiserstadt* and *zlatá slovanská Praha*, *Prag Dreivölkerstadt* is a representational mode based on legendary and historical references. It combines the Czech and the German discourses with several hints regarding the role of the Prague Jewish community in Prague history and culture. It includes, for example, the famous Rabbi Löw and his relationship to emperor Rudolf II, the Golem legend as well as other ghetto stories (Schmitz and Udolph 2001, 172–94). These references are the basis of Prague's image as a magical city (163–7), of the romanticized and exoticized Prague that finds followers among both Czech and German authors (164, 167), as well as all over Europe (Demetz 1997, 318–22). The attitude of the *magisches Prag* narrative toward the city's multiethnicity seems quite ambivalent. On the one hand, it represents Czech-German-Jewish coexistence as something picturesque, which is itself a kind of magic that does not really correspond to the reality of the modern world. On the other hand, it also alludes to the sociopolitical and ethnonational dynamics of the city.

One of the best-known representations of the *magisches Prag* is the above-mentioned novel *Der Golem* by Gustav Meyrink. Meyrink sets his story mainly in the Prague ghetto and depicts it as a gloomy and spooky place suspended between reality and magic. He employs the conventions of romance literature to combine Jewish mysticism and legend with Christian superstition about Jewish diversity and/or perverseness. The novel's characters, some of them Jews, speak German if they belong to the upper classes but either German or Czech if they come from the lower classes. Meyrink (1995, 206) also refers to the differences between standard German and Prague German dialect and to the possibility of Czech/German bilingualism, for example mentioning the German spoken by the Czechs from Vienna:[20] "'You gentleman appear to be acquainted, if you allow the remark,' said the prisoner with uncombed hair in the slightly stilted [dialect] characteristic of Viennese Czechs, sketching a mocking bow in my direction. 'Permit me to introduce myself: Vossátka's the name, Black Vóssatka. Arson' he added an octave lower, his voice throbbing with pride."[21]

Novák's dislike for *Der Golem* is understandable. The novel's setting is clearly the old city: Meyrink even shapes his story as an evocation of a place that is definitely lost in the past since he concludes his story with the ghetto's renovation. Furthermore, the plot is a mixture of eroticism and mysticism in which the Czech language is associated with the lower classes. Meyrink neither celebrates the glory of the Czech city nor represents in a realistic way its modern complexity and challenges. Nevertheless *Der Golem* is not a German nationalist text that seeks a binary distancing of superior Germans on the one hand and inferior Czechs on the other. Meyrink undoubtedly plays with German stereotypes, but he exaggerates them by means of the romance and fantastic structure of his novel. His playfulness relativizes the German national perspective implicit in his representation of the Czechs as socially subaltern. Moreover, *Der Golem* makes no rigid distinction between the different Prague linguistic, social, or national groups. Rather, it shows how they regularly come together in the ghetto slums and dives, or in prison.[22] Finally, through the whole novel the Jewish element complicates the binarism of the German-Czech Prague identity frame. The fictional displacement of the Prague national issue is typical not only for Meyrink but also for all authors working on the image of the *magisches Prag*, including the Czech authors that Novák seems to forget when he compares the "decadent" German authors with the "realist" Czech writers.[23] This feature of the *magisches Prag* discourse can be read as a political and polemical statement about the overcharged atmosphere of the ethnonational struggle in Prague (Řezníková 2004).

The Czech/German conflict and the Jews' precarious position in the national struggle has led some Prague intellectuals to reflect in a new way upon the ethnic diversity of their city. They partly renounce the exoticism of *magisches Prag* or reshape it in an explicitly political way (Colombi and Řezníková 2010). Their *Prag Dreivölkerstadt* narrative claims that it is not possible to found Prague's history on the prominence of one ethnic group over the others. According to this discourse, it is risky to shape the city's present and future on a national competition that produces artificial identities and mutual isolation (68–9). The intellectuals who support the idea of a Prague of three peoples suggest that a better way to understand the city would be to accept and respect its multiethnic structure, the very coexistence of the Czech, German, and Jewish cultures as three elements that have an equal right to set their seal on Prague (Řezníková 2013, 122–3).

The cosmopolitan Czech and Czech-Jewish intelligentsia have tended to be quite open to the three-peoples discourse while continuing to stress the driving role of Czech culture in Prague.[24] Many German-speaking advocates of *Prag Dreivölkerstadt* accept and sustain Czech cultural and political rights. They recognize the Czechs' right to political emancipation in polemics against both the German hard-core nationalism from the Bohemian province and the soft-core nationalism of the Prague German liberals:

> We began again to speak Czech as we had in our childhood. We breathed more freely and more naturally than before. We felt firm ground under our feet – we were no longer suspended in the air of social illusions as our mothers and fathers had been. We now knew, as the most humane and liberal among our Czech friends told us: Old Austria had unfortunately come to an end in Prague and Bohemia. And this was also our fathers' fault, though they were not solely responsible. The main culprits were the German Nationals in Aussig [Ustí nad Labem in Czech language], Eger [Cheb], and Vienna. And we had the same reasons as our Czech friends to hate these anti-Semites and Hitler's forerunners. (Haas 1957, 36, my translation)[25]

This quotation by the Prague German-Jewish journalist, screenwriter, and literary and film critic Willy Haas exemplifies the political complexity of the *Prag Dreivölkerstadt* discourse. This narrative, on the one hand, supports the cultural and political specificity of each Bohemian ethnic group/nation, including the Jews, but, on the other hand, tries not to think of ethnonational relations according to a hierarchical scheme. The *Prag Dreivölkerstadt* perspective seeks to avoid both the ethnic violent competition and mutual exclusions supported by radical nationalism and the gradual cultural assimilation for which liberalism strives. This political challenge determines the great heterogeneity of the *Prag Dreivölkerstadt* image depending on its different interpreters. As a matter of fact, the city of three peoples constitutes the starting point for several different cultural-political proposals: humanist nationalism, Zionism, or Socialism, along with various combinations and paths in-between (Spector 2000). The two common features of all these statements on the challenges of Prague's multiethnicity seem to be (1) the conviction that the dialogue among Czech, German, and Jewish cultures in Prague is inevitable, and (2) the question of how to make that dialogue fruitful (Colombi and Řezníková 2010, 66). The Prague Jewish man of letters Max Brod, one of Kafka's closest friends and the posthumous editor of his literary work, writes about the meaning of Prague's multiethnic dialogue in his autobiography *Streitbares Leben* (Combative life, 1969). He claims that the greatest opportunity Prague gave to its dwellers was precisely the possibility of having an everyday multiethnic dialogue. This dialogue could undoubtedly be very polemical and did not necessarily lead to mutual comprehension, yet it allowed dwellers to be immersed in cultural complexity from childhood onward:

> All my life, quite against my will, I have had to struggle with someone. Thus, I can and must call myself an unwilling polemicist. It seems to me that this is less my fault than the fault of the city where I was born and where I spent the longest time of my life. It is Prague's fault. Old Austrian Prague was a city where not only individuals were polemical against each other but also where three nations were fighting against each other ... As young people growing up in the early 1900s, we often discussed these and similar difficulties, because life, the problem of bilingualism, had already brought us face to face with cultural decisions that inhabitants of a monolingual region are spared. Prague, the city of three nations, Prague, the polemic city. (Brod 1969, 74, my translation)[26]

Brod's emphasis on Prague's cultural disquiet is not at odds with his intimate connection, his respect, or even his enthusiasm for the polemical multiethnicity of his hometown. It is, on the contrary, the very reason for his positive feelings toward Prague. His warm praise of the city is surely also due to the fact that multiethnic Prague no longer existed at the time he was writing his memories after World War II. The Third Reich annihilated most Prague and Czechoslovak Jews, and most Germans were banished from Czechoslovakia in 1946. Brod escaped Nazism by emigrating to Palestine in 1939, and his autobiography belongs to that group of texts in which Prague migrants evoke a now-forgotten city of three peoples (Tramer's *Die Dreivölkerstadt Prag* is also one such text). These works tend to represent Prague's multiethnicity in a more conciliatory way than those written while still living in Prague. The latter depict national polemics less idealistically, as an inspiring though often frustrating daily effort (Colombi and Řezníková 2010, 73–5).

Nevertheless, *Prag Dreivölkerstadt* supporters seem to have played a furthering role from the very beginning. From 1900 on, negotiation among different cultures has clearly been central to their discourse, even though this cultural convergence is not necessarily presented as satisfying but rather as challenging and sometimes even annoying. The furthering intent of the *Prag Dreivölkerstadt* discourse is particularly evident in its commitment to translation as a form of positive mediation between different identities. Several intellectuals took part in this work, occasionally or regularly, by translating Czech literature into German and/or vice versa (Džambo 2010; Spector 2000, 195–233). Combining translation with literary criticism and essayistic engagement, these scholars presented texts written by "the other" in a way that transcends the conceptual schemes of German and Czech nationalism. This mediation process is fuelled by the deep conviction that Prague needs an intense cultural dialogue among its linguistic-ethnonational groups, albeit one that is neither stable nor linear. This shift in perspective reveals the mediators' diversity, as well as their polemics with colleagues and individual struggles – every single cultural actor comes to grips with their own political conscience (Koeltzsch 2012, 179–251). However, the cultural furthering of *Prag Dreivölkerstadt* does not go so far as to definitively blur the boundaries between different national identities. As Scott Spector (2000, xi) states, the aim of the *Dreivölkerstadt* authors is not to examine Prague's many in-between spaces in order to completely displace its ethnonational identities. These writers do not want to reach a condition of permanent transmutation and deterritorialization. Rather, they reject certain territorializing concepts in favour of approaches that are more suitable to addressing the linguistic duality and ethnonational triality of their city. They seek alternatives to the *Prag deutsche Kaiserstadt* and *zlatá slovanská Praha* models. The reterritorialization of these authors follows different patterns according to the individuals and the (more or less hybrid) *Weltanschauungen* they rely on (238).[27]

The German-assimilated Jew Max Brod, for example, embraced Zionism in the 1910s and resituated himself in Prague as a Jew. Nevertheless, he still considered himself deeply tied to both Czech and German culture, and mediated between them. Working mainly as a talent scout, arts critic, and occasional translator, he was instrumental in introducing Czech author Jaroslav Hašek and his novel *Osudy dobrého vojáka Švejka za světové války* (The good soldier Švejk, 1921–23) to the German public. He also contributed to composer Leoš Janáček's fame throughout Europe (Šrámková 2010; Kundera 1993). Brod's concept of *Prag Dreivölkerstadt* is undoubtedly based on cultural furthering, yet also allows some space for cultural distancing. He defined his relationship with Czechs and Germans as a form of *Distanzliebe*, a "distant love" that he feels for both his non-Jewish fellow citizens' communities and to which he also owes his native language (Brod 1968, 52–3).[28]

FRANTIŠEK LANGER, OR NOT EVERYONE LIKES PRAGUE IN THE SAME WAY

František Langer represents a stimulating case study of how the three representational models of *Prag deutsche Kaiserstadt*, *zlatá slovanská Praha*, and *Prag Dreivölkerstadt* can interact together. Langer belongs to the group of Czech intellectuals that gave full cultural support to the politics of the first president of the Czechoslovak Republic, Tomáš Garrigue Masaryk.[29] He sustains Masaryk's idea of a humanistic democracy based not only on codified law and social freedom but also on an ethic of mutual respect and solidarity among citizens. He shares with Masaryk both his engagement for a modern Czechoslovak state that breaks with the *ancien régime* legacy of the Habsburg empire and his scepticism toward uncontrolled capitalism (Lehár et al. 1996–98, 550–2). Langer's literary works – the best known are plays – are thus engaged in the Czech cultural debate on modernity (Holý 1991, 301–6). His work also contributes to the Czech literary discourse about Prague, for example through the drama *Periferie* (Periphery, 1925), which is based on the metropolitan social conflicts between the rich city centre and the poor suburbs. Langer's approach to *zlatá slovanská Praha* is strongly based on the ideal of a modern democratic "civilism" that overcomes ethnonational conflicts. He seems to consider the struggle between the Czech majority and the German minority in Prague as a problem that was solved by the proclamation of an independent and democratic Czechoslovakia after World War I, a nation-state committed by law to protect its minorities.

Langer's literary indifference to the Czech/German topic corresponds to a general, although not absolute, trend of Czech interwar literature. Czech writers tended to concentrate on subjects other than the old national conflicts, focusing on the perceived urgency of political and ideological class struggles and the necessity of a new aesthetics able to represent modern life (Colombi 2009, 156–7). The relative indifference of interwar Czech literature toward the topic of the Czech-German struggle constitutes a significant discrepancy between the literary discourse and Czech politics from the 1920s and 1930s. Politicians and political activists continued to highlight the national conflict in Prague. In 1932, the Czech nationalist Prague mayor Karel Baxa praised the Czech masses that visited Prague for the ninth meeting of the Sokol sporting association, shouting "Ať žije slovanská Praha" (Long live Slavic Prague!) (Adam 2013, 107). Many Prague Czech citizens protested when a cinema showed a sound film in the German language in 1930 (Gruša et al. 1993, 65–6; Koeltzsch 2012, 240–2).

Langer comments in "*Demonstrace proti německým filmům*" (Demonstrations against German movies), an article for the pro-Masaryk newspaper *Přítomnost* (The present):

> Every nationalism becomes one of the most disgusting things in the world the moment that it comes out on the streets roaring national songs and demonstrating with stones against another nation ... Thus, the patriotic spirit has turned against German movies simply because German speech on the screen represents a threat to the Slavic character of Prague just as German conversation on a tram or in a café would. And because of that protesters have also managed to have *Two Hearts in Waltz Time*[30] removed from the movie program, although everyone has to recognize that it was a "fully fledged" German film.[31] It had been showing at the theatre for several months and was seen not only by 50,000 Prague Germans but also by 100,000 pure Czech citizens. There is a certain irony in it ... The irony is that people were singing the praises of Czech cinema but rejecting films that could work as a bridge. (Langer 2001, 273–76, my translation)[32]

This quotation exemplifies Langer's tolerant attitude toward the German minority in Prague, which was also central to Masaryk's political program that encouraged dialogue between all Czechoslovak minorities, including the Jews. Langer's point of view on Prague's multiethnicity goes further than the idea of fair competition between Czechs and Germans promoted by Černý in the 1880s. Rather, he favours mutual collaboration between both ethnic groups for the sake of a modern civil society (and good films). According to him, the Masarykian vision of democracy has to become the common identitary goal of Czechs and Germans in Prague as well as in the whole Czechoslovak Republic.

Langer's criticism of nationalism finds an indirect expression also in his novel *Zázrak v rodině* (Miracle in the family, 1928–29), one of the few texts in which he deals at least tangentially with the Czech-German topic. The novel's protagonists, the Hejda family, move from Vienna to Prague after the end of World War I. Mr and Mrs Hejda, born into Czech families in middle Bohemia and Vienna, respectively, meet in the Austro-Hungarian capital where Mr Hejda works in the Habsburg administration and Mrs Hejda is associated with the upper middle class society of the imperial city. Langer presents the family's relocation to Prague not as a result of Czech national engagement, but rather as a way to maintain a standard of life and social status comparable to that enjoyed in Habsburg Vienna. The young Czechoslovak state needs qualified public servants like Mr Hejda and is willing to give them good professional opportunities without making them prove the depths of their patriotism. Through the figure of Mr Hejda, Langer alludes to the relative continuity of the administrators' mentality from the Habsburg time up to the Czechoslovak *zlatá slovanská Praha*. Langer remarks that Czech public servants from the interwar period had a Habsburg education, regardless of whether it was in the Czech or German language, or both. They still share a common attitude toward the state and are influenced by the values of Habsburg society. Langer is somewhat ironic about the reverent loyalty that Mr Hejda feels for the state's institutions, whether imperial like in Vienna or republican like in Prague. He seems to consider his character's mentality, at least to a certain extent, as one of those relics from the Habsburg time that should be "integrated" by a new democratic consciousness.

Yet Langer is not only (benevolently) critical of the cultural values of the Habsburg period. In *Zázrak v rodině*, he also questions the nationalistic celebratory representations of Czech *zlatá slovanská Praha* as a city that has nothing left from German culture. It is not only Mrs Hejda, he seems to suggest, who in Prague "spoke Czech in the same way she could talk in German, she did not put any emphasis on the language problem" (Langer 2001, 6).[33] Langer reminds of the fact that interwar Prague may not have been the Habsburg *Kaiserstadt* of Rudolf's time, but for centuries it was a city ruled by the Habsburg dynasty. This very fact determined the continuous exposure of Prague and its Czech population to German culture and vice versa, a practice already established in the Middle Ages. Indeed, Langer is not particularly interested in the Prague national issue, yet he remarks in

Zázrak v rodině that no image can grasp the city's complexity if it completely ignores its double Czech-German historical background.

Langer actually had intimate exposure to Prague bilingualism since his younger brother Jiří, also a writer, wrote in both Czech and German. Jiří also learned and could write in Hebrew, making him a perfect example of *Prag Dreivölkerstadt*, even more than some Prague Zionist propagators who did not always have a good command of Hebrew. Jiří spoke German very well and could easily move between the Czech and the German Prague milieus. He shared with many German-speaking Jewish writers such as Brod and Kafka an interest in Jewish history and Yiddish culture. Yet he questioned his own assimilation in a more radical way than his contemporaries. He was fascinated by Eastern European Chassidism and went to Galicia to live in a Chassidic community for the first time in 1913. Afterward, he spent his life mediating between Czech and German culture as well as between assimilated and unassimilated Jewish culture, first in his hometown Prague and later in Palestine, where he emigrated during World War II and died in 1943.[34]

Langer spoke about his brother for the first time in 1959–60, when he included some comments about him in a Czech Jewish yearbook. His text was published as the introduction to the English translation of Jiří's collection of Chassidic tales *Devět bran* (Nine gates, 1937) in 1961.[35] This work represents a lively document of cultural mediation between František's *Weltanschauung* – based on the values of Masarykian democracy – and his brother's strong fascination for the Jewish mysticism of east-central Europe. Langer (1993, ix) states from the outset that the world his brother devoted himself to was not the "enlightened" and civilized world to which the rest of his family felt committed:

> To write this book my brother Jiří Langer had to transport himself from the living reality of the twentieth century into the mystical and ecstatic atmosphere of the Middle Ages. Nor could this be effected merely in a metaphorical way, on the wings of fantasy. It had to begin with the reality of purchasing a railway ticket at a station in Prague to a little place in eastern Galicia. [Such a thing was easy at that time, it did not require any formality. Bohemia was then part of the Austro-Hungarian Monarchy that joined together various distant regions, nations, and levels of civilization.] Thus, it was that after twenty-four hours of travel, or a little

> longer, in a dirty train, Jiří found himself five hundred kilometres away to the east, and simultaneously two, or even five, centuries back in time.[36]

Langer's reference to the extent and diversity of the Habsburg monarchy is surely due to the need to provide some historical background for the anglophone readers. Yet his words also suggest that the dual monarchy was a strange world that tried to keep together incompatible realities like (Czech) high and (Galician Jewish) low civilization, and still it was the latter that Jiří elected as his own in 1913. He came back from Galicia to Prague dressed like a Chassid. He wore a black kaftan, a black hat, and a long beard. He did not wash his hands before eating, he always turned his back when speaking with women, and he sang his prayers in a sort of trance. Jiří wanted to live in Prague not as a Czech, German, assimilated Jew, or even a westernized Zionist but, rather, as a Prague Chassid, which was quite unique in Prague despite the diverse identities that inspired and defined its inhabitants.[37]

Langer mentions that the German-Jewish writers that were interested in the *Prag Dreivölkerstadt* and in the Jewish discourse, for example Kafka, found his brother's conversion to Chassidism quite stimulating. It was more difficult for the Langer family to get used to Jiří's way of life, since their relationship to Jewishness was quite distant. Langer's memoirs vividly describe the sense of embarrassment he and his family experienced when Jiří strolled through Prague in his kaftan. Relatives never refused Jiří but they could not really interact with him until he partially re-Westernized his look and accepted a post at Prague's Hebrew school. The teaching profession was something that suited the worldview of the Langer family, who were still concerned about Jiří's blurred social position. It is revealing that Langer prized among all his brothers' writings the Chassidic legends written in the 1930s. As he remarks, they were written in a (Czech) language that was also comprehensible to general readers as well as Jewish mystics, and he likes these texts even more because they had "to tell something different about the Jews from that which Nazi anti-Semitism was endeavouring to smuggle across the Czechoslovak frontiers" (Langer 1993, xxvii).[38] From the 1930s on, Langer was able to see in his brother's cultural engagement with Chassidism a civilian commitment to democracy against anti-Semitism, and this allowed him to "translate" part of Jiří's world into his own.

The conclusion of Langer's memoirs suggests once again that he could not but consider Chassidism as a worldview and life practice that had become anachronistic in the contemporary world. Yet the last sentences of his text also convey a certain understanding for the idealizing fascination his brother felt for the Chassidic way of life. The text's final words express Langer's acceptance of the fact that archaic social structures may still exist in the twentieth century, even if they are disappearing in Western society. As long as these structures survive or are remembered, Langer (1993, xxxiv) claims, there will also be people like Jiří who find them more attractive than modernity:

> It may be that among the Jews in Israel or New York there are a few handfuls of the old Chassidic believers still adhering to the customs that they have brought from their old homes. But these are merely so many reminiscences of the past. The mystical reality of the *chasidim* cannot last under the blue sky of Israel or amid the bustle of the streets of Brooklyn. It could only exist in the utter isolation from the world and time that it enjoyed in Galicia, in that poverty in which all were equal, in that freedom in which they were subjected to naught save the will of God, and in that spiritual grandeur that came to dwell in their villages through the wisdom and miracles of their saintly rabbis. And thus is what that my brother Jiří depicted it for the last time in his sweet and smiling book, thereby erecting for the *chasidim* an eternal monument to preserve their memory for all time.[39]

Langer's identification with Czech culture and Czech Prague corresponds to the hegemonic discourse of interwar Czechoslovakia. Yet he follows the Masarykian cosmopolitan and civilian version of this discourse, including a certain attentiveness toward the minority cultures of Prague and Czechoslovakia. This openness allows Langer not only to distance himself from Czech nationalism but also to recognize how deeply intertwined the Czech and German cultures were within the Habsburg Empire. The empire fell but Czech's mentality is still tied to it. Moreover, Langer recognizes that his family, despite its assimilation to Czech culture, is in some way still Jewish, especially since his brother attempted to revive his ancestor's traditions. Langer thus realizes that his ideal of a democratic and pluralistic *zlatá slovanská Praha* based in the interwar period has had to evolve and accept other images of Prague. He now has to consider not only the

German but also the Czech hidden nostalgias for the old *deutsche Kaiserstadt*, and be flexible enough to include Jiří's Chassidic version of *Prag Dreivölkerstadt*. Langer, a Czech citizen, seems to hold for both German/Habsburg and Jewish Prague that kind of *Distanzliebe* that Brod, for his part, claims to feel as a Jew and Zionist for Czech and German culture – a kind of lively distancing-and-furthering mediation that attempts to translate their own expectations into the others' and vice versa. Brod and Langer, as well as other Prague social actors, rely on this strategy to cope with the ethnonational tensions of their city of three peoples. In practising *Distanzliebe*, they seek that balance between a longing for identity and an opening to diversity.

NOTES

1 "An zwei Seiten müßten wir es anzünden, am Vysehrad und am Hradschin, dann wäre es möglich, daß wir loskommen" (Kafka 1958, 14). The quotation belongs to the famous passage beginning: "Prag läßt nicht los. Uns beide nicht. Dieses Mütterchen hat Krallen" (Prague doesn't let go. Neither one of us. This little mother has claws).
2 Hradčany plays an important role in the Czech nationalist narrative, too. It can be assumed that Kafka is not thinking of it in his letter because he wants to stress the opposition between German and Czech nationalism in Prague. Yet it is also possible that Kafka just thinks of Hradčany as a symbol of oppressive power, whether German or Czech.
3 Jewishness is, of course, a tricky category since it has both an ethnic and a religious valence. I focus in this analysis on the former, this being crucial for the Jews' condition in Prague from the nineteenth century onward. Both the Czech/German national struggle and anti-Semitism tend to subordinate the religious aspect of Jewishness to the ethnic one. Zionism is for its part quite ambivalent on this issue. Its secularized wing tends to subordinate religion to the ethnonational discourse while its spiritual wing tends to connect the religious and the ethnonational aspect or even to base the latter on the former. On the reception of this debate within the Prague Jewish community, see Baioni (1984, ch. 1).
4 Cohen also includes in the calculation of Prague inhabitants residents of municipalities like Smichov/Smichow and Královské Vinohrady/Königliche Weinberge, which in 1910 were still autonomous although they de facto constituted Prague suburbs. They were incorporated into the Prague munic-

ipality after World War I. For other statistics in relation to the Prague ethnonational groups, see Koeltzsch (2012, 356–65).

5 The statistics comprise the German speakers not only from Bohemia but also from the other regions of Czechoslovakia.

6 The Austrian constitution is valid only in the Austrian part of the Austro-Hungarian Empire, that is in *Die im Reichsrat vertretenen Königreiche und Länder* (The kingdoms and lands represented in the imperial council), the Bohemian Kingdom being one of them. The Hungarian part of the empire has its own constitution and different ethnonational policies.

7 Kořalka (1997, 112–13) remarks that Germans felt discriminated against by the Czechoslovak law although they basically had the same rights in the new state that they had in the Habsburg period. The reason is that the empire was by its constitution a multiethnic state, in which most ethnic groups were – at least in the Austrian part – legally equal. By contrast, Czechoslovakia was by law the Czechoslovaks' nation-state in which Germans were only a national minority. Within the new Republic, Germans had to renounce not only the privileged status they had de facto – although not by law – in the Habsburg Monarchy. They also had to cope with the status of a minority de jure, a legal position they felt was precarious.

8 White and red are the colours of the Bohemian Kingdom. In the nineteenth century, they gradually become a symbol of Czech patriotism.

9 "Aber auch so bleibt dem Deutschen das alte Prag eine vertraute Stätte. Mag man es auch weiß auf rot auf jeden Eckstein schreiben: 'Wandrer, denk dir: ich bin ein tschechischer Stein! O, daß du mich ja nicht übersetzest!' – die alten Steine lachen den Schreiber an und reden eine andere Sprache zu dem Wissenden!" (quoted in Adam 2013, 109).

10 Strobl did not come from the German-populated border of Bohemia. He was born in the town of Jihlava (Iglau in German) that constituted like Prague a bilingual city surrounded by a Czech-speaking countryside. Yet the large majority of the Jihlava population spoke German and the town counted fewer Jews among its members than the Prague German linguistic community. Therefore, German city dwellers from Jihlava shared a mentality similar to that of the Bohemian Germans living at the border of the region.

11 "Prag – hie galt vorzeiten deutsches Recht und heilig war hier die deutsche Sitte" (quoted in Jaworski 2010, 216).

12 On the relationship between Charles IV, his Přemyslid descent, and Czech culture, see Demetz (1997, 72–7).

13 Schmitz and Udolph remark that the evolution from the historical image of *zlatá slovanská Praha* into the image of the modern city has not gone com-

pletely unchallenged. Some Czech intellectuals protest against the demolition of old buildings and the whole ghetto (Schmitz and Udolph 2001, 84). The polemics against urban modernization become an area of complex competition and collaboration between different Czech and German cultural agents – with the latter also interested in preserving the historical fabric of the city that they tend to consider "German" (Adam 2013, 111–12).

14 Gustav Meyrink was not a Prague or Bohemian German and he did not have Jewish origins. He was born in Vienna and lived in Prague from 1884 to 1904. Prague is an important subject in his prose, together with Jewish mysticism and other forms of esoteric knowledge.

15 "Zrozené k rozkoši ducha i těla ... dnes vztahující lačné ruce po všech ženách a zítra opájející se mystickými sny."

16 The German Prague novels Novák speaks of seem to depict Prague in a decadent way that diverges from the *deutsche Kaiserstadt* narrative presented above. This narrative indeed looks to the past of the city, but it does not necessarily have decadent features. The fact is that Novák here partly relates to another Prague narrative that strongly influences Prague German literature, i.e., the *magisches Prag* (magic Prague, see below in this chapter).

17 "Uvědomiti si a prostudovati společenskou skutečnost zdejší," "v dramatickém dialogu dneška s dávnými věky."

18 Wenceslas Square was not an exclusively Czech space either in Habsburg or in modern Czechoslovakia. Yet it functions in the Czech national discourse as an icon of the nineteenth-century Czech renaissance.

19 "Viele der germanisierten Familien innerlich Čechen blieben" (quoted in Thomsen 2010, 236).

20 More than 100,000 Vienna inhabitants had Czech as their language of common use according to the Habsburg census of 1900 (on the Czech minority in Vienna see Csáky 2010, 137–44).

21 "'Die Herrschaften kennen einand, wie ich bemerkö,' sagte der Ungekämmte, dem dies auffiel, in dem geschraubten Dialekt eines tschechischen Wieners und machte mir spöttisch eine halbe Verbeugung: 'Erlaubens mich vorzustellen: Vóssatka ist mein Name. Der schwarze Vóssatka. – Brandstiftung,' setzte er eine Oktave tiefer stolz hinzu" (Meyrink 1983, 237). The English translation uses "manner" instead of "dialect." I maintain "dialect" to make clear that the text refers to the way Vóssatka pronounces certain words when speaking German. The English text does not reproduce the morphologic and phonetic particularities of Vóssatka's speech ("einand" instead of "einander" and "bemerkö" instead of "bemerke").

22 On the other hand, *Der Golem* does not say anything about the way the Ger-

man and Czech middle and upper classes interacted with each other in Prague.

23 On the Czech writers relating to the *magisches Prag* discourse and their relations with the Prague German authors, see Řezníková (2000) and Vojtěch (2010).

24 On the reader response of Czech literates to the subgenre of the so-called *Prager Roman* (Prague novel) in the German language, see Krolop (2010). On the ethnonational positioning of Czech-Jewish intellectuals, see Měšťán (2002). On the ethnonational thinking of President Masaryk and his entourage, see the considerations on Masaryk's idea of a humanistic democracy in the chapter on Langer in this article. Finally, the Czech Catholic culture has examined the history of Czech-German coexistence in Prague as part of its reflection on the role of tradition in modernity.

25 "Wir begannen wieder, Tschechisch zu sprechen, wie einst als Kinder. Wir atmeten freier und unbefangener als vorher. Wir fühlten festen Boden unter unseren Füßen – wir hingen nicht mehr in der Luft der gesellschaftlichen Illusionen, wie unsere Mütter und Väter. Wir wussten nun – und auch die humansten, liberalsten unserer tschechischen Freunde und Freundinnen sagten es uns: dass das alte Österreich in Prag, in Böhmen, leider ausgespielt hatte. Auch durch die Schuld unserer Väter – wenngleich sie nicht die Hauptschuldigen waren. Die Hauptschuldigen waren die Deutschnationalen in Aussig, in Eger, in Wien. Und diese Antisemiten und Vorläufer Hitlers hatten wir ebensoviel Grund zu hassen wie unsere tschechische Freunde."

26 "Mein Leben lang habe ich mich, sehr gegen meinen Willen, fast immer mit dem oder jenem herumzuschlagen gehabt. Ich kann und muß mich daher den Beinamen geben: ein Polemiker wider Willen. Es scheint mir, daß das weniger meine Schuld als die Schuld der Stadt ist, in der ich geboren wurde und die längste Zeit meines Lebens zugebracht habe. Die Schuld Prags. Das alte österreichische Prag war eine Stadt, in der nicht nur die einzelnen gegeneinander polemisierten, sondern drei Nationen standen im Kampf gegeneinander ... Über diese und verwandte Schwierigkeiten wurde unter uns, der um 1900 heranwachsenden Jugend, viel nachgedacht und diskutiert – denn das Leben stellte uns schon durch das Problem der beiden Sprachen vor Entscheidungen in Fragen der Kultur, die den Bewohnern eines einsprachigen Milieu erspart bleiben. Prag, die Stadt der drei Nationen, Prag, die polemische Stadt."

27 Spector's conceptual frame of de/reterritorialization refers to Gilles Deleuze's and Félix Guattari's interpretation of Kafka in their seminal essay

Franz Kafka: Pour une littérature mineure (1975). Deleuze and Guattari (1986, 16) define as minor a literature "which a minority constructs within a major language." They ascribe to this literature the power to subvert the majority culture from inside. According to them, Kafka's use of the German language and his relationship to German culture displace (deterritorialize) them since he is both a Jew and a dweller of a city in which the majority of the population speaks Czech. Deleuze and Guattari juxtapose in their essay Kafka and the rest of Prague German-language literature (mentioning only Meyrink and Brod). They consider Kafka the only German-language Prague author to really deterritorialize the literary discourse in which he is set. The others attempt a "symbolic reterritorialization, based in archetypes, Kabbala, and alchemy, that accentuates its break from the people and will find its political result only in Zionism and such things as the 'dream of Zion'" (19). Spector agrees with Deleuze and Guattari that authors like Meyrink, Brod, and their colleagues look for a way to relocate their Prague identity. He remarks, though, that also the literary practices of these literates work in a displacing way. This subverts German culture both in Prague (liberalism) and the rest of Bohemia (nationalism). Moreover, Kafka's literary strategies are not as exclusively deterritorializing as Deleuze and Guattari state. Indeed, Kafka shows a lively interest for different *Weltanschauungen* – mysticism and/or Zionism and/or something else – but finally does not commit himself to any of these to recompose his own displacement. Nevertheless a relevant part of his work – last but not least his interest for Jewish culture – reveals a (frustrated) desire to find a way to reterritorialize himself. It is surely true that Kafka became "a nomad and an immigrant and a gypsy in relation to [his] own language" (19) and that his literary deconstruction of his and others' attempts at territorialization was very effective. Nonetheless Kafka is a modern(ist) and not a postmodern(ist) author – at least in the sense Peter V. Zima (1992, 278) distinguishes between them: "Thus, it is not the refusal of meta-narratives as such that is at the core of postmodernity ... but the very fact that the longing for metaphysical sense through *master narratives* has been abandoned" ("Es ist also nicht die Ablehnung der Metaerzählungen als solche, die den Kern der Postmoderne ausmacht ... sondern die erloschene Sehnsucht nach metaphysischer Sinngebung durch *Großideologien*. My translation). Kafka may share Deleuze's and Guattari's postmodern metaphysical longing for deterritorialization as a goal, yet he shows a very strong modern striving for reterritorialization too.

28 Brod's *Distanzliebe* refers primarily to the author's relationship with German culture that Brod defines as closer than his relationship to Czech cul-

ture. Yet in many writings, Brod emphasizes his attachment to Czech culture as well, so that the inclusion of both Czechs and Germans in Brod's *Distanzliebe* seems logical, the difference he himself makes between the two cultures notwithstanding.

29 On Masaryk, see Demetz (1997, 329–38).

30 *Zwei Herzen im Dreiviertel Takt* (Two hearts in waltz time, 1930), directed by Géza von Bolváry. It is an operetta written directly for the screen, with music by Robert Stolz.

31 Langer (2001, 275) makes an ironic allusion here to a Czech newspaper article on demonstrations against "not well-rounded" or "not fully fledged" ("neplnohodné") German films. He makes a pun on *neplnohodný* and *plnotučný* (full-fat).

32 "Každý nacionalismus, jakmile vyrukuje na ulice s řevem národních písní a demonstruje kameny proti jinému národu, je jedna z nejodpornějších věcí na světě ... Tedy vlastenecký duch se obrátil jen proti německým filmům, když německá řeč z jejich pláten ohrožovala slovanský ráz Prahy podobně jako německý hovor v elektrice nebo v kavárně. A proto byl demonstranty odstraněn z programu i film Dvě srdce v tříčtvrtečním taktu, o kterém však každý musí přiznat, že to byl film plnotučný, když běžel po plátně čtvrt roku a kromě padesáti tisíc pražských Němců jej vidělo i sto padesát tisíc svérázných českých občanů. Je v tom jistá ironie ... Nuže, ironie je v tom, že se volalo sláva českému filmu a vyhodily se filmy, které mohly být mostem."

33 "Mluvila stejně česky jako švadronila německy, na jazykovou otázku nekladla žádný důraz." On the ethnonational characterization of the Hejda family in *Zázrak v rodině*, see also Koeltzsch (2010, 17).

34 Koschmal (2010) provides a detailed survey on Jiří's work.

35 See Holý (2003, 328).

36 I have put in square brackets the text where I have deviated from the English translation by Stephen Jolly. I have chosen a more literal translation to better illustrate my interpretation of Langer's text. The original reads: "Aby mohla kniha Devět bran vzniknout, musil se můj bratr Jiří Langer přenést z životní reality dvacátého století do mystické a extatické atmosféry středověku. A to nikoli jenom metaforicky, na křídlech fantazie. Naopak, zcela ve skutečnosti, která se začala zakoupením jízdního lístku na nádraží v Praze do jakéhosi městečka ve východní Haliči. To bylo tehdy snadné, bez formalit, na počátku tohoto století Čechy byly částí rakousko-uherské monarchie, která spojovala všelijaké odlehlé kraje, národy i stupně civilizace. Za dvacet čtyři hodin nebo o něco déle ve špinavém vlaku se tedy Jiří

octl v roce 1913 o půl tisíce kilometrů dále na východě a zároveň o dvě či dokonce o pět století nazpět v čase" (Langer 2003, 172).

37 Prague Jews and Chassidim from Galicia became closer during World War I when the latter escaped from the war front and found refuge in Prague. Tramer remembers the cultural distance the two communities experienced in relation to each other (Tramer 1961, 169–73). This situation made it all the more difficult for the Prague Jewish community to understand Jiří's conversion to Chassidism.

38 "Měli jim povědět o židech něco jiného, než co se nacistický antisemitismus snažil pašovat přes československé hranice" (Langer 2003, 186).

39 "Snad někde v Izraeli, snad v New Yorku se mezi židy najde desítka starých chasidských věřících, kteří ještě zachovávají zvyky přinesené ze starých domovů. Ale to jsou už jenom reminiscence. Pod modrým nebem Izraele ani v pouličním ruchu Brooklynu už nemůže trvat mystická skutečnost, jakou chasidský nárůdek mohl prožívat jen ve své haličské odloučenosti od světa a od doby, v chudobě, ve které si všichni byli rovni, v svobodě, v níž byli podrobeni jen vůli boží, a ve vznešenosti, která na jejich obce padala z moudrostí a ze zázraků jejich posvátných rabínů. Jak je ještě naposled zachytil a jak jim tím věčný pomník postavil a navěky jejich památku uchoval ve své úsměvné knize můj bratr Jiří" (Langer 2003, 191–2).

4

Language Edges: Reading the Habsburg Border City

SHERRY SIMON

The edge of empire always lies in a metaphysical landscape. As an image of the elusive line dividing self from other, it exerts a special fascination at moments of historical transformation. For the Ancient Greeks, as for the nineteenth-century Habsburgs, the edge of the world was a line drawn in the sand of language. Language was given the powers of a garrison – standing guard on the brink of the unfamiliar.

Two twentieth-century writers famously took up the myth of the language border in the wake of the dissolution of their respective empires. This chapter is devoted to one of them, Joseph Roth (1894–1939), and his fictional reinventions of the Habsburg border city. But it is worth recalling, at the start, the work of a figure who was in some respects Roth's Mediterranean counterpart, the diasporic Greek poet Constantine Cavafy (1863–1933).

A Greek-language poet who lived in Egyptian Alexandria, a city whose Hellenic identity was progressively lost through his lifetime, Cavafy invested borders with special powers. He saw the cities at the margins of empire as busy, populous, and polyglot – places not only of commerce among peoples and ideas, but also of mystery and illumination. Cavafy was a poet of the urban, and he experienced his own Alexandria as a template for the border city – an Egyptian place infused with the spirit of its classical Greek past. Equally fascinating for him were cities even more distant from the centre of the Hellenistic world, cities like Antioch, Sidon, and Beirut, where fragments of the Greek tradition persisted among the "Syrians, migrated Greeks, Armenians and Medes" who lived there (Cavafy 1975, 102). These cities at the edge of empire represented a kind of ideal for Cavafy. They were creations of the mind, witnessing the sensuous dramas unfolding between rival gods. To be distant from a cultural centre meant the freedom to live with contradictions: "Ask your heart / didn't you feel happier / the farther we got from Greece?" (187).

Cavafy's attention to the margins of the empire was nourished as much by his readings of classical history as by his daily experiences of social, literary, and linguistic alienation. He was also vividly aware of the times he was living through. He experienced the Balkan Wars and then the 1918 fall of the Ottoman Empire, which transformed the modern Hellenic world. Greece regained sovereignty, and the population exchanges of the 1920s saw the expulsion of the Greek-speaking communities from Asia Minor. His own diasporic existence as a Greek writer in Alexandria changed as the city became increasingly Arabic-speaking. Yet Cavafy's allegiance to his city remained as steadfast as ever. His poetic universe was constructed out of the drama of distance that he experienced as the citizen of the diaspora, a Greek speaker living far from the matrix of Greek thought and yet stimulated by the mixture of tongues in which he found himself. And so Alexandria remained a model of his dream city, a model of "poetic cities cast in its image, cities that imitate it as it can be, or even ought to be, in its essence" (Keely 1995, 6).

Like the ancient Greeks, the edge of empire for Cavafy was also associated with language. But rather than pitting "our" language against theirs as did the ancients, he revelled in the impure mixtures of post-classical Greek. In his reimagined Hellenic world, Cavafy found in the polyglot condition the very basis for his aesthetics. What defines his border city is less its nearness to the world of the barbarian than the many miles that separate it from that of the capital. What interests him are the kinds of translation that occur between the border and the centre of power, between the distant, impure version of culture that prevails at the border and the authorized version in the capital.

Cavafy and the Greeks provide distant reference points that echo the experience of another great empire that fell in 1918. During this same period, the Austro-Hungarian Empire was living out its death throes in a frenzy of border disputes centred on questions of language. Here, too, the edges of empire were endowed with particular cultural significance, as frontiers whose unruliness was to be tamed – or cultivated. Here, too, the myth of the border became the dramas of literature.

Roth was a writer and journalist whose imaginative world dialogues with Cavafy's through their common fascination with the regions where values are tested and a special knowledge is to be gained. Cavafy's palace windows and boisterous procession-filled streets correspond to Roth's taverns, casinos, garrisons, and tawdry hotels. These twilit outposts give rise to dramas of seduction and betrayal where "refugees travel between past and future, between a known past and a highly uncertain future, the passengers crossing a wobbly plank from terra firma into a strange ship" (Robinson 2007, 88).

Far from Where? is the title of the book that the Italian essayist Claudio Magris devoted to Roth and Eastern European Jewish culture in 1975. Magris explains that the title comes from an old Jewish joke (Gruber 2002, 37): "You're going all the way there?" asks a man. "You'll be so far away." "Far from where?" is the reply. This question was for Magris a metaphor of the diasporic Jewish condition, that of a people whose homeland is not a nation on the map but rather a community created within and among individuals, wherever they are.

The title can equally be applied to border cultures, whose identities are often measured in relation to their distance from the capital, and imbued with the ambiguous romanticism of the flyblown recesses of empire, but which flourish as blends of distinctive, local influences. One might wonder if the meaning of Cavafy's famous poem "Waiting for the Barbarians" (1904) takes on some clarity in this context. He describes the agonized wait of the citizens of the capital, convinced that the barbarians are about to attack. Nevertheless, at the end of the day: "Some of our men just in from the border say, there are no barbarians any longer" (Cavafy 1992, 18). What happened to the barbarians? Could it be that, after years of coexistence in the borderlands, they have become one identity among many, their language blended into the variegated soundscape?

HABSBURG LANGUAGE BORDERS

Language and languages were an obsession in all parts of the Austro-Hungarian Empire in the early years of the twentieth century, from the philosophical and moral debates of Karl Kraus and Wittgenstein (Janik and Toulmin 1973), to the political struggles for language rights in the various parliaments of the realm in the final years of the empire. Yet, because much of Habsburg historiography was long focused on national histories, only recently has work turned to the actual language interrelationships of the multilingual cities of the empire (Prokopych 2009; Wolf 2012; van Drunen 2013; Fellerer 2014).[1]

The Habsburg borderlands were especially diverse in their populations, especially Galicia and Bukovina with their respective capitals of Lemberg and Czernowitz. Roth's reports on these border zones and their cities were concerned with language questions – how could they not be? But as always, Roth's own imaginative universe shaped his angle on such matters. Roth was an emphatically German-language writer, and quickly abandoned the Yiddish of his early family life. Yet his writings retain a sense of the translational nature of the borderlands he so affectionately portrays.

JOSEPH II, BRODY, ROTH

> Eibenschütz had long since ceased to listen. But it did him good that a man was speaking beside him, just as it sometimes does one good when the rain is pouring down, even if one does not understand the language of the rain.
>
> Joseph Roth, *Weights and Measures*

When Joseph II (1741–1790) acquired Galicia in 1772, he set out on a six-week mission to inspect the new outer edge of his lands. The territory had been wrested from Moldavia in negotiations with the Ottomans (Glajar 2004, 18). This was new, quasi-savage land and, as Larry Wolf (2010) recounts, Joseph set out on what was a pioneering voyage of exploration. In his journal, Joseph noted both the natural and the human environment, in particular observing the abilities of his freshly acquired peasants, artisans, and merchants (87).[2] Throughout the journey, Joseph took special interest in the border. He wanted to eliminate the Polish coats of arms and replace them with Habsburg insignia, to institute procedures for border surveillance, and to open quarantine stations (88). The border that he marked out in 1773 would remain in place with only a short interruption for 140 years (117). It was the eastern border of the empire, a space that would be endowed with a special mission to protect the empire militarily – and culturally.

A picture postcard of this eastern border at the city of Brody (the cover image of *Getrennt und doch Verbunden*[3]) evokes the unexpected ambiguities of border life. The image, probably taken in the early years of the twentieth century, shows a relaxed, festive group. Uniformed guards from both sides pose at the open crossbars, accompanied by civilian officials, women, and children in Sunday dress. One wonders what might have been the occasion for such an event. What kind of celebration would bring together the border guards and their families? Perhaps fresh coats of paint applied to the border marker, or the visit of a photographer charged with recording novel views of picturesque or typical sites? The legend on the postcard simply says "border" in three languages: Polish, Ukrainian, and German. The fact that Russian and Yiddish are missing indicates that the postcard was to be sold on the Habsburg side of the border, and that Jewish consumers were assumed to speak German.

In the terms used by the social theorist Richard Sennett, the postcard has turned a "boundary" into a "border." While the boundary is a place of stark divides, of rarefied population and relatively inert exchanges, a border is "a more active edge, as at the shoreline dividing ocean and land; this is a zone of intense biological activity, a feeding ground for animals, a nutrient zone for plants. In human ecology, the eight-lane highway isolating parts of the city from each other is a boundary, whereas a mixed-use street at the edge between two communities can be more of a border" (Sennett 2012, 79). Sennett's double sense of the "edge" shows that a dividing line can be either an unequivocal barrier or a point of contact. But what he might have added is that the same edge can turn from border to boundary and back again. The same physical zone, considered from the standpoint of trade, religion, language, or politics, peace or war, can give rise to radically different behaviours and interpretations. While this Russian-Austrian border could be the site of rigid divides and violence, it also saw much friendlier kinds of exchanges. In an unpublished memoir relating to the city of Ushiatyn, another Galician border town, Manny Zornberg (1975) describes the relatively lax behaviour of border officials in regard to some aspects of cross-border traffic. In his stories and novels, Roth also conveys a vivid sense of the border as a site of conviviality and translation, a contact zone at the edge of empire.

THE RADETZKY MARCH: SCENES OF TRANSLATION

Brody was Roth's birthplace and the prototype of the Habsburg border city in his work – a place defined by its distance from the centre of power and its proximity to temptation. Brody was a small city, mainly populated by Jews,[4] ten kilometres away from its twin city Radzivilov across the Russian border, a city with which Brody's life was intimately intertwined through trade and smuggling.[5] The Austrian military was a strong presence in the city. When Roth was a schoolboy, both the Galizianer-Bukowiner Feldjägerbataillon and three squadrons of Ulan regiments were stationed there (Bronsen 1975, 5). Images of Brody in Roth's illustrated biography show the comfortable house in which he was raised and the busy marketplace at the town centre, but also the imposing architecture of military barracks and the familiar presence of army regiments in the town.

Raised within a multilingual context, Roth early entered the exclusive precincts of the German language. In Brody, he attended one of only two German language high schools in Galicia, the Imperial-Royal Crown Prince Rudolph Gymnasium. He went on to study German literature in the capital of Galicia, Lemberg. After one semester at the university there he transferred to Vienna. Though born into a Yiddish-speaking family, Roth became a German-language thinker and writer, one of Europe's best known and most highly regarded journalists, and a prolific fiction writer.

Brody remained a strong imaginative presence for Roth, and the source of his lifetime fascination for the borderlands and *Grenzmenschen* (borderlandspeople). Among the characters that reappear in his fiction are many border-types: "Lonely and adulterous wives, migrant hucksters, unscrupulous moneylenders, border traders or smugglers, aristocrats living on borrowed time, idling and dissolute soldiers, refugees, Jewish innkeepers, matronly brothel-keepers and idealistic men soon corrupted" (Robinson 2007, 67). These characters, as well as the geographical landscape of the borderlands, receive vivid and detailed presence in Roth's work. But his friend Josef Wittlin (n.d.) notes, as have many critics since, that the border was much more than a physical reality for Roth: "The border fascinated Roth for it was the border between the Austro-Hungarian monarchy and Czarist Russia. It was the border between two worlds and two cultures, the Western and the Eastern. In addition the mysterious figures of those border people, smugglers, guards and the whole world of contraband, fascinated Roth. It was like a border between life and death."

The borderland for Roth was a true contact zone, an in-between space with its own culture, its own language. In *The Radetzky March*, Roth (2003, 144) describes the area between the Russian and Austrian garrisons as a place of meeting: "The respective garrisons even kept up reciprocal comradely relations. Sometimes it was the Austrians who crossed the border in little canvas-topped baggage carts, to watch the riding skills of the Cossacks and to drink Russian schnapps ... There the Tsar's officers gave the officers of His Apostolic Majesty a lesson in Russian hospitality." Conversely, Count Chojnicki organized frequent parties in his home, where the aristocratic officers of the Russian dragoons regiment and the middle-class officers of the Jagers "formed lifelong emotional ties" (148).

This description of cross-border military connections corroborates the tone of the postcard discussed earlier. The border was indeed powerless to effectively separate the populations, just as it was inefficient in stemming the flow of illegal goods and people. The passage of deserters from the Russian army into Austria was particularly common and seems to have been somewhat tolerated. This in-between identity is particularly acute in one of the most significant sites and imaginative topos in Roth's writing: the border tavern. Like the hotel and the coffee house, the border tavern appears over and over. Lying beyond the limits of the city and outside of bourgeois order, it is open day and night. It brings together a cast of disreputable characters – smugglers, deserters, gamblers, disaffected army officers – and here languages meet as well (Beug 1991).

The conviviality seems to be made possible also by the sense of boredom and dislocation that reigns over the troops: "Any strangers who came to this part of the world were slowly but irresistibly doomed. No one was a match for the swamp. No one could stand up to the border" (Roth 2003, 141). This sense of distance and gloom extends even to language. Though German is a minority language in these regions, it remains the administrative tongue and the language of the army. Still, Roth notes that "cut adrift from the ways of home, from their German mother tongue," the soldiers fall into "a kind of militarese" – in the same ways as they are "exposed to the endless drabness of the swamps, they had fallen prey to games of chance, and the powerful schnapps that was produced locally" (144). Their language is degraded through isolation, but also through exposure to the many tongues around them.

Roth's affection for the borderlands, the peripheries, is rooted precisely in this incapacity to uphold divisions, in particular the resistance to nationalism. His rosy-tinged portrait of the Jews of Eastern Europe in his essay "The Wandering Jews" (1926–27) is a product of his admiration for the impossible national identity of the Eastern Jew. As a soldier who saw two years' service during World War I, as a journalist who visited the Soviet Union only to discover the exhaustion of revolutionary hopes, Roth (2002a, 66–7) came to see national "liberation" as so much "foolish glee." In a story fragment that takes place in Brunn but might have applied to any of the myriad cities of Central Europe, he describes the pathetic theatricality of the transformation of empire into nation: "On 1 November, he had returned to his native Brunn. What he saw there – the Revolution in the little capital of the erstwhile Crownland, the procession of the army band dressed in its old Imperial uniforms and playing a new nationalist anthem, the Czech soldiers who went about plucking the old cockades from the officers' hats, the whole foolish glee of the liberated nation" (66–7).

LANGUAGE BORDERS

> The Habsburg sun sent its beams as far east as the border with the Russian Tsar.
>
> Joseph Roth, *The Radetzky March*

One of the consequences of the emergence of nations after World War I was the new powers given to their languages, along with the elimination of German as an administrative language in imperial lands. This change is nicely prefigured in a comic translation scene toward the end of *The Radetzky March*. Count Chojnicki was hosting a party at his home when the rumour of Franz Ferdinand's assassination in Sarajevo began to percolate through the borderlands. The count decided to assemble a few of the higher-ranking guests in a separate room to share the news. The drunken Count Battyani reacted by beginning a long harangue to his compatriots in Hungarian. As this speech went on for some time and the guests who could not understand a word grow impatient, someone asks him to continue the conversation in German. "Benkyo who had just been speaking stopped and replied: 'All right, I can say it in German too: we were just agreeing, my compatriots and I, that it's a good thing if the son of a bitch is dead!'" (Roth 2003, 327).

The irreverence of the translation is a clear sign of what the assassination means: the end of the empire and Austrian dominance: *finis Austriae* and *finis Deutsch*. The withholding of translation and the shocking words to the assembled guests prefigure the breakdown of imperial solidarities.

But while mindful of the political dimensions of language and the tensions that were so much a part of borderland plurilingualism, Roth also gives attention to the affective dimensions of language. The young von Trotta, Carl Joseph, who is the novel's protagonist, feels a sentimental attachment to Slav languages. He had hoped to be posted to Slovenia, but when he arrives at the eastern border with the Russian tsar he feels consolation in this "home of the Ukrainian peasants, with their mournful harmonicas and their unforgettable songs: it was a kind of northern sister to Slovenia" (138). When Joseph finally leaves the army, he takes a post as steward on Chojnicki's estate and becomes familiar with the Ukrainian language. The last words he hears as he falls to his death in war are a Ukrainian blessing from his troops. To their cries of "Praise be to Christ Jesus!" he wanted to say "for ever and ever, amen!" as he often had on his strolls through the estate. "They were the only words of Ruthenian that he knew. But his lips could no longer move" (351).

The affection for Slav languages is also erotic. In Roth's (2002a, 186) "Stationmaster Fallerayer," the stationmaster's passionate attachment to the Countess Walewska is aroused by her voice. "She spoke German in a strange, low voice, with a harsh and strange Russian accent. All the splendour of distance and the unknown were in her throat." Later, "he learned the woman's mother tongue and he imagined he was speaking to her, in her language. He learned endearments, sweet nothings, love whisperings in Russian ... With every new sound of the foreign language he was learning, he was coming closer to the strange woman" (189).

The exciting women in Roth's fiction often speak a foreign language – the Russian revolutionary Natasha of *Flight without End*, the Circassian gypsy Euphemia of *Weights and Measures*. The most explicit – and moving – evocation of language and the borderlands is surely the story of the inspector of *Weights and Measures* (first published in 1937) who loses himself among languages he does not understand. His experiences on the frontier lead from his idealistic beginnings as a fervent enforcer of the law to a downfall infused with the pathos of loneliness and betrayed love. The tale highlights the contrast between the inflexible bureaucratic system, bent on applying the letter of the law, and the community of the border that sees the world through tradition and solidarity – but also of flexible measures. Gradually, the inspector loses his hold on the correct measures (literal and figurative) and becomes caught up in the seedy world of illicit cross-border traffic. The border is a place of perdition, where smuggling, drinking, and illicit love flourish in taverns and dark forests. Roth's bureaucrat finds himself between two systems of values and loses everything. He dies in utter loneliness.

From the start, we are led to understand that the drama of Anselm Eibenschutz will be one of language. "For the first few days, Eibenschutz went about like one who has suddenly been struck deaf. True, he understood the language of the country, but what mattered was to understand not so much what the people said as what the land itself uttered. And the land spoke a terrifying language: it spoke of snow, darkness, cold and icicles, even though the calendar said it was spring" (Roth 2002b, 13). Eibenschutz does not understand the language of this district of Zlotogrod. Here he is betrayed by his wife and discovers the exciting world of the border tavern, where Euphemia speaks not so much with her voice as with the swirling of her gypsy skirts and the tinkling of her jewellery. But Eibenschutz cannot keep his hold on this elusive music either, and he becomes a victim of his official position when he is finally assassinated.

This story, more than any other, shows Roth's imaginative attachment to the ambivalence of the border as a place of contradictory knowledge and untrustworthy translations. For instance, while the people on the border are going to suffer from the devastating violence of war, they may also in some way profit from it. "At that time, the important people in Vienna and Petersburg were already making their preparations for the Great War. The people on the border felt it coming before anyone else did; not just because they were used to sensing things early, but also because every day they could read the signs of the impending catastrophe with their own eyes. Also they profited from these preparations" (2003, 141). The exchange of information across distances gives rise to conflicting interpretations, just as the movement across languages can be treacherous. Translation in Roth's novels takes place less as a transaction from one tongue to another than as the awareness of living in and through a plurality of idioms. Roth's *Grenzmenschen*, inhabitants of the polyglot zones far from the centre of power, express the productive disorder of the spaces where the empire may in fact be most fully itself (Robinson 2007).

LANGUAGE AFTERLIFE

The language relations of Roth's novels extend into their afterlife as translations. Roth's celebrity as a journalist and his almost constant travels across Europe and beyond resulted in the early translations of his novels into English and French (Viking Press in New York, Heinemann in England). His French translator Blanche Gidon (1883–1974) was a steadfast friend and productive worker (translating among others Gottfried Keller, Bruno Frank, Emil Ludwig, Rene Schickele, and Heinrich Boll). Of Roth's works, she translated two novels: *Radetzky March* (*La marche de Radetzky*, Plon) and *The Hundred Days* (*Les cent jours*, Grasset 1938). She kept every paper from Roth that Friderike Zweig had gathered after Roth's death.

It is notable that Roth's German was almost immediately translated "back" into the border zones he came from. He maintained his relations with the borderlands, corresponded with family in Lemberg, and often travelled east. From December of 1936 to mid-March of 1937, Roth made a final voyage with his companion Irmgard Keun to Warsaw, Wilna, and Lemberg. He gave interviews and speeches in which he both denounced National Socialism and praised monarchist ideas (Lunzer 1994, 252). He visited Lemberg but not Brody. Perhaps as a result of this trip, Roth's work was translated into Polish – and into Yiddish. A typewritten note on letterhead from the magazine *Hajnt* (Today) in Warsaw, addressed to Roth at the Hotel Europejski in Lemberg (Lwow) and dated 10 March 1937, refers to a manuscript translated into Yiddish for a payment of 400 zlotys, another 400 to be delivered upon printing. It was the *Geschichte von der 1002* (253). In fact this novel appeared in Poland before it appeared elsewhere, in an original, longer version, because of the war. Roth's work was also translated into Polish by his friend Jósef Wittlin (1896–1976), a Polish Jewish poet and author of the Nobel-nominated novel *Salt of the Earth* as well as a gifted translator, and by Isidor Berman.

This suggestion of an immediate, almost spontaneous reception for Roth back at the edges of empire conjures up an image of circulation across vast terrain. It evokes an audience eager to bring Roth's work back to his roots, and of the creative power of Polish and Yiddish to engage with German modernity. Translation was indeed one of the mechanisms through which the many "minor" languages of the empire fortified themselves and established their legitimacy. In some cases, writers' language conversions were a more direct path to the same goal. And so Czernowitz author Olha Kobylianska took to writing in Ukrainian, after being educated in German; Itzik Manger, also from Czernowitz, chose Yiddish; Wittlin, like Roth raised in Brody, chose Polish. Translating Roth "back" into Yiddish, his mother tongue, recast his work in the language in which he did not choose to write, but which is in a sense his source language. Had the Holocaust not put an end to Yiddish-language culture, in Europe and worldwide, this translation would have been part of an expanding response to the great German-language literary tradition in Central Europe.

Struggling with the consequences of the death of empire, both Roth and Cavafy evoke myths that have enduring resonance today. With a similarly keen sense of irony, they direct their readers to zones of the imagination that resist confining definitions.

NOTES

1 While Wolf's work on translation and interpretation in the monarchy focuses on official, paid translation, she also devotes considerable attention to informal practices of interpretation that were manifold. Fellerer (2014) seeks to dispel the image of rigid divisions that historians of national histories have imposed, focusing not on the rival national associations but rather on the structure of urban space that might promote contact. His vision of Lviv as a city of layered interactions, structured especially by class, stresses the language overlaps that occurred in many everyday situations. Using evidence from court records, he suggests that there was frequent interchange between Polish speakers and native Ukrainian and Yiddish speakers at the lower end of the class spectrum. For the middle class, he surmises that there was also a "degree of urban-cultural integration and community that did exist among the nations," for instance in the southern historical district of Lviv where fine villas were inhabited by Poles, Ukrainians, and Jews of similar class and tastes – all of whom were competent in several languages.

2 Larry Wolff (2010, 13) begins his book on Galicia with Joseph setting off on this voyage. "'Je vais partir pour la Galicie; *altri guai!*' wrote Emperor Joseph II to his brother Leopold, Grand Duke of Tuscany, in July 1773. Joseph had never been to Galicia before, and neither had Leopold – nor indeed had any but a very small number of recent travelers. For Galicia did not exist until 1772, when it was constituted and named as the Habsburg share in the first Polish partition. If there was some sense of occasion in Joseph's French

announcement of his imminent departure, it was because Galicia was truly a new world, newly created the year before, invented in the rational spirit of enlightened statecraft. Joseph himself was one of its principal creators, now to become also one of its first discoverers and explorers, and certainly its most grandly distinguished visitor." He covered 1,881 kilometres in Galicia alone.

3 A rich study that investigates trade, smuggling, and religious travel, but makes scarcely a mention of language.

4 In 1900 its population was 72 per cent Jewish. Most of the mayors were Jews and most of the streets were named after Jews (Lunzer 1994).

5 But several of the border cities were in fact themselves traversed by the border – they were cities halved by decree when Joseph II and his administrators laid down the line of demarcation in 1772. These cities contained borders within them, extending the line of fracture into the very texture of the city. This was the case, for example, for Husiatyn and for Podwoloczyska (Adelsgruber, Cohen, and Kuzmany 2011). In these cases, the border was part of the city's very fabric. The unpublished memoir of life in Husiatyn by Manny Zornberg mentions the border police walking back and forth, trying to prevent smuggling. But most of the illicit activities went on at night, in particular the smuggling of Jewish boys out of Russia. There was also a huge amount of commercial traffic from Russia into Austria.

PART TWO

Moving Fault Lines of the Global City

5

Digital Dublin: Translating the Cybercity

MICHAEL CRONIN

So This Is Dyoublong?
Hush! Caution! Echoland!

James Joyce, *Finnegans Wake*

In 1848, the year known as the springtime of nations, two thousand Poles left Russian-occupied Poland to fight with the Hungarians against their Austrian overlords. The rising failed and many of the defeated Poles went into exile in Turkey, Britain, and the United States. Ignacy, a character in Bolesław Prus's novel *The Doll* (1890), is one of these wandering insurgents, and later in his life back in Warsaw he reflects on his period of exile: "A few days after Katz's death, we reached Turkey and for two years I – alone now – wandered through Europe. I was in Italy, France, Germany, even England, and everywhere I was troubled with poverty and devoured by homesickness. Sometimes it seemed to me I would go out of my mind listening to the flood of foreign tongues and seeing faces that were not ours, costumes not ours, earth not ours" (Prus 2011, 138). This is a classic description of the emigrant experience as involving brutal rupture, disorientation, and loss. In listing what he had left behind, Ignacy is quick to mention language. He fears drowning in the "flood of foreign tongues," his native speech carried away on the riptide of displacement. Forced into exile by political circumstances, Ignacy realizes that the *translatio* of space means inevitably, and in his case tragically, the translation of tongue. In this chapter, I suggest that the schismatic paradigm of migrant language experience implicit in the reflections of the former Polish exile – the radical abandonment of mother tongue for another language or languages – is undergoing a significant readjustment in the contemporary digital moment and that this readjustment has major implications for the way we think about the city as translation zone. I illustrate my remarks by specific references to the city of Dublin, which has witnessed a remarkable upsurge in inward migration in the first decades of the twenty-first century. In evaluating the change in paradigm, three factors inform my analysis: communication, presencing, and virtuality.

COMMUNICATION

Castells et al. (2006, 246) claim that fundamental to what we communicate is how we communicate: "Because communication is the fundamental process of human activity, the modification of communication processes by the interaction between social structures, social practice and a new range of communication technologies, constitute indeed a profound social transformation." Communication is not separable from the means that allow it to happen. Each time the technologies of conveying meaning change, the meanings themselves change. As a form of communication, translation is no exception to this rule, and as I argue elsewhere web-based technologies have profoundly altered both the practice and the reception of translation (Cronin 2013). If the city is, among other things, a forum for and enabler of communication, then the advent of new forms of information and communications technology in urban spaces will impact the nature, breadth, and intensity of communication that takes place. Therefore, any attempt to understand the nature of migrant communication and translation practices in the contemporary metropolis must factor in changing communication technologies.

PRESENCING

A customary way to understand migrants is to think of them as having been born in one place and having chosen, willingly or unwillingly, to live and work in another. The dialectical relationship is between presence and absence, present in one place, absent from another. However, it is possible to contest this polarity and suggest that it conceals a more processual form of being in the contemporary world that is captured by the term "presencing." By this I mean forms of presence that do not involve actual spatial or corporeal displacement, but that bring someone or something into the field of attention of others at another point in space and/or time. A notable feature of digital technologies, for example, is the extensive use of presencing, such as Skyping distant relatives. Thinking through the notion more fully, we can conceive of translation itself as a form of presencing, a making present in one language of what has been absent because it was initially expressed or formulated in another. In other words, presencing calls into question the dichotomous absolutism of presence and absence by suggesting that there are ways of being present that are not captured by the physically defined either/or of home and away.

VIRTUALITY

One of the most notable developments in the last two decades has been the shift from stand-alone personal computers at fixed work stations to distributed computing in the form of laptops, tablets, smartphones, and so on. It is not only humans but also our machines that are on the move. As Dennis and Urry (2007, 13) put it, "This trend in distributed computing is developing towards a shift to ubiquitous computing where associations between people, place/space, and time are embedded within a systemic relationship between a person and their kinetic environment." Ubiquitous computing is sometimes referred to as the "third wave of computing," one "whose cross-over point with personal computing will be around 2005–2020" and which may become "embedded in walls, chairs, clothing, light switches, cars – in everything" (Brown and Weiser 1996). Adam Greenfield (2006, 18) talks of "everyware," where information processing is embedded in the objects and surfaces of everyday life. (This is already partially with us in the form of Amazon Dash Buttons and Nest home security and alarm systems.) The probable social impact of everyware can be compared to the electricity that passes invisibly through the walls of every home, office, and car. The transition from fixed locations of access to increased wireless presence coupled with the exponential growth of Internet capability means that greatly augmented information flows become part of an information-immersive environment.

A consequence of the emergence of ubiquitous computing is that computing capacity dissolves into the physical surroundings, architectures, and infrastructures. Marcos Novak (2010) uses the term "trans-Architecture" to signify "a liquid architecture that is transmitted across the global information networks; within physical space it exists as an invisible electronic double superimposed on our material world." William Mitchell (1995, 46–105) in the 1990s spoke of a "city of bits" where the combination of physical structures in urban spaces with the electronic spaces and telematics would be known as "recombinant architectures." Cities, then, exist at two levels of reality: the physical and the virtual. When locating migrant experiences within the city's translation zone, this duality must be taken into account if we are to understand fully the multiple modes of inhabiting a city implicit in the recombinant worlds of the physical and the virtual.

IRISH MIGRATION

Ireland is a country famous for migration, but usually in one direction: outward. At the beginning of the nineteenth century, Ireland had a population of around eight million, but by 1861 it had almost halved to 4.4 million, the result of the deaths and disease from the Great Famine (1845–48) and extensive migration to other regions of the anglophone world. By 1961, the population had dropped to 2.8 million. The situation did not change greatly with Ireland's accession to the European Union in 1973, and even in the early 1990s Ireland was the only member state of the European Union to have a net outward migration rate (Ruhs and Quinn 2009, 1–2). The economic boom that began at the end of the 1990s and continued on until the dramatic 2008 financial crisis led to a marked shift in Ireland's migration fortunes. For the first time since the colonial plantation of settler populations in the seventeenth century, there were significant population inflows. By 2007, with 14.5 migrants per 1,000 members of the population, Ireland had the highest net inward migration rate in the European Union after Spain and Cyprus. The flow peaked in 2006 and 2007 with around 100,000 migrants arriving each year. However, despite the prolonged recession that accompanied the European Union and International Monetary Fund bailout of the Irish economy, the overall number of migrants has declined only slightly. While 172,000 migrants left Ireland between 2008 and 2012, 140,000 arrived (Crosbie 2013, 3). Foreign-born persons accounted for only 6 per cent of the population in 1991, rising to 10 per cent in 2002, 15 per cent in 2006, and 17 per cent in 2013 (Ruhs 2009; Crosbie 2013, 3). The rise in the number of migrants has been accompanied by a notable linguistic diversification, and there are now upward of one hundred languages spoken in the Dublin metropolitan area. Of the 544,357 non-Irish nationals living in the country in 2013, 122,585 were Polish, 112,259 were British, 36,683 were Lithuanian, 20,593 were Latvian, and 17,642 were Nigerian (Crosbie 2013, 3). Given the recent and dramatic change in the size and nature of the migrant population in Ireland, how have communication, presencing, and virtuality impacted the experiences of migrant communities in Dublin, and what might these impacts say about the contemporary nature of the city as translation zone?

DEMATERIALIZATION

One of the most common ways to conceive of migrant presence in cities is through the notion of ethnic enclaves (pejoratively referred to as "ghettos") that make up the ethnoscape of the city. These are areas where there are typically high concentrations of particular ethnic groups, often accompanied by schools, shops, and religious buildings that cater to the various needs of the community. Public and private signage in the language of the migrant community is the most immediate visible evidence of difference. "Chinatown" in various cities across the globe is the most frequently cited example, but in many cities particular communities tend to be associated with specific areas (see Simon 2006, 2012). When we begin, however, to look at cities from the point of view of altered forms of communication and the rising incidence of virtuality, how the ethnoscape is conceptualized or indeed visualized is bound to change.

Lee Komito (2011), in a detailed study carried out on the use of new technology by a representative group of non-nationals living in Ireland, based predominantly in the Dublin area, found that the majority of the migrants tended to socialize with fellow nationals or other migrants. However, the way in which this communication was happening was changing, with a significant amount taking place via mobile phone or texting:

> Of course, mobile phone and texting is a widespread means of coordinating social life for most people, but, in the context of migrants, it enables individuals who are geographically dispersed to still meet face to face. Such a circumscribed social life is what many migrants said they desired. This facility was not previously available at such a low opportunity cost; previously, it requiring

> the close residential proximity characteristic of ethnic enclave communities. Now, mobile phones enable migrants to organise a social life that can include only fellow non-nationals, even when those non-nationals are dispersed throughout the city. (1080)

One of the effects, then, of the shift to virtual forms of communication was not the elimination of face-to-face communication, but rather the removal of one of the motivating factors for "close residential proximity characteristic of ethnic enclave communities." Cheap, virtual communication meant that the logistics of interaction no longer depended on spatial proximity, thereby weakening the communicative rationale of physical agglomeration. In a sense, arguably what is at work here is the operation of a triple shift in logic, namely a move from a logic of disjunction to a logic of dispersal, a move from a logic of trace to a logic of link, and a move from a logic of fixity to a logic of nomadism. In other words, the subjects in Komito's study no longer inhabited distinctive, disjunctive spaces that were the preserve, for example, of the Filipino community or the Polish community. They were now dispersed throughout the city but could remain in constant contact by means of low-cost information and communications technology. In this respect, the virtual link takes increasing precedence over the physical trace. Though there are shop signs and notices (traces) in the city in Polish, they are extremely few in number compared to the relative importance of the Polish community in the city and in the country generally. Finally, the shift from fixed to ubiquitous computing noted earlier is manifest in the move away from Internet cafés and call centres (fixity) in the urban spaces as the obligatory portals of Internet connectivity to the more widespread use of smartphones, tablets, and laptops (nomadism) as a way to access the Internet and other members of a language or ethnic community (Komito 2004). In a sense, what is happening is a gradual displacement of the signifiers of language alterity from the physical space of the city to the virtual space of the online world. Komito (2011, 1079) notes, for example, with respect to social media, "Social network sites were relevant for most migrants: 30% of Polish respondents use a social networking site (SNS) once a day, and another 26% several times a week, while 37% Filipinos use a social networking site daily, and another 26% several times a week."

The forms of virtual communication other than the mobile calls and texting that Polish and Filipino migrants used included instant messaging (usually Yahoo! Messenger), Gadu-Gadu (a Polish instant messager), Nasza Klasa (a Polish social network), email, webcam (such as via Skype), and Facebook. In other words, while the quintessential representation of the city as translation zone or cosmopolitan centre presents a seductive collage of different signs and characters and shop fronts, in the digital age there is arguably a new kind of linguistic transarchitecture where webs of virtual language connectivity envelop the physical spaces of the metropolis. One of the challenges, indeed, in visualizing the contemporary city is that of how to envision or capture these multiple language connections that are not subject to former or more conventional regimes of visibility. It is furthermore the hidden nature of these forms of language relatedness not actualized in physical traces that can make the real translation labour of the migrant less visible than it might be. In the next section, I consider how this dematerialization of language difference impacts forms of presence that are reconfiguring the city as a site of translation.

PRESENCING

Dana Diminescu (2008) is deeply critical of what she views as the fixation with fixity in migration studies. That is to say, she views as inaccurate and unhelpful the tendency to establish strict delimitations between presence and absence, settler and nomad, migrant mobilities and sedentary mobilities. She argues that, on the basis of research she conducted in France, researchers need to be much more aware of how migrants continuously renew their bond with the place or community they left behind through information and communications technology:

> This "virtual" bond – via telephone or email – makes it easier than before to stay close to one's family, to others, to what is happening to them, at home or elsewhere, and even allows one to do this better. The paradigmatic figure of the uprooted migrant is yielding to another figure – one that is as yet ill defined but which corresponds to that of the migrant on the move who relies on alliances outside his own group of belonging without cutting his ties with the social network at home. (567)

Not only has the dialectic between presence and absence altered, but the nature of presence itself has changed: "The idea of 'presence' has

... become less physical, less 'topological' and more active and affective, just as the idea of absence is implicitly altered by these practices of communication and co-presence" (572). The altered notion of presence is bound up with the shift from conversational methods where communication compensates for absence, and is primarily centred on the exchange of knowledge, to connected modes where information and communications technology services maintain "a form of continuous presence in spite of the distance" (572). As Christian Licoppe (2004, 141) points out, increasingly when users have recourse to forms of digital communication, they "talk about a feeling, an immediate emotion, the state that one is in." What is striking is that these forms of connected presence are very sensitive to modes of remote presence, and change their "cognitive and emotional nature in accordance with the richness of the interaction" (142). The more complex the interactions permitted by digital technologies (sound, vision, text, the bidirectionality and user-generated content of the contemporary web), the greater the emphasis on forms of phatic communication where emotional presence was as important as the transmission of instrumental knowledge. These claims were borne out in a study by Carla De Tona and Andrew Whelan on the use of the Internet and mobile phones in migrant women's organizations in Ireland. In their study, which draws heavily on the experience of migrant women in the Dublin metropolitan area, they note that texting was the favoured mode of communication because of its rapidity, spontaneity, and sense of greater proximity in real time to the recipient. Expressions of emotional support were as important as pragmatic and purposive responses to requests for information. As De Tona and Whelan (2009, 14) argue, "the emergence of *mediated* social networks" leads to a "a *reconfiguration of the experiential rupture* of migration," and "re-mediation implies that migrant women act collectively to create space for themselves in their new country of destination, to remediate the dislocations and fractures of translocation, creating institutional space for self-representation and agency." If De Tona and Whelan emphasize the logic of dispersal in imagining new networks of solidarity for migrant women in urban spaces, that same logic in terms of the "connected" migrant means the possibility of a constant, low-level monitoring of events in the place left behind. Richer content (for instance, photos and other visual materials on Facebook), higher speeds, and lower costs facilitate for the departed migrant forms of ambient presence or *presencing* that Lee Komito (2011, 1083) compares to the "background knowledge that exists in face-to-face communities, where people notice who is talking to who in a village meeting place, be it pub, coffee shop, market or post office." What are the implications for translation of these forms of presencing that accompany the rise of digital technologies in migrant settings?

First, the notions of the connected migrant and presencing imply frequent or continuous contact with the mother tongue through frequent virtual communication, either with other members of their language group dispersed throughout the city or with individuals or groups from their place of origin. Thus, rather than the dichotomous, schismatic model of the melting pot involving the brutal rupture with one language and the assimilation of another (see Cronin 2006, 52–6), current developments indicate the migrant is aware of translation not as a state but as a process. That is to say, the changing time-space compression of the digital means migrants have far greater possibilities for experiencing the liminal position of oscillating between two or more languages. They become part of everyday virtual life. Translation becomes less a state of assimilation where the mother tongue is increasingly remote as both memory and experience, and more a process where the migrant constantly moves or negotiates between languages and cultures in the real and virtual spaces of the city and of the place left behind.

Second, presencing suggests that a more comprehensive notion of translation is needed to capture the nature of the translation that takes place in the contemporary, urban translation zone. Traditionally, the discussion of translation and migration has occurred within the remit of interlingual translation, the passage from the language of the migrant to the different, foreign language of the host. However, if there is continuous linguistic interaction between members of a community and those who leave it, how does migrants' language use affect nonmigrants' language use? Is there a sense, within languages and not just between them, that there are processes of change, alteration, and mediation that are best captured under the rubric of intralingual translation? Moreover, reconsidering the role of intralingual translation in the digital age could open up lines of inquiry into earlier periods of migration where speakers of a specific language (for example, English migrants in Australia or Irish anglophones in Britain) experienced a variety of translation problems centred around intralingual difference. A more inclusive notion of translation also helps to capture the different forms of social capital that operate in translation environments. Robert Putnam (2000) differentiates between "bonding capital," which focuses on strengthening collective membership within a group, and "bridging capital," which links diverse groups. Arguably, forms of presencing that feed into intralingual translation are examples of bonding capital, whereas forms of interlingual translation that allow different language groups to communicate in the city illustrate the potential of bridging capital.

Third, it is possible to argue that presencing points up the role of translation in what Diminescu (2008, 571) calls the "relational settlement," or "the social device by which the migrant organizes his life of mobility." How migrants organize their movement, orient themselves in space, set up fruitful encounters, and avoid harassment or discrimination or worse are all part of the relational settlement. The role translation plays in relational settlement becomes even more acute when there are notable changes in migration patterns. One of these is the emergence of "circular migration." Piyasiri Wickramasekara (2001, 1), in a discussion paper prepared for the International Labour Office, defines circular migration as "temporary movements of a repetitive character either formally or informally across borders, usually for work, involving the same migrants. While it can be distinguished from permanent migration (for settlement), and return migration (one trip migration and return), there are nevertheless interfaces between them with circular migration in some cases leading to permanent migration or final return. By definition, all circular migration is temporary migration." Circular migration is fraught with many issues relating to workers' rights and conditions, denial of citizenship and integration, and the instrumentalist exploitation of vulnerable human beings for economic gain. However, due to the changing nature of international labour markets, there is little doubt that temporary labour migration or circular migration is on the increase (58–64) and the "intermittent integration" (Diminescu 2008, 571) that it favours generates increased pressure for appropriate relational settlements. In other words, in increasingly disruptive and flexible labour markets, migrants are forced to factor in translation as a permanent rather than a temporary state of being.

ACCESS

Cities are defined by access. If they develop in particular places at particular times, it is because from there you can access (resources) or be accessible (by traders). Much of the infrastructure development in cities centres on facilitating access, whether by land, sea, or air. Some, over the centuries, has also centred on limiting or blocking access, with drawbridges, moats, and city walls. Translation throughout its long history has been similarly preoccupied by access. During the Reformation, the infrastructural possibilities of the printing press in conjunction with the strategic mobilization of vernacular languages were harnessed to provide wider access to sacred scripture (McGrath 2001). In sixteenth-century China, an imperial court eager for access to Western astronomical knowledge in the drawing up of a new calendar co-opted Western Jesuit translators into the administrative infrastructure of empire (Laven 2011). The infrastructures and strategies of access that underlie both the construction of cities and the practice of translation must be considered anew in the digital moment. In particular, what characterizes notions of belonging today are the conditions and possibilities of access. As Diminescu (2008, 573) points out:

> Whether we are concerned with communication, information or access, these terminals that we wear about ourselves interconnect us, giving us access to different services (transportation, banking, traffic, monitoring) and to different spaces. They are the material support of our connection to our spheres of belonging – urban, national, banking, social, familial, and so on. The portability of the networks of belonging is a feature of all our lives. Migrant or non-migrant, practically everyone finds themselves subject to a logic of access: to circulate, take money out of the bank, to get medical care, to enter one's home, to call etc.

Central to this logic of access are the codes that will let you into your computer at work or your online bank account or your apartment building lobby. In thinking, then, about city as virtual translation zone, translation too becomes part of a particular logic of access for natives and newcomers. How does translation facilitate or obstruct access for the connected migrant? A response to this question incorporates three elements: internalized translation, externalized translation, and traceability.

Internalized translation is the folding of translation functions into digital devices or sites that act as a kind of language prosthetic. For instance, migrants might use dictionary or translation apps on smartphones. Or they might access multilingual documentation through health care, immigration, or educational services websites (McAreavy 2009, 1–22). Technology in these instances allows for a form of mediated access to information in a specific environment, where the migrant does not have to actively recruit or engage an external agent to do the translation for them. For Nicholas Ostler (2011), digitally enabled internalized translation offers one possible scenario for cities of the future as linguistically diverse translation zones. Drawing on the figures for the exponential growth in Internet use by non-English-language speakers, Ostler claims that "the long-term tendency is for information-technology developments to lessen the inaccessibility of the world's languages, to break down language barriers, but without abolishing the languages that cause them" (263). In this view, the availability of cheap and ubiquitous digital technology would remove the need for a global lingua franca as the "frustrations of the language barrier may be overcome without any universal shared medium beyond the compatible software" (261).

Fundamental to this conception of the demise of a global lingua franca is a serviceable model of machine translation. The shift from rule-based machine translation approaches to a greater reliance on machine intelligence, enabling inference engines to derive their own rules from exposure to very large amounts of translation equivalence data and the greater use of statistical matching, has meant an exponential growth in machine translation usage in our age (Wilks 2008; Koehn 2009). Central, of course, to any debate on the future of internalized translation as a form of linguistic access is the question of who gets access to the access. Will there be digital ghettos of disenfranchisement as economically and/or ethnically dominant groups become the gatekeepers to the new city of bits, pulling up the digital drawbridges when their interests are threatened?

Externalized translation is the devolution of the translation to a person who is external to the migrant but whose activities are partly or wholly mediated through technology. For an example of the latter, telephone interpreting is widely used, particularly in the medical field, in the Dublin metropolitan area (Zimányi 2005). Community interpreters use mobile phones, Skype, or other voice or video call apps to translate or mediate between patients and health care workers who do not speak the same language. Another form of externalized translation is what might be termed blended externalized translation, where a particular individual translates orally while interacting with a website. In De Tona and Whelan's study on migrant women's organizations in Ireland, they report on forms of interaction where a migrant leader acts as mediator/translator between online information and non-English speakers in migrant communities. One migrant leader in the African community in the Dublin area, for example, was reported as saying: "The women I worked with have poor English, if you are giving them a leaflet to read is not going to work ... it can be a bit intimidating if you have language barriers ... Sometimes it is just by word of mouth that works out ... So the word of mouth works a lot and then integration really is just about providing information" (quoted in De Tona and Whelan 2007, 13). This "word of mouth" is frequently conveyed by mobile phone, which is a further blending of externalized translation with information and communications technology. Externalized translation, like internalized translation, is subject to an ethics of access, and questions arise, from who does the translation (frequently family members) to what form it takes (what confidentiality is there when interpreting over a mobile phone using public transit) to who is prepared to pay for it (see Pöchhacker and Shlesinger 2007). What is significant is that the type of access afforded by translation is bound up with different tools that allow or prevent translation from being offered to potential users.

Traceability in the context of this chapter is understood to mean the use of both translation and digital technology to track a person's movements, status, and/or opinions. Traceability originated in the business world, where software was designed to track goods as they moved along a distribution chain, collecting information and metrics like delivery, transport, distribution, and sales. In our contemporary world, traceability has become a key component in the deployment of national and transnational security technologies (Cehan 2004). Traceability has become an integral part of the extraterritorial logic of the contemporary nation-state, where the border is everywhere. That is to say, an immigration officer or a customs official with a laptop and a wireless connection is now a border post. Traceability is bound up with access as the justification lies in being able to track and therefore decide who has legitimate access to a society and who does not. There is little point, however, in tracking what you cannot understand (see Cronin 2013, 126–7), so translation becomes an integral part of the surveillance apparatus that tracks the movement of people and opinions in multilingual cities. If in a previous era debate centred on the idea of translation and identity, in our mobile and digital age it is perhaps more appropriate to speak of translation and traceability. This new configuration captures both the surveillance capacity of translation co-opted into new technologies and also the sense in which nomadic inhabitants of the contemporary city leave multiple digital traces (mobile phone calls, texts, emails, video calls) that need to be addressed and archived in any attempt to capture the changing configuration of language and culture in those cities.

Dematerialization, presencing, and access are three parameters that are helping to define the new emerging kinds of translation zones, not just in Dublin but also across the planet. Like the Polish clerk Ignacy, we must be forever mindful of how the "flood of foreign tongues" leads not so much to new Noahs as to new arks, new vessels of translation communication in our changed worlds.

6

Monolingualism and Plural Narratives: The Translation of Suffering in the Language of the City

SIMON HAREL
Translated by Carmen Ruschiensky

CITIES, TRANSLATION, AND THE *DIFFÉREND*: HOW CAN THE REFUGEE BE HEARD?

In this era of globalization, cities are marked by diverse languages that give rise to dissonant forms of expression that share no common denominator. The city has been transformed, under the impact of transnationalism, into a site of global trade in divergent narratives that, through their very heterogeneity, contribute to the creation of a new urban imaginary. This imaginary is transnational but also translational, in the sense that translation highlights and extends dissimilarities. Our worlds are no longer the expression of clearly defined differences.

Exploring the relationships between cities and translation raises the question of the subalternity of the subject of the enunciation. The act of speaking always implies translating from one idiom to another, regardless of the language or languages in use. Subalternity, however, is often associated with the problematic notion of the nonright to speech. But is it true that the subaltern subject cannot speak, is condemned to silence? Is this not in some respects an essentialist claim? We are speaking subjects. The expression of speech, which we perceive as volatile, loose, and spontaneous, is deceptive, an empathetic enacting of discourse that seeks to situate and animate an interlocutor.

Refugees, regardless of their geopolitical and discursive position, are from the outset speakers. As I show, the figure of the refugee, which I study below as a topos of certain fictional discourses, is obligated to speak of the harm that he or she has endured. This obligation, however, is a trap. Refugees have the right to speak insofar as they conform to the habitus of regulated speech forms. Conformity is assured by a legal process that determines the validity of their stories. In this respect, refugees, unlike native subjects protected by national borders, are particularly dependent on translational interventions, translational "prostheses," that determine their acceptance or rejection by governing, primarily legal authorities. An important factor that contributes to reframing the role imposed on refugees within the discursive but also contentious space of translation is that the act of translating positions the foreign language as external, as though it were an accessory, an unnecessary inconvenience for the host country's subjects.

How can the refugee be heard? Is it a question of listening with compassion? The familiar discourse of empathy implied in these words excludes the possibility of regarding translation as a site of conflict. In Dave Eggers's (2007) novel *What Is the What*, this empathy is omnipresent. The American characters who welcome the novel's protagonist, Valentino Achak Deng, make every effort to be helpful and share in his painful memory of a massacre, which they perceive as a "serial narrative." In the many scenes describing this reception on US territory, the question of language is barely mentioned, as though the refugee's linguistic integration were secondary. Indeed, it is through the filter of the second language (English) that Deng's emotional experience emerges as a story that conforms to the expectations of a compassionate audience.

Though Rawi Hage's (2008) novel *Cockroach* presents a very different situation – the story unfolds against the backdrop of a Middle-Eastern immigrant community in Montreal – the main character undergoes a series of psychotherapy sessions during which the therapist, Genevieve, takes on the role of an investigator examining her patient's unconscious. In both novels, difficulty abandoning the foreign mother tongue appears as a deficiency, and translation is treated as an aside. While the other characters are content in their monolingualism, refugees are forced to go beyond their familiar linguistic universe. They must speak the language of the others, relying on dictionaries and grammar manuals that will, ideally, assure their integration into the world of culture, of plurality.

I take a different perspective on these questions. The refugee who is "charitably" welcomed into a community is obliged to compromise his or her linguistic idiom and make it an instrument of negotiation. With respect to the official, state-sanctioned pluralism that often serves as the ideological justification for this welcome, the refugee's situation raises troubling questions. Refugees, even more so than immigrants, have become the emblematic figures of transnationalism, and of its violence and mercantile digressions. How does translation affect the refugee's status and precarious position in a globalized urban context?

Translators are often described as traitors, unfaithful to the material they are required to transfer from one language into another. Whether or not this accusation is justified, the translational intervention, like any utterance, is subject to discursive formations (in Foucault's sense) and regulated meanings that should be contested. Translation and power go hand in hand. In manifesting a desire to speak and in assuming a linguistic position, individuals and communities inevitably confront the dynamics of a *différend*, an element of dispute between languages, cultures, and ways of being in the world.[1] Translation that ignores the *différend* quickly becomes a technique, a process bound to habitual thought, as though the subject, having returned to a primal identity and failing to travel across languages, is condemned to repeat his or her original, monolingual language.

Within this comfortable universe, translation takes on the familiar forms of crossing, transition, and nomadism. Though these concepts are not necessarily inadequate, they have not aged well. They characterize translation as an activity to be used in so-called favourable conditions: in contexts of plurilingualism and cultural hybridity. In the two novels under discussion here, *Cockroach* and *What Is the What*, this plurilingualism is an illusion, an intellectual's utopia. Translation is not the inevitable outcome of plurilingualism, and cultures are not spaces that, in and of themselves, elicit exchange between predefined territories.

Refugees are subjects who are trying to survive (and end intolerable situations of oppression) in the hopes of having a better life, of merging into the background of the urban landscape. Their efforts, however, are often in vain. Refugees who want to go unnoticed are soon found out. They wander the city in search of refuge. They do not speak the language of native subjects. They have to be translated to be understood.

I hypothesize that the refugee poses a challenge to the habitual speech of the monolingual, who, taking meaning to be literal and uncontested, denies any possible enunciative ambivalence between the speaking subject and the utterance. Monolingual subjects speak with the certainty that no one will question what they say. They understand one another in the home, in the workplace, in the enclosed, entrenched spheres of the national space. Monolingual subjects perpetuate the idea of a source language, as it provides a sense of belonging that corresponds to their self-image.

When translation becomes mechanical, it is transformed into a passion for the referent, denying the aporia that is the source of any enunciation. Monolinguals do not question their position. They expect language to provide an efficient, unhindered form of communication. The figure of the refugee disrupts this efficiency. As Robert Barsky (2000) demonstrates, refugee claimants must justify their existence to the administrative and legal authorities of the host country. Yet, even the concept of a host society is misleading. Refugees must defend their case in the *templum* of the tribunal, implying that they are positioned, from the outset, as liars. This last point is important, because the narrative that establishes communication between subjects is, from the beginning, associated with doubt and deception.

In the novels under consideration here, writing takes the form of a narration that attempts to represent the refugee's speech. However, this narrative is created through a third party, transforming the refugee's testimony, the enunciative transcription of violence endured, into fiction. We are confronted with an ambivalence between truth and fiction. In the context of the asylum hearing, judges presume to recognize the truth. They have one obsession: to find the flaw in the refugee claimant's account, to note contradictions in the various versions of the story that are, in the end, irrefutable proof of the power of the imagination over the literal testimony.

Narcissistic affectation, the origin of all dreams, of all untamed thought (see Bion 1998), contributes to the failure of translation here. The refugee has difficulty explaining his motives, trips over his own words, doesn't seem credible – in short, he possesses all the traits of a liar. Though this situation is far from the realm of the literary enunciation, it still merits consideration. Any utterance of a testimonial nature faces this vertigo of imposture, as if the subject rising to speak is destined to say it wrong, to misrepresent his or her innermost truth. While the tribunal's judges oversee the "normality" of the process, the refugee loses his train of thought, is taken by surprise, and finds himself unable to respond to the questions he is obliged to answer.

This portrait of ambivalence is at the heart of my reflection. Every instance of speech is circumstantial. The utterance represents an anchoring point in our individual histories that enables us to construct a credible discourse. What would happen if we were no longer ourselves? If we were overcome with doubt about who we really were? Our personal narratives are also fictions, insofar as we are fallible subjects having fallen into the abyss of language. From this point of view, literary fiction has the capacity, in a very serious way, to register this ambivalence that briefly reconciles the real and the figural. In a situation as crucial as the quest for refuge (a territory, a place of residence, but also a psychological reassurance), the novels considered here reveal that ambivalence is a basic element of self-expression.

THE CUSTODIAN-NARRATOR

In a language foreign to academic discourse, Eggers's *What Is the What* reveals the lot of the destitute, those beings who, as refugees, cannot claim to participate in or even aspire to the great dream of cosmopolitanism. The novel's narrative structure is complex. Eggers's narration represents a previous telling: Deng's personal account. This carefully structured narrative raises questions regarding the status of the testimony but also the role of (Eggers's) monolingualism in altering it. Deng's mother tongue is erased. This act of violence is presented as the necessary price to pay to gain acceptance in the host country. The very real constraints of translation become evident here. Deng is not in a position to write his own story. Lacking proficiency in English, he has to entrust it to another. Through this questionably transparent process, he is dispossessed of his story and becomes what I refer to elsewhere as a public writer.[2] He accepts losing a part of himself: the inscription, in his mother tongue, of an emotional suffering dissociated from its root of origin. Of course, suffering and exploitation have no language, and the testimony itself cannot be reduced to its linguistic formulation. Those who have lived through expulsion from their native countries understand that their stories are fluid and mobile, not fixed or bound by territorial logic.

As in the context of the asylum hearing discussed above, it is once again this ambivalence – the refugee not trusting his own discourse – that casts doubt on his testimony. The characters in Hage's *Cockroach* inhabit a Dostoyevskian universe. Any well-articulated utterance – indeed, any confident use of language – can fail, though the loss of equilibrium this implies is inconsequential. Instead of failure or breakdown, it might be more accurate, as I suggest elsewhere (1994, 1997, 2001), to speak of a claustrum,[3] that abysmal swamp of self-hate and guilt (in the name of what error?) without depth or density that appears intermittently in the novels under consideration here. The refugee wakes up one day and wonders if he is not someone else, if his survival is not simply the consequence of another's death. The question might seem futile. Isn't the important thing to have survived? To have crossed land and sea to escape imminent death?

In this cosmopolitical homage to alterity, in the passage from one language to another, the subaltern subject is forgotten. The subaltern is the one whose mouth is filled with rubble, the one grovelling, crawling, barely walking, roaming the city's streets or fleeing totalitarian regimes, border zones, civil wars, and other brutalities. In Eggers's *What Is the What*, Deng is this subaltern. He cannot use his mother tongue to recount his own story. His suffering can only be expressed through another – Eggers, acting as his spokesperson. This raises serious questions regarding the role of monolingualism in representing this emotional suffering, the affective aspect of words and their mental representation as understood by psychoanalysts. In *What Is the What* this monolingualism is not a constraint; it is the source of an aporia.

How is this addressed in *What Is the What*? The dream of becoming an American is the ultimate priority, from the human zoos of the refugee camps where the forgotten are left to rot, to the culmination of a long journey in Atlanta. But what about the refugee's account? Is it not silenced by a betrayal? The denial of Deng's mother tongue also effaces his signature, his symbolic being. His story can only be told through the intermediary of a master translator, an omnipotent narrator like Eggers. This representation of Deng's suffering in *What Is the What* reveals sites of translation in the narrative. Translation appears to be a process that filters out the subaltern's mother tongue.

Both novels depict refugees in urban settings. We might question, however, the refugee's role in contributing to the cosmopolitan future of the world's globalized cities. While European encyclopaedism emphasized the cosmopolitan aspect of cities, today we must explain the demise of this cosmopolitan humanism, which has been ransacked, plundered, and transformed into a spectacle of diversity. In place of this universal humanism, we now see the emergence of multiple singularities and an attention to countless and immeasurable differences. Has translation become a smoke screen in this era of triumphant neoliberalism? In appealing to the diversity of the new urban agora, its celebration of difference and similarity, disagreement and consensus, translation seems to participate in the effacement of the subject. Translation is representative of the mobile, agile, and efficient forms of communication that erase uncertainty, the suffering inherent in the refugee's experience.

The underlying enunciation of violence in the refugee camp, "the human zoo" as Peter Sloterdijk (2000) describes it,[4] must be taken seriously. The refugee always, in these situations, depends on intermediaries to be heard, whether they be representatives of nongovernmental organizations, humanitarian associations, or other international groups. The refugee's speech cannot be taken at face value. It is not a form of free expression. It has been shaped by mistreatment, misunderstanding, and betrayal. Those who manage to escape the human zoo of suffering, the no-man's land of the refugee camp, have not seen the end of their ordeal.

In *What Is the What*, Deng's departure for the United States is decisive. Does this mean he is welcomed and accepted? Not really. For Eggers, Atlanta represents a universe without tensions, a "soft power" where a festive ambiance is subjected to the law of consumerism and neoliberalism. The refugee thus takes part in a spectacle of misery and exploitation, recalling the antihumanism described by Alain Badiou (1997). In the cosmopolitan universe of the humanist era, debate revolved around questions of immanence and transcendence, the single and the multiple, the sacred and the profane. Humanism is the expression of this juxtaposition of seeming contradictions. It is also with reference to these categories that translation, following Berman (1984), can be understood as a "trial of the foreign."

In *What Is the What*, Deng's story must be retranscribed and narrated by a writer-subject – a custodian. By assuming responsibility for the refugee's story, the narrator performs an act of linguistic and cultural translation. Does this narrator also revise the original account by transforming it into an acceptable work of fiction? Who establishes the conditions of its reception? Who sets the expectations and assures its readability as fictional discourse? Eggers is a well-known writer. Deng's story is one among thousands that have not been transformed into celebrated publications. As the preface explains in *What Is the What*, the choice to fictionalize the story was the result of long discussions during which Eggers came to better understand the intolerable realities of the massacres and community violence that Deng experienced. My intention, therefore, is certainly not to portray Eggers as a thief of someone else's words.[5] There is nothing in this novel that suggests bad faith on his part or crass exploitation of another's misery. On the contrary, it is clear that Eggers sought to produce a cocreation in which Deng played an important role. Nevertheless, the book's publication, sales, and distribution all point to one fact: Eggers is the author, and Deng is anonymous. Meanwhile, Deng's narrator-character in the novel is the result of a skilful substitution. While Eggers speaks in the name of the refugee, the narrator's character (Deng) is a fictional construction who "uses" Deng's words. This strategy is clearly not an attempt to deceive. Nor is it an act of bad faith. This would be a misinterpretation of Eggers's intention.

Literary discourse on the subaltern typically takes the form of pious declarations that seek to establish the subaltern subject's rightful place in society. This position, however, becomes esoteric rather quickly. The only way to escape the subaltern condition is to occupy the place of the author, to establish a non-negotiable place for oneself at the heart of the discursive universe. This place is symbolically confirmed by both a signature and a name, insofar as the author's civic identity is the toponymical indicator that determines, in the world of letters, who is considered a writer and who is not. From this perspective, one naturally concludes that Deng is not a writer. His role is simply to provide a crude account of his experience of intercommunity violence, mass murders, and life in the refugee camps. Does this mean that the writer's title depends on a work's status as an aesthetic object? This question is open to endless debate. We might ask, rather, what the refugee has to do to escape his or her harsh destiny, to be miraculously transformed into an author or narrator.

Though Eggers's project is commendable, it is based on the questionable premise that empathy can be a basis for literary creation. Eggers is a custodian: he assumes responsibility for Deng's speech. But he reifies this speech in some way and condemns it to oblivion, in spite of his good intentions. This effacement is the inevitable result of a literary protocol that imposes its own rules in much the same way that the asylum hearing process determines the outcome of a status claim. The interpreter hired to translate the refugee's speech performs this task within the official context of the asylum hearing. In this role, he or she also acts as a custodian, transferring the other's speech and seamlessly integrating it into a circuit of communication that must be direct and immediate. What exactly takes place in this act of translation? We presume that interpreters do not lie or intentionally deform refugees' words, but, in their attempt to be faithful to the other's speech, do they actually speak the truth?

In everyday life the refugee's speech is fragile. It is threatened. I have described the role of individuals who act as custodians. Within a strictly symbolic framework, these custodians are the legislators of speech, like the judge whose authority frames the tribunal process. The interpreter's role is to translate his or her client's speech, to respect every word of the testimony. But is this always possible? To continue with the above example, what if the refugee speaks too quickly, and the interpreter is unable to keep up with the whirlwind of thoughts? Would the interpreter in this case be tempted to eliminate the seemingly unnecessary details? Or would he or she be inclined to make the statement more coherent? Given the spontaneous exchanges and interrogations of the asylum hearing, it is reasonable to assume that interpreters, in spite of their professional obligations, sometimes unintentionally simplify the other's speech to make it more expressive or more easily understood.

Meanwhile the writer, in this case Eggers, pleads on Deng's behalf with all the good faith in the world. Like any good lawyer, he hopes to convince his audience of the cruelties and abuse that his client has endured. But while the lawyer is obliged to conform to the norms and jurisprudence of the tribunal, the writer enjoys considerably greater freedom. This illusion of freedom is perhaps granted too quickly in the world of arts and letters. *What Is the What* is ultimately based on an indifferent narrative mechanism that attempts to translate the refugee's voice but, in the end, silences it. Consider the following passage from the novel:

> From there the questions went deeply into my experiences as a refugee:
>
> Who were the groups that wanted to kill you and what made them want to kill you? What kind of weapons did they carry or use? Before you left your village, did you see people killed by these attackers? What motivated you to leave Sudan? Which year did you leave Sudan? When did you arrive in Ethiopia and by what means? Did you ever fight in the wars of Sudan? Do you know of

> the SPLA/SPLM? Were you ever recruited by the rebel army? What security issues do you face in Kakuma? ...
>
> I answered all of the queries without distortion, it was over in twenty minutes. I shook their hands and left the room, puzzled and impressed. Certainly that was not the sort of interview that would decide whether or not a man traveled across the world and became the citizen of a different nation. I stood, dazed, the interpreter opened the door and caught my arm. – You did very well, Dominic. Don't worry. You look worried. I'm sure this will be straightened out now. (Eggers 2007, 493–4)

The refugee takes part here in a drama that is violent and intrusive. This questioning, as Roland Barthes (1970) observes, functions like a summons. The institutional constraints of this interrogation, in which Deng's survival is at stake, recalls the *outside-technè* proofs (*preuves hors-la-technè*) of ancient rhetoric: the most raw violence, beyond words, that scars, cuts into the subject's body.

What Is the What is also the story of an interminable journey, that of the African refugees known as the Lost Boys of Sudan. The failure of translation is again evident here. In what language can these massacres be described? Who can be the spokesperson for something that at times escapes the order of discourse? As readers of *What Is the What*, we accept being led into places of danger and death, from the graveyard of South Sudan to the survival zones of the refugee camps, the human zoos endured while awaiting shipment to North America. The refugees in *What Is the What* are constantly on the move, but do not travel. They are transported, displaced, and manufactured. They inhabit the cargo hold of a ship, the undercarriage of an aircraft.

What do refugees do after leaving these confined spaces of isolation, after finding themselves, against all odds, in a host country? In *What Is the What*, the refugee's mental suffering receives little attention. The monosemic language of indifference eclipses it. In one of the novel's first scenes, Deng is the victim of an armed robbery in his apartment. He is beaten, bound and gagged, and subjected to a verbal violence that deprives him of all dignity:

> "Get the fuck down, motherfucker!"
>
> And my face meets the floor once more. Now the kicking begins. He kicks me in the stomach, and now the shoulder. It hurts most when my bones strike my bones.

> "Fucking Nigerian motherfucker" ... "Fucking Nigerian, so stupid!"
>
> He is heaving, his hands on his bent knees.
>
> "No wonder you motherfuckers are in the Stone Age!"
>
> He gives me one more kick, lighter than the others, but this one directly into my temple, and a burst of white light fills my left eye.
>
> In America I have been called Nigerian before – it must be the most familiar of African countries – but I have never been kicked. (Eggers 2007, 9)

The crudity of the insult is amplified by the racism and physical violence, all accompanying this very singular welcome in the language of Empire. This "motherfucker," this "fucking Nigerian," is the background noise against which the barely audible refugee is to be eradicated.

One conclusion may be drawn from this act of violence. The cosmopolitics that once engendered endless discussion and debate, establishing the basis for a community of meaning, has been discarded in favour of plundering, aggression, robbery, and rape. Following this logic, the heterotopias of hospitality and community (the haven, the refuge, the sanctuary) are replaced in Eggers's universe by the psychopathy of burglary and violence carried out in the rented space of an apartment. This violence represents a radical form of desubjectivation that corresponds to Michel Wieviorka's (2004) concept of the antisubject.

RESISTING TRANSLATION

What role does translation play in this context? It is clearly not based on dialogue or mutual understanding. In this scene, Deng is not so much subject to the principle of translation, which assumes the meeting of two subjectivities capable of maintaining an expressive commensality, than he is confronted with the degrading impact of insults. The degree zero of translation, the enunciation of a coarse language, seems, from the first pages of *What Is the What*, to be an integral part of American life. Figures of vertical power (the American Empire) give way here to the representation of small spaces and sites of confinement: waiting rooms, small apartments, and customs bureaus. One passage offers a particularly absurd description of

American life. Following the attack, Deng goes to the hospital for treatment. After a few hours of waiting, he realizes that not only is his presence unwelcome, but he is not even acknowledged as a person, a complete subject:

> I have been to this hospital. Shortly after I arrived in Atlanta, Anne Newton brought me here to get a physical. It is the finest hospital in Atlanta she told me ... it is the finest we have, Anne said, and I'm happy to be there. In the hospitals I feel palpable comfort. I feel the competence, the expertise, so much education and money, all of the supplies sterile, everything packaged, sealed tight. My fears evaporate when the automatic doors shush open ... It is four o' clock when we step into the reception area. An African-American man, about thirty years old and wearing short-sleeved blue scrubs, is at the receiving desk. He looks us over with great interest, a curious grin spreading under his thick moustache. As we approach, he seems to register the injuries to my face and head. He asks me what happened, and I relay a brief version of the story. He nods and seems sympathetic. I feel almost irrationally grateful to him. "We'll get you fixed up quick," he says. (Eggers 2007, 240–1).

The man at the reception desk appears sympathetic and compassionate. His attitude seems to contradict the indifference and solitude of monosemic language that I have described up until now. However, this benevolent attitude, this apparent hospitality is insincere: "We have been in the waiting room for two hours. The pain in my head has not diminished, but is less sharp than before. I expected help from you, Julian. Not because you are of African descent, but because this hospital is very quiet, the emergency room virtually devoid of patients, and I'm one man sitting in your waiting room with what I hope are minor wounds. It would seem to be easy to help me and send me home. I can't imagine why you would want me here staring at you" (244). This hospital waiting room is the antechamber of all those other anonymous rooms where refugees, crammed together in the camps, wait in the hope of finally meeting the NGO representatives, the diplomatic spokespeople who can provide some form of safe conduct. Refugees are familiar with this interminable waiting. In these situations, the refugee represents a problem, an annoying reminder of international guidelines on the protection of persons in danger. Officials will often certify a name or birthdate only to be rid of the problem sooner, to delete it from the system.

While Eggers's novel has the city of Atlanta as its backdrop, Hage's refugees inhabit the slums of Montreal. His depiction of Montreal is at odds with theoretical conceptions of the contemporary cosmopolitan city as a site of hybridity and transculturality. In this era of technological dematerialization of the self, through the Internet in particular, translation becomes just another way to reduce the subject, to transform the subject into a *parfum de poussière*.[6]

Hage's portrayal of the refugee in *Cockroach* is therefore significant. This novel addresses the necessity of the production of alterity.[7] To begin with, the city is the site of an ambivalent hospitality. The vision of the translational city as hospitable is the most implausible fantasy. It discards the myth of Babel and suggests that the impurity of languages no longer poses a problem. From this perspective – consider Google's metacommunication network that now provides portable translations in languages ranging from Cheyenne to Basque – we might envision a day when everyone will be expected to be completely understood, heard, and perceived in their entirety, and any form of illegibility, absence of meaning, or communication breakdown becomes unthinkable.

In this era of translational cities conceived of as sites of metacommunication, as self-reproducing systems void of any human intervention, it is important to consider elements that resist translation, particularly with respect to the refugee's status and its administrative and political determination. The concept of resistance may seem surprising here. It contradicts the idea that we should embrace translation, grant it a special pacifying role in contexts where refugees face violence. From this point of view, translation should be regarded as an aide, a form of support that ensures the recognition of the refugee's dignity and legitimacy as a citizen. The fantasy of hospitality is based on accommodating the refugee, on making every effort to facilitate his or her integration into the shared language of the city.

The ideal of the translational city is based on an omnipotent discourse. In its present form, the desire to understand the other, to know every detail, justifies the idea of a new servitude, a pacification of languages in the name of an absolute understanding of the refugee's suffering. Perhaps we should consider, rather, the difficulty in understanding the other, the so-called authenticity of the primordial enunciation. The refugee is, in some respects, a subject beyond language, a figurative motif that, like the foreigner, both repels and attracts. The refugee, in fact, is not really welcome, because he or she represents something we want to combat, annihilate, with all our might. The refugee most likely arouses in us the sentiment that Freud ([1926] 2002) refers to as infantile distress, the subject's sense, at times, that his or her familiar, welcoming environment (initially represented by the mother but eventually including the surrounding world) does not exist. We often reject the foreigner, who reawakens in us this infantile distress that we want to ignore. We associate the refugee and the foreigner with all that is dark, with a black box of abuses, torture, dungeons, catacombs, and other places of death.

The refugee is the one we refuse to translate. This refusal is a fact of daily life in every so-called translational city, because the production of the other in the context of the administrative tribunal,[8] in Canada as elsewhere, rests on the assumed falsehood of the refugee's claim. Refugee claimants are often accused of inventing stories of persecution. They are depicted as fabulators and manipulators. They are often perceived as the very incarnation of the liar, as subjects who, in the name of their culture, are bound to produce lies instead of embrace truth. This has major consequences for the production of an order of discourse, as Foucault (1981) describes. Refugees who present a status claim, accompanied by a lawyer for the occasion, are doubly hindered by constraints inherent in the asylum hearing process itself. They are subjected to the most violent discursive constraint – having to explain to a commissioner, in a self-narrative marred with inaccuracies, that they fear for their lives.

Both of the novels considered here situate the refugee's story in the heart of the city. Have the *passages obligés* of migrant literature[9] perhaps given way to other modes of representing the foreigner? What is the city's relevance in this new context? In the modern era, cosmopolitanism was mandatory. One traversed the city's spaces and delved into its inner recesses, which were a reflection of one's own instincts, trajectories, and desires.[10] Artists, from the Zurich Dadaists and the surrealists to Jackson Pollock, saw in modern cities like London and New York the ideal translation of their unique creative experiences, as though by giving free reign to their desires through various forms of transgression[11] they could reclaim an identity purified in the face of death and reborn in poetic reverie on their travels through the city's secret spaces.

The exfoliated city revealed that, while the plurality of trajectories observed day after day in metropolitan life could be discovered, detached, dissected even, the violence at the heart of urban life resisted abstraction. Benjamin explored this terrain, as did Stephan Zweig. The surrealists, starting with André Breton ([1928] 1998), tried to suspend the moment of this urban violence, as witnessed, for example, in *Nadja*. Wandering was a way of translating the surprise, anxiety, and fear that these encounters with the city's strangeness sometimes provoked.

But yesterday's cities have given way to sites of metacommunication that are apparently independent of megacities. The image of urban organicity has been replaced by a form of nonhumanity, and the subject has been dematerialized, reduced, as we shall see in *Cockroach*, to a thin layer of dirt. Likewise, the city's sharpness, monumental aspects, and architecture of verticality have given way to a world in which the human being has lost all consistency, has been transformed into a fluidity, as envisioned, for example, by Bauman (2000). This concept of fluidity, however, is based on a questionably optimistic discourse. In place of liquid fluidity and crumbling ruins, we should perhaps retain that which remains of the self in the wake of this violence, this silent trauma.

The idea of resisting translation implies that the refugee's stories can be heard in other contexts, beyond the tribunal. In the contemporary translational city, this means creating sites of alterity and illegitimacy that question common sense. My critique of forms of metacommunication that dematerialize the body, mind, emotions, and instincts is not based on a nostalgic longing for an era when the body did not depend on prosthetic support to exist, when feeling alone could give rise to full, complete enunciations. This appeal to embodiment, as it is called today – this reclamation of the body as a site of diverse emotional experiences, identities, and genres – is not intended to obscure the impurity of the foreign or the foreigner's communication.

THE JOUISSANCE OF THE FOREIGN

Consider the following passage from Hage's (2008, 52) *Cockroach*:

> I can live in filth and hunger, I assured her. My mother lives far away, and if we ever get married, no one has to clean because I can

> tolerate filth, cockroaches, and mountains of dishes that would tower above our heads like monumental statues, like trophies, testifying that we value lovemaking and a hedonistic existence, and that all else can wait! And even if you were my sister, I wouldn't mind hearing your most intimate fantasies.
>
> Shohreh laughed and called me crazy. You are so dirty, she said softly, and suddenly her long, black hair fell away from her face, her thick, arched eyebrows smiled at me and pierced my chest, her laugh escaped her and slapped me in the face, kicked me in the gut, mopped the floor with my hairy chest, dipped me in sweat and squeezed my heart with unbearable happiness.

In this passage, the filth of the foreign takes the form of a jouissance, a pleasure in blending into the surrounding mess, dirty apartment, yellowing walls, piled-up dishes, and accumulating garbage. This jouissance allows two unique, authentic beings to share their differences, their sexuality, and their abject, magnified eroticism in a way that unites them:

> I will sleep with you, said Shohreh, but you have to tell Reza all about it. Reza and his like need to understand, once and for all, that I am not their virgin on hold, not their smothering mother, not their obedient sister. I'm not a testament to their male, nationalistic honor.
>
> I will! I will! I shouted, and I mimed Reza's reaction upon hearing all about it, I stood up and did his baffled eyebrows, his itching armpits, and his squeaky voice like a mouse in a trap. Shohreh laughed again. (52)

There is a jouissance in the refugee's life that lies beyond translation, that precedes the metacommunication systematically manipulated by power structures that standardize and control. The romantic ambiance that envelops the dirt, residue, and waste in the above passage suggests an alternative form of translation: it embraces – and thus subverts – the stigma of filth and impurity in traditional representations of the foreign.

The foreigner represents a threat to the ethnic, national human community. The foreigner is the outsider who, in an affront to usual thinking, introduces new forms of communication for which translations do not yet exist, as in the following passage:

> The therapist annoyed me with her laconic behaviour. She brought on a feeling of violence within me that I hadn't experienced since I left my homeland. She did not understand. For her, everything was about my relations with women, but for me, everything was about defying the oppressive power in the world that I can neither participate in nor control. And the question that I hated most – and it came out when she was frustrated with me for not talking enough – was when she leaned over the table and said, without expression: What do you expect from our meeting? (4–5)

Do you hear me? Do you understand? Can you relate to what I'm saying? This questioning on the part of the therapist at the very beginning of *Cockroach* is relevant to my reflection on translation. Recall the premise of the novel: a man is living in Montreal. He is a refugee. Following a suicide attempt, he is ordered by the state to undergo therapy with a psychologist, an individual who, over the course of scheduled meetings, is required to assess his mental health. The element of misunderstanding is central to the narrative insofar as the concept of free expression, as conventionally defined within the context of the therapeutic space, quickly takes on a more complex aspect. This so-called free expression, within the immediacy of the therapy session, here involves the intervention of a third party represented by the legal system:

> I burst out: I am forced to be here by the court! I prefer not to be here, but when I was spotted hanging from a rope around a tree branch, some jogger in spandex ran over and called the park police. Two of those mounted police came galloping to the rescue on the backs of their magnificent horses. All I noticed at the time was the horses. I thought the horses could be the answer to my technical problem. I mean, if I rode on the back of one of those beasts, I could reach a higher, sturdier branch, secure the rope to it, and let the horse run free from underneath me. Instead I was handcuffed and taken for, as they put it, assessment.
>
> Tell me about your childhood, the shrink asked me.
>
> In my youth I was an insect.
>
> What kind of insect? she asked.
>
> A cockroach, I said. (5)

The patient has no choice but to speak. On the one hand, he is undergoing an evaluation, awaiting judgement, and subject to the requirements of a speech belonging to the order of discourse, and, on the other hand, he is obliged, in his state of house arrest, we might say also therapeutic arrest, to respond. This freedom of speech barely masks the betrayal of confidentiality. This speech is reduced, through the intermediary of the therapist, to its instrumental and utilitarian form. The truth the therapist solicits is not so different from that required of the narrator-protagonist attempting to prove his refugee status in an asylum hearing.

This translational confrontation takes place in a Montreal portrayed as a crowded space, populated with foreigners who squat in slums and live in precarity:

> I looked for my socks, and goddamn it! They were still moist. I usually put them under the bed covers and sleep on top of them to dry them out, but last night I forgot and just tossed them on the floor. Perhaps I was thinking a little fresh air would do them good. I dug around in my laundry and found an older pair that were dry – dirty but dry ... I walked down St-Laurent and approached the Artista Café. Inside it was smoggy with smoke and warm breath, and the glass of the window dripped water. I stuck my face close to the glass (so as to see others and not my own ghostly reflection for once), and I moved my eyes left and right, searching to see if any lost immigrants had arrived. No one I knew was there yet, so I continued walking. (85–6)

The above description of marginal life calls to mind the usual Bohemian stereotypes, as depicted, for example, in the writings of Henri Murger (1988), among others. We recognize this famished individual wandering the streets, leering into restaurant windows along St Laurent Boulevard. Similar descriptions can be found in Murger's nineteenth-century prose and in the novels of his numerous imitators in Brussels and London. Hage's approach is therefore not particularly original in its description of this precarious, Bohemian life. More interesting, in *Cockroach*, are these quasi-atmospheric images of dampness and humidity, dryness and dust that point to the nonhuman presence of the cockroach. These atmospheric motifs also suggest a nonhuman way of walking (that of the refugee?), as if wandering were a form of repressed violence, a return to inanimate existence. Any community bound by norms of meaning, interpretation, translation, or signification faces the untranslatability that this foreigner embodies.

When refugees speak, they must be translated. This applies not only to their words but also to their being and, even, to their *désêtre* (nonbeing), at the risk of abusing the expression. The violence they endure is presented as a form of aphasia, an interruption of thought in its inception. The therapist, Genevieve, relies on note taking. Discourse here is a transcription of the patient's orality: "Let me look at my notes, Genevieve said, dismissing my attempt at joy and laughter. Okay, so last time when you burst out of the office here – do you remember that? You were telling me about your sister and her husband, Tony" (98). This note taking introduces an aspect of anamnesis (retrospective understanding). It is the therapist's personal translation of her patient's discourse, in all its strangeness. Is this not a form of psychoanalysis? This therapist, however, also has to provide an evaluation. As Genevieve explains, she is performing an assessment: an activity that involves reporting her patient's intentions to a third party.

Hage's novels question forms of subjectivation that occur through translation by representing the cosmopolitan city as an illusion. *De Niro's Game* takes place in Beirut and Marseille, cities marked by conflict between languages, cultures, and religious traditions. *Cockroach* takes place in Montreal, which, for once, is not presented as an exotic destination for literary migrants or Bohemian travellers:

> As I strolled, a few clouds moved over the sky and covered the sun. All of a sudden, things started to turn grey and damp, and the darker side of nature appeared on people's face. I saw some looking up at the sky and muttering for themselves. Then, a few streets later, drops of water fell. You could see the drops dotting the pavement. At first they were distinct and visible because there were only a few of them, but then the whole city was taken over by thunder and homogeneous wetness that swallowed everything and changed the city's color and odor. Tin roofs sounded like snapping lashes across a monster's back. Car windows looked like cascading water. A few human silhouettes with invisible heads hurried down cobblestone streets. The edges of the sidewalks harbored little streams that soon became swollen and fast. I followed them, oblivious to the water falling from above. I am interested in water's flight, not its source. Everything became wet, the walls, my hair and clothing, even the gun beneath my jacket was wet. My pants stuck to my legs. My socks made squelching noises. Then

> the rain stopped, suddenly. And I walked back home to the tempo of my wet feet. (187)

SELF-TRANSLATION

The narrator clearly has difficulty walking and is transformed at times into a cockroach. The underlying fantasy is one of survival. While it is possible to forget the past, the present appears banal and the future is unpromising and hopeless. What does it mean to live in a city in which isolation is a persistent reality, as it is in Hage's Montreal? I have already discussed the need to critique this increasingly commonplace desire for total communication, for an urban language without conflict and in perpetual movement like the ebb and flow of the tide. The narrator's silence in *Cockroach* suggests a distrust of any form of contact, which is perceived as a threat and reveals the protagonist's difficulty in recognizing the other's subjectivity. It is no coincidence that Hage's cockroach penetrates the psychotherapist's apartment, invading and contaminating its inhabited space. The subject incapable of living in the present moment is fixated on relating to things instead of relating to other people.

Ultimately, in order to tell his or her own story, the refugee must perform a self-translation, one shaped by the revelations of the unconscious and open to the violence of desubjectivation. I prefer this expression, though somewhat convoluted, to the now-cliché description of traumatic rupture. Though I have referenced this term in relation to discourse myself, the idea has become rather commonplace. It seems to imply that in order to live, one has to already have been annihilated, weakened, and resigned to the fait accompli of death over life. I would propose, rather, that the refugee-subject inhabits a space in which he or she can develop a personal discourse, a translation of the violence endured.

The refugee has to adapt to the new world into which he or she has been plunged. I prefer to call this adaptation a form of self-translation. Both Deng and the protagonist of *Cockroach* find themselves confronted with new realities that demand adapting to an unfamiliar lifestyle and learning a foreign language, among many other factors. Refugees must become desensitized to their past. This process is fraught with risk. Those who distance themselves such are often accused of disloyalty and betrayal. This accusation does not necessarily come from a real person (though it can); it also exists in the imagination, in the form of a fictional description, for example. The subject who becomes desensitized to his or her past subconsciously reinforces the initial traumatic violence.

In *Cockroach*, the narrator's indifference to his psychotherapist seems to express a world without hope, as if the harsh reality of the present moment accentuated a rift between the words and their utterance. The narrator is very mistrustful of his therapist. He is careful, in the context of this therapeutic evaluation, this assessment, to hide his flaws and never let his guard down. Nonetheless, his cockroach fantasy is still revealed. As both a waking dream and conscious simulation, this fantasy readily brings to mind Lacan's definition of foreclosure. Its violent repression plunges the subject back into the real, back into a world of waking nightmares.

In *What Is the What*, the transplantation onto US territory also has an important impact on the small community of South Sudanese survivors. The different styles of clothing and the intensive use of gadgets and technologies (cell phones, MP3 players, high-definition televisions, etc.) are novel and surprising:

> There was one group among us who were dressed differently than the rest, wearing sweatsuits, visors, baseball hats and basketball shirts, accentuated with gold watches and chains. These men we called Hawaii 5-0, for they had just returned from Hawaii, where they were working as extras in a Bruce Willis movie. This is true. Apparently one of the Lost Boys Foundation volunteers knew a casting director in Los Angeles, who was looking for East African men to serve as extras in a movie directed by an African-American man named Antoine Fuqua. The volunteers sent a photo of ten of the Atlanta-based Sudanese men, and all ten were hired ... Now they were back in Atlanta, determined to make clear that they had been somewhere, were now of a different caste than the rest of us. (Eggers 2007, 168)

These are individuals who, only a few months ago, were living in refugee camps and accustomed to going without. Their idea of America was a vague fantasy. Suddenly, they've metamorphosed:

> To see all these men there – it was tremendous. I could glance across the crowd and see a pair of brothers I had coached in soccer when we were teenagers. They were boys I knew from English

> classes, another from my Kakuma theater group, another who sold shoes in the camp. This was the first time I had gathered with more than a dozen or so boys from Kakuma, and it almost knocked me over. That we had all survived, that we were all wearing suits, new shoes, that we were standing in a cavernous glass temple of wealth! We greeted with each other with hugs and open smiles, many of us in shock. (168)

Deng wonders how this change could have happened so quickly. It is not a question of being able to adapt, which would imply a gradual adjustment. The basic concepts of integration, acclimatization, and adaptation have no place here. The change is unexpected, as if the refugee's very physique, not so long ago clothed in rags, was suddenly transformed into a sign of incontestable wealth. This wealth is deceptive in that it transforms the newly arrived subject into an object of consumption. This is not, however, a mundane sociological observation. As already noted, the subject who is vulnerable to traumatic rupture (or desubjectivation) is threatened in his or her entire being, as in the following passage:

> I had walked in the dark many times before. I could walk under the moon or in the blackest night. But so far from home, without a path, the strain was extreme. I had to lock my eyes to the back of the boy in front of me, and to maintain my pace. Slowing down for even a few moments would mean losing the group. It happened through the night: a boy would fall off the pace, or would step out of line to urinate, and then would have to call out to find the line again. Those who did this were scorned and sometimes punched or kicked. Making a noise could bring attention to the group and this was undesirable when the night had been retaken by the animals. (128)

In this context, Deng is part of a larger human entity: the group of desperate children who cling to one another in an attempt to become one. In this situation, the objective is not being-with-others, as in the usual definition of community. This struggle to survive takes the form of a visceral symbiosis beyond translation. The fused group becomes an envelop of protection against death and loss of identity. How to describe this primal experience? Translation does not suffice.

TRANSLATION BEYOND LANGUAGE

This brings us full circle. A refugee claimant applies for asylum. Throughout the process, the refugee must justify his or her existence, try to be understood, and provide proof of an identity that is continually called into question. He or she also faces interrogation, questioning, and the life-threatening possibility of being denied asylum and deported. Of course, being offered refuge status is not the same as having refugee status, especially if the refugee's situation does not conform to established discourse. How, then, can the refugee be heard? Is there a form of translation beyond language? Clearly, words alone are not enough. Words cannot describe, for example, the shortness of breath of children wandering through the night, grasping onto each other's hands as they flee from their adult torturers.

In a literal sense, translation beyond language does not exist. However, I have shown that in narrative representations of the refugee's speech, the refugee's subjectivity, like a fragile vessel, risks being shattered into a thousand pieces. I have focused, specifically, on the space of the city and the relations that emerge in contexts of violence to reveal the fragile yet resilient and resistant subjectivity at work in the refugee's being. Like Deng plunged into a world of vulgar consumption and superficial empathy, the refugee always seeks refuge. In the case of the Lost Boys of Sudan, holding hands and making their way single file through the darkness of the jungle, it is the immaterial presence of the other, always in view nonetheless, that assures their survival. Later, in the United States, these boys are completely transformed. Having survived, they are in a position to recount their experiences, to make their presence felt in narrative form. In America, however, this survival story is transformed through an act of translation, an intervention that was unnecessary in the forests, jungles, and plains of Africa, where survival was central, and the shared idiom was the fear of dying, of being crushed in a tiger's jaws, kidnapped by a hostile tribe, or dying of thirst.

The journey through these precarious zones, in a world without borders or places of refuge "in-between," is a test of survival. Refugees are clandestine subjects continually on the move, seeking out a path, and clinging to their lives. Translation has no place in this desperate struggle to stay alive, except, perhaps, in the form of an internal witness, as Jean-François Chiantaretto (2005) describes. Being faced with the constant threat of violence and death, especially when the attack is coming from another person, requires an internal resilience, an ability to stand up to the other with unexpected self-confidence. In a certain way, the child survivors that Deng describes were able to create a space of refuge among themselves. This memory sustains him in his day-to-day life in the United States.

In reflecting on these questions concerning refuge and the refugee, I have attempted to go beyond a pacifying humanist perspective and to describe the effacement of the subject against the backdrop of a horizontal *mise en scène* that echoes the flatness of the plains traversed by the Lost Boys of Sudan in their flight from their torturers. Translation depends on the possibility of mediation. Refugees seek acceptance in any country that would deign to receive them, as in the two novels discussed here. Most often they are not offered refuge. They live, rather, in human zoos that destroy individual subjectivity. For the host country, refugees are often of no interest beyond the image of pacifying empathy they evoke. They are confronted with the fait accompli that is the nontranslation of their mental and emotional suffering. They try to be heard, knowing their efforts are in vain, that others cannot really understand what it means to simply survive. Almost as unbearable as the violence endured in Sudan or Ethiopia, this false empathy is just background noise, a caricature of cosmopolitanism rather than a lived and felt experience.

NOTES

1 See Lyotard (1983).

2 This expression was used in my analysis of the work of Émile Ollivier in Harel (2005).

3 See Meltzer (1999).

4 Sloterdijk's analysis is relevant here, though the refugee is excluded from the humanistic vision underlying the cultivation or training of the individual.

5 It would be unfair to depict Eggers in this light. As a cofounder of 826 National and founder of McSweeney's, he has been a committed activist for many years.

6 *Parfum de poussière* (Scent of dust) (2007) is the title of Sophie Voillot's translation of Hage's first novel, *De Niro's Game*. Voillot also translated Hage's *Cockroach* (Le cafard) (2009).

7 See Barsky's (1994, 2000) work on the argumentative aspects of the refugee's asylum claim in its regulated, administrative form.

8 See, once again, Barsky (2000).

9 See Harel (2005), *Les passages obligés de l'écriture migrante* (The rites of passage of migrant literature).

10 As described, for example, by Walter Benjamin (1999).

11 From the surrealists to Georges Bataille.

7

The Exilic City

ALEXIS NOUSS
Translated by Carmen Ruschiensky

All exile is experienced through language, at least two languages: "What is it called, your country / behind the mountain, behind the year? ... your mother's threeyearland, that's what it was, / what it is, / it wanders off everywhere, like language" (Celan 1989, 219). The exilic experience cannot be spoken, but only expressed in translation. All exile is an exile of the language of the exiled, which must therefore be translated: "Into yourself / language-scale, word-scale, home- / scale of exile" (Celan 2005, 95).

The city knows nothing of exile. This can be understood in two ways. First, the city ends exile by receiving the exiled subject and erasing his or her exilic condition or retaining it only as folklore. In offering asylum and refuge, the city bestows a new identity on the exiled, which for an artist can mean acquiring a specific profile. Examples in contemporary culture are numerous. In Quebec, for example, critics have even invented a new category known as *écriture migrante*.

Second, the city can welcome the exiled but not exile. Home excludes whatever lies outside it. In the urban order, there is a place for everyone, and everyone has a place. However, exile is precisely an absence of place, in not only its empirical but also its metaphysical dimension: exile declares the impossibility of place. "No one can stay in himself: the humanity of man, subjectivity, is a responsibility for the others, an extreme vulnerability" (Levinas 2003, 67). The ethics that Levinas proposes here suggests a concern for the other, a feeling that perhaps I am usurping the other's position. I am no longer comfortable in a place that I thought was mine and from which I am now expelled by my conscience and compelled to leave, because it has become a nonplace for me. This expropriation of identity can be described in terms of exile: "The I approached in responsibility ... dis-locates itself, loses its place, is exiled, relegates itself into itself ... emptying itself in a no-grounds, to the point of substituting itself for the other, holding on to itself only as it were in the trace of its exile" (Levinas 1991, 138). The city erases traces of the other or the elsewhere, because these are incompatible with the kinds of circulation indispensable to the urban order.

We might, however, consider a contrary view – the city as the fruit of exile. Saint-John Perse wrote *Exil* (Exile) in 1941 while exiled in the United States. The poem, as though following its theme's destiny, was published the following year in various cities (Chicago, Marseille, Buenos Aires, Neuchâtel, Paris). *Exil*, however, was preceded by *Anabasis* (Anabase). Perse composed this earlier work in 1921 while in China, where his diplomatic postings allowed him to undertake long journeys to Manchuria, Mongolia, and Korea. *Anabasis* narrates the conquest of a territory and the founding of a city, in an epic poetry that unites the sword and the word, sweat and song. In the first song, the conqueror addresses his followers: "O seekers, O finders of reasons to be up and be gone, / you traffic not in a salt more strong than this, when at morning with omen of kingdoms and omen of dead waters swung high over the smokes of the world, the drums of exile waken on the marches / Eternity yawning on the sands" (Perse 1970, 25). Various episodes lead to the mythical moment of the fourth song: "Thus was the City founded and placed in the morning under the labials of a clear sounding name" (33). The theme of exile, however, is still present: "The founders of asylums meet beneath a tree and find their ideas for the choice of situations. They teach me the meaning and the purpose of the buildings" (35). Once the city is founded, the conqueror moves on, because the city is only one step. The last stanza of the final song concludes: "Plough-land of dream! Who talks of building?" (65). Still, exile has blended with sand and water to build the city. It marks the exilic city with its songs and languages, because exilic is the city that yet knows how to sing, knows it is founded on words: "And the earth in its winged seeds, like a poet in his thoughts, travels" (39). The poem, along with the conqueror and the priest, gives a role to the "grammarian" and the "poet."

Stories from mythology support the idea of exilic cities. Cain is condemned by divine wrath to wander the earth after murdering his brother. During his exile, he founds the first city mentioned in the Bible, which he names after his son Enoch (Gen. 4:17), as though decreeing, through this filial legacy, an end to exile. Between Cain the sedentary cultivator and Abel the nomadic shepherd, economic history confirms this relation between a sedentary economy and the first cities. Another fraternal story is that of Remus and Romulus. Driven out of Alba Longa by their great-uncle Amulius, the brothers are discovered and raised in the desert at the foot of the Palatine Hill, where they found the city of Rome at the very site of their childhood exile. Romulus, attempting to increase Rome's population, is said to have later opened an asylum on Capitoline Hill where exiles and refugees were welcomed and immediately offered citizenship. The Hellenistic tradition also provides rich examples. Cadmus embarks on the path of exile when his father, the king of Tyre, enjoins him to find his sister Europa, who has been kidnapped by Zeus. Though Cadmus is unsuccessful, his journey results in the founding of Thebes, a city known for its importance in ancient Greek history and mythology.

The city, however, resists. The urban order must erase any trace of exile to ensure its vocation, which is based on principles of permanence, durability, and immutability, a stasis that shares its dogma with the state. This foundationalist objective is at odds with the exilic experience and its defining ethos, "exiliance" (Nouss 2015). Exiliance refers to both a condition and a state of consciousness that do not always coincide. While it is possible to feel exiled without having abandoned one's residence, it is also possible to have left without feeling exiled. This is the existential core of the experience shared by all migrants regardless of their reason for migration, whether expatriates or deportees, outcasts or refugees. Exiliance is the manifestation of a topo-ontological tension, to use a Derridean term. Exile is not bound to a specific place (of either origin or arrival). It represents a bipolar reality, a phenomenon that encompasses both a source and a destination. Though sociological discourse on migration recognizes these points of departure and arrival in tracing the journey between the two, it tends to emphasize one pole or the other. This polarity is reproduced in politics, with republican integration privileging the identity of arrival, and communitarian multiculturalism, in the identity of origin. The exilic experience, however, unites the two, creating and sustaining a dynamic of multiple belonging, a complex reality that is not always appreciated by citizens of the nation state, as evidenced on a smaller scale by crises of cohabitation in large urban centres.

Exiliance is characterized by oscillation between passivity toward a new, unfamiliar cultural landscape that one is never sure of mastering, and the intense preservation of one's connection to the past culture for fear of losing oneself in the new landscape. It is like using a map of London to orient oneself in Paris, or a map of pre-war Berlin to navigate the city in 2016. Exilic nostalgia is what inspired Joseph Brodsky (1992), in a familiar reflex of Russian culture, to see Saint Petersburg in the canals of Venice. Likewise, in Chico Buarque's (2004) novel *Budapest*, the protagonist's feelings and memories about the Hungarian capital are intermingled with those of Rio de Janeiro. On a much larger scale, the founding exilism of North America is evident in the toponymical duplication of cities' names (New Orleans or Paris, Texas), with little regard for environmental resemblances.

The existential multipolarity of the exilic experience is completely at odds with the urban order's unitarism and centralism. If exile, as some argue, is linked to a hope of return, integration in the city presupposes a definitive installation, excluding the possibility of return. However, according to the exilic genealogy outlined here, cities are acquiring a different status – today's capitals are becoming world cities. Experimentation with new lifestyles, along with their accompanying problems and eventual solutions, continues to be an urban phenomenon (Soja 2001; Médam 2002). If exiliance is to provide a model for constructing identities beyond the monoterritorial subject, the city will be its testing ground. The city typifies sedentary civilization, because it establishes boundaries (neighbourhoods, suburbs, and peripheral zones) that act as borders. These borders, in turn, reproduce the enclosed space that guarantees the city's integrity. The city excludes the outside, without which it could not exist, all the while regenerating itself from within through the possibilities of its nomadic space. This is the space of Apollinaire's (1995) and Benjamin's (1999) flâneur, or of the wanderers Aragon (1970), Desnos (2005), and de Certeau (1988) describe. Like the protagonist of Paul Auster's (1987) *City of Glass*, these figures recreate urban alphabets to express their desires. Now entire exterior languages accompany the migrant crowds of contemporary cities to the point of changing the urban fabric.

When Arjun Appadurai (1966) proposed the term "ethnoscape" to describe the frameworks that shape migrants' collective identities in a contemporary globalized world, he highlighted the need for flexible borders to allow these communities to exist beyond rigid territorial limits. In the context of the host city, migrant communities create their own ways of living based on the tastes and colours of their cultural landscapes of origin. The notion of the ethnoscape enriches our analytical vocabulary, particularly in contrast to the concept of habitus, conceived by Bourdieu (1990) as encompassing the interiorized practices and representations of distinct groups within the social space. However, habitus, insofar as it is defined in relation to a specific social class (the middle class, the academic, the artist, or the poor, for example), is based on a logic of monobelonging that is no longer relevant to contemporary urban realities in which immigrant populations struggle to maintain links to their origins as they adapt to new cultural identities. In this sense, the pluralism of the urban setting allows for the creation of hybrid subjectivities (Nouss 2005). In other words, a habitus is read; an ethnoscape is translated. While the ethnoscape tends to juxtapose two distinct contexts of belonging, the migratory experience creates a tension between them that is better reflected in the concept of exiliance. In addition, there are gaps in the contemporary urban fabric. Beyond ethnographically defined groups like migrants, there are also those excluded from work, accommodation, or citizenship who escape traditional sociological classification. We might refer to these gaps in the urban landscape as exoscapes, sites that generate a dialectic between place and nonplace and combine imaginaries from here and elsewhere in the construction of the real.

If the flâneur can be said to bring back the outside within the city's interior, Benjamin's analysis of this figure in *The Arcades Project* (Das Passagen-Werk) develops this idea in revealing how the city gives rise to and sustains exiliance. For the subject as for the city, exiliance is the persistence of exteriority experienced from within. Among the quotations Benjamin includes to introduce the section on the flâneur is Victor Hugo's line from *Les Misérables*: "All that can be found anywhere can be found in Paris" (quoted in Benjamin 1999, 416). In other words, the French capital not only accommodates difference without losing its specificity; its ability to do so is part of what makes it exceptional. When Benjamin defines flânerie as "anamnestic intoxication" (417), he notes that it is not a unidimensional experience, since it incorporates the recollection of other places, and gives rise to displacements not *in* space but *of* space. It constitutes a shifting of the terrain.

Two aspects of this spatial mobility stand out. "The 'colportage phenomenon of space' is the flâneur's basic experience ... Thanks to this phenomenon, everything potentially taking place in this one single room is perceived simultaneously" (418). Constantine Cavafy (2003, 156) provides an excellent example of this, and imagines, in the spirit of other poet-flâneurs like Baudelaire or Pessoa, that the Alexandrian décor of his modern love affairs, its shops and taverns, open onto past centuries, "bringing the days closer together," from the second century BCE up to the seventh CE, from the cities of Hellenistic antiquity and Macedonia to the farthest reaches of the Orient. In this immense space unified by the vernacular *koine*, cultures beyond understanding translate one another: "We the Alexandrians, the Antiochians, / the Selefkians, and the countless / other Greeks of Egypt and Syria, / and those in Media, and Persia, and all the rest: / ... / and our Common Greek Language / which we carried as far as Bactria, as far as the Indians" (Cavafy 1975, 127).

In the first chapter of *Civilization and Its Discontents*, Freud (1989, 16) explores a similar phenomenon in his discussion of the "problem of preservation in the sphere of the mind." Imagining a visitor in Rome simultaneously perceiving the successive architectural strata of the city, from Antiquity to the Roman Empire, he is quick to question this comparison between the city and the mind, noting that a city's history is always marked by "demolitions and replacement of buildings" (18). Benjamin disagrees. The space, he says, "winks at the flâneur," becomes a theatre for events that may have transpired there (Benjamin 1999, 418). Exiliance also refuses to erase the past, which persists in the present. The effect is a dramatization: place is no longer a location with precise coordinates but becomes a stage on which various scenes unfold, a nonplace. In Merleau-Ponty's (1962, 244) terms, nonplace is not a position determined by a spatializing space but, rather, a situation in its concrete context, a spatialized space with its "irreducibly manifold variety" of experiences. Exiliance naturally encompasses this internal plurality, born of diverse personal experiences of different exterior realties.

Indeed, in a broader sense, exiliance introduces a theatricalized world. For those in exile, the place they occupy is a stage on which they play a role they did not play in their former countries, and the uncertainty of it continuing forever or being abandoned is always fuelled by memories of their place of origin and the possibility of return. Similarly and simultaneously, the former place loses its sense of coherence and reality because it lies beyond concrete experience and therefore also becomes a theatre of desires, dreams, and fantasies.

The second aspect is related to the concept of aura that Benjamin (1999, 419) develops in several works: "We know that, in the course of flânerie, far-off times and places interpenetrate the landscape and the present moment."[1] Exiliance also denies any instinct to supress distant times and places. Baudelaire's (1919, 45) depiction of the swan as a figure of exile in his poem from "Parisian Scenes" reflects a similar sensibility: "Paris may change; my melancholy is fixed. / New palaces, and scaffoldings, and blocks, / And suburbs old, are symbols all to me / Whose memories are as heavy as stone." In this sense, the space that exiliance claims and legitimates is linked to the fluidity of nonplace (Nouss 2014). This is not a lack of place, a rejection of the idea of place, or a denial that a place can be inhabited. A place, as opposed to a simple space, is precisely that which can be humanly inhabited, either concretely or virtually, but which also juxtaposes present and previous locations. In other words, in the nonplace, the exile inhabits both a present and a past or, rather, a past and a present inhabit and coexist within the exile, contributing to and legitimized in his or her process of subjectivation. Exile is a nonplace, because the exilic experience is defined by a tension between two or more territories to which no exiled subject can claim to entirely belong. Exile empties place of its territoriality, of the territorial function that makes it a specific location, a *lieu-dit*, and creates other spatial possibilities, in particular those traces of possibility that the exilic memory retains.

My interest in the exilic city, as distinct from the city of exile, is precisely its quality of nonplace. The second term, unlike the first, refers to a destination for exiles whose urban reality is profoundly and visibly influenced by the presence of exilic communities. Semantically, "city of exile" emphasizes "city," while "exilic city" highlights "exilic." The city of exile assimilates; the exilic city juxtaposes. The point here is not to impose rigid or absolute definitions on a changing reality.

The distinction between fusion and contiguity, between the city of exile and the exilic city, is operational, not decisive. A city, for example, can be exilic at one time only to later adopt the uniform sheen of postmodern, urban globalization. The exilic city is usually confined to a neighbourhood or neighbourhoods, to this or that area of town. It rarely encompasses an entire city, especially with increasing urban agglomeration and expansion.

If the city of exile assimilates and the exilic city juxtaposes, this distinction affects, in particular, the status of subjects who arrive from outside. The foreigner's affective experience, for example, is not the same as that of the exile. While the foreigner provokes a rupture or confrontation between two orders, the exile is understood more in terms of a contiguity, natural or artificial, between two symbolic regimes. The foreigner adopts the dominant language; the exile translates. Between departure and arrival, the exile lives in a state of anticipation to prevent being engulfed by overwhelming anxiety. The exile's trajectory is particular because it is autonomous in relation to the two cultural contexts, its purpose being based, precisely, on the connection between the two. The exilic experience is an experience of limits at the limits of experience. There are no guarantees of formalization, transmission, or reception.

This simultaneous belonging to both inside and outside that is central to our understanding of the exile's experience has also been studied over the past century by two important figures in sociology, Georg Simmel (1984) in 1908 and Alfred Schütz (1972), exiled to the United States in 1944,[2] both of whom attributed this spatial ambivalence to the foreigner. Between then and now, the elsewhere that the foreigner represents has changed. While the foreigner is still brandished as a threat in reactionary and extremist discourse, another response is to assimilate this figure as an importer of elsewhere, of foreign culture. This is the domesticated foreigner of consumer globalization whose abundance of goods – whether in the form of cuisine, fashion, or music – contributes to Western cultural consumption and entertainment. By contrast, the exile's elsewhere maintains its elsewhere. The exile's nonlinear trajectory and fragmented identity disrupt this game of international, postmodern culture.

The assimilating culture of the city of exile, in contrast to the exilic city, has a particular impact on communication. Interaction between languages is not a given, the inevitable outcome of multilingual situations resulting from migration. The exilic city, benefiting from the facilities of a host language, does not translate; it juxtaposes languages, as it does cultures and individuals. One speaks Tamil or Kurdish without breaching minority or dominant codes. In the city of exile, however, the urban is born of an elsewhere that it suppresses or rejects, with or without violence, as part of a regulating process. The *Urbi* must oppose the *Orbi* in a confrontation that inevitably leads to a hierarchization. Indeed, any city's destiny is to be a capital (of a district, department, region, or state), that is, not only a site of centralized power that assures the efficient management of its governed territories, but also a site that accrues the symbolic capital associated with this spatial division. From this point of view, the elsewhere maintains its agonistic function. It cannot integrate the here and now. The city is the ultimate depository of symbolic capital. It is, first and foremost, the guardian of semiotic codes, the protector of language or languages. In this sense, the city of exile, if it is to allow translation, can only translate in one direction – from other languages/the languages of the other into the host language/the language of order. This politics of assimilation contrasts with the exilic city's dynamic of juxtaposition.

Two museums located in the exilic cities of New York and London illustrate this. The Lower East Side Tenement Museum on 97 Orchard Street in Lower Manhattan displays the reconstructed lives of successive immigrants who inhabited the building from 1860 to the 1930s. Spanning five floors, it includes re-creations of the apartments, workshops, and stores of Jewish, Irish, and Italian exiles. It highlights comparison through juxtaposition in a way that brings exilic memory to life. The same inspiration seems to have guided the creation of the Museum of Immigration and Diversity on 19 Princelet Street in East London, where traces of previous inhabitants, in this case Huguenot Protestants from France followed by Eastern European Jews, are also preserved. Its exhibition *Suitcases and Sanctuary* traces the waves of immigration from Europe, Africa, and Asia that, over three centuries, shaped London's Spitalfields district, a neighbourhood that exemplifies multicultural England and the exilic city.

A third example of an exilic city on a third continent is Buenos Aires, shaped from its inception by the arrival of European immigrants and, later, an influx from the surrounding countryside. The city's exilic spirit is most evident in its symbol: the tango. Developed by Italian immigrants on the shores of the Río de la Plata, the origins of this artistic form born of exile are well known. Carlos Gardel, whose voice and lyrics defined tango music, was born in

Toulouse to the French laundress Berthe Gardes and arrived in Argentina at the age of two bearing the name of Charles Gardes. Roberto Goyoneche, his successor from the 1950s to the 1990s, was nicknamed El Polaco (the Pole), a playful reference not to his origins but to his Slavic physique. In the history of tango, close to 80 per cent of the musicians are of Italian origin (Anibal Troilo and Juan d'Arienzo being among the most admired masters), and Jewish artists make up a good part of the rest: Arturo Bernstein, known as El Alemán (the German); the Rubinstein brothers; Raúl Kaplún, born Israel Kaflún; and Carlos Bahr, the most prolific lyricist in the history of tango; not to mention Astor Piazzola and Osvaldo Pugliese, both of Jewish-Italian origin.

From these beginnings in the Americas, the tango of exiles followed its own path of exile, migrating to places as far as Japan and Scandinavia. Tango returned to Europe, laying down roots to become, among others things, the Yiddish music of Jewish communities expressing their sorrows and fears in song. Yiddish tango, Russian tango, French tango. Who does it belong to now? Buenos Aires weeps to the rhythm of tango, and Borges (1977), in "The Mythical Founding of Buenos Aires," evokes Juan Diaz, devoured by Indians, and the thousands upon thousands of migrants who crossed the oceans, before concluding the following: "A mí se me hace cuento que empezó Buenos Aires: / La juzgo tan eterna como el agua y el aire." Literally: "For me it's a fable that Buenos Aires had a beginning: / I believe it to be as eternal as water and air." Or in a more musical translation: "Never born was Buenos Aires / The city is eternal like water and air." Water and air: the great channels of exile that both translate and define it. The exilic city is founded on them. Stones come later.

NOTES

1 A few pages later in the same section, Benjamin defines aura: "The aura is the appearance of distance, however close the thing that calls it forth" (Benjamin 1999, 447). This is the same definition that appears in "The Work of Art in the Age of Mechanical Reproduction," which is the essay usually associated with Benjamin's concept of aura.

2 Schütz's (1944) essay represents a good example of cultural transfer: it was written in English and published in 1944, while Schütz was teaching at

Adorno's New York School for Social Research. It was later translated into German and published in 1972 (Schütz 1972, 53–68). Another essay followed the same trajectory: "The Homecomer" (Schütz 1945) was translated into German as "Der Heimkehrer" and published in 1972 in the same volume as the previous text (Schütz 1972, 70–84). Writing in a language that is different from that of your neighbours is also part of the exilic experience.

8

Media Networks and Language-Crossing in Montreal

WILL STRAW

The big city is a fantastic hive of words which never shut up. Without pausing, they stir the energies of the city and are in turn stirred by them. In the endless cycle of the talking city, its current spirit, which rules over the layers of older significations, inscribes itself within words. Language in movement is immobilized in writing which captures within itself the dynamism of the city, just as cold finds itself held within ice.

Karlheinz Stierle, *La Capitale des signes: Paris et son discours*[1]

Montreal is both a site for the encounter of languages and a place of linguistic division. Those who write about Montreal – as scholars of urban space or culture, poets, novelists, or screenwriters – usually highlight one of these dimensions of the city's life over the other. Across various genres of writing on Montreal, I suggest, a preferred focus has been those occasions in which the city's languages intermingle and lose their exclusivity. This preference is easy to understand. The interweaving of languages offers both a more convivial image of social life and a more interesting complexity than does the presence of strict divisions between languages. Scholars of Montreal-based literature or theatre have charted those practices of writing that thematize or perform the breaking down of linguistic barriers, often seeing this breakdown as a key mission of creative expression in the city.[2] Those who study public space in Montreal will often seek out ways in which languages are seen to mix, either in everyday speech or in the overlaying of linguistic communication on city surfaces.[3] In journalistic writing on

Montreal, linguistic mixing is celebrated (as the source of distinctive, local versions of English and French) or condemned (as proof of an ongoing erosion of one language at the expense of another).[4]

At the same time, the sense that real or virtual walls divide the French and English languages has a long history in Montreal folklore. It was once common to designate St Laurent Boulevard ("The Main") as a linguistic wall dividing the francophone and anglophone parts of the city. (More recently, people invoke this designation in order to quickly update, refute, or complicate it.) At a more anecdotal level, the claim that the French division of the National Film Board of Canada worked on Apple computers while the English division used Windows machines has circulated for two decades, invoked as emblematic of the incommunicability between the two language communities. In 1963, a reporter for the Montreal newspaper *La Patrie* wrote in bemused fashion of the opening of one of the city's first multiplex cinemas, the Versailles, which contained one screening room for each language and a hall that served to divide them. How one saw this hall depended on one's view of the state of Montreal's language politics. In *La Patrie*, one writer wondered whether it would become "le salon de la bonne entente" or a "champ de bataille" (a happy meeting place or a battlefield) (Maître 1963, 32).

MEDIA AND LANGUAGE-CROSSING IN MONTREAL

Our natural interest in those spaces (or occasions) in which languages meet and mingle sometimes obscures those forces which work in Montreal to keep languages apart, to reinforce their exclusivity. Key among such forces are media of all kinds, from print and broadcasting to most examples of digital. In Stierle's evocative words, quoted at the beginning of this chapter (and slightly adapted here), media are places in which the flow of language through social space is momentarily stopped and held in immobile form. Media are places for fixing and freezing linguistic expression. Through this freezing, they bind units of expression to each other, setting them in physical adjacency (as on a newspaper page) or in temporal sequence (as in radio or television programming) in relation to others. In some media, as I will show, this adjacency or sequence is marked by a multiplicity of languages, such that the freezing of expression produces a durable image of linguistic copresence. More often, this same freezing produces clusters of expression characterized by monolinguistic exclusivity. In this way, the media of Montreal may be seen as hieroglyphs for the variety of linguistic relations possible in the city.

We might undertake an inventory of Montreal media in terms of their forms and levels of French-English bilingualism. From the outset, it is tempting to develop a number of observations or hypotheses. One of these is that those media in which French and English sit alongside each other in roughly equal proportions tend to be peripheral or "minor" in terms of their communicative complexity or cultural centrality. More crudely: bilingualism is strongest in those textual forms whose wordage is lowest. Thus, as a result of federal law, French and English appear in close proximity and with equal presence on the packaging of consumer goods, on currency and postage stamps, and in the signage systems of federal institutions like train stations, ports, and airports. Elsewhere, homemade announcements of yard sales or missing cats typically convey an imperfect and usually uneven attempt to communicate in both French and English. Commercial signage and restaurant menus in Montreal, since the passage of Bill 101 in 1977, are very often marked by the effort to come as close to full bilingualism as the law (as modified by the amendments and court rulings to which it has been subject) allows.[5]

As one moves toward media of higher levels of audience reach and sociocultural importance, linguistic exclusivity becomes stronger. I refer here, for the most part, to what we might all the great media of the twentieth century, like television, radio, magazines, and the daily newspaper. The most popular examples of these media in Montreal operate with near-exclusivity in either French or English. Of the most-listened-to radio stations in the city during the period November 2013 to February 2014, half broadcast with their spoken word content exclusively in French and the other half in English (BBM 2014). The language of vocal music, as I will show, complicates this situation somewhat, but regulators and the advertising industry nevertheless classify stations as uniformly English or French. While industry measurements of television viewership, which focus more on the popularity of individual programs than of individual stations, are much less easy to compare directly, the dominant stations likewise operate in either French or English exclusively. The same is true for Montreal's six daily newspapers and for all mass-circulation magazines published or available in the city.[6] The online versions of these media are almost always marked by the same linguistic exclusivity.

While the future viability of these media is less and less certain in the face of the Internet, they continue to play a major role in the circulation of discourse and in the routines of Montrealers' lives. In their linguistic exclusivity, they pull the heterogeneous language practices of city life into the linguistically uniform time/space of broadcast programming and of print forms such as the newspaper or magazine. Montreal's large-scale media do not simply resist the intrusion of one language upon each other; by absorbing the heterogeneity of social and cultural phenomena within the discourse of a single language, they produce systems of inter-reference that reinforce the coherence and self-sufficiency of that language. The more that information or entertainment media may appear to cover the near-totality of phenomena in a single language, the less likely they are to encourage practices of language-crossing, whereby individuals might seek out media in a second language in order to access specific kinds of content. Even when this language-crossing is common, however – when people switch between French- and English-language media in their daily lives – media maintain their linguistic uniformity.

The exceptions to this monolingualism in Montreal media are usually "marginal" in reach. The copresence of French and English often characterizes self-defined multilingual media, like community radio programming or "ethnic" newspapers. Here, the presence of languages that are neither French nor English frequently serves as an alibi for the additional presence of both. Elsewhere, and for obvious reasons, French-English bilingualism may be found in limited circulation print media aimed at a tourist readership, like the entertainment or shopping guides distributed in hotels. The sector of magazines covering the cultural sector offers a more complex state of affairs. Quebec-based magazines that specialize in music, theatre, cinema, or literature are typically unilingual and, with very few exceptions (such as the *Montreal Review of Books*), published in French. At the same time, there is a principled (if costly) commitment to French-English bilingualism in many of Montreal's magazines covering the visual arts, like *Esse*, *CV Photo*, or the long-defunct *Parachute*. The anomalously high bilingualism of the art magazine confirms the apparently greater bilingualism of Montreal's visual arts institutions and scenes relative to those in which theatre and literature are embedded.[7]

A curious feature of Montreal, then, is that a city that offers so many everyday experiences of linguistic multiplicity and bilingualism has so few examples of bilingual media. Attempts to produce bilingual media with extensive audience reach in Montreal have almost always floundered for a variety of reasons. These include their perceived economic nonviability, audience indifference, or regulatory intervention. The *Montreal Gazette*, at various points in its history, has experimented with limited French-language content, but no longer does so. In radio broadcasting, as I will show, attempts to broadcast in both languages have run up against the opposition of advertisers and regulators. In some cases, the bilingualism of a media artefact has not allowed it to escape factors that anchor it much more strongly in one language community than another. The film *Bon Cop, Bad Cop*, bilingual from its title through much of its dialogue, grossed twelve million dollars in Quebec, most of that from francophone audiences, and a little over one million in English Canada. While, by the standards of anglophone Canadian cinema, the film's appeal to English-speaking Canadian audiences was high, the unevenness of its success suggests that any dream of a bilingual cinema that resonates in roughly equal measure with both language communities is elusive.

BROADCASTING AND MEDIA BILINGUALISM IN MONTREAL

The history of radio and television broadcasting in Canada is punctuated by short-lived moments in which key television and radio stations broadcast in French and English. In the chaotic early days of radio, before the consolidation of public broadcasting across the country, programming that moved between the French and English languages was relatively common. Richard Collins (1990, 58) has suggested that Western Canadian resistance to the prevalence of bilingual broadcasting in the 1930s was one of the key motives for the introduction of public regulation of broadcasting in Canada. After World War II, the Canadian Broadcasting Corporation and Société Radio-Canada initiated new experiments in bilingual broadcasting. These usually followed similar paths of development. As radio or television service was introduced to a particular region, French and English programming shared a single channel, with blocks of several hours devoted to each. Subsequently, after these services were established and additional resources become available, services were split, with French and English channels operating in parallel.[8] Thus, in 1952, Canada's first television station, CBFT, began by broadcasting in both languages in Montreal, with programming blocks in English and in French. This would continue until January of 1954, when

CBMT, a Montreal-based English-language channel, commenced operations, leaving CBFT to broadcast in French only (Canadian Communications Foundation 2013).

The introduction of FM radio broadcasting in Montreal followed a similar pattern. The CBC launched its first "national" FM network in 1960, as a link between stations in Montreal, Ottawa, and Toronto. The network operated only during the evenings on weekdays and from noon to midnight on weekends, with programming in both languages. (During non-network times, Montreal's CBM-FM simulcast programs from its English-language AM equivalent, CBM-AM.) The introduction of a single FM service that operated in both languages was rooted in part in a scarcity of resources, but also expressed the CBC's conviction that bilingual broadcasting was an ideal for the country whose time of realization had come (see Cote 1961, 7). In his review of the FM service shortly after its launch, the *Globe and Mail*'s long-serving music critic John Kraglund (1960, 8) notes the ways in which bilingual programming highlighted differences in sensibility between Montreal and Toronto and their respective uses of language:

> It is too easy to pass any serious judgment on what is being offered and the way in which it is being done. However, we wonder why it is that Toronto announcers come across blasting in like high-pressure commercials, while those from Montreal retain the same volume level as their programs. And Jean Valleraud's Montreal broadcast, an informative talk with recordings, on the survival of the gallant style in French music, suggested that Montreal is more effectively bilingual than Toronto, since he spoke and translated at a frightening pace.

This experiment in bilingual FM broadcasting in Canada ceased in 1962, when the CBC went back to simply simulcasting its AM stations on the FM network. On 1 October 1964, distinctive FM networks in each language were launched (CBC 2014a). By this point, and until CHOM-FM's experiment with bilingualism in the 1970s (discussed below), day-long dual-language broadcasting in Montreal could be found only on a single private station. CKVL-FM, launched in 1947, broadcast announcements in both French and English and for many years presented a bilingual program live from the Simpson's department store downtown (CBC 2014b). By 1969, CKVL-FM possessed the most powerful radio signal in Canada, was the only FM station in the country to broadcast twenty-four hours a day, and was considered the only bilingual station in the country. In 1973, it switched to French-only broadcasting (ibid.).

In the late 1960s, the program *Jazz en liberté* was one of the last vestiges of bilingual broadcasting on the Montreal stations of Canada's public radio service. Broadcast on both English-language CBM and French-language CBF, *Jazz en liberté* is interesting in part because its content was seen as particularly suited to language-crossing. In 1966, the *Montreal Gazette* published a lengthy article about Montreal-based jazz musician Nick Ayoub, who had recorded performances for the program. Under the headline "Need No B and B Commission to Understand Jazz – Nick Ayoub," Wylie (1966, 13) quoted Ken Withers, program director for Montreal's CBC-FM, who argued for the special place of jazz in a country marked by linguistic and cultural divisions: "On a jazz program, no B+B Commission is needed to bring French and English together. In Canada, jazz is the only true national expression of brotherhood among majority and minority groups. Language differences don't really exist. The jazzman projects his feelings through music, and his message is readily understood." The B+B Commission referenced here was, of course, the Royal Commission on Bilingualism and Biculturalism, which at this historical moment was preparing a report demonstrating that francophones were underrepresented in Canadian business and politics.

There is, here, a somewhat curious justification for the exceptional bilingualism of *Jazz en liberté*: that a music not notably Canadian, and thus relatively untouched by Canada's linguistic duality, could serve as the cultural token around which bilingualism was practiced. At the same time, as a music shaped by relations of majority to minority whose local equivalents went unspecified, jazz was seen as partly healing the divisions that otherwise made bilingualism impossible. In its emphasis on tone rather than words, jazz also seemed to transcend language and the differences carried within it. Roughly similar claims would be made in the 1970s about disco and in later decades about other forms of dance music, such as house.

RADIO, MUSIC, AND THE CASE OF CHOM-FM

Radio broadcasting in Montreal has been the terrain on which the successes and impasses of bilingual media have played themselves out with greatest intensity. The particular status of radio in the city has much to do with the important role played in radio broadcasting by music, a key element in radio programming. Music sits in a complex relationship to language. Important historical forms of music seem to contain no linguistically marked expression (classical symphonic music, for example), and others do so only occasionally (jazz or electronica). Other genres of music are important carriers of language (such as folk music or the francophone tradition of the *chanson*). In those forms of popular music that have achieved the greatest commercial success in the last half-century (rock and pop), vocal expression is prominent. However, language-based expression often grounds the meaning and reach of popular music much less than do its markers of genre, style, and fashionability. Listeners and fans use musical tastes to express cosmopolitanism, up-to-date-ness, and political solidarities. These often generate affinities with music that take listeners outside of their primary language group.

The peculiar relationships of music to language, and of radio broadcasting to language communities, were central to one of the most important controversies around media and language in Montreal history – that which surrounded FM radio station CHOM-FM's attempt to broadcast in both French and English in the 1970s. CHOM was the successor to CKGM-FM, and was launched in Montreal in 1963 by the Maisonneuve Broadcasting Corporation, Limited. CHOM developed its own album rock format (a programming strategy later formalized in radio industry discourse as "album-oriented rock") and for a time was the only Montreal radio station playing so-called progressive rock music.[9] From its inception, CHOM let announcers move back and forth between French and English, a policy that the station claimed reflected the bilingual character of its listenership and city. This language switching was also part of the station's wilfully adopted free-form approach to radio broadcasting.

By the early 1970s, the Canadian Radio and Television Commission (CRTC), which granted and renewed broadcasters' licences and devised policies to guide the growth of each broadcast medium, confronted several challenges in dealing with radio. One of these was the increased commercialization of the medium, which encouraged a clear division of audiences and advertising markets. Radio broadcasters whose audiences crossed linguistic lines were viewed at best as confusing to advertisers, at worst as seeking to poach listeners from one linguistic group for stations operating in another. During the same period, political struggles over language, particularly in Quebec, became intensified, with bilingualism receding as an ideal and each of Montreal's dominant language groups seeking entrenchment of their right to be served in their own language. It was in this context that the CRTC took up the question of CHOM's experiments in bilingual broadcasting. In its renewal of CHOM's licence in 1973, the regulator refrained from stating in explicit terms that it approved of the station's use of both languages. It simply authorized continued use of the station's "experimental type of programming"; any reference to the explicitly linguistic character of that programming was diluted within the ruling's acknowledgement that the station's broader approach to radio bent the rules in an experimental fashion. Without using the word "French," its ruling said: "During this period [the two years for which its licence was now renewed] the applicant may carry on broadcasting in the language of the majority within its coverage area." Canadian rock critic Ritchie Yorke (1973, 60), reporting for *Billboard* magazine, saw the decision as one with "far-reaching implications" insofar as it seemed to authorize broadcasting in both languages without saying so openly.[10] Indeed, in its renewal ruling, the CRTC's interest in language seemed directed more at the broadcasting of speech whose content some listeners deemed offensive. The station was warned that it might be pandering to a "growing permissiveness in [its] subject matter and language" and should be attentive to possible infractions (ibid.). A station spokesperson suggested this warning was prompted by CHOM's broadcasting of excerpts from albums by George Carlin and the National Lampoon comedy troupe (*Globe and Mail* 1973, 8).

By the mid-1970s, CHOM had become the most listened to FM radio station in Montreal (and the third most-listened-to English-language station on either dial) (*Billboard* 1975, 70). Its announcers often spoke in French, and while advertising in that language had been prohibited in the 1973 ruling, its introduction of music and freeform conversations with its listeners were marked by high levels of bilingualism. CHOM's listenership among francophones had grown amidst an increase in the extent to which it played music of British origin or of a generally progressive bent: "Pink Floyd, Genesis, Shawn Phillips, Babe Ruth, Gentle Giant, the Rolling Stones" (ibid.). The appeal of this music to francophones, explained CHOM's program director Les Sole, had to do with the ways in which the linguistic marking of this music was weak: "The young Quebecois enjoys British rock with a classical base like the Strawbs and Genesis ... That's almost bilingual music. A lot of times I would say that the Rolling Stones' music is illiterate anyway. Unless you have a lyric sheet in front of you, you have no idea what Jagger is saying even if you understand the English language. The French also like a good theatrical presentation by an act" (ibid.).

In the 1960s, the producer of CBC's *Jazz en liberté* had based jazz's appeal across language groups in its universalism and emphasis on "feelings." For Sole, progressive rock crossed the linguistic divide in part because of the incomprehensibility of its lyrics (which made its instrumental dimensions that much more important) and in part because of its theatricality, which involved nonlinguistic forms of communication like costume and record jacket design. Unsaid in this discussion, but arguably inflecting it in important ways, was the sense that, in its explicit intellectualism and artfulness (however pompous these might be on occasion), English-language progressive rock from Europe was not an obvious villain in the struggle to preserve the French language from the inroads of popular, commercial (and usually American) culture.

In 1975, the CRTC acknowledged CHOM's commitment to bilingualism in a new licence renewal. The station had asked for permission to begin broadcasting advertisements in the French language. The regulator denied this request, but allowed the station's programming to continue in both languages: "In its application the licensee requested authority to continue to broadcast programming in both the English and French languages and to commence broadcasting commercials in the French language. The Commission APPROVES the continuation of the experiment of programming in both languages and DENIES the right to commence broadcasting commercials in the French language."[11]

CHOM's 1975 renewal was for a period of short duration, ending 31 March 1976. The CRTC claimed it wished to re-evaluate the station's overall programming policies in the light of a new, broader consideration of FM programming in Canada. In early 1976, the owners of a number of French-language radio stations in Montreal complained to the CRTC that CHOM threatened their viability by attracting francophone listeners and thus harming their ratings and advertising revenues. The very structure of the radio broadcasting and advertising industries in Montreal was then – as now – based on a clear division between language groups. Advertisers counted only the English-speaking listeners for English-language stations when targeting their advertising and determining a station's ratings (and the same held true for francophone listeners of francophone stations). Bilingual broadcasting and audiences' language-crossing had real effects on station revenues – by drawing away listeners who were part of their target audience – but produced no benefits for stations able to attract listeners across the language divide inasmuch as those crossover listeners were not counted in audience measurements.

In a 29 July 1976 ruling that renewed CHOM's licence until 1980, the CRTC put an end to the station's experiment in bilingualism. The commission, its ruling noted, "is of the opinion that the interest of both English and French population of Montreal are best served by not renewing CHOM-FM's authority to broadcast in the French language over and above its use in proper names and those expressions, quotations, words and phrases that are common currency."[12] Reference to those uses of the French language "that are common currency" betrayed the difficulty of enforcing unilingualism in a context in which French and English were often interwoven. French-language stations, particularly those (like the newly "progressive" CKOI-FM) that featured a good deal of new music by anglophone musicians, had regular recourse to English in designating new generic categories (like "New Wave") or in interviewing stars as part of their programming. The CRTC's denial of CHOM's bilingualism nevertheless allowed the station to deliver "such announcements as station identification and time-checks" in both languages ("CHOM" 1977, 31). Here, as with airport signage and consumer packaging, bilingualism was confined to its briefest forms and to those most restrained in rhetorical and affective terms.

In a 1977 section devoted to Canadian music, *Billboard* spoke favourably of the CRTC's commitment to a prohibition on bilingual broadcasting: "The licensing policy of the [CRTC] to give stations licenses to broadcast in either French or English but not bilingually has on the whole enormously helped the retention and development of the Quebecois culture and the music industry in particular" (18). If this was the noble purpose of the CRTC's 1976 ruling against CHOM's bilingualism, the station nevertheless responded in an obstinate fashion, announcing its intention to fight the ruling in court and making its protest known to national media (*Billboard* 1976, 62). Under the headline "A French Voice Strangled," a 1976 *Globe and Mail* editorial suggested that it was a "disturbing notion that the CRTC had actually succumbed to pressure from the French stations." CHOM station manager Leslie Cole stated that the station intended to "keep on doing bilingual radio and [that] we will go beyond the CRTC if necessary to do so" (*Globe and Mail* 1976b, 2). Program director Peggy Colson told the *Montreal Gazette* (1977) that the station's "on-air staff whose mother tongue is French find it a bit frustrating always having to make sure they are speaking English." In the same article, she estimated that 60 per cent of CHOM's listenership consisted of francophones.

While the question of CHOM's bilingualism appeared to have been settled by the CRTC's ruling, it would erupt in a sideshow that captured the messy political character of the affair and the absurdities to which the CRTC sometimes appeared to resort. In March 1977, *Billboard* reported on an exchange of letters between Sole and Canadian Prime Minister Pierre Trudeau. Inspired by a speech in which Trudeau laid out his dreams for a bilingual Canada, Sole wrote to the prime minister:

> Your statements last evening on an emerging progressive culture, and the spirit of brotherhood in Canada have been sentiments close to our hearts at CHOM-FM for the past six years. In that time, we developed a unique medium that was based on bilingual and bicultural foundations ... In light of recent developments, with regard for the essence of your national unity goals, we are planning to ask Mr. Boyle and the Commission to reinstate our mandate to use Canadian French in the radio in Montreal along with Canadian English and maintain our role as our audience defined it. (quoted in Melhuish 1977, 109)

In a reply that skirted close to government interference in a CRTC decision, Trudeau expressed his contentment with Sole's decision to appeal and announced that he was sending a copy of Sole's letter to Jeanne Sauvé, who was minister of communications and the cabinet official responsible for media policy. While nothing came of this exchange, CHOM's efforts to link its regulatory troubles to the national question of Canada's bilingualism marked an apparent shift in its rhetoric, four months following the election of an independentist government in Quebec. Earlier justifications of CHOM's experiment in bilingualism had been couched much more modestly in relation to the communities of progressive radio listeners to which CHOM appealed across linguistic lines, or with reference to the bilingual character of its own on-air staff.

It is tempting to explain the CRTC's shift of policy toward CHOM's bilingualism in terms of the change of chairs at the Canadian Radio and Television Commission (which became the Canadian Radio-Television and Telecommunications Commission in 1976). Pierre Juneau, who served as chair between 1968 and 1975, was a close colleague of Trudeau and shared the latter's commitment to official bilingualism. In 1975, Trudeau named Juneau to his cabinet as minister of communications, but Juneau's failure to win a by-election resulted in his replacement as minister by Sauvé. Harry Boyle, who succeeded Juneau as CRTC chair, had worked for several years in public broadcasting, but had begun his career in private radio and was seen as someone with an intimate understanding of the issues facing commercial broadcasters. In any event, the CRTC's increased reluctance to extend CHOM's experiment in bilingualism came amidst the ascendancy of FM broadcasting as a lucrative activity whose players preferred markets free of ambiguity.

In 1982, the CRTC allowed CHOM to broadcast one thirty-minute program per week in French. In the ruling granting this permission, it acknowledged the "bilingual and cultural character" of Montreal. In 1984, following a renewal hearing, the CRTC reminded the station that any other uses of French were to be restricted to the aforementioned "proper names and those quotations, words and phrases that are common usage." It admonished the station for letting French words that went beyond common usage slip into the ongoing discourse of announcers who, it appeared, could not help themselves. Over a three-day period in May 1983, the CRTC had monitored the station's programming and found a number of such violations (*Globe and Mail* 1984, B1).

Since the 1970s, linguistic diversity on Montreal radio has persisted and flourished mostly in the programming blocks of *radio communautaire*, like Radio Centre-ville. Language-crossing on the part of listeners of commercial radio continues, as does intermittent speculation about the viability of bilingual radio broadcasting in the city. In 2012, a report on the state of the Montreal radio market noted that large numbers of young, francophone Montrealers were listening to anglophone radio stations. CHOM, it was noted, had more francophone than anglophone listeners – something that the station had claimed since the 1970s – and the same was true for other English language stations whose programming was dominated by music rather than talk. The question was posed, again, as to why the regulating body, the CRTC, might not allow bilingual radio broadcasting in the city. The answer, given by an industry analyst, was simple. If the CRTC permitted bilingual broadcasting, the result would be a local radio dominated by francophone hosts playing anglophone music (Ducas 2012). The average radio listener in Montreal, it appears, wants French-language talk and English-language music.

Under current regulations governing radio, broadcasting in the French language is inseparable from the public goal of promoting French-language music. This project is enforced by French-language content regulations that govern the music playlists of stations designated as francophone. (Currently, French-language radio stations are required to ensure that 65 per cent of all music played is in the French language.) English-language stations play no similar, prescribed role in relation to music in the English language (which is not perceived as threatened, though its Canadian versions are). English-language broadcasters must, instead, play a certain percentage of Canadian music (which, incidentally, may be in French). To give radio stations the option to broadcast in either language, it is believed, would lead them to speak in French, like the majority of their audience, while still playing the English-language music widely believed to be more attractive to francophone listeners. The refusal to allow bilingual broadcasting means that more and more young francophones listen to English language music on English language radio stations, where the news, commentary, and advertising speak to them in incomplete ways.

In its editorial bemoaning the end to CHOM's experiment in bilingualism, the *Globe and Mail* (1976b) spoke of the CRTC dropping "the portcullis between the two languages." This wording invoked the language of walls and borders that has long seeped into accounts of Montreal's language relations. For the foreseeable future, it appears, radio broadcasting in Montreal will continue to be marked by the linguistic classification of stations, even if listeners themselves are language-crossing to an extent made easier by music's uneasy status as linguistic address. In radio, nevertheless, this crossing takes place to a much greater extent than it does with television, the newspaper, or others of those twentieth-century media I referred to earlier. These other media, I argue, produce lines of flight that carry attention across a single language, producing bounded spaces of language-specific experience, celebrity, and civic engagement. These lines of flight are reinforced, of course, by the monopolistic corporate ownership of the television stations, celebrity magazines, live performance operations, and other cultural channels through which the tokens of Quebec life pass.

Montrealers regularly resolve to consume media in the "other" language as a way to expand their linguistic abilities. This is particularly true for anglophones new to the city, for whom the commitment to watching French-language television or reading *Le Devoir* every day offers a seemingly convenient way to improve one's French. Unscientific observation suggests that these commitments are rarely upheld for long periods of time. Arguably, exposure to media in the other language exposes one to complex systems of inter-reference (to celebrities, films and television programs, political impulses, regions and neighbourhoods, and so on) that are often of limited intelligibility and interest. Rather than serving as pathways of orientation, then, Montreal's linguistically divided media produce coherent and rarely overlapping symbolic universes that only serve to intensify estrangement.

Large numbers of Montrealers will move back and forth between media in the French and English languages. This is particularly common among those for whom neither language is a mother tongue. This movement, as I have show, is widespread among radio listeners who, in seeking out the music they prefer, will cross linguistic boundaries in order to find it. In this switching, we find another site (like street-level conversation) in which the boundaries between language are challenged. Most of the time, however, this switching does little to weaken the linguistic exclusivity of Montreal's media themselves. These media rarely represent, within their own programming, the language-switching that is a deeply rooted feature of everyday life in Montreal.

NOTES

1 My translation. The original reads: "La grande ville est une ruche fantastique de mots qui ne se taisent jamais. Sans trêve, ils attisent les énergies de la ville et sont attisés par elle. Dans le cycle sans fin de la ville qui parle s'inscrit en eux, imperceptiblement, l'esprit actuel de la ville qui domine les strates de significations anciennes. Le langage en mouvement est immobilisé dans l'écriture qui fixe pourtant en elle le dynamisme de la ville, tout comme le froid se trouve fixée dans la glace."

2 See, among many other examples of scholarly works that deal with linguistic mixing in Quebec writing, the essays collected in Ireland and Proulx (2004).

3 On mixes of language in everyday street terminology in Montreal, see Médam (2004, 49). On the overlaying of languages on city surfaces, see Darroch (2010).

4 For one among many discussions of "Montreal English" and its borrowings from the French, see Hayhoe (2013). For warnings about the erosion of French by English, see, for example, Rolland (2013).

5 For one among many other interesting accounts of this process, see Artières (2014).

6 It is worth nothing that Montreal has more daily newspapers than most cities of comparable size in North America. *La Presse*, *Le journal de Montréal*, *Le Devoir*, and the *Montreal Gazette* are all available six days of the week. *Métro* and *24 heures* are free dailies aimed at commuters, the former owned by the Quebec-based Transcontinental corporation and the latter by Québecor's Sun Media Corporation.

7 This bilingualism may also be an effect of the extent to which magazines devoted to the visual arts circulate through international networks of gallery bookstores and other venues in which English has become a shared language of communication.

8 For an extended discussion of bilingual broadcasting in Canada, and of English-language resistance to the practice, see Raboy (1990, 130–1).

9 In 1977, CKVL-FM renamed itself CKOI-FM and offered roughly similar programming in the French language (see *Globe and Mail* 1977b, 67).

10 See also CRTC Decision 73-80, 19 March 1973.

11 CRTC Decision 75-32, 28 January 1975.

12 CRTC Decision 76-498, 29 July 1976.

9

Medial Translations and Human Unsettlements: Planetary Urbanisms in McLuhan and Flusser

MICHAEL DARROCH

The problem of translation and translatability takes on the cosmic dimensions of all existing issues: it encompasses everything.

Vilém Flusser

I expect to see the coming decades transform the planet into an art form.

Marshall McLuhan

Scattered across Marshall McLuhan and Vilém Flusser's writings on language, media, technology, and communication are images of cities and of urban life on the verge of massive transformation.[1] These two communication theorists each came to imagine an emergent planetary urbanism, a social space that is networked, non-site-specific, dynamic, and deeply dialogic. In each case, the image of a planetary urbanism is represented by new systems of thought grounded in topologies rather than geographies of urban space. While McLuhan's notion of the global village is distinct from Flusser's concept of a posthistorical telematic society, both invoke understandings of translation – between languages, senses, codes, and media forms – as a metaphor for processes of communication deeply connected to urban life.

Flusser was nine years younger than McLuhan and died eleven years after him in 1991, that much closer to the launch of global network culture. In his many writings on communication and technology, he largely shares McLuhan's stance that cultures rooted in the linearity of writing and print were on the brink of transformation into an electronic or digital network society. For this reason, Flusser has occasionally been labelled a European McLuhan (van der Meulen 2010). McLuhan predicted that electricity would rekindle the interplay of our senses, reawakening a long-lost audio-tactile sensibility that would bind us together as a global community. In contrast, Flusser believed that technical images (*Technobilder*) would displace writing as the predominant form of information flow. This distinction between McLuhan's emphasis on acoustic space and Flusser's emphasis on technical images provides a starting point for a discussion of their approaches to translation, language, and urban media cultures.

In McLuhan's theorization of media, the city – like language, clothing, and other material forms – is a technology that acts as an extension of the human. As technologies are extensions of our bodies and senses, they create environments in which we are immersed. Media act as a nervous system that surpasses the body and surrounds us, but also works us over. They are immersive devices that have direct influence on our sense of self, on what it means to be human. Cities, then, are extensions of our thought patterns as much as any other media forms. McLuhan was among the first to argue that new media of the postwar period – above all, live television – would collapse our sense of social space, with direct implications for the shape of our cities based on town centres and progressive margins. Networked communication was leading us toward a total reorganization of social space, ultimately rendering the infrastructure of our old cities obsolete. As he suggests in his 1954 pamphlet *Counterblast*, "The metropolis is OBSOLETE. Ask the Army / The INSTANTANEOUS global coverage of radio-tv makes the city form meaningless, functionless. Cities were once related to the realities of production and inter-communication. Not now" ([1954] 2011).

Despite McLuhan's continual engagement with oral linguistic traditions, rhetoric, and the idea of an emerging nonlinear acoustic space, his references to translation do not stem in any obvious way from his personal cultural experiences in specific cities. Edmonton, Winnipeg, Cambridge, St Louis, Windsor-Detroit, and Toronto – these sites of McLuhan's urban experiences are tied to his relatively stable trajectory of academic training and employment; indeed, the Toronto in which McLuhan developed his keenest insights into media forms and environments was hardly the multicultural sphere to which it now claims ownership. As Janine Marchessault (2005, 77) aptly puts it, "One can scarcely imagine a more dismal and bland place than Toronto in the 1950s." His encounter with theories of language and translation stem rather from multiple sources: cross-contaminations between the language games of Joyce, symbolist poetry, Sapir-Whorf's theory of linguistic relativity, and the related ethnolinguistic anthropology of Edmund Carpenter and Dorothy Lee. At the same time, notions of a global urban condition reach back to McLuhan's earliest encounters in the 1950s with architecture, environmental studies, and town planning through the influence of Sigfried Giedion and Jaqueline Tyrwhitt. Tyrwhitt was a key collaborator at the University of Toronto and coeditor of the journal *Explorations* (with McLuhan, Carpenter, political economist Thomas Easterbrook, and psychologist D. Carlton Williams). She provided a link not only to the CIAM movement – the Congrès international d'architecture moderne, founded by Giedion and Le Corbusier – but also to the Ekistics movement, the science of human settlements, led by the radical town planner Constantinos Doxiadis. In her own projects, Tyrwhitt consolidated a vision of the city as network, interconnected through a combination of media and architecture. In the 1960s McLuhan would join Buckminster Fuller at the famous Delos symposia in Greece, organized by Doxiadis and Tyrwhitt, to consider the Ekistics vision of *ecumenopolis*, the future worldwide city or expanded planetary settlement network.

In contrast, in the multilingual landscape of Flusser's writings, theorization of the urban oscillates between references to his experiences of specific cities (in particular Prague and São Paulo) and his own conceptualization of the urban as a vast medial network (Darroch 2008). Unlike the stability of McLuhan's urban experience, Flusser's life in cities is characterized by displacement, groundlessness, loss, migration, and unsettlement. Flusser would characterize the city as a space of not concrete but rather communicational structures, a network of information flows and patterns of intercultural communication. Like McLuhan, we could think of this city as an environment, a "landscape of inter-subjective relationships that are mutually interdependent" and that are deeply connected to the abundance of technical images or *Technobilder* in late twentieth century media culture (Araujo 2008). This image of the city as a relational field is connected to Flusser's broader conceptualization of communication and media as intricate and overlapping networks of relations.

While Flusser's metaphor of the city as network extends beyond specific sites to encompass a global field of intersubjective relations, his commitment to thinking about and between languages ("nomadic thinking"), modes of communication, and media forms as fundamentally translational and processual invites us to reconsider McLuhan's writings on the ways in which hybrid media and perceptual and cultural forms of interpenetration fostered a new acoustic space within the global village (Guldin 2008). In order to weigh McLuhan and Flusser's approaches to the metaphor of translation as communication and the changing dynamics of urban space, we must first take a detour through their approaches to history and posthistory.

DYNAMIC HISTORIES, POSTHISTORICAL IMAGINATIONS

In *The Gutenberg Galaxy* ([1962] 2011), McLuhan expands his nonlinear, "mosaic," or "field approach" to historical phenomena as "the only practical means of revealing causal operations in history" (lxii). Chronological history, he claims, is a product of writing: "The linearity of writing (in contrast with the multidimensionality of experience) and the linearity of the logic it expresses reflects neither the nature of experience nor, for that matter, of history, but rather the limitations of the medium" (157). His understanding of history as nonlinear and dynamic comes from many sources, but one often overlooked early influence on his field approach – with direct links to the shape and history of cities – is Sigfried Giedion, a historian of art, architecture, and town planning. With his seminal works *Space, Time, and Architecture* (1941) and *Mechanization Takes Command* (1948), Giedion ([1941] 1982, 5) himself develops an approach to history as dynamic, as a pattern of living and of changing attitudes and interpretations. Drawing on models of space-time relations from mathematics and physics, Giedion wanted to reconceptualize our relationship to space through the perspectives of simultaneity and many-sidedness. It was a deeply seductive approach for McLuhan, who immediately offered Giedion the writings of T.S. Eliot. Giedion (1943) valued Eliot's notion of a unified sensibility, agreeing in a letter to McLuhan that artists and historians should allow feelings to "enter into new combinations": "We need in our own arguments that clarity and at the same time that many 'senseness' – if I can say so –

in our treatment of problems." It is Eliot's (1989, 39) emphasis on the mind of a mature poet as a "finely perfected medium in which special, or very varied, feelings are at liberty to enter into new combinations" that captures Giedion's own belief that artists, town planners, and historians must seek out relationships of meanings across time, rather than linear and contingent conceptions of historical progress. For Giedion, a many-sided understanding of space presents objects from multiple points of view, and is thus composed of simultaneous relationships. He would take up the notion of a dynamic, simultaneous environment through the notion of "anonymous history" in *Mechanization Takes Command*. History itself can no longer be the pursuit of a single point of view; it now "reveals itself in facets, which fluctuate with the vantage point of the observer" (Giedion 1948, 2). Historians should engage with anonymous history by uncovering these relationships: "These relations will vary with the shifting point of view, for, like constellations of stars, they are ceaselessly in change. Every true historical image is based on relationship, appearing in the historian's choice from among the fullness of events, a choice that varies with the century and often with the decade, just as paintings differ in subject, technique, and psychic content. Now great historical panoramas are painted, now fragments of everyday things suffice to carry the feeling of an epoch" (ibid.). As with astronomers, historians "may see new constellations and hitherto invisible worlds appearing over the horizon" (2). What Giedion calls "many-senseness" in his message to McLuhan references what he had previously called *Durchdringung*, or cultural interpenetrations of space and time. Such interpenetrations or interfaces between historical periods and technological systems resonated with McLuhan's notions of technological and cultural environments – especially the interface between the cosmic, dialogic medieval world of simultaneity and the modern, linear conditions of the printed word. For McLuhan, print culture's visually dominated orientation had disrupted a simultaneous sensibility, resulting in the separation of the senses. This was already an act of "translation or reduction of a complex, organic interplay of spaces into a single space" (McLuhan [1962] 2011, 51). Ultimately, repairing this separation would require a new form of translation or "interplay" between the senses, which McLuhan believed to be announced by the electric galaxy: "Today, such translations can be effected back and forth through a variety of spatial forms which we call the 'media of communication'" (51–2). For

McLuhan, such major transitions in media history always represent moments of hybridity or interpenetration, as points of resonance. His notion of translation between both media formats and human senses is predicated on their very interpenetration.

Flusser developed an analysis of media forms and codes that in many ways resembles McLuhan's approach to media history. In the lexicon of concepts at the end of *Towards a Philosophy of Photography* ([1983] 2000), Flusser defines history as the "linear progression of translation from ideas into concepts" (83), where translation represents "switching over from one code to another; hence, jumping from one universe into another" (85). Images mediate between humans and the world; their peculiar space and time presents a magical world "in which everything is repeated and in which everything participates in a significant context. Such a world is structurally different from that of the linear world of history in which nothing is repeated and in which everything has causes and will have consequences" (9). Like McLuhan, Flusser argues that writing produced a linear sense of history as progress or, in Flusser's terms, a process of translating images into texts. The advent of the alphabet and writing challenged pictorial, magical experience, an idea that McLuhan refers to as typographic man.[2]

Flusser would develop a theory of technical images, starting with the introduction of photography in the nineteenth century. Technical images represent another moment of translation, a jump into a new universe. Here, we might contrast Flusser's technical images with McLuhan's belief that "translations can be effected back and forth" in the electric age. Technical images are "instruments for turning the messages of texts imaginable" (Flusser [1983] 2013, 95). In a chapter entitled "Images" (conceived originally as a dialogue with McLuhan), Flusser argues that if texts were originally designed to explain the world of images, then technical images will retranslate the world of texts into a new imagination. This transcoding or translation takes place within the apparatuses of technical images: in television, for example, where "material is translated into images and irradiated. It is transcoded from symptom and history into post-history" (97).

Posthistory is a key concept for Flusser, which must be distinguished from the thesis of the end of history that Francis Fukuyama initiated at the same time. Posthistory does not refer to the demise of history, but rather a period after linear, chronological historical thinking.

Whereas McLuhan argues that we are re-entering a kind of acoustic or audio-tactile space through the conditions of electric media, Flusser foresees a turn where the linearity of written history is finally displaced by the emerging networks of technical images. While Flusser's theories of communication are oriented to dialogic encounters, he nonetheless envisions translation as a series of jumps or leaps from one language, experience, code, or format to another – an idea that contrasts with McLuhan's emphasis on cultural interpenetrations. As I discuss below, Flusser's philosophical reflections on posthistory provide not only a point of connection between the transition from a universe of texts to a universe of technical images, but also what he will later call the end or disappearance of the city as we know it.

MEDIAL TRANSLATIONS, URBAN TRANSFORMATIONS

To explore these connections inherent in Flusser's work, I turn first to the metaphorics of translation that McLuhan employs in building a theory of a simultaneously mediated global village. I finally connect this discussion to Flusser's writings on the city and his concept of a telematic society.

In McLuhan's hands, the alphabet translated multidimensional space into a single space. Electric media, particularly computing, promised to resolve discrete differences between media. "With the new media it is also possible to store and to translate everything" (McLuhan 1964, 65). Furthermore, translation operates as a two-way system: "Language as the technology of human extension, whose powers of separation we know so well, may have been the 'Tower of Babel' by which men sought to scale the highest heavens. Today computers hold out the promise of a means of instant translation of any code or language into any other code or language. The computer promises by technology a Pentecostal condition of universal understanding and unity" (83–4). The key suggestion here is the possibility of universal understanding, reintegrating the senses into the common sense:

> "The common sense" was for many centuries held to be the peculiar human power of translating one kind of experience of one sense into all the senses, and presenting the result continuously as a unified image to the mind. In fact, this image of a unified ratio among the senses was long held to be the mark of our rationality,

> and may in the computer age easily become so again ... Having extended or translated our central nervous system into the electromagnetic technology, it is but a further stage to transfer our consciousness to the computer world as well. (McLuhan 1964, 67)

As we will see, McLuhan connects this notion of the *sensus communis*, a cultural space that fosters the constant and simultaneous translation or interplay of our senses, to the future shape of a global city. This is a catholic gesture that embraces a universalizing or Pentecostal technological promise: a moment when the segregation of languages, senses, and individual experiences will be overcome.

McLuhan also contends that "all media are active metaphors in their power to translate experience into new forms" (64). In this regard, his theory of translation oscillates between processes of convergence and processes of transformation or transposition. As medial forms collide, they transform into hybrid states: "Media as extensions of our senses institute new ratios, not only among our private senses, but among themselves, when they interact among themselves." Radio, he argues, "changed the form of the news story as much as it altered the film image in the talkies. TV caused drastic changes in radio programming, and in the form of the thing or documentary novel" (61). Translation as transposition resists total synthesis, producing hybrid medial forms. As information passes from one state to another, it undergoes such transposition.

McLuhan's metaphor of translation encapsulates the dream that languages, and other media, will reconverge into a universal form, while acknowledging that this transfer always produces change. The media environment of the twentieth century kindled this debate through the discourse of a universalizing digital code. This debate resuscitated the ancient model of linguistic universals, the search for the perfect language, in which we might reconstitute the city (Babel) as a global environment. Conversely, following Flusser, we must always attend to the recurrent failure of this search and the persistence of dialogism. By embracing the economy of shifting meanings through the circulation of linguistic exchanges, we also acknowledge the impossibility of total translation in local and global contexts. The metaphors of translation as embodying the possibility of a global universality must be juxtaposed with a planetary urbanism that is processual and represented by perpetual transposition and circulation.

McLuhan's metaphor of translation also binds media and technologies to his understandings of the city itself as a medial form. From his first reflections on media as art forms in the 1950s, McLuhan developed the view that cities in history are already translations: from orality to literacy, a translation of sound into particular visual spatial terms. Such translations made possible the initial organization of town spaces, as McLuhan writes to Tyrwhitt in an 8 December 1953 letter (Tyrwhitt). At McLuhan, Tyrwhitt, and Carpenter's Culture and Communications Seminar in 1954, translation between media formats and spaces was at the forefront of their discussions about post-literate, acoustic space. Notably, at one of the group's meetings in November 1954, Williams initiated a sequence of connections by reading "a paper on auditory space." Carpenter followed by reading "a paragraph from Kandinsky connoting color with sound," McLuhan "said that the translation of one sense in terms of another was the origin, in scholastic philosophy, of the term 'common sense,'" and Tyrwhitt presented her paper "The Moving Eye," providing a cinematic description of the multidirectional sense of space in non-occidental cities. In the same year, McLuhan's pamphlet *Counterblast* ([1954] 2011), inspired by the Vorticists and released just prior to the images of Sputnik, first articulated a concept of simultaneous planetary urbanism: "Simultaneity compels sharp focus on effect of thing made. Simultaneity is the form of the press in dealing with Earth City. Simultaneity is formula for the writing of both detective story and symbolist poem. These are derivatives (one 'low' and one 'high') of the new technological culture. Simultaneity is related to telegraph, as the telegraph to math and physics. Technological art takes the whole earth and its population as its material, not as its form" ([1954] 2011). In a later letter to Tyrwhitt on 23 December 1960, McLuhan recounts his interpretation of the city as *sensus communis*:

> Now that by electricity we have externalized all of our senses, we are in the desperate position of not having any *sensus communis*. Prior to electricity, the city was the *sensus communis* for such specialized and externalized senses as technology had developed. From Aristotle onward, the traditional function of the *sensus communis* is to translate each sense into the other senses, so that a unified, integral image is offered at all times to the mind. The city performs that function for the scattered and distracted senses, and

> spaces and times, of agrarian cultures. Today with electronics we have discovered that we live in a global village, and the job is to create a global city, as center for the village margins. The parameters of this task are by no means positional. With electronics any marginal area can become center, and marginal experiences can be had at any center. Perhaps the city needed to coordinate and concert the distracted sense programs of our global village will have to be built by computers in the way in which a big airport has to coordinate multiple flights. (McLuhan 1987, 277–8)

Like Flusser, McLuhan argues that new media would alter the ratios and arrangements of city life, encapsulated in the notion of the global village and his emphasis on city spaces as learning environments.

The cities of Flusser's nomadic life, particularly his native Prague and his adopted São Paulo, are rife with linguistic layerings that cross both public and private life, a major influence on his experiments in multilingual writing and translation. The particular cultural and linguistic constellations of Prague that produced the German-Jewish intellectual class into which Flusser was born also affords him keen insight into the influence of language on the intellectual sphere of São Paulo. These experiences of living between languages nourished his early passion for developing a theory of translation (Guldin 2004, 2005) and contributed to the metaphors of wandering, nomadic thinking, leaps, and bridges to which he continually returns. As he expanded his philosophy of media, he extended the metaphor of translation from language and multilingual relationships to encompass communication, art, information, and technologies that were constantly producing new mediated, dialogic experiences. Toward the end of his life, before his tragic death in a car accident in 1991, he turned increasingly to cities and the conditions of emerging media: new technologies constantly exert pressure on the dynamics of public and private urban spaces. Flusser's philosophy of media history, or rather posthistory, and its implications for the future of the city, invites us to imagine a shift from alphanumeric codification to the telematic society.

Flusser gradually expanded the concept of translation beyond linguistic parameters to embrace notions of transference, dissemination, and mediation across media such as photography, film, and computing. As Rainer Guldin (2005, 205) notes, he commonly turns to the metaphors of bridges and leaps (Brücke und Sprünge). Bridges describe connections (between humans, languages, media, experiences, cities), yet are constantly threatened by collapse. If bridges offer the possibility of synthesis, ultimately only leaps from one situation or condition to another can guarantee transference. Flusser invokes the metaphors of bridges and leaps in his frequent references to "entropy." While entropy is the predictable or "probable" process toward disorder in a system, the production and accumulation of information is its unpredictable or "improbable" counterpart. We have the capacity to counter entropy not only by constantly producing new information but also by storing it in memories and databanks. Information is not random, but is produced through the particular contexts of dialogue, which Flusser juxtaposes to the discursive processes that disseminate it. Every social structure, including the city, is a constellation of dialogic and discursive processes. Thus improbable or negentropic dialogue is made increasingly probable through its discursive dissemination. As an inherently dialogic (and therefore negentropic) process, translation does not merely transfer information, but is itself a producer of new information. Translations may strive to be loyal by building bridges, but ultimately must take a leap of faith into a new situation. In this sense, translation, as mediation, always creates "noise" that accumulates as new information in the system. Translations and retranslations are cybernetic feedback loops.

Being-at-home in language(s) is core to Flusser's philosophy of communication and, albeit indirectly, his theories of the transforming fabric of urban space. His writings about cities shift between his commitment to thinking about and between the interconnectedness of languages, on the one hand, and his own later conceptualization of the city as a planetary network or intersubjective field of relations, on the other hand. While Flusser did not overtly combine these two areas of philosophical reflection, his preoccupation with translation and with cities invites us to consider their relationship. Both Flusser and McLuhan consider the transposition of mediated urban space through the lens of human settlement and, ultimately, human unsettlement.

SETTLEMENT, UNSETTLEMENT

McLuhan's vision of a global city image takes shape in part through Giedion and CIAM's unwavering emphasis on building new cities at a human scale, and in part through Tyrwhitt and Doxiadis's ekistical models of networked global settlements. The world city as a space of unity is a "translation of our entire lives into the spiritual form of information [making] of the entire globe, and of the human family, a single consciousness" (McLuhan 1964, 67). Flusser similarly proposes a new city model, a universe in which technical images refashion and emphasize intrahuman relationships and diminish individual subjectivities.

In McLuhan's hands, villages and cities are settlements that are formed primarily as nodes in transportation networks or as collective shelters. In keeping with his metaphor of translation, he describes the traditional formation of city settlements as a transition from nomadic to sedentary, specialized, and individualized patterns of living. In contrast to Flusser's reflections on migration, in which nomadic life and thinking are persistent and always present human experiences, McLuhan associates nomadism with tribal, agrarian societies, and the all-at-once conditions of acoustic space to which electric media will hearken back. "Man the food-gatherer reappears incongruously as information-gatherer. In this role, electronic man is no less a nomad than his paleolithic ancestors" (248). As noted in his 1960 letter to Tyrwhitt, this insight applies to cities' changing shape and spaces. Emphasising a new interplay between the senses in "Five Sovereign Fingers Taxed the Breath," McLuhan and the *Explorations* researchers interpreted the old city form as obsolete faced with an emergent planetary space-time: "We are back in Acoustic Space" (McLuhan [1954] 2011). As Mark Wigley (2001, 99) says, "Electronics was the new form of traffic and therefore the new form of the city."

In his deliberations with Doxiadis and Tyrwhitt at the Delos symposia in the 1960s, McLuhan argued for recognizing the changing paradigms of human settlements. CIAM's modernist emphasis on building settlements at a human scale, and Doxiadis's science of human settlements, needed to shift focus. As Wigley puts it, "CIAM thinking had to be retooled for an electronic world. The Delos meetings would turn the CIAM idea of settlements held together by transportation networks into the idea of inhabitable information networks" (97). As McLuhan would suggest at the Fourth Delos Meetings, it is the "speed-up of information that reduces the planet to the scale of a village," where "a global consciousness thus becomes the new human scale ... Since the central purpose of human settlement in the electronic age becomes learning, human settlement must be a projection, a multi-dimensional model of our new global consciousness" (quoted in Bell and Tyrwhitt 1972, 527). This projection or model is imagistic: through electric speed-up and movement, the global village is not simply connected, but also imagined. As he wrote to Tyrwhitt on 23 December 1960, the city as *sensus communis* "translates each sense into the other senses, so that a unified, integral image is offered at all times to the mind" (McLuhan 1987, 277). McLuhan follows Heidegger here in arguing that the world has transformed into a picture, an entire network or system within which we come to imagine our own position. The radical architect Buckminster Fuller, a regular contributor to the Delos symposia, shared McLuhan's standpoint. By the 1970s, McLuhan and Fuller began to criticize the Ekistics vision of *ecumenopolis*, a concept they felt was too beholden to the history of human settlement. After all, settlements, with their emphasis on specialization and sedentariness, were ultimately incongruous with planetary consciousness and an electric galaxy. As Fuller would write in 1978, it was time to "accommodate" formless and strategic systems of human unsettlement (see Wigley 2001). "Human settlements were inherent to agrarian and mill town ages: now *unsettlement* is occurring" (Fuller 1978, 57).

In contrast, Flusser (2003, 40) juxtaposes nomadism to settledness in both historical and contemporary terms: "The settled are localized, and nomads wander." Nomadism and wandering are themes closely connected to his life experiences, suggesting constant migration as much as states of settledness in different cities and languages. He reclassifies human existence as a three-part division between the Palaeolithic age, a period of humanization "up to the invention of agriculture" and "characterized primarily by the use of stone tools"; the Neolithic Age, "the creation of civilization ... characterized above all by life in settlements"; and the Immediate Future, which (at the time of his writing in 1990) "has as yet no fitting name; it is characterized primarily by the fact that our world of habit is becoming uninhabitable" (39). As with McLuhan, settlements in Flusser's eyes were initiated as hunter-gatherers transitioned to agriculture and animal breeding. Flusser's redefinition of the Neolithic Age as spanning 8000 BC to 1990 – a "10,000-year interruption in nomadic life" (40) – suggests that the present moment (then 1990) was on the verge of transformation. Like McLuhan, Flusser envisages this transformation in terms of changing landscape or environment of information and communication, but he also invokes Benjamin's thesis of the storm of historical progress. Amid the "media storm" of our posthistorical moment, the "information that is delivered into the home must be carried by material or nonmaterial channels, which puncture roofs and walls. The home has become drafty, as gales of media sweep through from all directions: it has become uninhabitable" (42). The new learning environment of the city, as McLuhan and Carpenter (1957) would say, is a "classroom without walls."

While the settled in Flusser's terms are identifiable in terms of the space in which they possess (store) both things and concepts, nomads are identifiable in terms of space-time and communication flows. "The settled have divided the world and themselves into sections, *nomai*, and concepts on which they sit, and they strive to possess ever more of these sections. And nomads experience concrete networked reality: they move about in it and travel over fields of potentiality" (Flusser 2003, 50). Yet Flusser also invites us to complicate the relationship between settledness and nomadism as a false dichotomy: nomads rest and settle, if only for a short time, while city dwellers are frequently on the move. Ultimately, for Flusser, human beings are unsettled creatures: "To be human in the true sense of the word, one has to be unsettled" (25). Unsettledness for Flusser represents a freedom that he associates with the state of being a nomad, migrant, or expellee. The city as the history of human settledness and sedentariness is on the verge of dissolving into the network of nomadic thinking and the worldwide flows of technical images. In this new environment, "we have begun to be nomadic" because "it is information and not possessions (software not hardware) that empowers" and "communication, not economics, now forms the substructure of village (society)" (43). Flusser's description of an emerging condition of unsettledness recalls McLuhan and Fuller's argument that the electric age is characterized by "stirring up rather than settling down" (Wigley 2001, 112). "Within the network," writes Flusser (2003, 51), "everyone is an omnipresent potential." Referencing Martin Buber's (1923) dialogic meeting of "I" and "Thou," Flusser (2003, 53) argues that the "form of nomadism is one in which dispersed potentials approach each other via a networked structure so that they may experience a mutual 'I' and 'you' and dialogue *above* history." The hope for dialogue, the constant migration between languages and also experiences, binds together subjects within the networked form of the telematic society. As with the sped-up informational flows of the global village in McLuhan's terms, Flusser's telematic society presents the world as a sphere of proximate relationships between humans, nature, and media:

> Let us imagine that our central nervous system were to extend around the globe like a net. Let us further imagine that it would constitute something like a *neurosphere* situated between the biosphere and the atmosphere. What I am suggesting is not science fiction but the model on which the telematics society now being built is based. What we need to do is imagine such a neurosphere as a network of human nerves as well as material and nonmaterial cables. And we must further imagine human brains and artificial intelligences at the nodal intersections of such a network. Such a neurosphere spanning the globe would function to compute into experience all stimuli incessantly streaming in from all directions and to transform these experiences into decisions and actions. Seen this way, the telematic society would be a mechanism for experience, a global machine for the realization of potentials. (67)

In the text "L'espace de la ville et les nouvelles technologies," composed in 1985, Flusser initiates his description of the transformation of city space into the telematic society. Recalling his discussion of settlement, he distinguishes between public and private: information is exposed, that is to say, made public or "published" – in the space of the city, but is saved or stored in the space of one's home. The telematic society, the rise of the flow of technical images, will transform this dialectical movement between private and public, between individuals and the world. New technologies will make the open space of the city (the marketplace) obsolete, resulting in a shift in consciousness. Flusser characterizes technologies in terms of their emphasis on dissemination (broadcasting) and on complex forms of exchange (network). Whereas broadcasting is a one-directional sender-receiver model that ultimately fosters fascist tendencies, a synchronized society characterized by centralized information, networking is multidirectional, a complex and dialogic web of "reversible channels" that produce new forms of intersubjectivity – a shift that McLuhan would identify as a centre-without-margins. In Flusser's work, there is only the Babelian dissemination, the dialogue of increasing information exchange. "If we wish to preserve (and augment) consciousness, freedom, we must commit ourselves not to saving the city, the republic, but to establishing reversible channels in a dialogue that is universal and open" (Flusser 1985, 2, my translation).

São Paulo appears as a particular case of a city trapped between old and new codes (Flusser 1992a). Flusser describes it as a kind of processor of linguistic materials: intellectuals (writers) "process" Portuguese in their everyday lives, but the information that nourishes their production stems from European sources in English, French, Italian, and German. Translation is thus an essential feature in the intellectual life (what he later calls the theoretical space) of São Paulo: without translations, these external sources could not enter into the city's intellectual discourse. The many writers of diverse linguistic backgrounds augment the city's capacity for translation, giving São Paulan Portuguese a peculiar plasticity and making the city a centre of poetic innovation. At the same time, São Paulo remains largely trapped in the alphabetic-representational field of Portuguese colonial history. It remains a city brimming with print media, the intelligentsia its information-producing "authors" who are not yet prepared to embrace the new codes of new technologies. "Should São Paulan writers succeed in advancing from the alphabet into new codes (from paper into new mnemonic devices), then São Paulo can be revived as an innovation centre" (208, my translation).

Flusser's belief that the "space of the city" will be transformed by telematics is further articulated in "The City as a Wave-Trough in the Flow of Images," first written in 1988. We must learn to think about the city in topographical, rather than geographical, terms. Subjects must be reinterpreted not as concrete individuals, but as knots of interrelations and information channels, a network out of which the city is woven. Again, this view emphasizes the dialogic nature of the city as a relational field:

> The threads of this net should be seen as channels through which information like representations, feelings, intentions, or knowledge flows. The threads knot themselves together provisionally and develop into what we call human subjects. The totality of the threads constitutes the concrete lifeworld, and the knots therein are abstract extrapolations. One recognizes this when they unknot themselves ... If one holds fast to the image of an intersubjective field of relations – we is concrete, I and you are abstractions of this – then the new image of the city gains contours. (325)

Following Buber once again, the dialogic structure of "we" as the mutual recognition of "I" and "you" becomes Flusser's compelling metaphor for the city's image. Again, this is an *image* of the global city as much as its form, an image that shapes our subjective self-awareness through our relations to others.

COSMIC VILLAGE, RELATIONAL FIELD

McLuhan suggests that a post-Gutenberg, postvisual society would mean the obsolescence of the old metropolis. Flusser also believes that media posthistory – the end of history as it has been written – signifies the end of the city as a historically defined spatial field. While Flusser does not write about the posthistorical condition explicitly in terms of transitions in the fabric of urban life, he points in this direction in the essay-interview "Ende der Geschichte, Ende der Stadt?" (1991). However, in another version of his thesis, "Designing Cities," also written in 1988, Flusser (2002) makes an important distinction between villages as spheres of culture and cities as spheres of civilization: "Why cities and not villages? Why not, as some alternative thinkers are suggesting, discard civilized life in favour of a cultivated life? Why not focus, for example, on McLuhan's cosmic village?" (175). While gesturing to their shared focus on the phenomenon of posthistory and a mediated planetary urbanism, Flusser argues that only cities produce a theoretical space, that is, the space needed for theorizing, the activity of creativity, and "leisure in the civilized sense" (177). Theory can thus be understood in terms of translation and retranslation: the dialogic process of mutual recognition. "Theory is the connecting force of intrahuman relationships, to which we owe the production of information" (176). While McLuhan's notion of the global village as a dialogic space thus has much in common with Flusser's planetary intersubjective field, Flusser's distinction between cities and villages highlights an important difference between their models of planetary urbanism. For McLuhan (1964, 67), the global village is a "translation of our entire lives into the spiritual form of information [making] of the entire globe, and of the human family, a single consciousness." This Pentecostal gesture is a unifying consciousness, a total interface, reintegrating human senses and meanings in a total awareness. The translative *sensus communis*, in Giedion's sense of interpenetration or *Durchdringung*, no longer defines the space-time of cities, but of the world. It is a village, for McLuhan, because it resembles the tribal characteristics of oral cultures, in which members understand themselves as part of a larger community defined by interdependence, interpenetration, and shared responsibility.

In contrast, while Flusser's theoretical project is oriented to overcoming knowledge gaps through synthesis, he equally stresses the impossibility of a final synthesis and the need to emphasize difference. At stake is not a "Pentecostal condition of universal understanding and unity" where the next logical step is "not to translate, but to by-pass languages in favour of a general cosmic consciousness" (84), but rather a Kabbalistic understanding of the basic multiplicity of languages, a possible totality only through the presence or harmony of differences. To be sure, acoustic space for McLuhan reflects a comparable field of multiple viewpoints, where the paradigm of configuration opposes lineal and uniform visual space. To this extent, Flusser may share Giedion's emphasis on the multiplicity of perspectives, but it is not Eliot's unified sensibility. His experiences jumping between different languages, cities, cultures, and disciplines led him always to emphasize and cherish the distinctiveness between them. Flusser wants to retain these distinctions rather than blur them. In his autobiography *Bodenlos* (Rootless), he describes the sensation of moving-between rather than being-in-between:

> Once one has transcended one's own culture (that is, one has lost one's footing) a different kind of cultural experience becomes possible. One hovers above a whole set of cultures, and at the same time one is consciously experiencing this drifting. One can perceive how the different cultures interconnect with each other, how they form groups and hierarchies, how they distance themselves from each other, how chasms open up between them and how they fight against each other. And at the same time one experiences the impossibility to assess cultures, that is, to choose between them. One perceives oneself adrift, and since one starts viewing oneself as an "I" created by one of the cultures one has transcended, the drifting itself is experienced as a progressive transcending of one's self, as a progressive self-estrangement. (translated in Finger, Guldin, and Bernardo 2011, 80)

This gesture of celebrating nomadism reflects cultures' fragmentation rather than reintegration, and shines through Flusser's thesis of a new urbanism. In the act of surrendering "geography in favour of topology," we are in a position to move between the nodes on the network rather than perceive the network as a single unity. "As soon as we are able to think topologically – that is, in terms of networked concrete relationships – the city to be designed allows not only localization, but also localization everywhere in the network" (Flusser 2002, 177). For McLuhan, technologies are extensions of the human; for Flusser, the individual is an abstraction of the concrete network of relations that constitute culture and civilization (174). "From a geographical perspective, the city will encompass the entire globe, but, from a topological perspective, it will initially be a barely perceptible fold in the all-encompassing intrahuman relational field" (179).

As Ben Highmore (2014, 26–7) argues in "Metaphor City," "it might well turn out that the 'city' most properly exists as a 'representation,' a representation that has very real consequences ... cultural workers (academics working on urban cultural matters, cultural critics, cultural producers, and so on) might find the work that they can most productively contribute to the future of cities is not to borrow the garb of urban planners but to work to find new, more productive metaphoric systems both for the city and within the city." While McLuhan and Flusser's theses of the translative characteristics of all media diverge at many fundamental levels, they ultimately offer possible metaphoric systems for understanding an emerging planetary urban condition. Their theses are seductively optimistic about renewed forms of dialogism leading toward open informational flows as the basis of a global network culture. Given their respective premature deaths – McLuhan in 1980 and Flusser in 1991 – just prior to the rise of Internet culture, we might question whether their optimism would have withered had they lived to witness contemporary debates about net neutrality, global investment, surveillance, and big data. Nevertheless, their writings urge us still to consider new metaphorics for the city – the image of the global village; topological thinking – that are grounded not in a dream of extending the human scale of the built city across the globe, but rather in recognizing the social and political transformation of collective space and urban media culture in an age of seemingly ceaseless information and data.

NOTES

1 The research for this contribution was made possible with support from the Social Sciences and Humanities Research Council of Canada (SSHRC)

and a 2015 Visiting Fellowship at the Institute for Modern Languages Research, School of Advanced Study, University of London.

2 Mersch (2008) argues that McLuhan and Flusser's historical treatment of media transformation resembles in many aspects a Hegelian approach to the philosophy of history.

PART THREE

Hybrid Urban Languages

10

Linguistic Zones of the French Atlantic

BILL MARSHALL

The term "French Atlantic" was developed as a conceptual tool to remap, decentre, and provoke debate about those objects of contemplation within French studies, namely France and "Frenchness." Previous work (Marshall 2009) involved (mostly) a journey between cities, and was attentive to the need for French-speaking populations and cultures to compose with other languages, and indeed new environments and rulers, in the situations – "archipelagos" – in which they found themselves on the American continent. A distinctly minoritarian (or "minor," as opposed to would-be majoritarian) position was faced by those other groups whose lives and very cultural existence or nonexistence were shaped by military and/or political defeat or economic subordination in the Americas: the Acadians, the Cajuns, the Creoles of New Orleans, and the French-Canadian immigrants to New England. These emphases link to Edouard Glissant's (1996, 43–4) use of "*archipélique*" to describe "une pensée non systématique, inductive, explorant l'imprévu de la totalité-monde" (a nonsystematic, inductive thought, exploring the unforeseen in the world-totality. My translation) and capable of undermining centripetal, "continental" forms of thought and culture. At work therefore was a crossing, movement, and even "settlement" – what Deleuze and Guattari (1980) call deterritorialization and potentially reterritorialization – that meant that those mobile, minimal particles of French language, culture, and narrative we might call Frenchness journeyed and became something else from the metropole, as with the *canadianité* that existed even at the time of Conquest in 1759, or as with the Creole cultures of the Caribbean. In the Americas, faced with the majoritarian fact, and even the positions of mastery, enjoyed by both English and Spanish, as well as vis-à-vis the cultural capital associated with metropolitan French, minoritarian French-Atlantic cultures might conceivably set in motion a process whereby "French" would be destabilized, in which seeds of becoming, in Deleuze and Guattari's terms, could trigger uncontrollable, unpredictable movements and deterritorializations of the mean or majority.

In this chapter, I revisit cities in the French Atlantic and track the specific workings of translation that illuminate both the particularity of those sites and also those aspects of transoceanic exchange and transformation that in urban contexts invent new forms and question old orthodoxies. To what extent do the sites I discuss here – New Orleans and Montevideo – generate particular energies that question the *doxa* associated with monolingual or monocultural existence? If "dual" cities are usually the product of conquest, or represent a legacy of empires that have competed with each other, or have been superseded by nationalism, what complex language relations – of distance, proximity, and mutual transformation – determine the apprehension of space, history, and memory? What is the particular role of translation – as opposed to simply bilingualism – in this process, and how frequently is the form of literary modernism taken as a prime expression of this radical cognitive, perceptual, and linguistic questioning? To the tracking of translation instances and practices, I add that of the relationship to the overarching and overweening real or imagined presence of metropolitan French, which is a far more centripetal cultural and linguistic force than that of any other European empire, and which in a sense represents a fourth term in these cities of translation in addition to the local version of French, the majority language (English or Spanish), or the multilingualism impelled by other minorities. For the French Atlantic is also a challenge to metropolitan French investments in an imagined "America," be it that, in French cultural history, of Buffalo Bill, jazz, or Disney. As the Quebec geographer Jean Morisset points out, "La véritable Amérique ne saurait exister en français aux yeux de la France, de peur justement que son rêve d'Amérique ne devienne un cauchemar indéchiffrable parlant joual ou créole" (Morisset and Waddell 2001, 288: The real America could never exist in French in the eyes of France, precisely for fear of her dream of America becoming an indecipherable nightmare speaking *joual* or creole. My translation).

Nineteenth-century Louisiana and New Orleans offer a French-speaking Creole population wedded to its Catholicism and invested in its linguistic expressions and indeed high-cultural forms of opera as well as theatre, poetry, and the novel. It shares histories of a (bloodless) "conquest," or rather two, with the same 1763 Treaty of Paris awarding Canada to the British and Louisiana to the Spanish (who did little to prevent the perpetuation of French), and then the Louisiana Purchase of 1803. Despite the influx of anglophone Protestant Americans, New Orleans remained a majority francophone city well into the 1840s. Until 1852 the city was separated into three distinct municipalities: two downtown dominated by French Creoles and one uptown dominated by Anglo-Americans. (Like St Laurent Boulevard in Montreal, Canal Street was a dividing line between the linguistic communities.) The "foreign French" were migrants from metropolitan France, particularly the south and west, and totalled 3,000 to 7,000 people a year from the 1830s. Among their ranks were a large number of political exiles, for whom New Orleans was a haven: royalists in the 1790s, anti-Bonapartists after 1799, Bonapartists after 1815, republicans after 1848. To these are to be added the large influx from Saint-Domingue that began in the 1790s (for example, Louis Guillaume du Bourg, born in Cap Français, was the founder of the city's first newspaper, *Le Moniteur de la Louisiane*, in 1794; the first mayor in the American period, James [Jacques François] Pitot, settled in New Orleans in 1796, via Philadelphia from Saint-Domingue, where he had been in the sugar business). This culminated in 1809–10, when Joseph Bonaparte's usurping of the Spanish throne led to war and the expulsion of exiles from Cuba, 10,000 of whom pitched up in New Orleans (in roughly equal numbers of whites, free people of colour, and their slaves), adding themselves to the 5,000 to 10,000 that had arrived since 1791 and doubling the city's French-speaking population. These arrivals swelled the ranks of the francophone merchant and professional classes, and contributed much to the cultural dynamism of the following decades, educational attainment and even literacy among the pre-1800 white Creoles being low, despite the *ancien régime* pretentions of the upper classes. There was thus an established readership for the rich (and under-researched) literary production in the French language, which peaked in the city between 1840 and 1850.

What of translation across the divide in this context? There was none, unless we accept the trans- or French-Atlantic translations in France of American works, for example the poet Charles Baudelaire's translation of Edgar Allan Poe's *Extraordinary Tales* (1857), which in turn influenced fellow but francophone southerner Alfred Mercier in some of his more gothic writing (*Hénoch Jédésias*, 1892). This is the tale of a dual city, where the linguistic communities turned their backs on each other and from where French as both a vehicular and literary language disappeared by the early twentieth century as a result of race, and civil war. As United States racial polarizations gradually overcame the more variegated French Caribbean codings that prevailed in the city, the significant population of free people of colour saw their own cultural capital severely restricted. In the run up to the American Civil War of 1861–65, invocations of an alternative, French Atlantic racial politics (slavery was definitively abolished in the French Caribbean and elsewhere in the colonies in 1848) became increasingly dangerous in a Louisiana that was virtually a police state. The French émigré Charles Testut's abolitionist novel, *Le Vieux Salomon*, was written in 1858 but not published until 1872, let alone translated. The Union army occupied New Orleans in 1862 and for a period closed down the separate French public school system. Creoles were financially ruined by the war and were unable either to send their children to France to be educated or to import French tutors, and after 1865 faced an economic onslaught from northerners. Moreover, white Creoles had to choose their side in the bitter and violent divide of southern racial/racist politics that marked the period through Reconstruction (when the south was occupied by the Union army and black political rights pushed through), its end in 1877, and beyond. The choice was to be white above all, and to deny any common ground, let alone ancestry, with the free Creoles of colour:

> The white creoles' fervent embrace of the Anglo-Americans' racial mores was doubly ironic. It was ironic, first, as an act of self-denial. Turning their backs on much of their own history, they rejected in the rush to whiteness the historic closeness, indeed interconnectedness, of the white and black creole communities ... Second, the antebellum ethnic, cultural, and political divisions among whites provided the space within which New Orleans' unique community of free people of color could flourish. The attempt to hijack the *creole* label for exclusive white use not only furnished evidence of the white creoles' Americanization but also meant that, to the extent New Orleans' creole character survived at all, it did so primarily among nonwhites. (Hirsch and Logsdon 1992, 98)

However, there is a coda to this story of nontranslation, and it is connected with looking back, with the memory of that antebellum world of linguistic duality and combination of racial hierarchy and fluidity.

This can be seen in the work of Sidonie de la Houssaye (1820–1894), whose extensive output began to be published only in her sixties. She wrote a version of the Acadian Evangeline myth, *Pouponne et Balthazar* (1888), and most importantly an examination of the fate of the "quadroons," mixed-race women who earlier in the century were "placed" as official mistresses to married white men, *Les Quarteronnes de la Nouvelle-Orléans* (published in serial form, 1894–98, under the pseudonym Louise Raymond). Born Hélène Perret into an old Creole slave-owning planter family north-west of New Orleans (her ancestor Jean-Baptiste Perret settled in Louisiana in 1723), she was married at age thirteen to Louis de la Houssaye, from a similar but, as it turned out, financially less solid background. Sidonie opened a girls' school in 1849, but the family fortune was ruined by the Civil War. She died shortly before the serialization of *Les Quarteronnes*, which uses the frame of the "author" discovering her grandmother's papers both to establish the narrative and also to create a distance from it. The novel's content was explosive, especially within the racial and political polarizations of the 1890s.

The view from the 1890s to the 1810s, 1820s, and 1830s is also about memory, the reconstruction of the Creole past in the context of "the rush to whiteness," and the emergence of new segregationist laws. De la Houssaye corresponded with George Washington Cable, and with Cable's publisher in New York, Edward Scribner. He translated and bought the rights to a diary written by de La Houssaye's grandmother, and with her permission included some of it in his 1889 book *Strange True Stories of Louisiana*. (Cable was also instrumental in helping de la Houssaye publish her work, and the two corresponded frequently.) His fiction about *plaçage*, "Tite Poulette" (1874), portrays a white man seeking to marry a coloured woman and thus taking on the whole system, although the final revelation is that she is really white after all. But Cable's project in *Old Creole Days* (1879) and *The Grandissimes* (1880) – both set in the years between the Purchase and the Civil War, with resonances between the fate of the free people of colour "then" and that of the freedmen "now," against the opprobrium of the Creoles sprinting to be white – is to disinter the secrets of New Orleans' past, its horrors, and its miscegenations.

Francophone New Orleans literary output petered out before World War I, and Louisiana imposed restrictions on the use of French until reversing policy actively to encourage it with the creation of the Council for the Development of French in Louisiana in 1968 (which is arguably more interested in the international French of immersion classes than its specific Louisiana forms, although the council's existence has accompanied the manifestations of the Cajun renaissance in the state). Between Cable's intervention in the 1890s and renewed academic activity from the late 1970s, the sole examples of English translations of French Creole work were those by African American poet Langston Hughes. In 1958, he included in his *Langston Hughes Reader* two poems from the 1845 anthology *Les Cenelles: Choix de poésies indigènes*, which is the first such work written by Americans of African descent. Armand Lanusse, its editor, had been educated at the École Polytechnique in Paris, and in 1843 had created a literary journal, *L'Album littéraire*, to publish work by Creoles of colour (it was also open to whites). Although the collection is diverse and the project mainly concerned to demonstrate the cultural legitimacy of the community from which it had sprung, it does include for example "Epigramme," a stinging piece by Lanusse on the practice of *plaçage* (the institution of the quadroon mistress explained above), and one of Hughes's selections. The other was Pierre Dalcour's "Vers écrits sur l'album de Mademoiselle ***," a love poem to the bearer of a "brune paupière/dark eyelid." In 1979, Regine Latortue, Professor of Africana Studies at Brooklyn College and then a postgraduate student in French and Francophone Literature at Yale, and Gleason R.W. Adams published a bilingual English-French edition of the collection with G.K. Hall Publishers of Boston. Other than these interventions in African American cultural politics, translations from the 1990s onward have been by academics inserting works by New Orleans writers into, first, debates within American studies (the rediscovery of the multilingual past and indeed present of American literature), African American studies, and, in more limited fashion, the "francophone turn" within French studies, helped by the work of the Editions Tintamarre in republishing nineteenth-century texts at Centenary College upriver from New Orleans in Shreveport. Norman R. Shapiro (2004), a professor of French at Wesleyan University, has translated a wider collection of poetry from that era in *Creole Echoes: The Francophone Poetry of Nineteenth-Century Louisiana*. As Shapiro points out in the preface, these rediscoveries have "dramatically altered our literary timeline" (xxxiv), and he gives the example of Victor Séjour's 1837 short story "Le Mulâtre," which is the first published work of fiction by an African American author, and is in French. Translated by Philip Barnard in 1995 for the *Norton Anthology of American Literature*, and by Andrea Lee in 2001 for *The Multilingual Anthology of American Literature* (Shell and Sollors 2001), its violent denunciation of plantation slavery set on Saint-Domingue, and its murderous rewriting of the family romance in that context, stand in some but not total contrast with the rest of Séjour's work as a successful playwright on the Paris boulevard scene. (Shapiro has translated two of these, *Le Juif de Séville* of 1844 [2002] and *La Tireuse de cartes* of 1860 [2002].)

Clearly, New Orleans as a dual city, with distanced rather than bridged communities, duality unravelling in historical circumstances as extraordinary as those which created it, can be understood in terms of translation only through a very elastic notion of space, and an extensive time lag. To an extent, the very existence of these texts, as much as their content, contribute to transformed perceptions, even as their absence of "minorizing" questioning of metropolitan French (the Atlantic is very much bridged – to Paris – during the relevant period, unlike this time in Quebec history), at the same time posits a radically distinct – and often republican – take on the racial politics of the time.

Surprisingly, perhaps a more fluid example can be found in another nineteenth-century site, and one that, among other characteristics, features a very early manifestation of literary modernism due, in no small part I argue, to questions of translation. In the seven-year period from 1835 to 1842, Montevideo received nearly 33,000 immigrants, of whom over half – nearly 18,000 – were French, more than the next largest groups (Spanish at just over 8,000, Italians at nearly 8,000) combined. In 1843 the French therefore represented over half the foreign population, and a quarter of Montevideo's as a whole. A large majority – 80 per cent – came from the western Pyrenees, that is the French Basque country, Béarn (the area south of Pau), and Bigorre (south-east of Lourdes). Many French immigrants from the southwest to Montevideo, their trades or businesses being squeezed by "modernizing" economic forces even in the mid-nineteenth century, and often began either as manual workers – roadworkers, bricklayers, stevedores, blacksmiths, carpenters – earning two or three times the wages they could earn at home or, in the case of village shopkeepers, setting up as hoteliers, bakers, *traiteurs*, hatmakers, tailors, or cobblers.

Many became upwardly mobile, assimilating well into Uruguayan society, aspiring to and attaining bourgeois comfort. By 1860, the French were still coming but in lower proportions: by then Uruguay's population was 221,000, including 77,000 foreigners, nearly 9,000 of whom were French. These figures underestimate the overall picture. Many had become naturalized Uruguayan citizens: many – such as deserting sailors, those evading military service, indebted shopkeepers, political refugees – were quick to lose their French nationality, and had little truck with French consular officials, especially before 1848. It is estimated that by 1860 more than a third of Uruguay's population, or their parents, had been born in France, and the figures were higher for Montevideo.

Into this mix came the Ducasse family, and the scion, Isidore, "Comte de Lautréamont." Isidore's father, François, was born near Tarbes in the Pyrenees in 1809 to a family of small farmers. By the 1830s he was a primary school teacher, but when local connections brought news of a vacant post as clerk to the French consulate in Montevideo, he left from Bayonne in 1839. François was promoted, and served as *chancelier* at the consulate from 1848 to 1873; Isidore's mother, Célestine-Jacquette Davezac, was born in 1821 and left Sarniguet near Tarbes for Montevideo in 1842, the peak year of French migration there. She married François in February 1846, and Isidore was born the following April; she died in December 1847. At the age of thirteen, Isidore left for the lycée at Tarbes, returning to visit Montevideo in the second half of 1867, where he received support from his father for his project of pursuing a literary career in Paris. The *Chants de Maldoror* were published in 1869 under the pseudonym, and the *Poésies* the following year, under his real name. Isidore Ducasse died in Paris in November 1870 at the age of twenty-four.

So little is known about Ducasse's short life that biographers often spend time sketching in the Montevidean context and then speculating, sometimes desperately, about what influence it had on his poetic development. Thus Edouard Peyrouzet in his *Vie de Lautréamont* (1970) homes in on realities such as the bloody tales of the siege and war that afflicted the city from 1843 to 1851, and the La Plata folklore that Isidore would have heard as a child from servants in a motherless household, as well as the impact of a yellow fever epidemic in Montevideo in February to March 1857 that left nearly 900 dead (Peyrouzet 1970, ch. 2). These factors would supposedly "explain" the violence and fantasy of the *Chants*. The situation is not helped by the work of the Uruguayans Álvaro and Gervasio Guillot-Muñoz (1926), who interviewed in the 1920s persons in Montevideo who allegedly knew Ducasse. Their highly unreliable concoction, full of local colour and enigma that served up to the idolatrous surrealists exactly what they wanted, was reprinted in *La Quinzaine littéraire* in 1972. And yet, after all, Lautréamont does – proudly but ambivalently – proclaim his origins at the end of the first *Chant*: "[The poet] was born on South American shores, at the mouth of the River Plate, where two peoples once enemies now struggle to outdo each other in material and moral progress. Buenos Aires, queen of the south, and Montevideo, the coquette, extend friendly hands across the argentine waters of the great estuary. But everlasting war has imposed his destructive rule upon the fields, and joyfully reaps his countless victims" (Ducasse 1983, 33). In her monumental study of Lautréamont and Mallarmé, Julia Kristeva mentions the Uruguayan connection twice in over 600 pages of text. (Significantly, these are to be found in those sections of the work absent from the 1984 English translation.) The first is embedded in a discussion of Lautréamont's death in the context of the Franco-Prussian war and the Commune that would come several months later. Thus the young Ducasse's childhood had been marked by another war: "That first war awakens in Lautréamont a general condemnation of injustice, for which he blames his father. But, implicitly, the poet is probably marked by it in many ways, if we think of the incessant upheavals of a life and discourse held back by no sense of fixity, unless it is to relaunch them towards other clashes" (Kristeva 1974, 411). In this section of her work, Kristeva draws analogies between the logics behind both the *Poésies* (where, unlike in the *Chants*, there is a positive embrace of the law that is open to both irony and transformation – she makes much of Ducasse's use of his real, father's name) and the Commune (a new, "impossible" positivity, more about movement than the conquest of power).

The second, more significant, reference, is in the section on "La traversée des frontières": "Neither Lautréamont nor Mallarmé possess a French national identity card, in the same way as the subject in process is never identical with itself. The Latin American, born of French parents on the banks of the Rio de la Plata and crossing [Kristeva here writes "perhaps"] the ocean twice, condenses in his own biography that tendency of the textual experience to be transnational as well as trans-subjective" (526). The reputation of *La Révolution du langage poétique* as a founding moment of a (feminist) appropriation of Lacanian psychoanalysis ought not overshadow the fact that it is also a highly sophisticated attempt to articulate relations between text and context, with sustained discussion (largely absent in the truncated English translation) of regime change in France (the end of the Second Empire, the early Third Republic), as well as of republican colonialism, and the development of nineteenth-century capitalism. Her poets' lack of explicitness about politics is surpassed by what is at stake in the nonidentical "subject in process," namely a dialectic between "la sémiotique" and "le symbolique." The "semiotic" is the domain of the pre-Oedipal *chora* associated with the mother's body, drives, and *pulsions*; the "symbolic" is the domain of language, which according to Lacan is structured like the unconscious, a homology thus established between the "lack" inherent to the signifier and the Oedipal castration scenario. The hinge between the two is the "thetic" phase, a break that for Kristeva produces the *position* from which signification is produced. Poetry before Lautréamont was reduced to "a decorative uselessness that challenged none of the subjects of its time" (Kristeva 1984, 83). The "positions of mastery" of capitalism, science, and colonialism needed therefore to be challenged via the unspoken psychic logic on which its order is based: "By signifying the violence of drives in and through codes – moral, scientific, everyday, journalistic, modern, familial, economic ... interminably" (84). Lautréamont's text is thus based on the rejection of the paternal function that underpins language and the social order.

Kristeva's analysis is valuable for its rescue of Lautréamont from the problematically easy canonization he received from Breton and the surrealists. The fundamental split in language and subjectivity that the dominant order disavows is the source of Kristeva's discussion of the dualities in the *Chants de Maldoror*: between Maldoror and the subject of the enunciation, and in the explicit references in the text ("the duality that composes me") (Ducasse 1983, 188): "Thus pluralised, 'I' is no longer an instance," but "a rhythmic movement, un undulating dynamic" (Kristeva 1974, 320), the bisexual, hermaphrodite dimension (470). However, there is an element that Kristeva fundamentally underestimates: Ducasse was bilingual. Her text hints at, but accomplishes a preemptive withdrawal of, this possibility: "If it is true that the cultural referent remains that of the mother tongue," she writes, "that referent undergoes a change of scene [*dépaysement*] which is certainly due to the specific economy of the subject and language, but which is achieved historically thanks to the collapsing of frontiers" (526), which events after 1870 intensified. There are problems here: French is Ducasse's "maternal" language in a problematic but not literal sense, as he barely knew his mother; and if the *Chants de Maldoror* are all about disrupting the paternal function, then to Kristeva's general argument about disruption of paternal language ("the specific economy of the subject and language") needs to be added an understanding of the language of the father as it was experienced in a bilingual context. Moreover, the emphasis on what we would now call "globalizing" developments in capitalism *after* the year of Ducasse's death automatically underestimates that element in his make-up that, quite apart from psychic fissures, makes him a "stranger to himself." The opening sections of Kristeva's *Etrangers à nous-mêmes* (1988), "Toccata and Fugue for the Foreigner," could indeed be revisited with the young Ducasse in mind, pitching up at the lycée de Tarbes in 1859, that site of a legitimate and integrated French national culture and language: the blank "confidence" of the *étranger* caught between humiliation and courage ("I do what *they* want *me* to, but it is not 'me' – 'me' is elsewhere, 'me' belongs to no one, 'me' does not belong to 'me' ... does 'me' exist?") (Kristeva 1991, 8); the "believer" who passionately aims for future success, but also the disillusioned "ironist" (a combination she describes as irreconcilable, except in the poetic ambition of Ducasse?) (10); the "orphan" (21–3).

To build on Kristeva's inchoate notion of *dépaysement*, more recent work on Lautréamont has been devoted to his relationship with Hispanic culture and language. Montevideo in the 1840s and 1850s was a Babel. To the Spanish/French diglossia in the early life of Ducasse can be added the presence of Pyrenean patois among certain recent immigrants; there is speculation that this is likely to have been the main language of his mother, who came from a lower social class than his father. This is Montreal rather than Paris (or Tarbes). A "fusion of horizons," which, along with migration itself, contributes to the unceasing dualization of reality noted earlier: Lautréamont is thus "an author who slips ceaselessly between two space-times, between two opposing ideas"; "any being that goes from the periphery to the centre engenders within itself two mobile and simultaneous instances" (Tachibana 1998, 443).

These dualizations, and the further splittings they evoke, permit the juxtaposition of heterogeneities, and a concomitant defamiliarization of language and its relation to the real: "The bilingual person maintains in their attitude to language that attention to the signifier that is typical of children, when they learn new words, and of poets, who keep forever that attention and that enjoyment. Whereas the monolingual person makes an indissoluble association between word and idea, the bilingual always conserves the 'sight' and 'hearing' of each signifier, in all its materiality and arbitrariness"[1] (Perrone-Moisés and Monegal 2001, 78). If Isidore thus had an "external" appreciation of French, this was also the case for his relationship to French literary culture, and this becomes clear via a translation. It is known, via annotations he made – in Spanish, as "Isidoro" – on a Spanish translation of the *Iliad*, that he was at least as familiar with the Spanish poetic tradition. Josef Gómez de Hermosilla (1771–1837), despite the anachronistic neo-classicist precepts of his 1827 *Arte de hablar*, which dominated the teaching of poetics and rhetoric in the hispanophone world in the nineteenth century, produced a translation of Homer that was much bloodier and violent than those that existed in French. The young Ducasse was therefore certainly familiar with the traditions of Spanish baroque poetry such as that of Balbuena and Lope de Vega. The authoritarian interlocutor of the *Chants* is associated with the kind of scholarly discourses Ducasse would have encountered at the lycée de Tarbes, whose *sixième* class he entered at the age, behind by two years, of thirteen. At one level, the tussle in the *Chants* can be read as that between a French classical tradition and baroque excess. We have seen that Ducasse in France can be seen as both *ironiste* and *croyant*. One side of the duality of his existence there, the foreigner/outsider whose word lacks support from his social environment, could therefore also be seen as partaking of the baroque, if Kristeva (1991, 22) is to be believed: "Under such conditions, if it does not founder into silence, it becomes absolute in its formalism, excessive in its sophistication – rhetoric is dominant, the foreigner is a baroque person. Gracián [Baltasar Gracián y Morales, 1601–1658, whose *Criticón* portrays France as a land of hypocrites and lunatics] and Joyce had to be foreigners." Even "Maldoror" is likely to have an origin in Spanish: *matador*, *mal dolor*, *mal olor*, mal d'horror, the Uruguayan place name Maldonado. There are numerous hispanisms: "get this into to your head" (*mets-te-le dans la tête = météTelo* or *póntelo en la cabeza*) (Ducasse 1983, 71); "remember this well" (*rappelle-toi-le bien = recuérdetelo bien*) (27); "can you possibly be breathing still?" (*est-ce possible que tu sois encore respirant? = ¿es posible que estés aún respirando?*) (119).

Lautréamont is in the lineage of an Atlantic minorization of French language and culture. As Deleuze and Guattari argue, bilingualism is simply a convenience here. Like Kafka writing German in a bilingual Prague, Ducasse was located in a nexus of major and minor forces and positions. French was a major language, the age of the second French overseas empire was approaching, and there were neo-colonial elements in the cultural and economic relations with South America. But in Montevideo French was in a minority, and even if some stable Uruguayan "French" had subsisted, it would have been "minor" in relation to that of metropolitan French, witness the case of Quebec. In addition, Pyrenean patois was also present. Thus Ducasse/Lautréamont was in the business of constructing "a continuum of variation, negotiating all of the variables [*variables*] both to constrict the constants and to expand the variables [*variations*]: make language stammer, or make it "wail," stretch tensors through all of language, even written language, and draw from it cries, shouts, pitches, durations, timbres, accents, intensities" (Deleuze and Guattari 1988, 104). This, and Edouard Glissant's (1996, 40) notion of writing "in the presence of all the world's languages," is the (Atlantic) key to Lautréamont's treatment of French.

Finally, let us return to the instances of translation that are common to these examinations of our dual cities. We have seen the comparative questioning of two languages and *doxas*, the disruption of "major" languages' claims to mastery and even hegemony, and the probing of language itself. Moreover, it is clear that the translation events – that of francophone Louisiana literature into English, of ancient Greek into Spanish and also French – have "added value" to these processes. One source for understanding this is to be found in work by a bilingual citizen of that eminently French Atlantic space that is Montreal. Charles Taylor (1995, 231), inspired by Gadamer's notion of the "fusion of horizons," writes of "learning to move in a broader horizon, where what we once took for granted as the background to valuation can be situated as one possibility alongside the different background of the unfamiliar culture."

However, it is possible to push beyond a potentially liberal-democratic understanding of these words and invoke Jacques Rancière's (2006, 152) notion of *le partage du sensible*, the partition or distribution of the sensible that sets the horizons of perception along which a common world, such as that of the city or *polis*, can be shared and grasped: "Politics resembles art in one essential point. Like art, politics also cuts into that great metaphor where words and images are continuously sliding in and out of each other to produce the sensory evidence of a world in order. And, like art, it constructs novel combinations of words and actions, it shows words borne by bodies in movement to make them audible, to produce another articulation of the visible and sayable." The work of translation literally renders audible, readable, and sayable that which could not be heard, read, or uttered by the other linguistic community. Changes to the conventions of meaning thus have political relevance because they form part of that movement of *dissensus* that reveals a hitherto excluded and repressed (invisible, inaudible, unsayable) social reality. Theories of consensus presuppose a common language in the literal and figural sense, whereas *dissensus* is a speaking out of turn: the "broader horizon" of the two linguistic worlds here becomes (or can become, depending on context), a "lodging" of one world into another, a rewriting of the distribution of the sensible via a demonstration of "a possible world where the argument could count as argument ... the construction of a paradoxical world that relates two separate worlds" (Rancière 2001).

In this chapter, we have seen these processes at work in relation to the place of African Americans in literary history; in an alternative, French Atlantic understanding of race relations and slavery; or in a baroque, excessive challenge to French classicism or even patriarchy. Indeed, Rancière (2011, 45) writes, "An art is never just an art: it is always at the same time the proposal of a world [*proposition de monde*]. And its formal procedures are often the remains of utopias which, more than the spectator's pleasure, aimed for the redistribution of the forms of collective sensible experience." The fundamentally urban origins of this promise raise further questions about the ways in which translation in these contexts negotiates the aesthetic and the political in its production of the new.

NOTE

1 See also Perrone-Moisés and Monegal (1983).

11

Antônio de Alcantâra Machado's *Brás, Bexiga e Barra Funda* as a Translation of São Paulo during Brazilian Modernism

ROCH DUVAL

> E é esta mescla de italiano e brasileiro que, prevalecendo sobre as outras raças – hespanhola, syria, allemã, franceza e outras – vae fixar o typo do paulista, do brasileiro futuro, nessas paragens da patria.
>
> Antônio Carneiro Leão, *S. Paulo em 1920*[1]

MODERNISM, LANGUAGE, AND IDENTITY

On 7 September 1922, the centennial of Brazil's founding was commemorated with great fanfare. Behind the glitz and glamour surrounding the event, O Centenário da Independência do Brasil (Centenary of Brazil's independence) altered the country's fate. This highly patriotic commemoration was a time to boast about the huge progress made over the past century, especially during the Second Empire (1840–90), and to shower Benjamin Constant Botelho de Magalhães (1833–1891) with praise for his constant efforts to introduce the Brazilian mind to progressive European ideas. It was also the perfect opportunity for politicians, intellectuals, and artists from all walks of life to celebrate a national identity in the making and take a stand in favour of what Mário de Andrade (1893–1945) terms *abrasileirar o Brasil* (to brazilianize Brazil) (Duarte 1971, 301). De Andrade foresaw that *abrasileirar a língua brasileira* (to brazilianize the Brazilian language) was an inescapable phase of this all-encompassing process of identity formation.[2]

This emotional call to brazilianize the (Brazilian) Portuguese language paralleled the desire to break all ties with the colonial past or, at least, with a debilitating feeling of subjection to the former rulers. According to the advocates of Brazilian modernism, the time was ripe to stop mimicking European culture, and particularly its prevalent aesthetic models. In the words of essayist Francisco de Assis Barbosa (1914–1991), "O principal objetivo dos modernistas era destruir o convencionalismo literário, desmoralizar a inteligência empalhada, acabar com os medalhões da cultura" (1988, 39: The main objective of [the] modernists was to eradicate literary conventionalism, discredit the embalmed intelligence and rid the culture of its pundits). More precisely, the modernists' main targets were, among others, figureheads of the neo-Parnassian movement such as Manuel Said Ali (1861–1953), Henrique Maximiano Coelho Neto (1864–1934), and Olavo Bilac (1865–1918).

The advent of Brazilian modernism coincided with a period of intense technological development in which unbridled industrialization drastically redefined the social fabric as a whole and gave rise to a new aesthetic movement – allegedly inspired by Italian futurism (Lages 2003)[3] and cubism – able to reflect upon and understand the era's *Zeitgeist*. Population growth; urban expansion; the emergence of a middle class that made its fortune in coffee growing culture and trade; a significant influx of immigrants; radical changes in social roles and labour; development of new means of transportation; and the emergence of new media, among many other factors, attracted the modernists' attention. A cult for speed, cities, skyscrapers, cars, airplanes, and mechanization, among other things, featured within this new aesthetic.[4] From the 1922 Semana de Arte Moderna (Modern art week),[5] the predominant and conservative view of the world, deeply rooted in rural and patriarchal society, was shattered, and modernist converts vehemently discredited symbols of the past.[6]

Although there are clear differences between the content and the concrete expression of avant-garde movements in Argentina and Brazil,[7] these two neighbouring countries shared a common element: the emergence of a new type of discourse, in particular during the 1920s, in which cities – both in their sheer materiality and in their unsettledness – became symbolic representations of translating modernity. As such symbols, and as two of the largest and most cosmopolitan cities in 1920s South America, Buenos Aires and São Paulo[8] were also sites of intense immigration (especially Italian), and so it is no wonder that their soundscapes – exemplified by the ceaseless interplay, and sometimes clash, between languages from all corners of the world – became a defining characteristic of urban sites.[9]

Where São Paulo and Buenos Aires differ is in the treatment the Italian language received from the mid-nineteenth century up to the end of the 1920s. In Buenos Aires, site of the interplay between Rioplatanese Spanish and Italian, there was, on one hand, the rise of a type of macaronic language surreptitiously relegated to a derogatory dialect (*cocoliche*), habitually used in vaudeville to mock Italian immigrants, and, on the other hand, the rise of a *lunfardo*, a sociolect characteristic of Bonaerense[10] slums and the underworld of *cafishos* (pimps), *linyeras* (bums), and *borrachitos* (drunkards) vividly portrayed in tango music. In São Paulo, through the urban chronicles penned by Antônio de Alcântara Machado (1901–1935) in *Brás, Bexiga e Barra Funda*,[11] there is rather a kind of *wertfrei* (nonjudgmental) and descriptive presentation of the macaronic (i.e., Brazilian oral language interspersed with Italian words or grammar, deforming and interfering with the original Luso-Portuguese discourse) language in force.[12]

In fact, the intent behind Machado's use of this nascent macaronic language can be interpreted in two ways. The first was, in conformity with the project to *abrasileirar o Brasil*, to shape São Paulo as a symbolic representation or an aural translation of the modernist spirit by identifying the emergent and hectic city as the the *locomotiva do Brasil* (Brazilian steam engine). The second was to recognize the role of the inter-relations between Luso-Portuguese and Italian in the making of a genuine Brazilian language in order to be consonant with Mário de Andrade's agenda to *abrasileirar a lingua brasileira.*

Let us now turn to Machado's *Brás, Bexiga e Barra Funda* as both a modernist attempt at *abrasileirar a língua brasileira* in welcoming a significant Other (namely the Italian immigrant and language) and also as an endeavour to aurally translate São Paulo.

THE INSOLENT MODERNITY OF *BRÁS, BEXIGA E BARRA FUNDA*

Machado once wrote, "Só as grandes cidades sabem rir" (1934, 2: Only big cities can laugh). He was not wrong. The emergence of modernist urban chronicles coincides with the search for new means of expression to better capture the inventiveness, humour, and elusiveness of *desvairada* (frantic) São Paulo at a turning point in its history. The main characteristic of urban chronicles is that they capture cities' dynamism and expansiveness in a radical new way. It is not surprising that many Brazilian modernists seized upon those chronicles as a medium to translate and express that sense of urgency.

It is also not surprising that many of these modernist urban chroniclers were journalists. Machado – and contemporaries such as Guilherme de Almeida (1890–1969) and Menotti del Pichhia (1892–1988)[13] – were anxious to witness the passage of time in a city devoid of landmarks, and the best way to capture the prevalent ephemerality, the eternal newness, was to put the day-to-day scenes of the city down on paper. For Machado, these daily scenes included the aural/oral dimension of the hybrid language that was spoken in São Paulo at the time.

Even if Machado did not take part in the groundbreaking Semana de Arte Moderna[14] in February 1922 in the Teatro Municipal (Municipal theatre) in São Paulo, he nevertheless proves himself, in retrospect, to be one of the most prominent Brazilian modernists. In fact, at the age of only nineteen, he was among the group of hostile and offended students who stormed the Teatro Municipal in order to protest the Semana de Arte Moderna while this emblematic modernist's celebration was in full swing (Barbosa 1988, 21).[15]

Machado began to publish articles in *Jornal do Comércio* as a theatre critic.[16] (The newspaper welcomed texts propagating the modernist credo.) At that time, he befriended Oswald de Andrade, a figurehead of the *Modernismo Brasileiro* and still at the height of his fame. We can speculate that the author of *Pau-Brasil* played an active role in Machado's conversion to modernism. During the golden age of modernism, between 1926 and 1928, Machado contributed to many (short-lived and sometimes eclectic) modernist journals and magazines, including *Terra Roxa e outras terras* (1926),[17] *Revista de Antropofagia* (1928–29),[18] *Revista Verde* (published sporadically 1927–29), and *Revista Nova* (1931–32), which he founded with Paulo Prado (1869–1943) and Mário de Andrade when modernism was already moribund in the 1930s. It is worth mentioning that in 1929 he had an ideological falling out with Oswald, befriended Mário, the other titan of modernism, and together they became the target of Oswald's attacks. In any case, the unity and heterogeneity of *Modernismo Brasileiro* were already threatened by internal dissension. The first, heroic phase of modernism was over.

Machado's novels in particular made him a respected and popular modernist author. *Pathé-Baby* (1926),[19] his first book and a collection of modernist travel chronicles inspired, to an extent, by Oswald's *Memórias Sentimentais de João Miramar* (1924),[20] displays virtually all of his modernist stylistic devices: short sentences; nervous writing; telegraphic, direct, and conversational style; clear predominance of action over psychological descriptions; journalistic writing; use of different fonts; and typography that mimics billboards and illustrations by Antonio Paim Vieira (1895–1988).[21] Many of these devices are apparent in the following excerpt: "No centro, o vapor apita e a Tower Bridge escancara-se. À direita, sobre o oceano de telhados se espraia a fumaça suja das fábricas. Em baixo, a multidão tapa as calçadas. Vendedores ambulantes. Berros. Rangidos" (Machado 1926, 80: In the centre of the city, the steamer whistles and Tower Bridge opens up widely. On the right, the dirty smoke of factories spreads over the sea of roofs. Below, the crowd hits the pavement. Hawkers. Shouts. Creaks.).

The title *Pathé-Baby* refers to a 9.5 mm home film system of the same name that went on the market in 1922. In an obvious aim to revolutionize the prose of *belles-lettres* (high literature), Machado went even further than the modernist poetic experiment Blaise Cendrars attempted in *Documentaires au Kodak* (1924).[22] Machado purposefully traded the Kodak for a film system in order to suggest speed, nervousness, and movement within his writing style. He preferred the moving images, instability, and quickness of the portable filming device to the static pictures of photography, and using it allowed him to pay tribute to the modernist cult of speed, machinery, and manufactured goods. With the title of *Pathé-Baby*, he transformed the Pathé-Baby film system into a kind of prosthesis of his own eyes that enabled him to capture the hectic nature, fragmentedness, and simultaneity of urban life.

Pathé-Baby was an important step in Machado's literary career. For the first time, the city became one of his favourite themes. From a theatre critic in *Jornal do Comércio*, he gradually transmuted himself into a modernist urban chronicler. Before undertaking his trip to Europe, he published three short stories – *Gaetaninho* (25 January 1925), *Carmela* (1 March 1925), and *Lisetta* (8 March 1925) – in the same newspaper. At the time, these pieces were presented as likely to appear in a book project entitled *Italo-Paulistas*.[23] Instead, they are among the eleven that make up *Brás, Bexiga e Barra Funda*. According to one of Machado's critics, "Esse escritor-flâneur capturou em suas histórias a nova espacialization e temporalidade da urbe tornando-se o prosador urbano de uma paulicéia já desvairada" (Carmo 2004, 16: This writer-

flâneur captured in his stories the new spatialization and temporality of the city by becoming an urban prose-writer of an already frantic[24] *paulicéia*[25]).

Machado's European experience in 1925 allowed him to develop a modernist style of writing to better grasp the spatial, fragmented, and hectic dimensions of the cities he visited in Europe.[26] With *Brás, Bexiga e Barra Funda,* Machado went a step further than *Pathé-Baby*.

BRÁS, BEXIGA E BARRA FUNDA AS URBAN CHRONICLE

In order to deal with the (quasi-)widespread diglossia in São Paulo – once called *a cidade dos italianos* – in the 1920s, the next natural step for Machado was to transpose – but not without some improvements – the telegraphic and photographic writing style he used in his first book to his second, this time to capture the city's dynamic and aural dimensions. If *Pathé-Baby* evoked the era of silent movies, *Brás, Bexiga e Barra Funda* evokes the emergence of sound movies.[27] Though the first talkie – *The Jazz Singer* – appeared in 1927, earlier cinematic devices had combined sound and image, including the Vitagraph in 1925 and the Vitaphone in 1926. Consequently, it is possible that as early as 1925 and his three published short stories, he had contemplated the idea of combining the photographic impression of Cendrars's *Documentaires au Kodak* and the moving impressions of *Pathé-Baby* in a writing style that anticipated the creation of a narrative frame similar to that of talkies.

What predominated in *Brás, Bexiga e Barra Funda* was the recording and editing of what the author saw and heard in the city, as well as the swift physical movements that were occurring on the urban territory. Consequently, what comes to the fore in the collection is a visual and aural/oral description – acting as symbolic translation – of the continual interplay between Luso-Portuguese, trying to break free from Parnassianism and academicism's shackles imposed by outdated and rigid European models in order to find its own identity, as well as the Italian language of the immigrants in their effort to domesticate the Brazilian language in the making.

Machado was right when he wrote, "E o jornal deve ser um resumo do mundo. Lido num instante, num instante esquecido" (1934, 2: And the newspaper must be a summary of the world. Read in an instant, and forgotten the next). It is precisely this quality of chronicles – their ephemerality – that allowed them to translate or to capture the haecceity of São Paulo in the 1920s. The urban chronicle as a modernist literary genre "não tem pretensões a durar, uma vez que é filha do jornal e da era da máquina, onde tudo acaba tão depressa" (Candido 1980, 24: has no pretension to last, because it is the daughter of newspaper and the age of the machine, where everything ends so fast).

The originality of *Brás, Bexiga e Barra Funda* stems from the fact that Machado presented his stories as if they were news articles. At that time, no one could imagine that a columnist would use such a writing style to express ideas in a book. Urban chronicles belonged in newspapers, not books, and crossing the line between these heterogeneous mediums was unthinkable. Because of this, Machado (1988, 77) upheld that *Brás, Bexiga e Barra Funda* "não nasceu livro: nasceu jornal. Estes contos não nasceram contos: nasceram notícias" (was not born book, it was born newspaper. These tales were not born stories, they were born news). He added, in an audaciously provocative gesture, that the book's preface was not born a preface but an *artigo de fundo* (leading article). In this leading article he expressed the main ideas behind his modernist agenda.

As early as 1924, in "O que eu disse a um comediógrafo Nacional," Machado referred obliquely to the *abrasileirar o Brasil* agenda. In this article, he maintained that it was important to brazilianize, or more precisely "SaoPaulistanize," Brazilian theatre. We can deduce from this early text that the project to SaoPaulistanize all sectors of the cultural life – and Brazil in general – was underway. In other words, many of the elements that appeared later in *Brás, Bexiga e Barra Funda* were already present in this early version, as the following excerpt from the piece shows:

> Abrasileiremos o teatro brasileiro. Melhor: apaulistanizêmo-lo. Fixemos no palco o instante radioso de febre e de esforço que vivemos. As personagens e os enredos são encontradiços, nesta terra de São Paulo, como os taxis, nas ruas de todos os bairros, procurando passageiros, quer dizer, autores ... Olhe: aí vai um, com a bandeirinha vermelha içada. Está livre. É toma-lo! É toma-lo! Não vê? Ali, ao longo do muro da fábrica. O casal de italianinhos. Ele se despede, agora. Logo mais vem buscá-la. Um belo dia mata-a. Traga este drama de todos os dias para a cena. Traga para o palco a luta do operário, a desgraça do operário, traga a oficina inteira. Pronto, ali vai outro. É um cavalheiro gordo, de gestos duros e gravata vermelha. Ontem engraxate; hoje industrial.

A escalada deste homem é o mais empolgante dos enredos teatrais. Dê passagem a mais este que ali vem. É um grileiro. Resume toda a epopéia da terra roxa. Saíu da cidade cheio de audácia; voltou do sertão cheio de títulos. Anhangüera moderno, mais inteligente, mais feliz. Atenção: mais um. Sim, mais um que passa. Nasceu na Itália. Três anos de idade: São Paulo. Dez anos: vendedor de jornais. Vinte anos: bicheiro. Trinta anos: chefe político, juiz de paz, candidato a vereador. (Machado 1988, 434–35: Let us brazilianize Brazilian Theatre! Even better: "SaoPaulistanize" it! Let's capture on stage the radiant moment of fever and effort we live. In this land of São Paulo, the characters and the plots are commonplace, like taxis on the streets of every neighbourhood looking for passengers, I mean, authors ... Look, here's one coming with the red flag hoisted. It's available. Take it! Take it! Don't you see it? There, along the factory wall. The couple of *Italianinho*.[28] He says good-bye, now. He'll fetch her soon. One day he kills her. Bring this everyday drama to the stage. Bring to the stage the workers' struggle, the misery of the workers, bring the entire workshop. There's another one coming right now. It's a fat gentleman, with a stern face and a red tie. Shoe-shiner yesterday; industrialist today.

The professional advancement of this man is the most exciting of theatrical plots. Give way to the other who's coming. He's a land-grabber. He summarizes the entire epic of the *terra roxa*. He left the city filled with high ambition; he came back from the *sertão* with an array of titles. A modern impostor,[29] more intelligent, happier. Watch out, another one. Yes, another one is coming. He was born in Italy. When he was three: São Paulo. At ten: newsboy. At twenty: lottery ticket vendor.[30] At thirty: political leader, magistrate, candidate for mayor.)

In this excerpt, some elements require special attention. Machado's use of neologisms (*apaulistazimô-lo*), popular language (*italianinho*, *Anhangüera*,[31] *bicheiro*[32]), and terms that evoke modernity and industrial urban life (*abrasileirar*, *taxi*, *fábrica*, *Anhangüera*) are irrefutable evidence of his modernist prose-writing. His prose evokes a disjointed, terse, telegraphic writing style. He uses the verb *fixemos* (let's fix), belonging to the lexicon of photography. He also uses terms that allude to São Paulo's hectic nature and chaotic frenzy ("instante radioso de febre e de esforço que vivemos"). Finally, he mentions the social unrest that marked São Paulo in the 1920s ("traga para o palco a luta do operário, a desgraça do operário, traga a oficina inteira"). The only element missing from a full description of modernist São Paulo is the aural/oral dimension of the city, found in *Brás, Bexiga e Barra Funda.*

Machado recalled Brazil's racial history in a few words. When the first settlers arrived and mixed with the Indians, the *mamalucos* (Brazilian mestizo) were born. Later, when the African slaves came to Brazil, they intermarried with the Indians and the European settlers, and so the second generation of *mamalucos* came to be. At the time, according to local popular belief, the common thread between these three groups was melancholy. During the great European migration, however, Brazil welcomed a merrier race: the Italians. They contributed to the emergence of the new *mamalucos*, and so "Nasceram os Italianinhos" (Machado 1988, 78: the Italo-Brazilians were born). Machado wanted to recount the day-to-day and concrete stories of these Italian immigrants in São Paulo, because they carried with them the values and virtues of the heroic *Bandeirantes* (Portuguese settlers in Brazil).

In *Brás, Bexiga e Barra Funda*, Machado depicts the daily life of Italian immigrants in a macaronic style. His stories written in the emerging Brazilian-Portuguese language are peppered with words that phonetically imitate the way Italian immigrants' grappled with the language of their new country. Besides Italianisms such as "*andiamo*," "*repito*," "*orra meu*," "*ciao*" (written "*tchau*" in Luso-Portuguese), and "*amore*," mixed or hybrid words that combine Italian and Portuguese appear in Machado's stories (Machado 1988, 87, 99, 85, 93). In the phrase "Ia *dimenticando de dizer*" (99), for example, one verb is Italian (*dimenticare*, forget) while the other is Portuguese (*dizer*, say); in standard Portuguese, it would read "*esqueci de dizer*." The same mix is apparent in the phrase "*Domani, na outra semana, quando quiser*" (98). Here "*domani*" is an Italian word that means "tomorrow." Occasionally, Machado plays with the language and it is not clear whether or not the word he uses retains an Italian or a Portuguese significance. In "Gaetinho" (Little Caetano) – a short story in *Brás, Bexiga e Barra Funda* – it is not clear if the verb "amassou" in the sentence "Amassou o bonde" derives from the Italian verb *ammazzare* (to kill) or from the Portuguese verb *amassar* (to knead, to deform, to squash). Examples of this type abound in *Brás, Bexiga e Barra Funda*. Machado's stories are a perfect example of the interplay between two communities/languages.

During the massive influx of Italian immigrants to São Paulo, the language that was spoken in predominantly Italian neighbourhoods was neither Italian nor Portuguese; it was a mix of both. The qualities of the language spoken in Brás, Bexiga, and Barra Funda are particular. The Italian immigrants had, for instance, difficulty with the plural form of Portuguese words (because in Italian the plural form is not marked by an enclitic "s" as in Portuguese), the palatization of certain phonemes such as "di" or "ti," etc. The following excerpt from an Adorinan Barbosa (1910–1982) song highlights the main characteristics of the language that was –and, to a certain extent, is – spoken in São Paulo, especially in Mooca: "U arnestu nus convidô prum samba/eli mora nu brais" instead of "O Ernesto nos convidou para um samba/ele mora no Brás" (Ernesto invited us to a samba/he lives in Brás). Other examples are "*nois vai*" instead of "*nos vamos*" (we go) or "*eu não vou pedí*" instead of "*eu não vou pedir*" (I won't ask).

Besides the aural/oral transcription of the hybrid language that Italian immigrants spoke in these neighbourhoods, *Brás, Bexiga e Barra Funda* made the most of all the stylistic devices of modernism compared to other texts of the same period. Different typefaces are used to convey different types of emotion. The replication of the typography used in advertising posters or storefronts is noteworthy. "As casas de modas – AO CHIC PARISIENSE, SÃO PAULO PARIS, PARIS ELEGANTE" (Machado 1988, 82–83: Fashion houses – at Parisian Chic, São Paulo Paris, Stylish Paris). For the sake of realism, real parts of the city are named: Rua do Oriente (a street in Brás), (Graveyard) Araçá (in Sumaré), Parque Antártica (a football stadium in Barra Funda), etc. Like the photographs of Militão Azevedo (1837–1905) that capture numerous scenes of São Paulo at the turn of the last century, *Brás, Bexiga e Barra Funda* is a unique account of a frantic and evanescent São Paulo. In this sense, Machado's dialogues in the collection help revive conversations and voices of the past.

CONCLUSION

In Brazil – and particularly in São Paulo – a massive influx of immigrants in the late nineteenth and early twentieth centuries had a lasting effect on economic and cultural life. Within the realm of literature, Brazilian modernism was especially sensitive to changes induced by the interplay between a large set of foreign languages and native dialects (such as *caipira*) on the one hand, and Portuguese (which was the language of the colonizers) on the other hand. Brazilian modernists, in a concerted effort to emancipate themselves from the language of the Portuguese rulers – an elitist language totally disconnected from the Brazilian-Portuguese vernacular –struggled to create a national literature representative of a country in search of its own identity as it grappled with unrestrained industrialization and urbanization. Mário de Andrade's groundbreaking collection of poems *Paulicéia desvairada* (1922) was an attempt to capture and express the changing nature of language. Prompted by *Pauliécia desvairada*, Machado adhered to the Brazilian modernist movement and became a zealous exponent of its aesthetic agenda. He was the first modernist who attempted to thoroughly and radically transpose Mário de Andrade's poetic experiments into prose – a task he undertook in his own collection of short stories, *Brás, Bexiga e Barra Funda*, in which he captured the minutiae of daily life in 1920s São Paulo. Moreover, the dialogue featured in his urban chronicles was mostly written in a macaronic literary style characteristic of how Italian immigrants spoke Brazilian oral language interspersed with Italian words or grammar, interfering with the original Luso-Portuguese language. And in so doing, they indirectly influenced that language.

In Brazil, Machado was not the first author to refer to the way Italian immigrants strived to communicate with their fellow citizens on a daily basis. The pre-modernist Alexandre Ribeiro Marcondes Machado (1892–1933), alias Juó Bananére, was the first to insert an imaginary language mimicking the way Italians spoke Luso-Portuguese into his chronicles, which were featured in *O Pirralho* magazine, and elsewhere, in the 1910s. However, the intent behind Juó Bananére's stylistic device was more ironic or satirical than purely descriptive (as was the case with Machado). For this reason, the chronicles included in *Brás, Bexiga e Barra Funda* are still considered a genuine kind of intersemiotic translation of 1920s São Paulo.

Although European – and especially Italian – immigration drastically declined after the World War II, nowadays Brazilian citizens of Italian descent still foster the idea that their *linguajar* (idiosyncratic mode of speaking) – namely *mooquês*, the *linguajar* characteristic of Mooca's *prefeitura* (administrative district) – should be preserved as intangible cultural heritage. Under the impulse of Juscelino Gadelha – Mooca *vereador* (city councillor) since 2005 – a proposal was submitted to the Conselho Municipal de Preservação do Patrimônio Histórico e Ambiental da Cidade de São Paulo (Municipal council for the preservation of the historic and environmental heritage of the city of São Paulo) in which *mooquês* was presented as a candidate for Unesco's list of intangible cultural heritage, though it was ultimately not accepted.

Much like the macaronic language (standing as a synecdoche and a symbolic representation of 1920s São Paulo) in Machado's *Brás, Bexiga e Barra Funda*, the aforementioned anecdote about *mooquês* points to the fact that language is a very sensitive issue in Brazil. Similarly, the fact that São Paulo has been home to the Museu da Língua Portuguesa (Museum of the Portuguese language) since 2006[33] suggests that Brazilians perceive their language, in all its dimensions and declensions, as an important part of their cultural identity. It should come as no surprise, then, that one of the Museu's objectives is to teach citizens that they are the genuine "owners and active agents of the Portuguese language."[34] In agreement with this objective, Machado's collection of tales in *Brás, Bexiga e Barra Funda* is to be perceived as a factual testimony of the role Italian immigrants played in the elaboration of a Brazilian language representative of São Paulo.

NOTES

1 Leão 1920, 13: It is this mix of Italian and Brazilian races, prevailing over other stocks – Spanish, Syrian, German, French and many others – that will determine the paulista type, of the Brazil to come, in this corner of the country. All translations are mine, unless otherwise indicated. The wording and spelling of this epigraph were not modernized. My special thanks go to Christal Chikani for stylistic improvements and corrections.

2 For a long time, Oswald de Andrade toyed with the idea of publishing a grammar of the Brazilian language. Unfortunately, his *Gramatiquinha da fala brasileira* was not published in his lifetime. To read Andrade's unfinished project, refer to Pinto (1990).

3 Oswald de Andrade brought Filippo Tommaso Marinetti's (1876–1944) *Manifesto del Futurismo* (1909) back to Brazil (particularly to São Paulo) in 1912 after a stay in Europe. It should be noted, however, that two previous translations of the manifesto appeared in two newspapers, first 5 June 1909 in Natal, and then 30 December 1909 in São Salvador da Bahia. They were respectively penned by Manuel Dantas (in *A República*) and Almachio Diniz (in *Jornal de notícias*), but they practically went unheeded. Cosmopolite São

Paulo provided fertile ground for the dissemination of futurism. The so-called *Futurismo Paulistano* was sometimes erroneously associated with Italian futurism. Consequently, before and after the Semana de Arte Moderna, some modernists took great pains to dissociate themselves from Italian futurism. Mário de Andrade in 1921 and Menotti del Picchia in his daily chronicles in the *Correio Paulistano* are among the most representative of this trend (see Barreirinhas 1983; Fabris 1994; Castro 2008).

4 Even though, on 5 April 1909, the Nicaraguan poet Rubén Darió published the first Spanish translation of Marinetti's manifesto in the prestigious Bonaerense newspaper *La Nación*, with the exception of the Chilean poet Vicente Huidobrod (1893–1948), futurism did not have the same impact on the rest of South American culture as it did on the Brazilian culture.

5 The key ideas of *paulista futurismo* were formulated during a banquet organized by Menotti del Picchia in the Trianon, 9 January 1921. Trianon and Villa Kyrial were highly esteemed places where the paulista intelligentsia gathered.

6 Paulo Menotti del Picchia's poem *Juca Mulato* (1917) was a poignant illustration of the clash between the traditional agrarian society and the rise of an industrial society in Brazil.

7 Refer to Miceli (2003, 2011).

8 While there were 677,000 inhabitants in Buenos Aires in 1900 and close to two million in 1930 (Mahieux 2011, 34), there were only 579,033 in São Paulo in 1920. It is important to stress here that even if Rio de Janeiro was more populous than São Paulo (1,147,599 inhabitants in 1920), it had less international immigration.

9 Examples of linguistic hybridization in Brazil in the first half of the twentieth century include the macaronic German/Portuguese satiric texts that were published in *O Pirallho* (*O Birallha. Xornal Allemong*) between 1911 and 1914 (in São Paulo) and in the Carioca newspaper *Manhã* (*Zublemmend to Alle ... manho*) between 1927 and 1947.

10 "From Buenos Aires."

11 Brás, Bexiga (or Bixiga), and Barra Funda refer to districts of São Paulo that were predominantly populated by Italian immigrants from Calabria, Venice, and Campania.

12 Roberto Arlt did almost the same thing in his urban chronicles *Aguafuertes porteñas*, published in *El Mundo* between 1928 and 1942. His intent was to portray the influence of "foreign" languages on Buenos Aires Spanish. Even though critics claimed that Arlt was unable to write properly it must be observed that Machado's aim (and aesthetic project) was larger and bolder.

13 The son of an Italian immigrant himself, Menotti del Picchia penned urban chronicles under the pseudonym Hélios in the *Correio Paulistano* between 1920 and 1930.

14 This cultural event marked the start of Brazilian modernism.

15 After a long period of neglect by scholars of Brazilian modernism, Machado and especially *Brás, Bexiga e Barra Funda* finally regained the prestige to which they were duly entitled. Among the scholars who helped lend credibility to his entire works, Cecília de Lara (1987) and Maria Inez Machado Borges Pinto (1999, 2001) must be mentioned.

16 After graduating from faculty of law, 4 April 1923, Machado had a change of heart and chose to become a journalist. Upon the recommendation of his friend Mário Guastini (1884–1949), he began to publish articles. A journalist and skilled polemicist, Guastini (2006) was also a fierce opponent of modernism.

17 Only six editions were issued.

18 Divided in two periods (or *dentição*, dentition), and a total of eleven editions were issued.

19 The texts included in *Pathé-Baby* were previously published in *Jornal do Comércio* in 1925. In fact, they were originally travel chronicles that he wrote during his eight-month trip to Europe between 25 March 1925 and 3 November 1925. As Cecília de Lara (1986) notes, the travel chronicles were rewritten with slight modifications before they appeared in February 1926 in *Pathé-Baby*.

20 Oswald de Andrade wrote *Pathé-Baby*'s introduction.

21 Besides Machado's book, he also illustrated many modernist poetry anthologies such as Guilherme de Almeida's *Meu* (1925) and Menotti del Picchia's *As máscaras* (1919).

22 Blaise Cendrars was a close ally to the Brazilian modernists. He made his first trip to Brazil, his "Utopiland," in 1924. Machado gave Cendrars an autographed copy of *Pathé-Baby* during his second visit in 1926. The purpose behind Cendrars's reference to the term Kodak in the title of his poetry collection was to introduce a new type of poetry intended to stand as verbal photographs.

23 Oswald and Mário de Andrade encouraged him to publish *Brás, Bexiga e Barra Funda*. It is also important to note that the impending publication of the collection was announced in *Pathé-Baby*'s table of contents: "Brevemente! Braz, Bexiga e Barra Funda (Contos) Brevemente!" (Soon! Braz, Bexiga e Barra Funda (tales) soon!). In a resolutely modernist style, the contents' design mimics film poster typography.

24 *Paulicéia desvairada* is the name of a famous book by Mário de Andrade, which was translated in English as *São Paulo Hallucinated* by Jack E. Tomlins in 1968. I prefer "frantic" as a translation of *desvairada*.

25 A nickname for São Paulo.

26 Las Palmas, Lisbon, Cherboug, Paris, London, Milano, Venice, Florence, Bologna, Pisa, Lucca, Sienna, Naples, Perugia, Assis, Roma, Barcelona, Seville, Cordoba, Granada, Madrid, and Toledo.

27 The advent of talkies had a direct influence, for instance, on Wittgenstein's philosophy of language. As Krystóf Nyíri (1994) suggests, talkies forced Wittgenstein to abandon the Picture Theory of Language.

28 In the oral language it refers to the Italians.

29 *Anhangüera* in the original.

30 *Bicheiro* (illegal bookie).

31 Originally it is a Tupi-Guarani word meaning "old devil." In the popular language it means either "devil" or "hooligan."

32 Retailers of lottery tickets.

33 On 21 December 2015 the Museu was destroyed in a fire. Fortunately, all exhibits and collections were saved. The Museu is still under renovation as of June 2016.

34 Museu da língua portuguesa, Estação da Luz, http://www.museulinguaportuguesa.org.br.

12

Artivism as a Form of Urban Translation: An Indisciplinary Hypothesis

MYRIAM SUCHET AND SARAH MEKDJIAN
Translated by Carmen Ruschiensky

I will build you a city out of rags, I tell you!
I will build you, without plan or cement
An edifice you will not destroy

Henri Michaux, *Darkness Moves*

The "language of Europe" is not a code but a constantly transformed system of crossed usages; it is, in other words, *translation*. Better yet, it is the reality of the social practices of translation at different levels, the *medium of communication* upon which all others depend.

Etienne Balibar, *We, the People of Europe? Reflections on Transnational Citizenship*

A city can be read as a collection of signs. Some of these signs are metaphorical, but most are extremely literal and concrete: billboards, logos, ads, and graffiti demand constant visual and verbal decoding. It comes as no surprise, then, that translation is a very visible part of the urban semiotic space. In the aftermath of Bill 101, Quebec "stop" signs were replaced with "arrêt" signs. In 1992, the minister of transport reversed this decision, maintaining that the Office de la langue française had considered "stop" a French word since 1976. Today, the use of either term is accepted as long as they do not appear together on the same sign, as Quebec is officially unilingual. In other provinces or territories, such as Ontario or Nunavut, the same sign can admit several terms in

Figure 1. Bilingual stop sign in Innu/French, photograph by the author.

different languages, thus including translations into French, English, Cree, Inuktitut, or Innu (see figure 1). To translate or not to translate urban signs is a political question, the effects of which are inscribed in the urban space itself. From Shanghai and Nicosia to Brussels, Johannesburg, and Pula, power struggles can be read through the presence or absence of translations in a city. This history of great conflicts and reconciliations, however, is not the only one written by urban translation.

On the margins of the tug-of-war between coexisting languages and their respective imagined communities, other translating practices transform urban spaces and reveal the potential of previously unseen spaces. Such practices as well as other urban art initiatives could be described as forms of "artivism" – activism through and by art (Lindgaard 2005; Augoyard 2000; Douay 2012; Lemoine and Ouardi 2010). Two Montreal-based initiatives of note are the FRAPRU (Front d'action populaire en réaménagement urbain) and the "socially acceptable terrorist" art collective ATSA (Action terroriste socialement acceptable) (see Pelletier 2007; for other examples, see Jacob 2011). If these translating strategies tend to be less visible than the famous stop-sign controversy, it is probably because the power games they engage are less familiar and because they call into question the very definition of translation. Exploring this uncharted terrain implies a certain degree of risk, but a risk worth taking. We are currently experiencing a period of "crisis" in which established theoretical frameworks are, by all accounts, becoming obsolete. Put another way, inherited paradigms seem to be out of step with our contemporary realities. Could artivism in its various forms provide new leads? Jorge Fernandes Torres (2012, 4), director of the Centro de Arte Contemporáneo Wifredo Lam and the eleventh Havana Biennial, seems to suggest it can when he asserts that "the crisis, the lack of any model or point of reference, forces us to rethink our aspirations and our future. Fostering action is not in vain. However, imagination precedes all theory."

The translation hypothesis, which is not typically part of geographers' and urban planners' theoretical arsenal, can provide a fresh perspective on artivism's critical impact. Innovative approaches in translation studies invite us to explore translation, beyond academic discourse, as a phenomenon firmly anchored in the city (see, in particular, Simon 2006, 2012).[1] We seek here to lay the foundations for a dialogue between translation theory (Myriam Suchet) and social geography (Sarah Mekdjian). This dialogue might be termed indisciplinary, for it not only bridges or connects two disciplines (as is the case in an interdisciplinary or transdisciplinary perspective) but also, more radically, challenges the authorized expertise of both, destabilizing their terminologies and tools to investigate third ways. This indisciplinary approach is itself experimental. Our aim is to bring different imaginaries and practices into contact. We use translation as a shuttle or a mediator to operate these connections, in lieu of a definitive theoretical framework.

To begin, we identify and document a number of current artivist practices that transform our experience of the city. Since we are exploring unknown terrain far from our usual areas of expertise (literature and geography), we have developed our methodological tools (maps and compasses) en route, disorienting ourselves. In the first part of this chapter, we together lay out our corpus or terrain, which consists of a typology of artivist forms organized around the hypothesis of translation. We then reconsider the very definitions of "translation" and "city" through the prism of this typology, and explore the new configurations that emerge. Myriam focuses on translation, redefined in terms of interval or interstices, while Sarah reflects on the city – urban art mapping in/as translation – with reference to an experimental workshop held in Grenoble, France, in 2013 that brought together a group of geographers, artists, and asylum-seekers (see Fischer et al. 2013). Our chapter is based on a series of photographic reproductions of the artivist works cited. Obtaining the copyrights for all the works mentioned was a challenge we did not fully achieve, and so when not reproduced here, we invite readers to discover and look at the works online. The reading experience we would like to engage is not only textual but also visual. The images we reproduce or refer to in this chapter are part of the indisciplinary approach we aim to develop.

Since we programmed our work-in-progress to be shared widely, we also invite readers to participate in the online version on Pearltrees.[2]

AN EXPLORATORY TYPOLOGY OF TRANSLATIONAL FORMS IN CONTEMPORARY URBAN ART

It is probably not enough to open our eyes, but we can learn to see (Foucault [1969] 1972) the proliferation of performative and experimental works that explore new ways to inhabit cities and build communities all over the world – particularly in Europe and North America, as we examine here. How and to what extent is translation implicated in these interventions, and what forms does it take? Drawing on results obtained from a search of the PLEPUC database,[3] we identified five categories of artworks, installations, and performances that implicate translation in an urban context, with a view to interpreting works through the lens of translation and, eventually, redefining translation in response to the works analyzed. The five categories range from those that incorporate the most literal forms of translation to those that use translation in a metaphorical sense, even though they still enact concrete, physical interventions that transform and redefine the urban experience.

1 Translational Installations Stricto Sensu

Certain art installations can be described as (pseudo) translational insofar as they explicitly incorporate translation in order to play with the shifts it engenders. An example of this type of work is Rachelle Viader Knowles's *Berlin Project* (2001),[4] realized in collaboration with three artists from Berlin, Germany, and three artists from Kitchener, Ontario. The link between these cities is grounded in the history of Kitchener, which up until 1916 was known as Berlin. Viader Knowles (2001) describes the project as follows:

> In both Kitchener and Berlin, local artists act as "guides," choosing a site of particular significance to them and recounting a story in their home language. The artists also act as "interpreters" by responding to the videos in the other language with a written simultaneous translation based either on their knowledge of the other language or by creative guessing. The written "translations" appear as subtitles. The video was produced for the council chambers of Kitchener City Hall, screened simultaneously on a large screen projection and on thirty monitors embedded into the architecture of the space.

The video screen is split in two.[5] At the beginning of the video, visual artist Ian Newton, on the left, recounts his first visit of Kitchener in English, while an artist from Berlin, on the right, takes notes that appear as subtitles in German at the bottom of the screen. The "interpreter" remarks that Newton is somewhere that resembles Alexanderplatz and, as more subtitles appear, it becomes evident that she does not understand English. *Berlin Project* makes use of translation on at least three levels. The first and most obvious is with reference to the different languages used in the storytelling and its interpretation. However, the lack of understanding transforms "interpreting" from a simple act of language transfer into a creative work on its own. The *mise en abyme* use of place also highlights translation, as Berlin and Kitchener reflect one another. Finally, translation works across time and memory, since the history of Kitchener is invoked by reference to its former toponym. In this way, the installation suggests a collapsing of space-time: Berlin (Germany) appears on the council chambers monitors of Kitchener/Berlin's (Ontario) city hall.

2 Subverted Signs: The Insurrection of Urban Signs

Altering street signs can be considered an act of translation even when no language change is involved, since it reveals the semiotic operation at work in the city. In his analysis of the proliferation of graffiti in New York in the 1970s, Jean Baudrillard (1993, 78–9) describes graffiti as an "insurrection of signs": "Invincible due to their own poverty, they resist every interpretation and every connotation, no longer denoting anyone or anything. In this way, with neither connotation nor denotation, they escape the principle of signification and, as *empty signifiers*, erupt into the sphere of the *full signs* of the city, dissolving it on contact."

The PLEPUC website presents two photographic images on billboard ads from the project *In Control*, curated by Lorenzo Buj and organized by the artist-run centre Artcite in Windsor, Ontario. Michael Fernandes's piece reads, "Inhabited by a spirit, worshipped by savages."[6] Jamelie Hassan's piece – a timely installation that coincided with the 1991 Gulf War in Iraq – features a photograph of the colourfully tiled dome and minaret of the Haidar Khan mosque in Baghdad taken in the 1970s, and reads, "Because there was and there wasn't a city of Baghdad."[7] Though neither of these works makes explicit reference to translation, both represent subverted signs and, therefore, are relevant to our typology and analysis.

Related examples are works by two Montreal-based artists, Gilbert Boyer and Peter Gibson. Boyer's 1988 piece, *Comme un poisson dans la ville* (Like a fish in the city),[8] is a permanent installation that includes a series of twelve text-engraved plaques affixed to different buildings at various locations around Montreal. One of the plaques – at the corner of St Laurent Boulevard and Laurier Avenue (figure 2) – reads: "QUELLE CHALEUR ! J'EN VIENS PRESQUE A RÊVER DE L'HIVER. JE ME SUIS ARRETE PRES D'ICI. UNE POUSSIERE DANS L'ŒIL. À LA POINTE DE L'ANCIEN HOTEL DE VILLE SE TIENT EN EQUILIBRE UN OISEAU NOIR. IL S'EVENTE LENTEMENT POUR SE RAFRAICHIR LES AILES DEPLOYEES" (It's so hot! I'm almost looking forward to winter. I stopped not far from here. Got dust in my eye. There's a black bird balancing on the turret of the old city hall. Fanning its wings to stay cool. Its wings spread out.). Rather than commemorating a monumental or official history of the city, Boyer's inscriptions record ephemeral moments. They invite passers-by to look at their city's architecture and its inhabitants from a different and unexpected perspective.

While Boyer subverts the function of commemorative plaques in Montreal, Gibson, aka Roadsworth, transforms road signs and surface markings and often intervenes directly on the pavement.[9] Though he works alone, Roadsworth situates his practice in a collective context and lays claim to public space in a unique way, such as by transforming the white lines that delineate parking spots into giant dandelions blowing in the wind, or adorning the broken line of a passing lane with an image of scissors cutting their way down the road.

Figure 2. Plaque from Gilbert Boyer and Peter Gibson's *Comme un poisson dans la ville* (Like a fish in the city), 1988, photograph by the author.

An example we came across by chance in the early stages of this research project is an exhibition held in October 2012 at Le Jeu de Paume in Paris: *Entre/Between*, a survey spanning over forty years of work by multimedia artist and translator Antoni Muntadas, originally from Barcelona and currently based in New York. Considered one of the first artists to develop media art in the 1970s, Muntadas explores, among other things, what anthropologist Marc Augé (1992) refers to as "non-place" and "nomadization." Muntadas's first video and television experiments involved direct interventions in the media landscape. According to the exhibition's curator, Daina Augaitis (2011, 14), "Muntadas' work suggests that in those situations that cannot be completely known, predicted or controlled, there exist possibilities for a multitude of engagements, especially if we consciously participate in deciphering and translating 'what we are looking at.'" The ongoing project *On Translation: Warning*, begun in 1999, exemplifies this aspect of Muntadas's work. Taking the pervasive influence of the "media landscape" on social life as a point of departure, the artist has acquired advertising spaces in various locales around the world to reach the widest audience possible. All of these works display, translated in each country's official language, "Warning: Perception Requires Involvement."[10] The typography employed is consistent with advertising and newspaper headline styles: the brief, catchy slogan is written in capital letters, with a uniform colour scheme of white text on a red ground. The words are translated according to the location, and displayed using a wide variety of media: posters, stickers, press inserts, building facades, windows, pamphlets, catalogues, books, magazines, newspapers, photographs, postcards, and banners. These works question *in situ* the manipulation and mediation of information in a way that engages the public and encourages participation.

3 Transforming and Creating Spaces: Guerrilla Gardening and Theatre Hacking

The third category of our typology takes us off the beaten path into less visible spaces: abandoned lots and buildings that have been transformed into gardens, bicycle paths, exhibition spaces, and temporary housing. Some of these projects, including three examples from PLEPUC, are the result of officially endorsed municipal initiatives. However, most forms of "guerrilla gardening" (Reynolds 2008; Hou 2010) are the result of more-or-less illegal tactics and interventions.

Trevor Gould's monumental work *Fable VII*, inspired by La Fontaine's fable *La cour du lion*, is installed in the courtyard of Ottawa City Hall and consists of three elements: an interior inscription in Latin that reads "Ex Oriente Lux," a bronze element in the exterior pool, and a lion with an accompanying frame.[11] The work establishes a reciprocal action between interior and exterior space, creating a dialogue between the architecture of the surrounding buildings. While the bronze frame evokes a sundial, the component in the pool constantly animates the surroundings, offering notions of constant renewal through sunlight and directional alignment. Translation, here, does not imply languages, since the Latin inscription remains untranslated. The numbering of the fable, however, differs from version to version: seventh in the English translation in a Penguin edition, but sixth in French. Translating also refers to a political situation: the monumental lion sculpture, surrounded by the city hall, is a metaphor of the empire, while the inscription (in English, light from the east) highlights the power relationships between East

Figure 3a. *Jardin de Lyon*, Montreal, 2000, by Jean-François Gavoty and Guerric Péré. Courtesy of the artist.

and West. Gould, born and educated in South Africa until his arrival in Quebec in 1987, explains:

> I work from the insight that sculpture is a form of social material and that producing exhibitions is an aspect of cultural research. The very act of putting objects on exhibition is comprehended as the substance of installation practice itself, in both its cultural and social variations. Working out from the perspective of Zoos, Botanical gardens, and World exhibitions as representations of a "geography of exhibiting," these sites are explored in their relationship to the contemporary museum through the significance of their related display practices.[12]

Another large-scale installation of note was commissioned for a project to mark twenty years of cooperation and exchange between Lyon and Montreal. Two gardens were created, the *Jardin de Lyon*[13] in Montreal by French artist Jean-François Gavoty and landscape architect Guerric Péré (see figure 3a), and the *Jardin de Montréal* in Lyon by Quebec artists Michel Goulet, Réal Lestage, and Julie SaintArnaud. Gavoty (2004) describes another ephemeral piece of his, entitled *Un*

Figure 3b. Detail, *Un jardin avec des ailes*, Lyon, 2004, by Jean-François Gavoty. Courtesy of the artist.

jardin avec des ailes (A garden with wings),[14] that he created for the *Festival des jardins de rue* in Lyon in 2004 (see figure 3b):

> For this garden, I recuperated a bunch of used, crumpled car wings of different colours. After a few pressings, I managed to flatten them out and assemble them to make a ground. Scattered wild flowers and grasses were planted in the cracks, between the irregular shapes of the fenders, and, in the centre, there was a metronome hidden in a waterproof case, timed to beat every second. Urban legend has it that passers-by could hear this muffled ticking sound, as if the little garden had a heartbeat. For a few months, it discreetly marked the time passed in traffic jams.

A third and somewhat less monumental example is Marlene Creates's *Boreal Poetry Garden*,[15] an ephemeral installation consisting of handwritten poems on cards, temporarily placed through the forest. According to Creates (2005), "The brief texts reflect some of the site's particular geophysical and climatic characteristics, its plant life, wildlife and social history, and my experiences here. For me, the location of the words in the specific spot to which they refer is fundamental to the radiating energy of their meaning and, of course, their beauty."

Beyond the threshold of official art, we find artivist groups engaged in subversive guerrilla gardening and insurgent urbanism. One of the groups active in Montreal is CRAPAUD (Collectif de recherche sur l'aménagement paysager et l'agriculture urbaine durable), an urban agriculture initiative begun in 2009.[16] Another well-known group is the San-Francisco-based art-design-ecology studio Rebar, organizers of the annual PARK(ing) Day event with the motto "Reclaim your city!" Rebar proposes to temporarily transform metered parking spaces into green spaces.[17] Its organizers obtained a creative commons licence that allows activists all over the world to join the movement, and PARK(ing) Day now occurs annually in hundreds of cities around the globe, including Toronto and Montreal (Hou 2010).

More ephemeral but no less spectacular are interventions that take the form of collective performance or "theatre hacking." Olivier Choinière, in addition to his collective "social theatre events," has organized several audio-guided walking tours, including *Ascension: pèlerinage sonore sur le Mont Royal* (Ascension: Mount-Royal sound pilgrimage) and *Bienvenue à (une ville dont vous êtes le touriste)* (Welcome to [a city where you are the tourist]). Each *spect-actor* walks alone, following the precise directions of the pre-recorded voices on the audio guide along the way. As Francis Ducharme (2009, v, 4) notes: "The audio guide not only provides an itinerary, it also imparts an ambiance through the sound and dramatic performance of the text ... The poetic and fictional nature of this text brings a literary dimension to street theatre. The text, the ambiance of recorded sounds, and the dramatization all produce effects of proximity and distance between real and fictional space ... The works' complex ambivalence and irony with respect to sense of place engage and provoke reflection without imposing a given position." The city here is the scenic backdrop of the activity, of the spect-actor's journey, but it also becomes a fictional decor seen through the lens of the text.

4 Alternative Narratives: The Polyphony of Unheard Voices

Some installations seek to give a voice to silenced subjects of history. For instance, the PLEPUC website registers *Double Blind*, a large-scale sculptural installation commissioned in 2008 for the atrium of the new Vancouver Community College's Broadway Campus building. Created by artist Antonia Hirsch, the work consists of mirrored acrylic domes arranged on a four-story-high wall to represent the Snellen eye chart used for routine eye exams – in Braille.[18] The title suggests a double bind: not being able to read the text in Braille when one can see it and not being able to see the text when one can read Braille. The irony, however, also targets the public space itself, which is structured as a Panopticon within which everything and everyone is to be seen at all times.

Sacrée montagne (literally sacred mountain, but also connoting damn mountain or hell of a mountain) is a collaborative and interactive work organized by the National Film Board of Canada. Joëlle Gauthier (2011) of the NT2 hypermedia art and literature lab explains:

> *Sacrée montagne* is a collaboration between writer/journalist Hélène de Billy and photographer Gilbert Duclos ... It takes the form of a virtual, interactive discovery of Mount-Royal, the famous "mountain" situated in the heart of Montreal. It addresses the "persistence of the sacred in our secular society." Different artists have identified six locations on the virtual mountain that serves as the main navigation interface: the cemeteries, the cross, Saint-Joseph's Oratory, the statue of Fame (the angel statue), Beaver Lake, and the mountain trails ... Each of these six virtual sites contains links to secondary sites that include content specifically created for the project: short films, photo albums, interviews with Québécois personalities, documentation of cultural events, and documentaries on the history of Mount-Royal, such as the canonization of Brother André in 2010.

5 Invented Maps and Trajectories

Imaginary maps and counter-cartographies have much in common with alternative narratives (as above), especially when drawing attention to blind spots in a city's official spatial representations. Stephen Foster's *Kiss and Tell*[19] is a map of Quebec City that represents, in place of official monuments, the locations of graffiti works Foster photographed. For him, these works are traces of personal and intimate history in public space: "Roaming the streets of Quebec City and photographing traces of personal history, the artist, whose work deals pri-

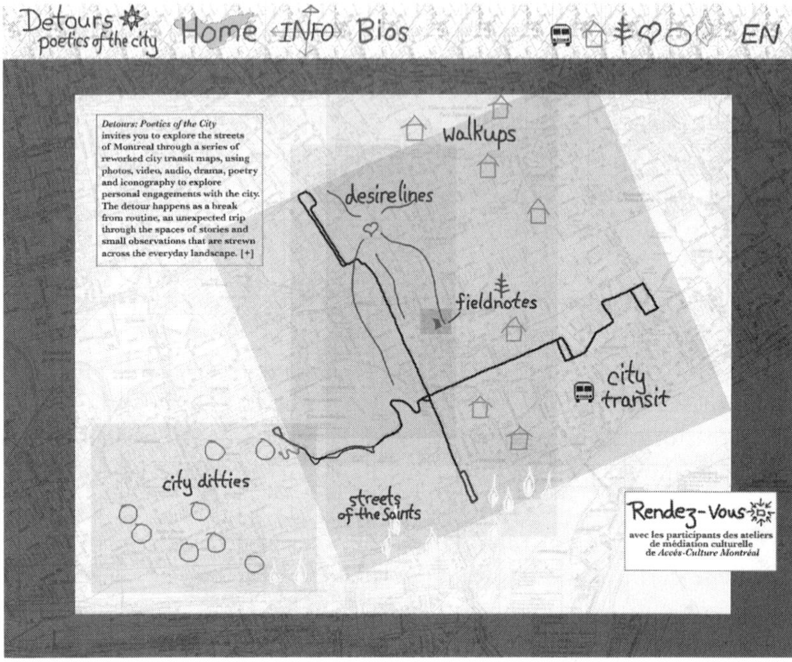

Figure 4. Taien Ng-Chan and Agence TOPO, *Detours: Poetics of the City*, http://agencetopo.qc.ca/detours/main_en.html.

marily with representations of Aboriginal people in popular culture, hopes to create a space of political and social dialogue. *Kiss and Tell* offers the internaut a photographic representation of graffiti practices intimately inscribed in and mapped across the city, personal histories woven together in the collective public space" (Galand 2009).

In *Detours: Poetics of the City*, a collective project organized with the support of Agence TOPO, a Montreal-based artist-run centre for new media, the participating artists map not places but rather itineraries, often combining visuals and sound archives.[20] Taien Ng-Chan, the project's coordinator, contributed two maps: *City Transit*, video poems about strangers on public transit (see figure 4), and *Streets of the Saints*, with Adrien Gorea, a poetic exploration of geography and hagiography. The project also includes *Field Notes*, a map within which Emilie O'Brien explores Le champ des possibles (Field of possibilities), a "much-loved" unofficial area of green space in Montreal's Mile End, with embroidery, textworks, images, and an interview with Emily Rose Michaud, creator of the *Roerich Garden Project*.

London-based artist Christian Nold developed a similar form of participatory map-making with his series of "emotional cartographies" that measure individuals' emotional arousal as they navigate the city. Combining two technologies, a Global Positioning System and a lie-detector-type sensor that measures Galvanic Skin Response, his maps represent temporal emotional reactions to particular environments and geographical locations.[21]

French artist-performer Mathias Poisson's urban maps are drawn in motion, while walking in cities. As Poisson (2010, 105) explains:

> I spend my days roaming city streets, discovering neighbourhoods, exploring marginal zones, finding lost or discarded objects, hanging out under bridges or in the woods, contemplating the landscapes around me. I note the sensations, preoccupations and observations that arise during these outings, and then I draw maps based on my experience, or I survey areas and map out new paths for possible future walks ... My drawings reflect the gestures and memories that seem important to me. They recount a journey, highlighting some parts, omitting others, deforming perspectives.

In a similar vein, choreographer Lauriane Houbey collaborated with visual artist Marie Moreau to produce *Géographies intérieures*, an exhibition based on mental maps and maps drawn in motion, held in Grenoble in 2012. In her text "Arpenter les recoins, les revers" (Exploring recesses, other sides), Houbey describes roaming the city with her sketchbooks: "I had a collection of standard spiral notebooks and felt pens that I carried around with me in my knapsack. I worked with the notebooks on my knees, or even on the ground, on the sidewalk, or on a step, often spreading them out, side by side, to allow the story to unfold across several frames. Sometimes, turning the page, landing on a new page, interrupted the process. So I would come back to it later, or not" (Houbey and Moreau 2012, 6). Both Houbey and Poisson create maps while walking and wandering (and getting lost) in cities. They focus on margins and interstices from a walking perspective, reinventing and subverting dominant urban landscapes. Their (disorientation/disorienting) maps involve the participation of urban dwellers met while walking or asked to walk with them. The mapping performances described above around walks and artistic journeys refer to the situationists' *dérive* (drifting) and psychogeography (see Simay 2008; Paquot 2010).

We will return to the situationists. Here, we revisit the concept of translation in light of the above tentative and exploratory typology of artivist translation forms.

FIGURAL INTERSTICES: INTERVALS OF URBAN TRANSLATING

When I say that translation seems to me intrinsic to any utterance, I am referring to solitude. Because utterances are rare. Not because there aren't many of them but because they can only be located in a rarefied space, a no man's land, a space without a subject ... a terrain that belongs to no one. *No man's land.* Not for sale, not for building. And especially not a site of meetings, exchanges, dialogues, discussion, or influences, in short, communication. But a space, first and foremost, of observation and reflection.

Emmanuel Hocquard, *Un bureau sur l'Atlantique / Ma Haie*

How do the above practices change our understanding of translation? To what extent is translation involved in urban artivism? The way translation operates in the above examples has little to do with a mere transfer. It even goes beyond explicit reference to language. In what sense, then, can these practices be referred to as forms of translation?

We might begin by trying to describe the role that translating plays in the different works included in the typology. These works – whether verbal or visual signs, graffiti, official architectures, marginal spaces, maps, installations, performances, or gardens – all introduce, though very briefly, a different dimension into the urban space. Translation, redefined in this context, thus changes the established order of things and expands our horizons beyond the existing range of possibilities. We can say that these works translate insofar as they do not simply suggest new approaches to familiar urban situations and activities bur rather enact or operate new situations and new modes of action. Translation, then, acts as an interval – a very concrete battement. In "urban" terms, we could say that translation operates as an interstice in the city.

Political scientist and sociologist Pascal Nicolas-Le Strat[22] (2009 [2007], 108–9) defines the potential inherent in interstitial space: "Interstices represent what is left of resistance in big cities – resistance to normativity and regulation, to homogenisation and appropriation. They embody, in a sense, what is still 'available' in the city. Their provisional and uncertain status allows for a glimpse of other ways of creating a city that are open and collaborative, responsive and cooperative. The importance of the interstitial experiment is borne out in this very register, in methodological, formative, political, as well as heuristic terms." While the notion of the interstices evokes a gap, rupture or interval in the saturated space of the city, its temporal dimension should not be overlooked. Hélène Hatzfeld, Marc Hatzfeld, and Nadja Ringart (1998, 36) emphasize both the spatial and temporal dimensions of the interstitial experience:

> From a spatial point of view, what is at stake [with interstices] are the fragments of urban space that fall outside officially regulated zones. There are many examples, from vacant lots, squats and hideouts, to unattended parking lots and other places transformed by various forms of marginality ... From a temporal perspective, interstices reveal the perpetual movement and plastic evolution of the city. In the wake of social and economic changes, for example, spaces that at one time had a precise function are transformed or abandoned, thus becoming pockets that invite marginal activities.

The power of the interstitial experience can be partly attributed to its ephemeral nature, which is also its limitation. But how can we understand translation as creating intervals and interstices without reducing these concepts to simple metaphors? Understanding translation as operating interstices involves shifting from a spatial representation – the linear transfer from a "source language" to a "target language" – to a temporal one that is disruptive. As a temporal process, the act of translating interrupts the utterance and denaturalizes the discourse. In other words, translation, in its artivist manifestations, is not so much about transferring from one language to another as it is about recognizing languages as forms of practice. As Meschonnic (2000, 31) puts it: "From a language, any language, we have nothing but discourse. It is this truism that must be stated, even at the risk of ridicule. Yet the so-called 'genius' and supposed clarity of the French language remind us that the distinction is not in vain: the mode of existence of a language is radically different from that of discourse." Elsewhere, Meschonnic (1997, 32) remarks that "language alone, with respect to the nominalism of discourse, does not exist. Words, alone, do not exist. Except in the dictionary. In this sense, the French language, like any other, does not exist."

Translation, then, has to be considered in terms of enunciation, and translating as a way to create new modes of speech that undermine the limits of naturalized "language." To establish the link between urban artivist translation and its subversive enunciative power, it might be useful to explore the notion of the interstices in relation to that of the figural, as discourse analyst Laurent Jenny develops in another context. Describing the enunciation event, Jenny (1990, 16) suggests we "think of an utterance as a 'deal,' a lexical *throw of the dice.*" While everyday language tends to conform to the rules of the game, literature transforms it, even to the point of setting the conditions under which the dice can be thrown. This is what Jenny refers to as the figural: "The figural, while grounded in the discursive event, also necessitates reflection on the form of language itself (its division into linguistic units, its combinatory rules). It drives us back to a 'first' decision with respect to form, since it gives shape to the emergent and arbitrary moment. By a kind of double effect, the discursive event lies in this reciprocity between the production of discursive meaning and the re-presentation of language that gives rise to it, between the power of naming and the opening of possibilities within the language" (20).

The interval created by urban artivist translation must be understood, in both its temporal and spatial dimensions, as a delimited, ephemeral, and disruptive event or space. By joining the sociological, urbanistic notion of the interstice (Pascal Nicolas-Le Strat) with the stylistic, enunciative notion of the figural (Jenny), translation can be redefined not as a linguistic transfer but rather as an enunciative upheaval of sedimented discursive practices. However, translation should not be conceived as "figural interstices" metaphorically, but as a plane of immanence (Deleuze and Guattari 1980, 89). In this respect, our approach differs radically from that of Homi Bhabha. As Bhabha (1990, 210) explains:

> [I'm using translation] not in a strict linguistic sense of translation as in a "book translated from French to English," but as a motif or trope as Benjamin suggests for the activity of displacement within the linguistic sign ... But for me, the importance of hybridity is not to be able to trace two original moments from which the third emerges, rather hybridity to me is the "third space" which enables other positions to emerge. This third space displaces the histories that constitute it, and sets up new structures of authority, new political initiatives, which are inadequately understood through received wisdom.

Despite the enduring interest in Bhabha's redefinition of translation, we believe that to reduce translation to metaphor is not the most productive way to explore translation in the urban space. Artivist translation in/of the city is a practice that reveals that "language" is not an entity or an essence. And it is as a practice that it gives rise to other practices.

THE (GEO)GRAPHIC TRANSLATION OF THE TRANSLATION HYPOTHESIS

> The question of what kind of city we want cannot be divorced from that of what kind of social ties, relationship to nature, lifestyles, technologies and aesthetic values we desire ... The metropolis is now the point of massive collision – dare we call it class struggle? – over the accumulation by dispossession visited upon the least well-off and the developmental drive that seeks to colonize space for the affluent. One step towards [a reinvention of urbanization] is to adopt the right to the city as both working slogan and political ideal ... The right to the city is far more than the individual liberty to access urban resources: it is a right to change ourselves by changing the city.
>
> David Harvey, "The Right to the City"

The subversive artivist practices discussed above constitute creative challenges to neoliberal urban capitalism (Brenner and Theodore 2002). How can the notion of translation help us understand other forms of urbanism and the social production of urban space? Can urban art retain its critical edge, or is it doomed to serve as a pawn, to be assimilated into the market economy? Is it possible to critique neoliberal models of urban development through art and imagination?

Urban planners, who work for the promotion of competitive neoliberal cities, are increasingly integrating art into restructuring projects. In his famous book *The Rise of the Creative Class: And How It's Transforming Work, Leisure and Everyday Life*, Richard Florida (2002) suggests that the Fordist city be transformed and restructured as a creative one. Florida's work can serve both as an introduction and a warning with respect to the possibilities for geographical thinking about the integration of art in contemporary urban contexts. Florida, who is director of the University of Toronto's Martin Prosperity Institute, describes the emergence of a "creative class" at the service of a "creative city," founded on artistic and cultural practices. Cities, he believes, should attempt to attract creative types – artists, journalists, artisans, and workers in high-tech fields, among others. The presence of this creative class enhances a city's "creativity index," and this, he says, is the key to economic urban renewal. Several municipalities have been inspired by Florida, transforming their images as post-industrial cities into new, competitive, "creative cities." Far from destabilizing contemporary urban capitalism, Florida's theory advocates using art and culture as economic tools to improve cities' commercial images and economies; using, that is, the symbolic and economic value of art and culture to accumulate capital, produce surplus value, and generate competition. Contemporary developers are looking to the symbolic power of art and culture to remake the urban image, and this "restructuring of Fordist production models has put cultural economies and creative industries at the centre of debates on the future of urban development" ("Présentation" 2013).

While the concept of the creative city has received a lot of attention, it has also been sharply criticized. Urban sociologist Jean-Pierre Garnier (2011) refers to the creative class as an urban myth, a "(self) proclaimed, avant-garde," and questions the kind of "life" it enables and what kind of survival it implies for those excluded from it. Geographers Anne Clerval and Antoine Fleury (2009) investigate links between gentrification, the eviction of low-income populations, speculation in real estate, and cultural policies carried out in Paris since the 2000s. The latter, they say, have not stopped gentrification as the left has promised since 2001, but have in fact contributed to it.

The translation hypothesis developed here conceives translation not as a transfer from one model to another (from a Fordist to a creative model of the city, following a process of creative destruction), but as a permanent ongoing practice. The idea is not to create a new city based on artivist proposals (functioning as designs for urban planners and architects), but to identify forms of urban practice that empower citizens to constantly question and destabilize the urban space. Translation, in this context, refers precisely to these everyday acts of deconstruction rather than to the construction of absolute or totalizing models. Translation is a critical process that destabilizes everyday relations and generates new sociospatial practices that are continually called into question.

Artivist projects that incorporate mapping processes are among the most interesting forms of urban translation. While urban planners often use prospective maps to design totalizing models of cities, artists and activists use maps to subvert their original uses and purposes. In *The Practice of Everyday Life* (*L'Invention du quotidien*), Michel De Certeau ([1984] 2011) critiques the map and its totalizing discourses that impose a disciplinary, "technocratic," and "functionalist" ideology on the city. He proposes, instead, a "return to practice," distinguishing the "walk," which lies beyond the visible and readable, from the map, which offers a panoptic image of the city in the service of modern urban planning (93). However, if maps are classical instruments of control, government, and panoptic totalizing urbanism, they are also used by researchers, activists, artists, and artivists who work on a critique of contemporary urbanism, neoliberal urban economies, and the apparatus of surveillance.

Counter-cartography projects have largely been involved in producing alternative visual narratives of social spaces, including cities. The Counter Cartographies Collective, for example, "uses what Deleuze (1988) calls a 'new cartography,' a practice that creates new (political geographic) possibilities and other (political geographic) realities, rather than *re*presenting already existing geographies" (Dalton and Mason-Deese 2012, 443). Process-oriented mapping practices like those of Poisson or Houbey seem to create possibilities for a critique of the modernist city by playing upon its sociospatial conventions. These mapping practices reactivate links between geography, map-making, and art, while at the same time introducing a social and critical dimension. Gilles Tiberghien (2010, 198) traces the critical use of maps in art to the beginning of the modernist era, and observes, "With modernism, conventionally starting with Manet, maps became an instrument of rupture, a critical mode in the regime of representation." According to Tiberghien (ibid.), "the map is based on an irreducible distance to its referent. Contemporary artists appropriate mapping practices not to bridge this gap but to circulate within it."

Many artivist maps, especially works based on the practice of wandering in the city, echo the mapping practices of the situationists, who took a critical stance on art and its commodification. In the 1960s, Guy Debord and the situationists used mapping practices to subvert the representational role of art, transforming it into a political practice. They invented a "map/card game" inspired by the writings of Henri Lefebvre, in particular *The Critique of Everyday Life* (La critique de la vie quotidienne), published in 1947. Lefebvre introduced the idea of the city as a place of play, inviting "players" to defy the rules and sociospatial conventions of modernist urbanism. Debord later developed the situationist *dérive*, a technique for losing oneself in the city. The rules of the game are as follows:

> In a dérive one or more persons during a certain period drop their relations, their work and leisure activities, and all their other usual motives for movement and action, and let themselves be drawn by the attractions of the terrain and the encounters they find there ... In the "possible rendezvous," on the other hand, the element of exploration is minimal in comparison with that of behavioural disorientation. The subject is invited to come alone to a certain place at a specified time. He is freed from the bothersome obligations of the ordinary rendezvous since there is no one to wait for. But since this "possible rendezvous" has brought him without warning to a place he may or may not know, he observes the surroundings ... The lessons drawn from dérives enable us to draw up the first surveys of the psychogeographical articulations of a modern city. Beyond the discovery of unities of ambiance, of their main components and their spatial localization, one comes to perceive their principal axes of passage, their exits and their defenses. One arrives at the central hypothesis of the existence of psychogeographical pivotal points. One measures the distances that actually separate two regions of a city, distances that may have little relation with the physical distance between them. With the aid of old maps, aerial photographs and experimental dérives, one can draw up hitherto lacking maps of influences, maps whose inevitable imprecision at this early stage is no worse than that of the first navigational charts. The only difference is that it is no longer a matter of precisely delineating stable continents, but of changing architecture and urbanism. (Debord [1958] 2006, 62–6)

The *dérive* creates the conditions for a disorientation that eventually gives rise to reinvented maps and reconfigures the city. The notion of play is a point of departure for possible urban practices. Renegotiating the rules of the urban social space through play can be understood as a form of translation operating in the city and in the social lives of the urban dwellers as an emancipatory practice.

As seen above, the *Detours* project, Poisson's travel drawings, and Houbey's sketched-out roamings, among other examples, recall the *dérive*, going beyond the rules of the game. Similar examples include

Bouchra Khalili's video mappings of covert journeys or Till Roeskens's video recordings of map drawings in progress, narrated by the drawers who also recount their memories, thoughts, and feelings.

These practices do not impose an omniscient view of the city as from a zenith. They offer, rather, a multiplicity of embedded, alternative narratives that integrate different points of view and modes of expression. Tiberghien (2010, 207) notes that "a number of contemporary artists have created roadmaps as a way of recording ... their subjective experiences while exploring different places or territories." He refers, in particular, to the work of artist Richard Long, whose maps "do not just represent the paths taken by the artist. They become paths in themselves, a conceptual analog" (ibid.). Jean-Marc Besse (2010, 7) proposes the idea of "itinerary maps," which represent "the territory in a way that does not depict it as independent of the activities that take place there ... the territory's very structure being defined by the practices of those who traverse it, leaving traces of their passage." These maps criticize the territorial and disciplinary conception of space enacted by conventional grid maps.

Taking these itinerary maps as a point of departure, artists, geographers, and people who face complex sociogeographic and administrative situations, most of them asylum seekers, were invited to participate in a series of experimental, interactive mapping workshops in Grenoble. Over a two-month period in May and June 2013, two researchers, three artists/performers, twelve participants, a photographer, and a research engineer met twice a week at the premises of the Association of Asylum Seekers in Grenoble.[23] These workshops were intended to create encounters around mapping practices and to produce alternative narratives on contemporary migrations and urban space. They were an experiment in reinvesting the city, providing a point of entry for people whose status was precarious, using mapmaking as a form of translation. Moreau, Houbey, and I worked with participants on themes related to migration experiences, border crossings, and living conditions in Grenoble. Moreau asked participants to make felt-pen drawings of their journeys on large white sheets, Houbey focused on the sounds heard during their travels and recorded participants' narratives, and I proposed a collaborative map key (using coloured stickers) based on words related to both their migratory experience and life in Grenoble. Participants then integrated the stickers based on this key into their drawings. Dozens of languages were present in these exchanges. Participants had lived or travelled in many different countries, and their past and present nationalities included Sudanese, Eritrean, Armenian, Congolese, Guinean, Algerian, Azeri, and Afghan. Some were asylum seekers or refugees, while others held no official administrative status. A range of linguistic, discursive, social, and administrative differences had to be negotiated by participants, artists, and researchers alike.

Creating the maps involved a double act of translation. First, map-making enabled us to frame our exchanges in a way that denaturalized participants' relationship to the administrative language and discourses of institutions governing the asylum process (Fassin and Kobelinksy 2012). Second, the maps themselves – particularly those of Grenoble, which were subsequently included in several exhibitions in the city – encouraged readers and spectators to critically engage with their daily environment. While asylum-governing institutions base their decisions on "the interpretation of the refugee's story in terms of conformity and deviance ... and an objectification of truth and falsehood" (Rousseau and Foxen 2006, 506), the maps produced in these workshops were not to be judged with reference to any horizon of "truth." These maps are neither true nor false, neither fictional nor imaginary. They allowed participants, within the unique context of the workshops, to express recollections, stories, feelings, demands, and discourses.

Houbey and Moreau had both already experimented with mapping as a means for establishing relationships with people living in the sociospatial margins of the city. Houbey, as we have seen, associates map-making with a form of roaming, while Moreau relates her interest in experimental mapping to a sense of disillusionment:

> At first I wanted to create works related to community centres, public health and social facilities, for example, that I thought had an important history and role in Grenoble. There were also some collaborations with Lauriane on landscape and territory around Grenoble. And this shared history of being evicted from one squat after another. A silencing operation that is still going on today. The city started to seem like a hollow shell. Anyways, it's a period that I went through. I was disillusioned. I needed to find new resource-spaces like vacant lots, passageways, unused zones where it was still possible to hang out, get lost, dream. (Houbey and Moreau 2012, 2)

With the workshops' participants, faced with the daily challenge of adapting to an exclusionary city and country, we tried to invent and map out spaces that could function as resource spaces, places of refuge/interstices. For Houbey, "resource-spaces are also spaces that stimulate the imagination. Environments where everything isn't already planned out and regulated, zones that seem like they're being used by other people for other purposes, or maybe even completely abandoned and serving no purpose whatsoever. Unaffected, in both the functional and aesthetic sense of the term" (ibid.). Moreau describes the maps created as part of an incomplete, referential, nonreferential, and anticonventional local atlas:

> The maps create ruptures. New stories emerge in these spaces. Sometimes, from one conversation to the next, two completely different maps are created by the same hand. The map-makers, who use the maps to "represent" (or represent themselves) use them for different reasons. They invent worlds that never existed before, worlds that don't exist in reality. The map represents and reconfigures a relationship to space in a given moment. It is a relative relationship that evolves. This is why the maps are exhibited and circulated. *Atlas local* is a work-in-progress. (ibid., 4)

As acts of translation that are by necessity relational, the maps we created are ideally presented to the public in a way that allows for interaction with their creators. They are tools that denaturalize both our linguistic relations and our interactions with the urban space.

One guide map was created by two of the workshop's participants (see figures 5 and 6). It is a tool intended to help newcomers arriving in Grenoble, unwelcomed immigrants in particular, settle in France and obtain rights. Unlike a conventional guide that outlines pre-existing itineraries and points of reference, this map cannot be used to orient oneself in Grenoble. Neither the scale nor the points of interest can be verified in relation to the terrain represented. Translation here does not consist in transforming one referent, the city of Grenoble as conceived by conventional maps, into another equally stable referent, the city of Grenoble as seen by asylum seekers. Translation plays a different role. Mapping becomes an act of translation insofar as it creates a displacement. On the one hand, it calls for using one's imagination to explore the city shown on the map. On the other hand, it invites us to abandon stable reference points in order to explore the city itself.

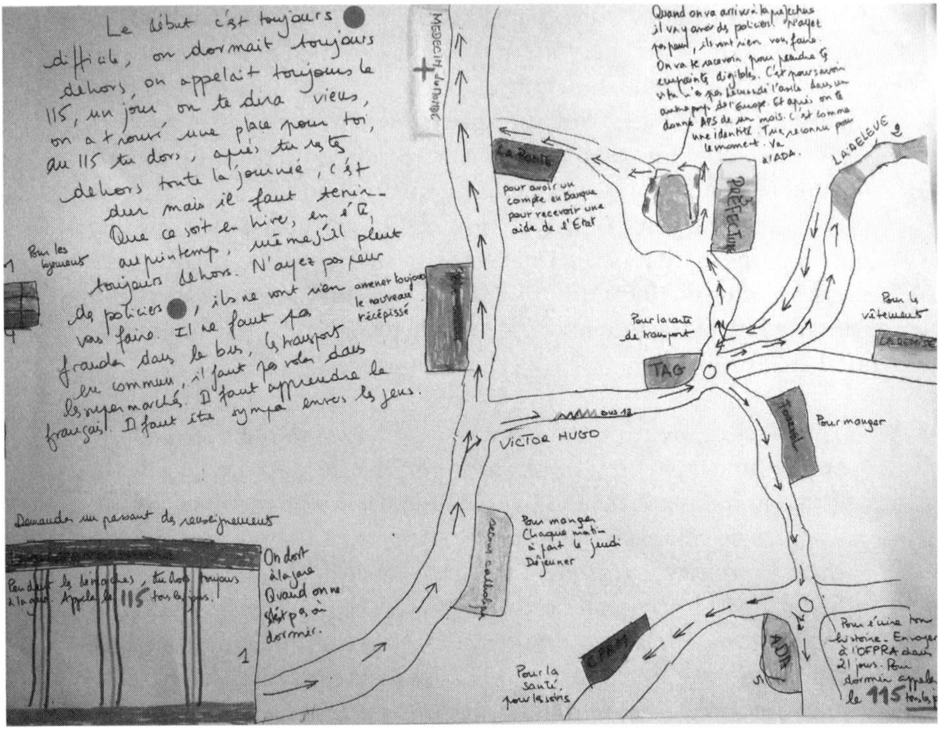

Figure 5. *Guide cartographique*, collective work, Grenoble's cartography workshops, 2013. © Mabeye Deme.

The guide offers tips for general attitudes to adopt in the city – for example, "don't be afraid of police officers" – and provides an itinerary that highlights several "resource sites" along the way.

The translational map, which offers no prescribed course, places its user in a precarious situation. The resource sites are options to be explored according to a continual re-evaluation of attitudes and responses to different interactive situations. The city does not pre-exist as an ordered whole. It is a terrain of possibilities that the reader, the traveller, anyone, and everyone can discover on the basis of a minimal range of social attitudes and interactions. Presented with the guide map, established residents of Grenoble experience disorientation and discover unknown places. The political idea of the "right to the city" developed by Lefebvre ([1968] 1996) is built on minute acts – movements, deviations, and rhythms in the very heart of the spaces where we live out our

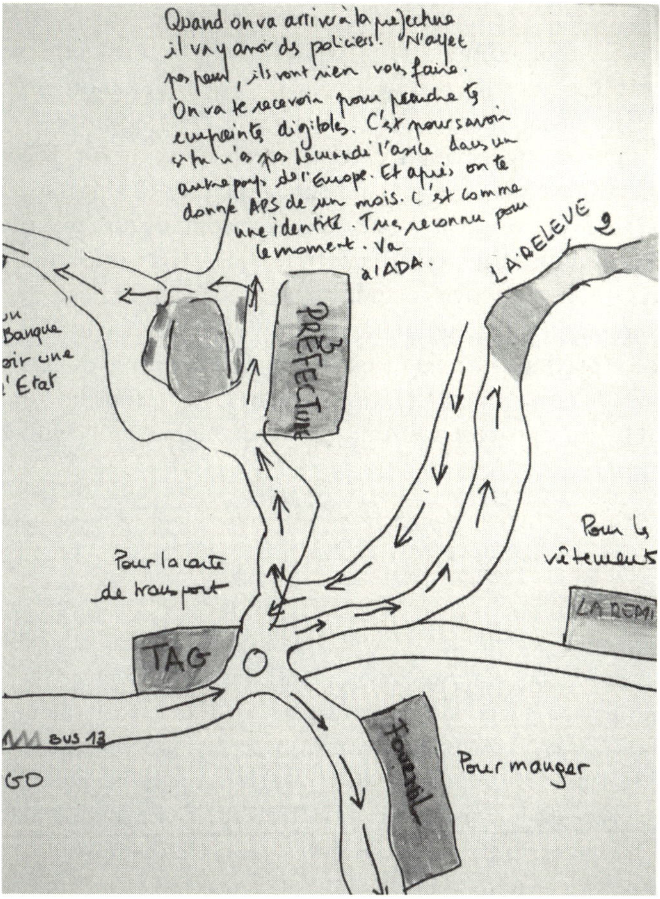

Figure 6. *Guide cartographique*, collective work, Grenoble's cartography workshops, 2013. © Mabeye Deme.

daily lives. (Counter-)mapping is one way to reinvent – i.e., translate – our everyday urban realities.

CONCLUSION

The respective reconfigurations of "city" and "translation" that we propose here, uniting different voices and drawing on numerous artivist examples, point to the important role of practice. Translation has been used to highlight the gaps, margins, intervals, interstices, and other shifts in the city's space-time. We have, in a sense, used translation as a temporary tool, useful as long as it can help to think otherwise. As soon as it loses its critical edge, we shall move on to another tool.

Scholarly research and, as it happens, this chapter propose that we think otherwise by leaving the comfortable room of our specialities to create a space for dialogue and the launching of alternative ideas. Without attempting to arrive at definitive conclusions, we recognize our responsibilities as researchers to engage with initiatives at the intersection of art, activism, and translation, where it becomes possible to reimagine collective alternatives. We feel that creating dialogue instead of playing the role of experts is a step in this direction, and we hope that this openness, resulting from a friendship too often masked by the apparent neutrality of academic research, will encourage response.

NOTES

1 Consider, among a multitude of examples: the volunteer translating collectives Translating the Printemps Érable (translatingtheprintempserable.tumblr.com) and Rouge Squad (rougesquad.org/fr) that emerged during the 2012 Quebec student protests; the Canadian Centre for Architecture's 2008 exhibition *Actions: What You Can Do with the City*; and the subsequent seminar at the same institution, Modernity in Translation: Geopolitical Interactions in Residential Culture (http://www.cca.qc.ca/fr/centredetude/355esraakcanmodernityintranslation).

2 "Art urbain et traduction," Pearltrees, http://www.pearltrees.com/msuchet/art-urbain-traduction/id7896025.

3 Présences du littéraire dans l'espace public canadien (PLEPUC) is a database of over 600 Canadian literary works created by a Concordia research group led by professor Marc André Brouillette. According to its website, PLEPUC aims to (1) contribute to the knowledge about the relation between various literary forms and their inclusion in public space; (2) encourage the creation of literary works by organizing multidisciplinary workshops that aspire to renew the connection between people and literature; and (3) publish information, articles and studies that can stimulate thought about the artistic, aesthetic, social, and urban issues surrounding this subject. "A propos," PLEPUC, http://plepuc.org/en/about.

4 See *Berlin Project* (2001), a site-specific video installation presented at the 2001 Contemporary Art Forum, Kitchener, Canada, http://uregina.ca/rvk/berlin.html.

5 To view the screen, visit "Berlin Project," PLEPUC, http://plepuc.org/fr/oeuvre/berlin-project; Rachelle Knowles, "Berlin," http://www.rachelleviaderknowles.net/berlin.html.

6 "Inhabited by a Spirit," PLEPUC, http://plepuc.org/fr/oeuvre/inhabited-by-a-spirit.

7 Jamie Hassan, "There Was and There Wasn't a City of Baghdad," PLEPUC, http://plepuc.org/fr/oeuvre/because-there-was-and-there-wasnt-a-city-of-baghdad.

8 Gilbert Boyer, "Comme un poisson dans la ville," PLEPUC, http://plepuc.org/en/artwork/comme-un-poisson-dans-la-ville.

9 Roadsworth, "Untitled," PLEPUC, http://plepuc.org/en/artwork/untitled-13.

10 Mutandas, "Warning: Perception Requires Involvement," http://ensembles.mhka.be/items/5945/assets.

11 Trevor Gould, "Fable VII," PLEPUC, http://plepuc.org/fr/oeuvre/fable-vii.

12 Trevor Gould, "Trevor Gould," Concordia, https://www.concordia.ca/faculty/trevor-gould.html.

13 Jean-François Gavoty, "Jardin de Lyon (Montréal)," http://jfgavoty.free.fr/nord-est/n2e1.html.

14 Jean-François Gavoty, "Un jardin avec des ailes (Lyon)," http://jfgavoty.free.fr/nord-est/n3e1.html.

15 Marlene Creates, "Virtual Walk of the Boreal Poetry Garden," http://marlenecreates.ca/virtualwalk/map.

16 "Blog du rucher collectif du CRAPAUD," CRAPAUD, http://www.crapaud.uqam.ca/?page_id=37.

17 "Portfolio: Park(ing) Day," Rebar, http://rebargroup.org/parking-day.

18 Antonia Hirsch, "Double Blind," http://plepuc.org/en/artwork/double-blind.

19 Stephen Foster, "Kiss and Tell," http://projets.chambreblanche.qc.ca/stephenfoster.

20 Taien Ng-Chan and Agence TOPO, *Detours*, http://agencetopo.qc.ca/detours/main_en.html.

21 Christian Nold, "Bio Mapping/Emotion Mapping," http://biomapping.net.

22 Pascal Nicolas-Le Strat is a member of Laboratoire d'Etudes et de Recherches en Sociologie et Ethnologie de Montpellier – EA 4584. He serves on the editorial committee of the politics, art, and philosophy journal *Multitudes*. His numerous publications on political and artistic practices and experiments are available through the COOP cooperative. For more on the notion of the interval, see also Atelier d'Architecture Autogérée (www.urbantactics.org) and Guillaud (2009).

23 The premises of the Association for Asylum Seekers in the Maison des Associations were used for the workshops. The Association for Asylum Seekers, financed mainly by state subsidies, is one of two associations in

Grenoble that help asylum seekers with their administrative procedures. Some of the main functions carried out by the Association for Asylum Seekers include drawing up and translating life stories, making appeals to the CNDA (French court reviewing appeals on refugee status), providing legal aid, supporting asylum seekers at meetings with the authorities, and financing the journey to the CNDA in Paris.

13

Montreal's Third Spaces on Foot

ANDRE FURLANI

RUELLES

The city dweller's immersive sidewalk perspective is adopted by an array of artists who wish to engage Montreal's linguistic diversity. Urban third spaces – those proximate, levelling, and convivial public areas between home (first space) and work (second) that foster passing encounters among habitués and strangers alike – are usually pedestrian, and these artists hone there a peripatetic enunciation that strays constantly from monolinguistic script. Theirs are works of textual itinerancy through varied linguistic ambiences that reveal a primary yet unacknowledged kind of knowing. "Knowledge is integrated *along* a path of movement," insists anthropologist Tim Ingold (2007, 91) in *Lines*. The pedestrian perspective is saccadic, tactile, resonant, restricted, and vulnerable, yet is also a powerful mode of knowing that picks up a consort of voices without segregating them wholly into discrete utterances. In the art of contemporary Montreal, relations are consonances of hazard and intent fortuitously established afoot.

The word *flânerie* retains an unflattering class bivalence: both genteel sauntering and contemptible "loitering," peregrination, and vagrancy. However, it no longer narrowly denotes decadence or a patrician imperturbability immune to the city's clamour and solicitations. The following examples of Montreal *flânerie* do not hearken back to genteel Second Empire strolling, where idleness provided a cavalier demonstration of resistance to the Taylorist imperatives of productive labour; the contemporary *flâneurs* and *flâneuses* are rather stalkers and foragers on the prowl for the composite character of a city that defies subordination to an ideologically totalized voice.

André Carpentier (2005, 16) rehabilitates *flânerie* to characterize his strolls over three years among the 400 kilometres of Montreal's alleys, a routine that organizes his *Ruelles, jours ouvrables* (Alleys: Working days): "*Flânerie* invites the stroller to discover public spaces, to wander aimlessly, without purpose, guided by intuition and acuity, and with full subjectivity. One becomes a perceiving machine colliding with places, because *the body unites us with things*, as Merleau-Ponty wrote."[1] Carpentier introduces the verb *flânoter* to denote the twin practice of loitering and notes: "J'aime à croire que le verbe clé de mon entreprise est flânoter, qui, à l'oreille, joint la flâne à la prise de notes" (102: I like to think that the key verb of my project is *flânoter*, which to the ear combines *flâner* and note-taking).

The laneways are an intermediary third space, public yet domesticated, a thoroughfare yet a playground, what Carpentier calls "les coulisses" (37: the street's backstage). "La ruelle et ses cours et galeries," he writes, "c'est déjà un peu la vie privée" (44: The alleys and its courtyards and balconies are already a bit of private life). They become the secondary setting of family relations and relaxed social propinquity. On several occasions Carpentier has to answer to the police for his presence. When, returning to the lanes of his childhood, he explains that he is taking notes toward a possible essay on them, an officer retorts that "ce n'est pas la place pour écrire un roman" (32: this isn't the place to write a novel). Only his Université de Québec à Montréal faculty card avails.

The *ruelles* are acoustic transmitters channelling a multiplicity of voices that tax the writer's plodding medium: "As night falls, I find myself in a neighbourhood of francophones of every walk of life, diphthongizing, lisping, hissing, gutturalizing, chewing over words, in a symphony of bass and nasal tones where the *whoms* perform the musical score of the *whose*. What a delight!" (105).[2] It is a reminder that the city incubates not only a host of languages but also a host of French idioms from the dialects of Quebec to those of the international *francophonie*. The alleys assume for Carpentier the character of a local resident embodying social hierarchy: "The alleys, in fact, behave very much like people, first addressing passers-by formally as *vous*, then more causally as *tu*, and often referring to them in the third person as a stranger: *Who's there?* So one assumes the stance of *I'm just passing through*, and the alleys respond *Go ahead then!*" (28).[3]

In other places the language is a macaronic jumble of colloquialisms, as when two "formidable jaseurs" puff cigarillos and chatter: "I hear one say that a roommate, lucky bastard! has *une date* with the *waitresse* from the deli, the one who has the top *stretché*. Apparently, she's totally hot, an *écoeurant de beau pétard*! As for the roommate, it seems he's fed up with the *coquerelles* – the *cucarachas*, via the English *cockroach*. 'If he doesn't like it,' says the other, 'he can go *crash* somewhere else!' I'd never heard that one before" (105).[4]

In Little Italy he admires the youths who function simultaneously "dans trois langues différentes" (186: in three different languages). Because Quebec's language Bill 101 requires them to attend school in French, Carpentier wryly calls French and English "la 101 et l'indispensable" respectively (186). A little further north the alley passes the garden of a cultural centre where immigrant pensioners who did not come under the jurisdiction of the law argue in several languages: "The insults and arguments are flying, in English mostly, but also in at least two or three other languages. The expressions *I can't believe it!* and *What do you mean, living apart?* are repeated over and over. Who is this couple of octogenarians creating such a scandal because they're going to separate?" (198).[5]

Carpentier invokes Deleuze and Guattari's concept of "lines of flight" (34), and Michel de Certeau's (1984, xviii) "lignes d'erre," wandering but efficacious lines that affront urban and state master plans; such rationalist teleologies often are aberrant draconian impositions incompatible with human circulation (see, e.g., Jacobs 1961, ch. 12). "For all of us, in reality, knowledge is not built up as we go across, but rather grows as we go along," Ingold (2007, 102) writes. Carpentier documents that growth step by step.

Along with Carpentier, some of the most innovative contemporary Canadian artists and writers register Montreal's meshwork threads and traces in an area Ingold, de Certeau, Deleuze, and Guattari do not broach: the itinerant plurality of languages. If wandering may be equated with knowing, as they show, these artists reveal, indeed revel in, the fact that linguistic third spaces are not confined strictly to spaces as determinate sites but extend equally to fluid situations, being no less directional than locative, indeed proving as kinetic as language itself. Languages are inflected not only by case but also by transitory pedestrian encounter.

Carpentier "flan-notes" the polyglot semi-private passages of the city while, in what follows here, a poet paces the mountainside park in another poet's steps, ethnographers record the still-reverberating locks of the former industrial canal, an audio artist stalks her own museum exhibit, a performance artist imprints canvas with his shoes in a bustling square, and a computer artist takes her dog around the digital neighbourhood. The linguistically plural lines of these artists are not ruled but digressive in the literal as well as rhetorical sense, sallyings forth with the "straight crookedness of a good walking stick," as in Robert Frost's (1966, 19) trope of the ideal poem. Although *Ruelles* is a prose travelogue, Peter Van Toorn's *Mountain Tea* a verse sequence, *Soundwalks* an acoustic ethnography, *Conspiracy Theory* an art installation, *LUNE* a performance piece, and *Entre Ville* a website, each contributes to the revival of the excursus, a genre that, because it is as protean as its peripatetic organizing procedure, has appropriately escaped categorization.

What one acquires fortuitously along the line is conventionally regarded as trivial, hence excursus denotes a brief departure from the dominant subject, a digression, that is, supplementary to what is systematically acquired at the end. Yet along the line hums a distinct and universal way of knowing. Potentially transgressive (literally the overstepping of a boundary), this knowledge is wont to affront preceptor, priest, or parliamentarian: an erratic clamour of meanings unintelligible or noxious to the ideologically pure administrators of uniformity. This includes linguistic uniformity. The third spaces of spontaneous, singular, and transient encounter make a festive mockery of system.

ENTRE VILLE

To the stoop, the street corner, the gallery, the park, and the revitalized industrial quarter has been added a virtual third space that includes locative media, digital apps, video games, and websites. The *flâneur* and *flâneuse* have wandered into the web, an extraterritorial domain no less governed than the city itself by principles of circulation.[6] J.R. Carpenter sets her electronic walk, *Entre Ville*, one of the earliest digital *déambulations*, in the former garment district of Mile End that now houses Ubisoft and other gaming companies. In it, the currents of languages merge with other sign systems to form a mutating ideogram of the ethnic but gentrifying neighbourhood.

The home page of the *Entre Ville* website, which premiered at an event at the Montreal Museum of Fine Arts in 2006, is a notebook surrounded by images of clotheslines, postal franking, a dog, a flower, gloves, a home address, a tattoo, and a signpost. The notebook includes a whimsical free sketch of adjoining row houses and scrolling poems. Several of the tenement windows and doors glow under the cursor and open onto a range of icons, including a street map.

The mutt – inquisitive, gregarious, and easily distracted – is the heraldic creature of aimless urban circulation. "Let's say our dog walks us up and down this alleyway three times a day," Carpenter writes. "We walk as if intent on studying every scent." For all the superb proficiencies of the species, the dog shares pedestrian limitations: neither as nimble as a cat nor as stealthy as a rodent nor capable of flight, the dog takes its readings from the ground up in lowly and restrictive stages. The "pedestrian point of view" that Carpenter maintains is canine.

As the creature of a tawdry interstitial territory, it is the real native of the alleys. The peripatetic philosopher Diogenes, epitome of the disenfranchised yet wily urban interloper, was a manumitted slave and *metic*; from this status is derived the French pejorative *métèque* (once a common ethnic slur). Subject to this legal discrimination in Athens, Diogenes identified himself as a cosmopolitan (he coined the word) and identified his philosophy with the curs that followed him and with the reproach that canine fellowship attached to him, "dog-like": *kunos*, cynic. Like the classical Cynics, Carpenter and her dog track a different city, foul but by no means abject. In a 2007 MIT lecture subsequently included on *Entre Ville*, Carpenter states that she and her dog "try to read between the alleyway's long lines." This equates the alley with writing. The lanes are lines of writing with hidden messages in plain sight.

The dog is the demoted yet stubbornly imposing element in the third space. There is pronounced sidewalk communication between pedestrians and pets. Social animals like their pets, dog-owners are seldom impeded by linguistic constraints, and manoeuvre between languages to establish informal courtesy and gratify curiosity. Dogs are triggers of encounter, quadruped third spaces and paragons of nonverbal communication. (Carpenter's novel is entitled *Words My Dog Knows*.)

Like the real mice infesting her neighbourhood the computer mouse slithers over the hand-scrawled sign À VENDRE, from which images of items on sale along the sidewalk (*vente à trattoir*) appear at a click. Sidewalk sales recirculate objects and turn the inside outside, encouraging a degree of intimacy. The maverick urbanist Jane Jacobs (1961, 56) challenges architectural modernism and rational urban planning by measuring the city's success by sidewalk traffic, and recognizes the sidewalk as a contact zone: "The sum of such casual, public contact at a local level – most of it fortuitous, most of it associated with errands, all of it metered by the person concerned and not thrust upon him by anyone – is a feeling for the public identity of people, a web of public respect and trust, and a resource in time of personal or neighborhood need. The absence of this trust is a disaster to a city street. Its cultivation cannot be institutionalized. And above all, *it implies no private commitments*."

There is much such trust in *Entre Ville*, but also surveillance implying suspicion and fear. Another door opens onto a handmade sign before an entrance: *ATTENTION UNE CAMERA VOUS REGARDE* (warning: you are on camera). The sign is pasted into the notebook, which contains an entry about collective surveillance in a neighbourhood where every balcony is a theatrical gallery "upon its neighbouring loge."

A house number opens onto the question "c'est quoi, ton numéro?" (what's your number). Click the Greek neighbour's window and a Greek-French dictionary page appears, a fifteen-cent postage stamp commemorating that most visible conjunction of the Greek and the French: the 1976 Montreal Olympic games. In *Beautiful Losers*, a novel cited in *Entre Ville*, Leonard Cohen includes entries from a Greek-English dictionary, which for its narrator becomes a litany and a prayer. Among the entries is a term of passing habitation: *epi'kata'meno*: *séjourner*. Click it and receive the cheeky gloss, "It's Greek to me," bane to Greek emigrants among English speakers. The stamp itself unites Montreal with Olympos, ancient capital of eirenic commingling of rival states under the sign of competitive play; when the image is clicked, that successor technology for distance communication, a prompt directly to Carpenter's email, appears.

A telephone indicates another modern apparatus of communication. To it a clothesline has been attached, and a synaesthetic motto: "Cooking smells and laundry lines crisscross the alleyway one sentence at a time." A line is both a string and a string of words. It is Carpenter's trope for a third space that is made up not only of verbal signals but material properties as well. Odours, echoes, garments, and telephone wires relaying between flats belong to a concatenation of fleeting yet defining exchanges, like the threads binding visibly every relation in Italo Calvino's (1971, 83) invisible city of Ersilia, where all civic ties are reticulated along coloured threads that eventually choke all passage into "una ragnatele di rapporte intricate che cercano una forma" (a spider-web of intricate relations seeking a form).

Having first arrived in Montreal to study fibres at Concordia University's Department of Fine Arts, Carpenter's lines are so many threads and scribal tracings. Her tenement is a sketch, not a photo, expressive of brisk shorthand ductus, strokes producing a continuous line and a trail of ink. A meshwork or woven text, *Entre Ville* is a set of knots and interlaced movements, not nodes in a static network. She threads her way through a prefabricated yet pliant environment whose uses have been adapted by the ingenuity of its various users.[7] While bureaucrats promote a single speech, its dwellers confect neighbourhood creoles and idiolects.

Carpenter's reader interface is a form of congress, i.e., of shared passage across a space Euclidian, virtual, and psychic. Her Mile End is not a happenstance boho utopia but defiantly topian: "*Entre Ville* is hot, loud, crowded and dirty," she underscores in the MIT lecture. The place too is mongrel, an unkempt and indiscriminate thoroughfare where Carpenter, exhilarated by the shabby élan of its cosmopolitanism, refuses to discriminate *tref* from *kosher*. "This is not quite a first-person point of view," she writes on the site. "Our proximity disallows singularity. We go about our business. *Nous autres*. We're poor. It's hot. No one has air conditioning. This is common, a shared experience." Humidity is the specific climate of this website about a city that, while associated with winter, has its torrid season. The heatwave effaces the work of partitions and sequestration. The street gets permeable; the inner-outer logic of the *ruelle* and the *gallerie* spreads through open windows, onto rooftops, and into the street.

The line between writing and reading is also eroded in a work of *Merzbau* bricolage[8] that borrows its heat wave not only from personal exposure but exposure to texts in the public library (local and university library stamps appear), including *The Street*, in which Mordecai Richler recounts a 1940s heat wave when the district was predominantly Jewish, and *La Grosse femme d'à coté est enceinte* (The fat woman next door is pregnant), in which Michel Tremblay recounts a 1950s heat wave when the Plateau was predominantly French working-class. Carpenter affirms the validity of de Certeau's claim for a pedestrian enunciation, writing, "*Entre Ville* is a text of walking, and a walk through texts."

Invitations to reply in real time meanwhile permit the reader to deposit an auxiliary layer of inscription. In her lecture, Carpenter notes: "Gossip is rampant on our street. Voices carry. Words get around, especially online. Occasionally the neighbourhood writes me an email." Such sedimentation transforms the site into a digital *carrefour* in which Montreal embodies the precarious conditions of global citizenship. The city becomes a rhetorical as well as a geographic topos.

That rhetoric is more than only polyglot, it is a heteroglossia of registers sounded off of the many resonant surfaces of the area. The urban text is indeed percussive. In "Sniffing for Stories," the pavement rings as poet and pet mutate into a city centaur on six feet: "That's eight-and-a-half years of up and eight-and-a-half years of down. Nine-thousand three-hundred laps of toenails clicking on cracked concrete, trail zigzagging, long tail wagging, long tongue lolling, dog tag clacking. Ears open, eyes darting, nose to the ground."

The pace, rhythm, duration, and echo of urban stravaging resists the division into discrete experiences. This is one reason for recourse to the web, an integrative medium for those "literalists of the imagination" that Marianne Moore (1982, 267) calls poets. "We walk like we own the place," Carpenter boasts. "We walk to write the place, to collect, collate and annotate the multitude of texts generated by the occupants of *Entre Ville*."

Among the texts quoted under the rubric *entre guillemets* (in quotation marks) is Cohen's poem "Snow Is Falling," in which the poet occupies a room with a nude woman: "She is eighteen. / She has straight hair. / She speaks no Montreal language." "What was a Montreal language?" Carpenter asks. "I was dying to find out." Settling a few blocks from Cohen's Montreal house, she writes: "I spent the next fifteen years learning the vocabulary of the neighbourhood. I don't mean French, English, Italian, Greek, Portuguese, Yiddish, or any other languages spoken in Mile End. I refer to the cumulative vocabulary of neighbourhood: the aural, audio, visual, spatial, tactile, aromatic and climatic vocabulary of community. I have attempted to present *Entre Ville* in this vocabulary."

This third space mingles aromas, ventilators, and laundry, it withdraws library books, clicks its heels and claws, posts signs on poles and online, and sends its detritus on the curb to be *telsquels* (recirculated).

The transitions between spaces and languages and even species, indeed the transitions between media, prove to be gradual, almost indistinct, like the franglaisword *balconville* popularized by David Fennario's eponymous, combative referendum-era play, from which Carpenter also quotes. "Poetry is not hard to find between the lines of fences," a graffiti pop-up utters in surrealist fashion.

MOUNTAIN TEA

Poetry is not hard for Peter Van Toorn to find between languages, and in *Mountain Tea* he does not simply represent the city's ensemble of languages but embodies it in virtuosic acts of translation. Many of its poems adapt canonical verse in the spirit of bebop variations on the Great American Songbook. The Dutch native, who arrived in Montreal in 1954 at the age of ten, has played tenor sax in a jazz band, and he himself draws the analogy in a 1983 essay while writing the poems:

> I aim at a text which will be native to the genius of contemporary English in Canada. My antecedents may be found in the "imitations" of Pound and Lowell. This kind of free interpretation should stand as a self-contained, autonomous poem: a transmutation or transposition, a new work in its own right – like the latest ad-lib of a "standard" in jazz. There exists no generally agreed-upon term for this kind of interpretation; but it aims to produce what the poet whose work is being translated might have done had he been writing in English in Canada at the present time. (Van Toorn 1983, 78)

In a book nominated for the 1984 Governor General's Award for Poetry, Van Toorn follows the lines of Basho, Goethe, Baudelaire, Ungaretti, and others as he follows the paths of Mount Royal park, *un dédale des voies et des voix* (a labyrinth of trails and voices). The feet are here no less bipedal than metrical. His off-course zigzags belong to a tradition spanning the itinerant renka poets of pre-modern Japan (several classical haikus are included), the *Minnesänger* and Troubadours, down to the *déambulations* of the Dadaists, surrealists, and their successors in the situationist international. Van Toorn also strolls in the convivial company of such Québécois contemporaries as Sylvain Gardeau, who has several poems of Montreal *flânerie*.

Mount Royal is the city's paramount contact zone, offering poets incentive to depart from protocol. A hillside park projects the illusion of suspended boundaries, sight lines hovering festively over the mundane city and toward the horizon. Like the furtive erotic interactions of its woods (substantially felled under Mayor Jean Drapeau in the 1950s to flush out fornicators, a harvest from which the mountain's ecology has never recovered), verbal interaction can be promiscuous. The park had been opened in 1876 as a bucolic antidote to social, economic, ethnic, and sectarian division in the rapidly industrializing city. Having recently designed Manhattan's Central Park, Frederick Law Olmsted sought to reconcile rural and urban, prole and patrician, French and English, Catholic and Protestant in the improving green theatre of morally legible nature.[9] Leisure had become an ethical category.

Van Toorn's choice of the mountain as the nexus of his Montreal poem is consonant with Olmstead's determination to translate the landscapes of Constable and the Lake Poets into an outdoor diorama. Inspired by the graveyard poets and the adjacent mountain graveyards, Olmsted aspired to make the park a vehicle for Rousseauvian reverie and Wordsworthian intimations of immortality. Simon (2006, 194) notes: "He conceived of the mountain as a poem whose meaning would progressively unfold as the viewer/walker followed its paths. The landscape was a work of art not only through the shapes that the author had scripted into it, but through the ever-changing readings that the viewers/walkers would create as a result of their particular trajectory and viewing positions." It is precisely the "ever-changing readings" that Van Toorn brings to what Simon calls Olmstead's *Gesamtkunstwerk* (ibid). De Certeau draws homologies between reading, writing, and walking, and in *Mountain Tea* the pedestrian speech act is exuberantly affirmed. Van Toorn does not so much translate the poems as take them along for a walk. They are invigorated by the alien semantic conditions.

Van Toorn grasps the insight of the Russian modernist poet Osip Mandelstam (1973, 115) that "to speak means to be forever on the road": "When we pronounce the word 'sun' we are, as it were, making an immense journey which has become so familiar to us that we move along in our sleep." The condition of speech is transit, for in uttering a word "we are living through a peculiar cycle" rather than volleying an "already prepared meaning," he insists (ibid).

Montreal poet Robert Allen (2005) defines the poem as a "standing wave," and the Poundian modernism that Van Toorn imbibes similarly gives priority to the verb. The optimal poet is then a wayfarer. Hence Mandelstam's (1973, 102) paeon to Dante: "The *Inferno* and especially the *Purgatorio* glorify the human gait, the measure and rhythm of walking, the foot and its shape. The step, linked to the breathing and saturated with thought: this Dante understands as the beginning of prosody."

As understood Rimbaud, marathon walker who has all but worn out another pair of shoes in "Ma Bohème," the peregrinating sonnet that Van Toorn takes on the inaugural hike of *Mountain Tea*. The principle of convertibility perpetuates the poem as "Mountain Going":

With rips in my pocket big enough to
put my fists through, my coat in great shape too,
I made for the mountains, Muse, true to you.
Jesus, the dreams of love I'd wake up to!
Skies I wore for hats! So who came by, hole
in his shorts, staying the night at the Hotel
Big Bear, to hear his stars swish and rustle?
Me, Tom Thumb, dreamer. Doodling my cuffs full,
leaning up against a ditch slope, left heel
under my bum, I'd smell valley wine, feel
it stick to my brows like a sweat, and start
deep shadow songs – rhyme them full of moon light,
twanging the red elastics of my right
running shoe, its sole just jammed to my heart.

(Van Toorn 2003, 91)

Rimbaud's poem is mum on origins and destination, it is all lines – of words, of (shoe) threads, of trails. Verlaine called his companion "l'homme aux semelles de vent" (the man with soles of wind), who already as a child had been an habitué of the public roads and admirer of the vagrants' perceived freedom from petite bourgeois morality. At fifteen Rimbaud fled 150 miles to Paris, and later led Verlaine on endless London dérives. In 1885 he abandoned poetry for vagabondage. "Like verse or music," writes Graham Robb (2000, 277; see Coverley 2012, 91–9), for the poet "walking was a rhythmical skill, a combination of trance and productive activity."

Translation in *Mountain Tea* is a mode of congress in the word's literal sense of a walking fellowship. Rimbaud and Van Toorn share something here more important than their twanging vocation; they share the succession of views and a companionable pace. Van Toorn's poem walks to the iambic step of Rimbaud's sonnet, the latter's Alexandrines curtailed into the pentameter of English accentual verse. The slightly modified Petrarchan stanzaic structure approximates Rimbaud's while the very freedom of the excursion invites semantic deviation and nonchalance. The opening sentence is more flippant and sardonic about the beggary that results from service to the muse. The topography too metamorphoses. These Quebec mountains rise out of the table lands of Rimbaud's native Meuse, near the Belgian border. "Ma Bohème" celebrates his defiant flight from Charlesville to Paris and then across the Belgian frontier. Sanctioned by Rimbaud's (1984, 57) invocation of the muse, Van Toorn transforms his downtown hill into Parnassus, seat of the classical Muses. Both poets will write Petrarchan love sonnets, but the result is a Whitmanesque "Song of the Open Road."

The legs are literally instruments of speech as well as locomotion. Van Toorn runs into Rimbaud and the French runs into English. Sloping lines of the mountain paths, iambic lines of handwriting (the cuff doodles), and plucked lines of shoelaces converge to unite French and English without the pieties of official bilingualism. When he wrote *Mountain Tea*, the park had not yet been subject to the signage that, since the 1990s, indicates directions, names, and landmarks in both languages. Olmsted opposed official language and monuments, and thus the mountain was still available to the poet for a personal cartography. A visual equivalent would be the situationist *Naked City* map. Van Toorn employs an unofficial language of literary encounter with a poet who, indexed by the Catholic Church and thus proscribed from libraries in ultramontane Quebec, assumed particular importance for the poets of the *révolution tranquille*, which occurred just as Van Toorn came of age.

"Readers are travellers," de Certeau (1988, 174) avers, while Umberto Eco (1994, 6) characterizes reading as a walk through the textual woods: "Even when there are no well-trodden paths in a wood, everyone can trace his or her own path ... The reader is forced to make choices all the time. Indeed, this obligation to choose is found even at the level of the individual sentence."

Van Toorn's convivial sequence of mountain strolls leaves a trail of reading, "from" Ronsard, Perse, Villon, Hugo, Baudelaire, and other

French poets who have entered the Quebec school curriculum. This is reading as production, de Certeau's (1988, xxi) "drift across the page" that achieves textual metamorphosis as the "wandering eye of the reader ... poaches on" the text. *Mountain Tea* presents an exemplary bipedal reader, a poaching nomad wandering through an established system (a literary canon, a plotted park). Pursuing the homology between pedestrian and reading habits, de Certeau declares that "every reading modifies its object" (169–70), and Van Toorn modifies Rimbaud's sonnet and Olmsted's park.

As a technique of translation, Van Toorn's substitutions, conversions, and poachings of Rimbaud epitomize what Simon (2006, 56) calls "warm" translation, "practices of pseudo-translation, deviant translation, and creative interference" that, in a way contrary to "cool" literalist practices, "activate circuits of exchange across the fragmented city." *Mountain Tea* descends from the poetics of A.M. Klein; like his Montreal precursor, Van Toorn uses slang, dialect, neologism, and polyglot locutions to create an extravagant diasporic language without ethnic hyphenation.

Thus Van Toorn insinuates an itinerant "Jesus" into Rimbaud's sonnet and plants "mountains" in his plain. The laces are now arterial "red," contiguous with the "heart" that the shoe ("*souliers blessés*" [Rimbaud 1984, 57]) is jammed against. "Doodling my cuffs full" is what Rimbaud often did, but not in "Ma Bohème." Van Toorn transfers Rimbaud's "*ombres*" from the path to poetry itself, as "deep shadow songs," and he adds "moon light" to the landscape.

Simon (2006, 151) states that "felicity rather than fidelity" governs warm translation, and felicity is both the theme of these poems and their mode of composition. Felicity is the Romantic promise of the ramble since Jean-Jacques Rousseau's *Rêveries d'un promeneur solitaire* and William Hazlit's "On Going a Journey." Fidelity in both poems is attached not to texts (an impossibility, as John Florio noted in 1576 in the preface to his translation of Michel de Montaigne's *Essays*),[10] but to agents encountered along the way: "Muse! J'étais ton féal" (Rimbaud 1984, 56) – "Muse, true to you" (Van Toorn 2003, 91). Fidelity is to forms of mediation founded in classical myth. "Mountain tea" is itself a kind of translation, for the book's title invokes Mount Royal, ceremonial tea services in the mountainous Japan of the peripatetic *renka* and *haiban* poets, marijuana, and the illuminated tee-shaped iron cross that, since 1929, has commemorated the arrival of the French.

SOUNDWALKS

"Reality is a sound, you have to tune in to it," Anne Carson (1998, 29) writes in *Autobiography of Red*, written while she was a professor of classics at McGill University. Andra McCartney and her collaborators in the *Soundwalks* seek the city's reality exclusively by means of a mini-disc recorder and stereo microphone, recording what, citing de Certeau, they call "les murmures de la vie quotidienne" (McCartney et al. 2002: murmurs of everyday life). *Soundwalks* captures the fragmentary, fortuitous harmonies of urban noise, tonalities without apparent coordinates. It is like an acetate version of William Carlos Williams's "Sunday in the Park" from *Paterson*, which also documented a decayed industrial riverside, in Paterson, New Jersey. Like Williams's poem, the recordings reveal rather than alter or augment the soundscape, realizing an immanentist aesthetic that collates and juxtaposes sensory data that usually stays in the background.

Free from narrative and tangible frame, the *Soundwalks*, in contrast to most modes of representation, impose no language hierarchy. The soundwalk is an art of contiguity, conjunction, and conversation. The walk is here dialectical and nonsynthesizing (see Robinson 2006, ch. 1), a mode of plenitude and presence. McCartney minimizes the imposition of a transcendent value by validating ear and foot, traditionally subordinate to eye and hand.

McCartney applies metaphorically the French gastronomic term *terroir* to the composite textures of the *Soundwalks*. The word is employed "to talk about food and wines, and how the tastes of the soil, the air, the water, and the vegetation of a region are mixed and transformed in the act of cooking or fermenting" (McCartney et al. 2002). This fermentation of the acoustic ecology, reduced to a murmur to ensure privacy, distils Montreal's linguistic zones into a quotidian yet almost utopian concoction.

For the *Balade Montréal Equinox Soundwalk*, her Soundwalk Interactions group congressed on 21 March 2013 along the lower Main to the Palais des congrès, Chinatown, and the Vieux Port. The improvised itinerary, itself rooted in Dadaist and surrealist practice, reversed the passage of immigrants to the city, for passenger steamships docked at the old port at the foot of St Laurent Boulevard. The disembarked passengers proceeded northward along what became the spine of industrialized, cosmopolitan Montreal, the Main informally dividing the French and English city into east and west. Speech occupies merely one stave in this diapason. In *Balade Montréal*, McCartney et al. (2014) invoke the concept of the ecotone: "The ecotone is a marginal zone, a transitional area where species from adjacent ecosystems interact. Some species in an ecotone are from neither ecosystem but thrive here and do not live elsewhere, because of the rich possibilities contained in such regions, which have characteristics of more than one ecosystem."

The polyglot Main ecotone is infused with peoples native to neither French nor English ecosystems who thrive in this transitional region that has characteristics of several ecosystems. It is just this ecology that the best writing about Montreal seeks to represent. Thereby is recovered what Francesco Careri (2006, 73) calls "terreni passionali" in "uno spazio liquido" (passional regions in a fluid space) that generate disorienting but productive affective tensions. Careri cites the precedent of the situationists in rediscovering this overlooked terrain: "*Elsewhere* is wherever, even in Paris, the exotic is always within reach; it suffices to lose oneself and explore one's own city" (72).[11]

Elsewhere is the Lachine Canal, where at the millennium McCartney and her collaborators recorded its reclamation from a defunct industrial quarter into a recreational area that has since attracted condominium development and tourism.[12] The resulting *Journées sonores, canale de Lachine* both documents and manipulates the soundscape over the several years of the revitalization.

The sounds of the Lachine Canal are fluently bilingual. In a section of the work entitled "Soundwalking at Night," McCartney's collaborator Sandra Gabriele paced the *terrain vague* on 25 October 2000, seventy-six years after the Dadaists inaugurated the motiveless ramble into *le terrain vague* of the St Julien-le-Pauvre quarter of Paris. Careri (2006, 48) notes that, by means of this pioneering 14 April 1924 walk, "one passed from the representation of movement to the practice of movement in actual space."[13]

As the Dadaists discovered a heterotopia not outside but within the city, so too does Gabriele, but it also conjures dystopia. The self-censoring dereliction of the Lachine Canal effectively excludes it from those "soft controls" that regulate circulation through urban North American areas. The mobility of the *flâneuse* is acutely subject to such controls, and Gabriele's evasion of this regimen at the volatile canal precariously increases her gendered visibility, even as the recording equipment, as McCartney notes, arrogates an ethnographic sense of "entitlement and access" (hernoise.org).

The recording apparatus picks up the gender of speech in the linguistic crucible of the dual city. A young man on a bicycle notices Gabriele walking in the shadows and turns back to approach her. He addresses her in French to her wary replies. And just as he had wheeled about abruptly, so now he rapidly code-switches to meet her in English. "I want to see what happens," he says. Gabriele takes refuge under a street lamp. He adds, "You want to stop recording?" She does not, for in a sense she wants the microphone to hear what happens. He asks what she is recording. "Just the sounds." "For school?" "For research." "For real?" He accedes to this imperative: "That's okay" ("Soundwalking at Night," *Journées sonores, canale de Lachine*).

"Powerful issues of ethics, entitlement, and privilege are brought into focus through the act of sound recording in public spaces" (hernoise.org), McCartney remarks upon retracing the canal walk with Gabriele in 2013. One of these privileges is linguistic, for the shift in dynamics occurs as well due to the code-switching. In 2013, McCartney and Gabriele do not discuss the bilingual nature of the encounter. Gabriele wonders whether moving into the light was meeting the stranger halfway, but she also took refuge in her native language, in order audibly not to meet the interrogator halfway. Doing so positioned their conversation outside his immediate territory, as the transition between languages momentarily re-established the linguistic relations that once prevailed between the anglophone management and the largely francophone labour force in an industrial quarter dominated by Redpath Sugar, Stelco, Dominion Textile, and Northern Electric. The English university researcher with sophisticated apparatus is menaced by the bicycling French plebeian. Gabriele's electronic carapace affords a measure of protection. The shift to English may be another one. She asserts herself by manipulation of an apparatus, by affiliation with a research institution, and by retrenchment in her native language in this federally administered territory.

Code switching is audible on the Parks Canada audio walking tour that now interprets the two-and-a-half-kilometre Lachine Canal trail. The tour contains the bilingual testimonials of Little Burgundy, Saint-Henri, and Pointe Saint-Charles residents. It complements the *Soundwalks*, in which talk is not heard but overheard. Steven High, Gabriele's colleague at Concordia University, collaborated on the canal guide and recognizes that a walking tour changes *le sens de la marche*: "When you are actually listening on site, you are hearing what was, you are seeing what is – and it ain't the same thing. There is a friction there. It's political" (quoted in Curran 2014). The pedestrian third space does not only dissolve but also coagulates political tensions that, in Montreal, routinely involve issues of language.

CONSPIRACY THEORY AND *LUNE*

The soundwalk records the mutating soundscape, an ethnographic practice akin to the recovery, in the contemporary fine arts, of bipedal locomotion as an instrument of creation, discovery, and recovery. When art goes for a walk in Montreal, its paths are the contact zone. A prominent linguistic contact zone in Montreal is the civic art gallery, hospitable to bilingualism and frequently mounting foreign exhibitions. By its nature fine art is at little risk of linguistic cantonization, and art galleries rarely can afford to court exclusively any single linguistic group, even the dominant one.

By making the museum and its patrons constituent elements in her audio *Walks*, Janet Cardiff harnesses the third space as a medium of fraught interaction. *Théorie du complot/Conspiracy Theory*, her 2002 audio *Walk* at the Musée d'art contemporain de Montréal transforms the gallery walk into the exhibit itself; the spectator, mobile and engaged in either or both official languages, becomes a witness, participant, and even accomplice in another of her ambiguous spectacles of innuendo and paranoia.

Cardiff's *Walks*, recorded with miniature microphones in collaboration with her husband George Bures Miller, are binaural recordings made with miniature microphones that reproduce sound in what appears to be three dimensions. The gallery visitor dons headphones and, in the case of *Théorie du complot/Conspiracy Theory*, circulates in and around the museum in obedience to the voice's prompting. Cardiff delivers instructions, observes, and chronicles occurrences in an even, contemplative, soothing but eerily dreamlike voice. The minutely planned, multilevel narrative is, as always, vaguely sinister and inconclusive. Carolyn Christov-Bakagiev (2002, 22) writes:

> Cardiff states that "the routes are designed to give the participant the physical experience of different types and textures of space." They also draw on earlier forms of entertainment such as radio plays, science fiction, "mad scientist" movies, funhouses and the haunted houses of theme parks. At the end of the Walks, a sense of loss and abandonment overwhelms you as you are left in a

> remote place and must find your way back alone from a bunker, from underground tunnels, from the corner of a library, from the middle of a forest, from the lakeside.

What begins as a didactic gallery tour soon becomes an autonomous, fragmentary narrative. Cardiff's instructions lead the auditor in, around, and below the museum in an atmosphere increasingly permeated by menace and intrigue. Disjunctions between the voice's description of the surroundings and the viewer's direct apprehension of them increase the disorientation, as does the mixture of ambient and fabricated sounds. Cardiff converts the neutral gallery corridors and exhibition spaces into a kinetic exhibit. The spectator becomes a possibly endangered and certainly manipulated co-conspirator in the elusive event, possibly a shooting, that takes place across the third space. "We wanted immersion," Cardiff explains in "Sculpting Sound," an 8 June 2010 CBC Radio broadcast of *Ideas*. "We're in the same sphere as the audience." Cardiff states: "In this type of work, synchronistic events play with the listener's understanding of reality. There is a sense of wonder and shock when events and scenes described on the audio tape coincidentally happen in the physical world. On the other hand, when something you hear is not there, the viewer is given a sense of displacement, as though they have been transported into someone else's dream" (Christov-Bakargiev 2002, 80).

Or translated there, for in the Montreal piece the disjunctions are also linguistic, as one traverses bilingual as well as binaural spaces. In the process, she furthers the museum rather as Van Toorn furthers Rimbaud's sonnet, in Simon's extended concept of translation as wayward "transmigration" between discrete civic alterities (Simon 2012, 157): "The city requires forms of furthering which will multiply points of contact between languages" (157). In Cardiff, the disorientations of a bilingual place, on the one hand, are magnified by the seductive and uncanny audio distortions, while on the other the place is transformed into a contiguous alternative place. One occupies a dual realm, both virtual and actual, in the bilingual museum, just as one occupies a dual realm in the bilingual city. As High says of the Lachine audio tour, the disjunction between what is heard and what seen is political. In officially unilingual Quebec, one reads the signs of State-legislated *francisation* but hears a multiplicity of tongues.

Conceptual and linguistic duality is also the spirit of another work exhibited at the Musée d'art contemporain. At the triennale Québécois held in 2011, the Montreal artist François Morelli hung tattered flags of his "lunar walks," LUNE. In his performance art, the walker himself becomes a kinetic third space. Raised in an Italian family in francophone east Montreal, the bilingual artist, who like McCartney and Gabriele is a professor at Concordia University, belongs among the first-generation of pedestrian performance artists. In the late 1960s, Richard Long in the United Kingdom and Robert Smithson in the United States pioneered very different forms of walking-as-medium (the bucolic *A Line Made by Walking* of the former, the post-industrial urban *Monuments of Passaic, New Jersey* of the latter). They inspired Morelli to reduce the dominance of the hand, classical standard of virtuosity, and recuperate the dignity of the foot.

"Before I compose a piece," said Eric Satie (quoted in Nicholson 2008, 129), "I walk around it several times." Morelli does not walk around it, he walks in it, simultaneous with the production of the artefact. In the 1974 ARBRE, he made the activity of walking both his subject and medium: he established a conceptual perimeter within the Hochelaga-Maisonneuve district of his youth and traced out a route with a canvas tied to one foot and calf, grinding a literal trace of his passage. He turned canvas shoes into painting canvas. "I was looking at ways of making or wearing or transcribing the environment around me in my day-to-day activities," he explained in a 2012 interview with Diaz-Bario. "The idea of walking with canvases and wearing them down" was, he continues, a way of working objectively, "without an interpretation of the hand, in terms of a kind of skill-based activity. It really is this notion of your feet touching the ground" (Diaz-Bario 2012). This breathtaking draftsman and painter sought a means of access to a place not restricted by intention.

Anticipating a central trope of Paul Auster's novel *City of Glass*, Morelli's itinerary through the working-class area traced out an ecological anagram, the French word for tree. *Les arbres* furnish the material from which Hochelaga-Maisonneuve and most other neighbourhoods are made. Softwood lumber is in Quebec a primary construction material, as hardwood lumber was the primary heating fuel before hydro-electricity. Cities cut down forests and consume their lumber. Deciduous canopies cast shade over sidewalks and streets. In Quebec the boreal forests are mythologized and, as English speaks of "old stock" settlers, French speaks of *Québécois de souche*, "stump" Quebecers who felled the Lower Saint Lawrence to farm the region. With a single noun and a pair of shoes, the first-generation Quebecer traces the history of the place.

One thinks "on one's feet" – that's alertness, spontaneity, resourcefulness; could one not also think *with* one's feet? This is Morelli's wager. He realizes Ingold's conception of knowledge as enmeshed along the flux of situations (see Ingold and Vergunst 2008, 5). "The storied world," he proposes, is one "of movement and becoming, in which any thing caught at a particular place and moment enfolds within its constitution the history of relations that have brought it there" (Ingold 2011, 160). Walking is the means by which stories are converted to a form of knowing that never forgets its basis and vitality in processes and embodiment rather than in hypostatized forms. It is the alternative to a Cartesian cartography and inventory of distinctly apprehended and anatomized extra-temporal objects in fixed, neutral space: "Knowledge is not classificatory. It is rather *storied*" (159). In *The Old Ways*, Robert Mcfarlane (2012, 24) similarly experiences "walking as enabling sight and thought rather than encouraging retreat and escape; paths as offering not only means of traversing space, but also ways of feeling, being and knowing." He urges that "walking is not the action by which one arrives at knowledge; it is itself the means of knowing" (27).

Morelli's walks link pedestrian mobility to politics. They transgress political, conceptual, or psychological boundaries, acts measured out in feet. *LUNE* revives the *ARBRE* regimen, again with a natural element, but one connoting romance, madness, and distraction (*avoir sa tête dans la lune* indicates dreaminess). In skullcap and casual dress, Morelli is a harmless crank limping along a downtown Montreal avenue, left foot on the ground, right foot on the moon: a white disk at the centre of a celestial blue flag under his shoe. Around Plaçe Emilie Gamelin, peopled with heavily policed marginalized groups, he traces out the word *LUNE*, a whimsical orbit that phlegmatically upsets the premises and portents of scopic cartography and the city planning that depends upon its gridded Cartesian abstractions. Morelli steps with peculiar immunity along Simon's (2012, 7) "translational city," alert to the linguistic variety urban theory and practice is often deaf to.

Morelli's performance art solicits interaction, and his lunar hobble excites bilingual exchanges that transform the walk into a convivial ambulatory third space. The chief artefact is the walk itself as a participatory mechanism that collapses binaries. He describes *LUNE* "as a kind of crazy idea of the moon and the earth touching each other and walking together, and the friction there" (Diaz-Bario 2012). Friction is the operative term, for Morelli's is a tribology of the contact zone. A smooth surface can only impede our step, Ludwig Wittgenstein (1984, 297) notes in repudiating analytic concepts of language for ordinary language philosophy: "We want to proceed; then we need *friction*," he declares in the *Philosophical Investigations*. "Back to the rough ground!"[14] A flawless logical language is unfeasible to us, as are the smooth surfaces of Le Corbusier's Radiant City. Simon (2012, 5) celebrates the sidewalk as just such an area of "friction." Friction is what gets Morelli around his lunar *parcours* and what gets his canvases painted.

Morelli shows that, in addition to a museum or a square, third spaces are portable, fortuitous, and convertible. Simply by walking about on a bandaged leg Morelli conjures a third space of saccadic encounter. *LUNE* provokes but poses no questions, as his extravagant step restores the original locomotive meaning of the word ambiguity: to pace back and forth (*ambigo*). The indecisiveness of Morelli's motives, and even of his materials, ensures a hesitation between possibilities. Is he injured, itinerant, lunatic? Is it art if painted not by hand, but by heel? Is he on earth or on the moon? Is it a bandage, a flag, a canvas? Is he strolling idly or intently composing?

Walking is writing here in de Certeau's sense of a pedestrian speech act, a rhetoric that is conjunctive, asyndetic, and phatic (see de Certeau 1988, 98, 101). Unlike, however, the allied performance artist François Alÿs, who trails punctured cans of paint along the Paris pavement before mounting the empty tins on a canvas, Morelli does not impose his signature on the environment. On the contrary, in his pedestrian ecology there is no defacement; the path leaves *its* signature on him and his lunar canvases.

Morelli's pedestrian is not the dominated, endangered subject of mechanized traffic and sprawl but is a fully fledged urban actor. And while enchantment engineering, like the encounter areas of Geneva and Montreal's Quartier des spectacles, confects fixed locations of festive public assembly, Morelli recuperates from the engineer a homely street-assembled aesthetic that generates bilingual enchantment out of a small piece of fabric.

Urbanist Michael Sorkin (2009, 27) notes that the dense, diverse city, mingling old and new, is never static but is instead a medium of exchange governed by Jane Jacobs's "golden rule" of "intensifying reciprocity." By modest means Morelli follows this principle. His lunar probes are anything but celestial, indeed they are happily sublunary; his walk links strangers into a kaleidoscope of stories. French and English, *promeneur* and astronaut, professor and madman, artist and idler, native and extraterrestrial, stalker and daydreamer: Morelli becomes a hybrid entity and thus a synecdoche for the city that he furthers just by going his way.

CONCLUSION

Third spaces and linguistic contact zones are as likely to be paths as places. The "third" is encountered *along* as well as *at*. The excursive pattern of the works here discussed is, as the word excursus implies (a "darting forth," "sallying forth," coursing along; rhetorically: digressiveness), borrowed from the pedestrian trail of idle reflection. Walking in these works favours juxtaposition, conjunction, and homology. It is somewhere between the loitering of the *flâneur* and the stalking of an investigator; forensic, evidentiary, yet fortuitous – materials in situ signalling stories the walker narrates. These excurses present a "storied world" in which the historical and personal narratives are not prior to circulation upon the pathways which channel their events, nor transmitted over a neutral, objective space. They are instead experienced as a confluence of ways and languages.

The Montreal peregrines "*flânotent*" the alleys and digitize the tenements, tape the polyglot canal murmurs and play them back in the gallery, hobble on a painted canvas and twang their laces, exempting themselves from the imposition of fixed linguistic subject positions and thus participating in equally mutable collective entities. The third space is then peregrine in the literal sense, deviating from the monitored zone of the tolerated, "integrated" *metic* (the Roman *peregrinatus*) into the porous passages of the unsponsored, free wanderer (the Roman *peregrinator*). The close resemblance of the Latin terms betrays the proximity of these purportedly discrete social classes, an instability that these labile Montreal excurses celebrate and extend to include the volatile channels of language.

NOTES

1 "Flânerie engage à conjuguer par la promenade des espaces publics, à zigzaguer sans but, sans calcul, prémuni de son flair, de son acuité, de sa pleine subjectivité, de sorte à enclencher sa function de machine à percevoir, aussi à se cogner aux lieux, puisque le corps nous unit aux choses, comme l'écrit Merleau-Ponty" (Carpentier 2005, 16).

2 "Au soir tombant dans un quartier de francophones de toutes les marches du pays, qui diphtonguent, zézayent, chuintent, grasseyent, mâchouillent les mots, dans une symphonie pour graves et nasals où les *que* jouent la partition des *dont*. Quelles délices!" (Carpentier 2005, 105).

3 "En fait, les ruelles se comportent comme des personnes, vouvoyant d'abord le passant, puis le tutoyant, et souvent le désignant à la troisième personne, celle de l'étranger: *C'est qui ç'ui-là?* Alors on se donne l'allure qui signifie *Je ne suis qu'un passant*, et leur air de rétorquer *Alors passez!*" (Carpentier 2005, 28).

4 "J'entends qu'un cochambreur, le bonyenne! a une *date* avec la *waitress* du delicatessen, celle qui a un top stretché. *Un écoeurant de beau pétard!* dit l'un. À propos du chambreur, y paraît qu'il est pas mal tanné des coquerelles – de *cucaracha*, via l'anglais *cockroach*. *Si y est pas content*, dit l'autre, *qu'y aille prendre une fouille ailleurs!* Celle-là, je ne l'avais jamais entendue" (Carpentier 2005, 105).

5 "Des invectives et des appels à la raison fusent de toutes parts, en anglais surtout, mais au moins dans deux ou trois autres langues. Les expressions *I can't believe it!* et *What do you mean, living apart?* sont répétés à la excès. C'est que ce couple d'octogénaires fait scandale parce qu'ils vont se séparer!" (Carpentier 2005, 198).

6 Will Straw and Alexandra Boutros (2010, 9–10) note that, unlike concepts of movement and mobility, which indicate human agents in Euclidian space, circulation also designates information, currency, and objects. Darren Wershler (2014, 1) adds that circulation concerns duration and takes "variations of intensity into account." Hence the hermeneutic value of the term as applied to the virtualized city of electronic literature.

7 The walk-ups are exemplary, the result of a legal loophole: having been required to reserve a plot between sidewalk and edifice, builders erected external stairwells on them to save internal space.

8 Kurt Schwitters collected much of his own interior *Entre Ville* on the streets of Hannover (see Gammard 2000, 87–114).

9 Yvan Lamonde (2013, 405) notes that the park did not initially attract a diverse public, being primarily "frequented by the anglophone middle class."

10 Calling translation "conversion," Florio (2014, 6) regards intellectual life as itself translation: "What do the best then but glean after others' harvests? Borrow their colors, inherit their possessions? What do they but translate?"

11 "L'altrove è ovunque, anche a Parigi, l'esotico è sempre a portata di mano, è sufficiente perdersi ed esplorare la propria città" (Careri 2006, 72).

12 Victorian Canada's predominant industrial quarter was rendered redundant in 1959 by the opening of the Saint Lawrence Seaway. Closed in 1972, its sluices were opened to become a dumping ground for the remaining factories. Areas of the bilingual working class Little Burgundy were demolished for public housing and expressways.

13 "Si passò dalla rappresentazione del moto alla pratica del moto nello spazio reale" (Careri 2006, 48).

14 "Wir wollen gehen; dann brauchen wir die *Reibung*. Zurück auf den rauhen Boden!" (*Philosophische Untersuchungen* #107).

References

Adam, Alfons. 2013. "'Slawisches Prag' versus 'deutsches Prag' – zwei konkurrierende Stadtmythen in der Zwischenkriegszeit." In *Mythen und Politik im 20: Jahrhundert. Deutsche – Slowaken – Tschechen*, edited by Edita Ivaničková Dieter Langewiesche and Alena Míšková, 101–21. Essen: Klartext.

Adelsgruber, Paulus, Laurie R. Cohen, and Börries Kuzmany. 2011. *Getrennt und doch verbunden: Grenzstädte zwischen Österreich und Russland 1772–1918*. Vienna: Böhlau.

Albrecht, Dietmar. 2006. *Wege nach Sarmatien – Zehn Kapitel Preußenland: Orte, Texte, Zeichen*. Munich: Martin Meidenbauer Verlag.

Alexander, Manfred. 1997. "Die Deutschen in der Ersten Tschechoslowakischen Republik." In Corsini and Davide, *Die Minderheiten zwischen den beiden Weltkriegen*, 117–31.

Almeida, Guilherme de. 2004. *Pela cidade*. São Paulo: Martins Fontes.

Apih, Elio. 1988. *Il ritorno di Giani Stuparich*. Florence: Vallecchi.

Appadurai, Arjun. 1996. *Modernity at Large: Cultural Dimensions of Globalization*. Minneapolis: Univ. of Minnesota Press.

Arad, Yitzhak. 1982. *Ghetto in Flames: The Struggle and Destruction of the Jews in Vilna in the Holocaust*. New York: Holocaust Library.

Artières, Philippe. 2014. *Les écrits urbains sous contrôle: L'Exemple de Montréal*. Rennes: Presses universitaires de Renne.

Augaitis, Daina. 2011. *Muntadas: Entre/Between*. Madrid: Museo Nacional Centro de Arte Reina Sofía.

Augé, Marc. 1992. *Non-lieux: Introduction à une anthropologie de la surmodemité*. Paris: Le Seuil.

Augoyard, Jean François. 2000. "L'action artistique dans l'espace urbain." In *Cultures en ville ou de l'art et du citadin*, edited by Jean Métral, 14–23. Paris: Éditions de l'Aube.

Badiou, Alain. 1997. *Saint Paul: La fondation de l'universalisme*. Paris: Presses universitaires de France.

Baioni, Giuliano. 1984. *Kafka: Letteratura ed ebraismo*. Torino: Einaudi.

Bakhtin, Mikhail. 1996. *The Dialogic Imagination: Four Essays*. Edited by Michael Holquist. Translated by Caryl Emerson and Michael Holquist. Austin: Univ. of Texas Press.

Balibar, Etienne. 2003. *We, the People of Europe? Reflections on Transnational Citizenship*. Translated by James Swenson. Princeton: Princeton Univ. Press.

Barbosa, Francisco de Assis. 1988. "Nota sobre Antônio de Alcântara Machado." In *Novelas Paulistanas*, edited by Antônio de Alcântara Machado, 27–52. São Paulo: Editora Itatiaia.

Barreirinhas, Yoshie Sakaiyama. 1983. *Menotti del Picchia: O Gedeão do modernismo 1920–22*. Rio de Janeiro: Civilização Brasileira.

Barsky, Robert. 1994. *Constructing a Productive Other: Discourse Theory and the Convention Refugee Hearing*. Philadelphia: John Benjamins.

– 2000. *Arguing and Justifying: Assessing the Convention Refugees' Choice of Moment, Motive and Host Country*. Aldershot: Ashgate.

Barthes, Roland. 1970. "L'ancienne rhétorique." *Communications* 16 (1): 172–223.

Baudelaire, Charles. 1919. "The Swan." In *The Poems and Prose Poems of Charles Baudelaire*, translated and edited by James Huneker. New York: Brentano's.

Baudrillard, Jean. 1993. *Symbolic Exchange and Death*. Translated by Iain Hamilton Grant. London: Sage.

Bauman, Zygmunt. 2000. *Liquid Modernity*. Malden: Polity Press.

Becher, Peter, and Anna Knechtel, eds. 2010. *Praha–Prag 1900–1945: Literaturstadt zweier Sprachen*. Passau: Karl Stutz.

Bell, Gwen, and Jaqueline Tyrwhitt, eds. 1972. *Human Identity in the Urban Environment*. Harmondsworth: Penguin.

Benedictsen, Age Meyer. 1924. *Lithuania, "The Awakening Nation": A Study of the Past and Present of the Lithuanian People*. Copenhagen: Egmont H. Petersen.

Benjamin, Walter. 1999. *The Arcades Project*. Translated by Howard Eiland and Kevin McLaughlin. Edited by Rolf Tiedemann. Cambridge, MA: Harvard Univ. Press.

Berghaus, Günter. 2000. "Futurism, Dada and Surrealism: Some Cross-fertilisations among the Historical Avant-gardes." In *International Futurism in Arts and Literature*, edited by Günter Berghaus, 271–304. Berlin: de Gruyter.

Berman, Antoine. 1984. *L'épreuve de l'étranger*. Paris: Gallimard.

Besse, Jean-Marc. 2010. "Cartographies." *Les Carnets du Paysage* 20: 4–9.

Beug, Joachim. 1991. "Die Grenzschenke: Zu einem literarischem Topos." In Chambers, *Co-existent Contradictions*, 148–65.

Bhabha, Homi. 1994. "How Newness Enters the World." In *The Location of Culture*, 212–35. London: Routledge.

Bihl, Wolfdieter. 1980. "Die Juden." In Wandruzska and Urbanitsch, *Die Völker des Reiches*, 880–948.

Billboard. 1975. "CHOM-FM Is Making Big Strides after Hurdling Obstacles." 11 October.

– 1976. "FMer Told to Drop French Broadcasts." 14 August.

– 1977a. "Broadcast and Print Media Focus on Mother Tongue French Audience." 29 January.

– 1977b. "Montreal Gets FM Outlet for New Quebecois Acts." 29 January.

Bion, Francesca, ed. 1998. *Pensée Sauvage, Pensée Apprivoisée*. Larmor-Plage: Éditions du Hublot.

Boothman, Derek. 2010. "Translation and Translatability: Renewal of the Marxist Paradigm." In *Gramsci Language and Translation*, edited by Peter Ives and Rocco Lacorte, 107–33. Lanham: Lexington.

Borges, Jorge Luis. 1977. *Obras completas*. Edited by Carlos V. Frías. Barcelona: Emecé.

Brenner, Neil, and Nik Theodore. 2002. "Cities and the Geographies of 'Actually Existing Neoliberalism.'" *Antipode* 34: 349–79.

Breton, André. (1928) 1988. *Nadja*. In *Oeuvres complètes*. Tome 1. Paris: Gallimard.

Brito, Mario da Silva. 1958. *História do Modernismo Brasileiro*. Vol. 1. São Paulo: Saraiva.

Brod, Max. 1969. *Streitbares Leben*. Munich: Herbig.

Brodsky, Joseph. 1992. *Watermark*. New York: Farrar, Straus and Giroux.

Bronsen, David, ed. 1975. *Joseph Roth und die Tradition. Aufsatz- und Materialiensammlung*. Darmstadt: Agora Verlag.

Brown, John Seely, and Mark Weiser. 1996. "The Coming Age of Calm Technology." http://www.ubiq.com/hypertext/weiser/acmfuture2endnote.htm.

Buarque, Chico. 2004. *Budapest: A Novel*. Translated by Alison Entrekin. New York: Grove.

Bureau of Broadcast Measurement (BBM). 2014. "PPM Top-Line Radio Statistics." 6 March. https://www.bbm.ca/_documents/radio_market_ratings/march_6_2014/2013-14_03_Radio_ME_MontrealToplineRadio.pdf.

Butler, Judith. 2004. *Precarious Life: The Powers of Mourning and Violence*. New York: Verso.

Calvino, Italo. 1971. *Le Città invisibili*. Torino: Einaudi.

Canadian Broadcasting Corp (CBC). 2014a. "Canadian Communications Foundation, Radio Station History, CBM-FM (Radio Two)." http://www.broadcasting-history.ca/index3.html?url=http%3A//www.broadcasting-history.ca/listings_and_histories/radio/histories.php%3Fid%3D477%26historyID%3D241.

– 2014b. "Canadian Communications Foundation, Radio Station History: CKOI-FM." http://www.broadcasting-history.ca/index3.html?url=http%3A//www.broadcasting-history.ca/listings_and_histories/radio/histories.php%3Fid%3D498%26historyID%3D679.

Canadian Communications Foundation. 2013. "Television Station History: CBFT-DT (SRC Network)." http://www.broadcastinghistory.ca/index3.html?url=http%3A//www.broadcasting-=history.ca/listings_and_histories/television/histories.php%3Fid%3D103%26historyID%3D105.

Canadian Radio-Television and Telecommunications Commission. 1976. Decision CRTC 76-498. 28 July. Ottawa: Canadian Radio-Television and Telecommunications Commission.

Canadian Radio-Television Commission. 1973. CRTC Decision 73-80. 19 March. Ottawa: Canadian Radio-Television Commission.

– 1975. CRTC Decision 75-32. 28 January. Ottawa: Canadian Radio-Television Commission.

Candido, Antônio. 1980. "A vida ao rés-do-chão." *Recortes*, 13–25.

Careri, Francesco. 2006. *Walkscapes: Camminare come praticaestetica*. Torino: Einaudieditore.

Carlucci, Alessandro. 2013. *Gramsci and Languages: Unification, Diversity, Hegemony*. Leiden: Brill.

Carmo, Eduardo Benzatti do. 2004. "A obra ficcional e jornalística do escritor Antônio de Alcântara Machado: letras e imagens." PhD diss., Pontifícia Universidade Católica de São Paulo.

Carpenter, J.R. 2006. *Entre Ville*. http://luckysoap.com/entreville.

Carpentier, André. 2005. *Ruelles, joursouvrables: Flâneries en ruelles montréalaises*. Montreal: Éditions du boréal.

Carson, Anne. 1998. *Autobiography of Red*. New York: Knopf.

Castells, Manuel, Mireia Fernández-Ardèvol, Jack Linchuan Qiu, and Araba Sey. 2006. *Mobile Communication and Society: A Global Perspective*. Cambridge, MA: MIT Press.

Castro, Ana Claudia Veiga de. 2008. *A São Paulo de Menotti del Picchia: Arquitetura, arte e cidade nas crônicas de um modernista*. São Paulo: Alameda Casa Editorial.

Cavafy, Constantine P. 1975. *Collected Poems*. Translated by Edmund Keeley and Philip Sherrard. Princeton: Princeton Univ. Press.
– 2003. *En attendant les barbares et autres poèmes*. Translated by Dominique Grandmont. Paris: Éditions Gallimard.
Cavell, Richard. 2002. *McLuhan in Space*. Toronto: Univ. of Toronto Press.
Cehan, Ayse. 2004. "Sécurité, frontières et surveillance aux États-Unis après le 11 septembre 2001." *Cultures & Conflits* 53: 113–45.
Celan, Paul. 1989. *Poems of Paul Celan*. Translated by Michael Hamburger. New York: Persea Books.
– 2005. "And with the Book of Tarussa." Translated by Joachim Neugroschel. In *Paul Celan: Selections*, edited by Pierre Joris, 95. Berkley: Univ. of California Press.
Certeau, Michel de. 1988. *The Practice of Everyday Life*. Translated by Steven Rendell. Berkeley: Univ. of California Press.
– (1984) 2011. *The Practice of Everyday Life*. Translated by Steven Rendall. Berkeley: Univ. of California Press.
Chambers, Helen, ed. 1991. *Co-existent Contradictions: Joseph Roth in Retrospect*. Riverside: Ariadne.
Chambers, Iain. 2001. *Culture after Humanism: History, Culture, Subjectivity*. London: Routledge.
Chattopadhay, Swati. 2005. *Representing Calcutta: Modernity, Nationalism, and the Colonial Uncanny*. London: Routledge.
Chiantaretto, Jean-François. 2005. *Le Témoin interne: Trouver en soi la force de résister*. Paris: Aubier.
Christov-Bakargiev, Carolyn. 2002. *Janet Cardiff: A Survey of Works Including Collaborations with George Bures Miller*. New York: P.S. 1 Contemporary Art Center.
Clerval, Anne, and Fleury, Antoine. 2009. "Politiques urbaines et gentrification, une analyse critique à partir du cas de Paris." *L'Espace Politique* 82. http://espacepolitique.revues.org/1314.
Clifford, James. 1997. *Routes: Travel and Translation in the Late Twentieth Century*. Cambridge, MA: Harvard Univ. Press.
Coetzee, J.M. 1982. *Waiting for the Barbarians*. Harmondsworth: Penguin.
Cohen, Gary B. 2000. *Němci v Praze 1861–1914*. Translated by Jana Mandlerová. Praha: Karolinum. (*The Politics of Ethnic Survival: Germans in Prague, 1861–1914*. Princeton: Princeton Univ. Press, 1981.)
Cohen, Israel. 1992. *Vilna*. Facsimile of 1943 copy. Philadelphia: The Jewish Publication Society of America.

Colin, Amy. 1991. *Paul Celan: Holograms of Darkness.* Bloomington: Indiana Univ. Press.

– 2006. "Czernowitz: A Testing Ground for Pluralism." In Cornis-Pope and Neubauer, *History of the Literary Cultures of East-Central Europe*, 56–7.

Collins, Richard. 1990. *Culture, Communication & National Identity: The Case of Canadian Television.* Toronto: Univ. of Toronto Press.

Colombi, Matteo. 2009. "Modernism and Multiethnicity? Interwar Czech Literature from Prague and Slovenian Literature from Trieste." *Primerjalna književnost* 32 (1): 139–62.

Colombi, Matteo, and Lenka Řezníková. 2010. "Tripolis Praga. Mýty kulturní plurality." In *Evropské město. Identita, symbol, mýtus*, edited by Blanka Soukupová, Hedvika Novotná, Zuzana Jurková, and Andrzej Stawarz, 64–80. Bratislava: Zing Print.

Cornis-Pope, Marcel, and John Neubauer. 2002. "History of the Literary Cultures of East-Central Europe: Some Theoretical Reflections." *ACLS Occasional Paper* 52: 14–16.

– eds. 2006a. *History of the Literary Cultures of East-Central Europe: Junctures and Disjunctures in the 19th and 20th Centuries.* Vol. 2. Amsterdam: John Benjamins.

– 2006b. "Cities as Sites of Hybrid Literary Identity and Multicultural Production." In Cornis-Pope and Neubauer, *History of the Literary Cultures of East-Central Europe*, 9–212. Amsterdam: John Benjamins.

Corsini, Umberto, and Zaffi Davide, eds. *Die Minderheiten zwischen den beiden Weltkriegen*. Berlin: Duncker & Humbolt.

Cote, Langevin. 1961. "FM Network Trial: CBC Venture in Bilingualism." *Globe and Mail,* 9 January.

Coverley, Miles. 2012. *The Art of Wandering: The Writer as Walker*. Harpenden: Oldcastle Books.

Creates, Marlene. 2005. "The Boreal Poetry Garden." Marlene Creates. http://www.marlenecreates.ca/works/2005boreal.html.

Cronin, Michael. 2006. *Translation and Identity*. New York: Routledge.

– 2013. *Translation in the Digital Age*. New York: Routledge.

Cronin, Michael, and Sherry Simon, eds. 2014. *The City as Translation Zone.* Special issue of *Translation Studies* 7 (2).

Crosbie, Judith. 2013. "The Growth of Intolerance." *Irish Times*, 29 June.

Csáky, Moritz. 2010. *Das Gedächtnis der Städte: Kulturelle Verflechtungen – Wien und die urbanen Milieus in Zentraleuropa*. Wien: Böhlau.

Curran, Peggy. 2014. "Lachine Canal Was Once Canada's Industrial Heartland." *Montreal Gazette*, 17 May.

Czarnecka, Ewa, and Aleksander Fiut. 1987. *Conversations with Czesław Miłosz*. San Diego: Harcourt.

Dalton, Craig, and Liz Mason-Deese (Counter Cartographies Collective). 2012. "Counter (Mapping) Actions: Mapping as Militant Research." *ACME: An International E-Journal for Critical Geographies* 11 (3): 439–66. http://www.acmejournal.org/vol11/CCC2012.pdf.

Darroch, Michael. 2008. "Language, Translation, and the Telematic City." *Flusser Studies* 6 (1): 12.

– 2010. "Language in the City, Language of the City." In Boutros and Straw, *Circulation and the City*, 23–47.

Dawidowicz, Lucy S. 1989. *From That Place and Time: A Memoir, 1939–1947*. New York: W.W. Norton.

Debord, Guy. (1958) 2006. "Theory of the Derive." In *Situationist International Anthology*, translated and edited by Ken Knabb, 62–7. Berkeley: Bureau of Public Secrets. http://www.cddc.vt.edu/sionline/si/theory.html.

Dějiny Prahy II. 1998. Praha: Paseka.

Dějiny Zemí Koruny české. 1993. Praha: Paseka.

Deleuze, Gilles. 1988. *Foucault*. Translated by Seán Hand. Minneapolis: Univ. of Minnesota Press.

Deleuze, Gilles, and Felix Guattari. 1980. *Mille Plateaux*. Paris: Les éditions de Minuit.

– 1986. *Kafka: Toward a Minor Literature*. Translated by Dana Polan. Minneapolis: Univ. of Minnesota Press. (*Kafka. Pour une littérature mineure*. Paris: Les éditions de Minuit, 1975.)

– 1988. *A Thousand Plateaus: Capitalism and Schizophrenia*. Translated by Brian Massumi. London: Athlone Press.

Demetz, Peter. 1997. *Prague in Black and Gold: The History of a City*. New York: Penguin.

Dennis, Kingsley, and John Urry. 2007. "The Digital Nexus of Post-Automobility." Department of Sociology, Lancaster Univ., 1–74. http://kingsleydennis.com/academic-writings.

De Tona, Carla, and Andrew Whelan. 2009. "Re-mediating the Ruptures of Migration: The Use of Internet and Mobile Phones in Migrant Women's Organisations in Ireland." *Translocations: Migration and Social Change* 5 (1): 1–20.

Diaz-Bario, Juan. 2012. "Interview with François Morelli." YouTube video. https://www.youtube.com/watch?v=uHsGtnww5T8.

Diminescu, Dana. 2008. "The Connected Migrant: An Epistemological Manifesto." *Social Science Information* 47: 565–79.

Döblin, Alfred. 1991. *Journey to Poland*. Translated by Joachim Neugroschel. New York: Paragon House.

Douay, Nicolas. 2012. "L'activisme urbain à Montréal: Des luttes urbaines à la revendication d'une ville artistique, durable et collaborative." *L'Information géographique* 76: 83–96.

Duarte, Paulo. 1971. *Mário de Andrade por ele mesmo*. São Paulo: Edart.

Ducas, Marie-Claude. 2012. "Frenglish Media in Quebec." *Headspace*, 22 May. http://whatquebecwants.typepad.com/whatquebecwants/2012/05/frenglish-media-in-qu%C3%A9bec.html.

Ducasse, Isidore, Comte de Lautréamont. 1983. *Lautréamont's Maldoror*. Translated by Alexis Lykiard. London: Allison and Busby.

Ducharme, Francis. 2009. "L'imaginaire de l'espace urbain montréalais dans *Bienvenue à* et *Ascension*, deux déambulatoires audioguidés d'Olivier Choinière." MA diss., Université du Québec à Montréal.

Džambo, Jozo. 2010. *Praha–Prag 1900–1945: Literaturstadt zweier Sprachen, vieler Mittler*. Passau: Verlag Karl Stutz.

Eco, Umberto. 2003. *Mouse or Rat? Translation as Negotiation*. London: Weidenfeld and Nicolson.

Edensor, Tim. 2008. "Walking through Ruins." In Ingold and Vergunst, *Ways of Walking*, 125–39.

Eggers, Dave. 2007. *What Is the What*. New York: Vintage.

Eliot, T.S. 1982. "Tradition and the Individual Talent." *Perspecta: The Yale Architectural Journal* 19: 36–42.

Fabris, Annateresa. 1994. *O Futurismo paulista: Hipóteses para o estudo da chegada da vanguarda ao Brasil*. São Paulo: Perspectiva.

Fassin, Didier, and Carolina Kobelinsky. 2012. "Comment on juge l'asile: L'institution comme agent moral." *Revue Française de Sociologie* 53 (4): 657–88.

Feichtinger, Johannes, Ursula Prutsch, and Moritz Csáky. 2003. *Habsburg Postcolonial: Machtstrukturen und kollektives Gedächtnis*. Innsbruck: Studien Verlag.

Fellerer, Jan. 2014. "One City United by Different Languages: Linguistic Practices in Late Habsburg Lviv." Paper presented at Cities as Cultural Spaces. Ukraine: History, Legacy, Literature. University of Vienna, Institute of East European History, 3–5 April.

Finger, Anke, Rainer Guldin, and Gustavo Bernardo. 2011. *Vilém Flusser: An Introduction*. Minneapolis: Univ. of Minnesota Press.

Fischer, Fabien, Lauriane Houbey, Sarah Mekdjian et Anne-Laure Amilhat-Szary, and Marie Moreau. 2013. "Crossing Maps/Cartographies traverses."

Antiatlas de frontières. http://www.antiatlas.net/blog/2013/09/20/crossing-maps-cartographies-traverses.
Fishman, David. 1998. *Dem Feuer entrissen: Die Rettung jüdischer Kulturschätze in Wilna*. Hannover: Laurentius-Verlag.
Florida, Richard. 2002. *The Rise of the Creative Class: And How It's Transforming Work, Leisure, Community and Everyday Life*. New York: Perseus Book Group.
Florio, John. 2014. "To the Courteous Reader." In *Shakespeare's Montaigne: The Florio Translation of the Essays, A Selection*, edited by Stephen Greenblatt and Peter G. Platt, 6–8. New York: New York Review of Books.
Flusser, Vilém. 1985. "L'espace de la ville et les nouvelles technologies: Table-ronde en Arles, passage du Mejan, 10/7/85." Unpublished manuscript.
– 1992a. "Alte und neue Codes: São Paulo." In *Städtische Intellektuelle: Urbane Milieus im 20. Jahrhundert*, edited by Walter Prigge, 196–219. Frankfurt am Main: Fischer.
– 1992b. *Ende der Geschichte, Ende der Stadt?* Vienna: Picus.
– (1992c) 2005. "The City as Wave-Trough in the Image-Flood." Translated by Phil Gochenour. *Critical Inquiry* 31: 320–8.
– (1983) 2000. *Towards a Philosophy of Photography*. London: Reaktion Books.
– (1983) 2013. *Post-History*. Translated by Rodrigo Maltez Navaes. Edited by Siegfried Zielinski. Minneapolis: Univocal.
– 2002. "Designing Cities." In *Writings*, translated by Erik Eisel, edited by Andreas Ströhl, 172–80. Minneapolis: Univ. of Minnesota Press.
– 2003. *Freedom of the Migrant*. Translated by Kenneth Kronenberg. Edited by Anke Finger. Urbana: Univ. of Illinois Press.
Foot, John. 2009. *Fratture d'Italia*. Milan: Rizzoli.
Foucault, Michel. (1969) 1972. *The Archaeology of Knowledge*. Translated by Alan Sheridan. London: Tavistock.
– 1981. "The Order of Discourse." Translated by Ian McLeod. In *Untying the Text: A Poststructuralist Reader*, edited by Robert Young, 48–78. London and Boston: Routledge and Kegan Paul.
– 2012. "Of Other Spaces." In *Theatre and Performance Design: A Reader in Scenography*, edited by Jane Collins and Andrew Nisbet, 73–81. London: Routledge.
Freud, Sigmund. 1989. *Civilization and its Discontents.* Translated by James Strachey. New York: W.W. Norton.
– (1926) 2002. *Inhibition, symptôme et angoisse*. Paris: PUF.
Frick, David. 2013. *Kith, Kin, and Neighbors: Communities and Confessions in Seventeenth-Century Wilno*. Ithaca: Cornell Univ. Press.

Frost, Robert. 1966. "The Figure a Poem Makes." *Selected Prose*, 17–22. New York: Holt, Rinehart and Winston.

Fuller, R. Buckminster. 1978. "Accommodating Human Unsettlement." *The Town Planning Review* 49 (1): 51–60.

Gabriele, Sandra. 2002. "Soundwalking at Night." In Andra McCartney, Owen Chapman, Anna Friz, and Sandra Gabriele, *Journées sonores, canale de Lachine*. http://www.andrasound.org/archive/Lachine%20Canal _ENG.pdf.

Galand, Sandrine. 2009. "Kiss and Tell." NT2 *Laboratoire de recherches sur les oeuvres*. http://nt2.uqam.ca/en/repertoire/kiss-and-tell.

Galofaro, Francesco. 2012. "Slavi si nasce o si diventa? La costituzione del Soggetto in 'Ritorneranno' di G. Stuparich." *E/C* VI (11–12): 97–101.

Gammard, Elizabeth Burns. 2000. *Kurt Schwitter's Merzbau: The Cathedral of Erotic Misery*. New York: Princeton Architectural Press.

Garnier, Jean-Pierre. 2011. "La 'classe créative': Un nouveau mythe urbain pour de nouvelles mystifications urbanistiques." *Terrains de luttes*. http://terrainsdeluttes.ouvaton.org/?p=447.

Gauthier, Joëlle. 2011. "Sacrée montagne." NT2 *Laboratoire de recherches sur les oeuvres*. http://nt2.uqam.ca/fr/repertoire/sacree-montagne-0.

Gavoty, JeanFrançois. 2004. "Un jardin avec des ailes." http://jfgavoty.free .fr/nord est/n3e1.html.

Geary, Patrick J. 1994. *Living with the Dead in the Middle Ages*. Ithaca: Cornell Univ. Press.

Giedion, Sigfried. (1941) 1982. *Space, Time and Architecture*. 5th ed. Cambridge, MA: Harvard Univ. Press.

– 1943. Postcard to Marshall McLuhan, 16 August. Marshall McLuhan Fonds, National Archives of Canada, MG31, D156. Vol. 24. File 65. Ottawa, Canada.

– 1948. *Mechanization Takes Command*. Cambridge, MA: Harvard Univ. Press.

Gilloch, Graeme. 1996. *Myth and Metropolis: Walter Benjamin and the City*. Cambridge, UK: Polity Press.

Girininkienė, Vida. 2004. *Vilniaus kapinės*. Vilnius: Atkula.

Glajar, Valentina. 2004. *The German Legacy in East Central Europe: As Recorded in Recent German-Language Literature*. Rochester: Camden House.

Glissant, Edouard. 1996. *Introduction à une poétique du divers*. Paris: Gallimard.

Globe and Mail. 1973. "Montreal Station Warned on Language." 20 March.

– 1976a. "A French Voice Strangled." 3 August.

– 1976b. "Montreal FM Station Is Ordered to Drop French Programming." 30 July.

– 1984. "Radio Station Gets Static over Slip of Tongue." 4 March.

Grade, Chaim. 2004. *My Mother's Sabbath Days: A Memoir.* Translated by Channa Kleinerman Goldstein and Inna Hecker Grade. Lanham: Rowman and Littlefield.

Gramsci, Antonio. 1971. *La costruzione del Partito Comunista*. Turin: Einaudi.

– 1992. *Prison Notebooks.* Edited and translated by Joseph A. Buttigieg. New York: Columbia Univ. Press.

Greenfield, Adam. 2006. *Everyware: The Dawning Age of Ubiquitous Computing*. Berkeley: New Riders.

Gruber, Ruth Ellen. 2002. *Virtually Jewish. Reinventing Jewish Culture in Europe.* Berkeley: Univ. of California Press.

Gruša, Jiří, Eda Kriseová, and Petr Pithart. 1993. *Prag. Einst Stadt der Tschechen, Deutschen und Juden*. Munich: Langen Müller.

Guasque Araujo, Yara Rondon. 2008. "The City as a Medium in McLuhan and Flusser." *Flusser Studies* 6, edited by Janine Marchessault and Rainer Guldin, 1–12.

Guastini, Mário. 2006. *A hora futurista que passou e outros escritos.* São Paulo: Boitempo.

Guillaud, Clara. 2009. "Interstices urbains et pratiques culturelles." *Implications philosophiques*. http://www.implications-philosophiques.org/Habitat/Guillaud1.html.

Guillot-Muñoz, Gervasio, and Alvaro Guillot-Muñoz. 1926. *Lautréamont y Laforgue*. Montevideo: Colección France-Amérique.

Guldin, Rainer, ed. 2004. *Das Spiel mit der Übersetzung: Figuren der Mehrsprachigkeit im Werk Vilém Flussers*. Tübingen and Basel: Francke.

– 2005. *Philosophieren zwischen den Sprachen*. London: Wilhelm Fink.

– 2008. "Die zweite Unschuld: Heilsgeschichtliche und eschatologische Perspektiven im Werk Vilém Flussers und Marshall McLuhans." *Flusser Studies* 6, edited by Janine Marchessault and Rainer Guldin, 1–24.

Haas, Willy. 1957. *Die literarische Welt: Erinnerungen*. Munich: Paul List.

Hage, Rawi. 2007. *Parfum de poussière*. Translated by Sophie Voillot. Quebec: Éditions Alto.

– 2008. *Cockroach*. Toronto: House of Anansi.

– 2009. *Le cafard.* Translated by Sophie Voillot. Quebec: Éditions Alto.

Hamon, Phillipe. 1992. *Expositions: Literature and Architecture in Nineteenth-Century France.* Translated by Katia Sainson-Frank and Lisa Maguire. Berkeley: Univ. of California Press.

Harel, Simon. 1994. *L'écriture réparatrice. Le défaut autobiographique: Leiris, Crevel, Artaud*. Montreal: XYZ.

– 1997. *Le récit de soi*. Montreal: XYZ.

– 2001. *La démesure de la voix. Parole et récit en psychanalyse*. Montreal: Liber.

– 2005. *Les passages obligés de l'écriture migrante*. Montreal: XYZ.

Harshav, Benjamin. 1990. *The Meaning of Yiddish*. Berkeley: Univ. of California Press.

– 2002. "Introduction." In Kruk, *The Last Days of the Jerusalem of Lithuania*, xxi–lii.

Harvey, David. 2008. "The Right to the City." *New Left Review* 53. http://newleftreview.org/II/53/david-harvey-the-right-to-the-city.

Hatzfeld, Hélène, Marc Hatzfeld, and Nadja Ringart. 1998. *Quand la marge est créatrice, les interstices urbains initiateurs d'emploi*. Paris: Éditions de l'Aube.

Hayhoe, Nathan. 2013. "Montreal English." *MLS une école OISE school*. http://mlsinc.ca/blog/english/montreal-english.

Highmore, Ben. 2014. "Metaphor City." In *Cartographies of Place: Navigating the Urban*, edited by Michael Darroch and Janine Marchessault, 25–40. Montreal: McGill-Queen's Univ. Press.

Hirsch, Arnold R., and Joseph Logsdon, eds. 1992. *Creole New Orleans: Race and Americanization*. Baton Rouge: Louisiana State Univ. Press.

Hirsch, Marianne, and Leo Spitzer. 2010. *Ghosts of Home: The Afterlife of Czernowitz in Jewish Memory*. Berkeley: Univ. of California Press.

Hocquard, Emmanuel. 2001. *Un bureau sur l'Atlantique / Ma Haie*. Paris: POL.

Holý, Jiří. 1991. "Svět Františka Langra." In Langer, *Byli a bylo*.

– 2003. "Ediční doslov." In Langer, *Byli a bylo*, *Spisy Františka Langra*, vol. 14, 32–9.

Hou, Jeffrey. 2010. *Insurgent Public Space: Guerrilla Urbanism and the Remaking of Contemporary Cities*. New York: Routledge.

Houbey, Lauriane, and Marie Moreau. 2012. "*Géographies intérieures*." Press release, 7 September. http://www.journee-art-contemporain.com/wp-content/uploads/2012/09/Dossier_presentation_Laa.pdf.

Ingold, Tim. 2007. *Lines: A Short History*. London: Routledge.

– 2011. *Being Alive: Essays on Movement, Knowledge and Description*. London: Routledge.

Ingold, Tim, and Jo Lee Vergunst. 2008a. "Introduction." In Ingold and Vergunst, *Ways of Walking*, 1–19.

– eds. 2008b. *Ways of Walking*. Aldershot: Ashgate.

Ireland, Susan, and Patrice J. Proulx, eds. 2004. *Textualizing the Immigrant Experience in Contemporary Quebec*. Westport: Praeger.

Jacob, Louis. 2011. "Art public et les transformations de l'espace urbain." *Les Plumes*. http://www.edredon.uqam.ca/upload/files/plumes/2011/jacob.pdf.

Jacobs, Jane. 1961. *The Death and Life of Great American Cities*. New York: Random House.

Janik, A., and S. Toulmin. 1973. *Wittgenstein's Vienna*. New York: Simon and Schuster.

Jaworski, Rudolf. 2010. "Aufgeladene Topographien. Prag-Motive auf alten deutschen und tschechischen Postkarten." In Becher and Knechtel, *Praha–Prag 1900–1945*, 213–28.

Jenny, Laurent. 1990. *La Parole singulière*. Paris: Belin.

Jurginis, Juozas, Vytautas Merkys, and Adolfas Tautavičius. 1968. *Vilniaus miesto istorija*. Vol. 1. Vilnius: Mintis.

Kafka, Franz. 1958. *Briefe 1902–1924*. Edited by Max Brod. Frankfurt am Main: Fischer.

– 1977. *Letters to Family, Friends and Editors.* Translated by Richard and Clara Winston. New York: Schocken Books.

Keeley, Edmund, ed. 1995. *The Essential Cavafy*. Translated by Edmund Keeley and Philip Sherrard. Hopewell: Ecco.

Klabjan, Borut. 2010. "Nation and Commemoration in the Adriatic." *Acta Histriae* 18 (3): 399–424.

Knabb, Ken, ed. and trans. 2006. *Situationist International Anthology*. Revised and expanded edition. Berkeley: Bureau of Public Secrets.

Koehn, Philip. 2009. *Statistical Machine Translation*, Cambridge, UK: Cambridge Univ. Press.

Koeltzsch, Ines. 2010. "Die gezählte Stadt: Tschechen, Juden und Deutsche im Prager Zensus (1900–1930)." In Becher and Knechtel, *Praha–Prag 1900–1945*, 17–19.

– 2012. *Geteilte Kulturen: Eine Geschichte der tschechisch-jüdisch-deutschen Beziehungen in Prag (1918–1938)*. Munich: Oldenbourg.

Komito, Lee. 2004. *The Information Revolution and Ireland: Prospects and Challenges*. Dublin: UCD Press.

– 2011. "Social Media and Migration: Virtual Community 2.0." *Journal of the American Society for Information Science and Technology* 62 (6): 1075–86.

Kořalka, Jiří. 1997. "Minderheiten als Notausweg: Grundsätze der Rechtslage und des Minderheitenschutzes in den böhmischen Ländern vor 1914 und in der Tschechoslowakischen Republik nach 1918." In Corsini and Davide, *Die Minderheiten zwischen den beiden Weltkriegen*, 95–115.

Koschmal, Walter. 2010. *Der Dichternomade: Jiří Mordechai Langer – ein tschechisch-jüdischer Autor*. Wien: Böhlau.

Kraglund, John. 1960. "CBC Introduces Bilingual FM, No Commercials." *Globe and Mail*, 12 April.

Král, Jiří. 1928. *Reiseführer durch die Čechoslovakische Republik*. Prag: Čedok.

Kristeva, Julia. 1974. *La Révolution du langage poétique: L'avant-garde à la fin du XIXe siècle: Lautréamont et Mallarmé*. Paris: Seuil.

– 1984. *Revolution in Poetic Language*. Translated by Margaret Waller. New York: Columbia Univ. Press.

– 1991. *Strangers to Ourselves*. Translated by Leon S. Roudiez. Hemel Hempstead: Harvester Wheatsheaf.

Krolop, Kurt. 2010. "Die tschechisch-deutschen Auseinandersetzungen über den 'Prager Roman.'" In Becher and Knechtel, *Praha–Prag 1900–1945*, 175–82.

Kruk, Herman. 2002. *The Last Days of the Jerusalem of Lithuania: Chronicles from the Vilna Ghetto and the Camps, 1939–1944*. Edited by Benjamin Harshav. Translated by Barbara Harshav. New Haven: Yale Univ. Press.

Kučera, Jaroslav. 1999. *Minderheit im Nationalstaat: Die Sprachenfrage in den tschechisch-deutschen Beziehungen 1918–1938*. Munich: Oldenbourg.

Kulbak, Moyshe. 1997. "Vilna." In *Vilnius*, translated by Nathan Halper, 17–19. Vilnius: Vaga.

Kundera, Milan. 1993. *Les testaments trahis*. Paris: Gallimard.

Kuznitz, Cecile. E. 1998. "On the Jewish Street: Yiddish Culture and the Urban Landscape in Interwar Vilna." In *Yiddish Language and Culture: Then and Now*, edited by Leonard Jay Greenspoon, 65–92. Omaha: Creighton Univ. Press.

Lages, Susana Kampff. 2003. "Entre Futurismo e Expressionismo: Ecos no Programa Estéticos do Primeiros Mário de Andrade e Jorge Luis Borges." In *Brasil & Itália vanguardas*, edited by Lucia Wataghin, 67–78. São Paulo: Ateliê Editorial.

Lalonde, Yves. 2013. *The Social History of Ideas in Quebec, 1759–1889*. Translated by Phyllis Aronoff. Montreal: McGill-Queen's Univ. Press.

Langer, František, ed. 1991. *Byli a bylo*. Praha: Státní pedagogické nakladatelství.

– 1993. "Foreword by František Langer. My Brother Jiří." In Jiří Langer, *Nine Gates to the Chasidic Mysteries*, translated by Stephen Jolly. Northvale: Jason Aronson. (*Devět bran*. Praha: Evropský literární klub, 1937, ix–xxxiv.)

– 2001. "Demonstrace proti německým filmům." In *Prostor díla: Úvahy a vyznání o culture*, *Spisy Františka Langra*, vol. 13, 273–77.

– 2003. "Můj bratr Jiří." In Langer, *Byli a bylo*, *Spisy Františka Langra*, vol 14, 172–92.

Lara, Cecília de. 1986. "Da realidade contada a transposição no texto literário Pathé-Baby: Correspondência e crônicas de viagem." *Revista do Instituto dos Estudos Brasileiros* 26: 35–45.

– 1987. *De Pirandello a Piolim: Alcântara Machado e o teatro no modernismo.* Rio de Janeiro: Intituto Nacional de Artes Cênicas.

Lazaroms, Ilse Josepha. 2013. *The Grace of Misery: Joseph Roth and the Politics of Exile, 1919–1939.* Boston: Brill.

Leão, Antônio Carneiro. 1920. *S. Paulo em 1920.* Rio de Janeiro: Annuario Americano.

Lefebvre, Henri. (1947) 2008. *Critique of Everyday Life.* Vol. 1. Translated by John Moore. London: Verso.

– (1968) 1996. "The Right to the City." In *Writings on Cities*, translated by Eleonore Kofman and Elizabeth Lebas, 63–184. Oxford: Wiley-Blackwell.

– 1991. *The Production of Space.* Translated by Donald Nicholson-Smith. Oxford: Blackwell.

Leftwich, Joseph. 1971. *Abraham Sutzkever: Partisan Poet.* New York: Thomas Yoseloff.

Le Goff, Jacques. 1986. *The Birth of Purgatory.* Translated by Arthur Goldhammer. Chicago: Univ. of Chicago Press.

Lehár, Jan, Jiří Holý, Jaroslava Janáčková, and Alexandr Stich. 1998. *Česká literatura od počatků k dnešku.* Praha: Lidové Noviny.

Lemoine, Stéphanie, and Stéphanie Ouardi. 2010. *Artivisme: Art, action politique et résistance culturelle.* Paris: Alternatives.

Levinas, Emmanuel. 1991. *Otherwise than Being or Beyond Essence.* Translated by Alphonso Lingis. Dordrecht: Kluwer.

– 2003. *Humanism of the Other.* Translated by Nidra Poller. Chicago: Univ. of Illinois Press.

Licoppe, Christian. 2004. "'Connected Presence': The Emergence of a New Repertoire for Managing Social Relationships in a Changing Communication Technoscape." *Environment and Planning D: Society and Space* 22: 135–56.

Lindgaard, Jade. 2005. "Artivisme." *Vacarme* 31. http://www.vacarme.org/article1269.html.

Lippert, Julius. 1909. "Prag, die deutsche Stadt." *Deutsche Arbeit* 8: 332–48.

Litovskaya SSR: Turistichiskaya karta. 1974. Moskva: GUGK.

Liulevicius, Vejas Gabriel. 2000. *War Land on the Eastern Front: Culture, National Identity, and German Occupation in World War I.* Cambridge, UK: Cambridge Univ. Press.

Lunzer, Heinz, and Victoria Lunzer-Talos. 1994. *Joseph Roth: Leben und Werk in Bildern.* Koln: Keipenheuer and Witsch.

Lyotard, Jean-Francois. 1983. *Le Différend.* Paris: Les éditions de Minuit.

Macfarlane, Robert. 2012. *The Old Ways: A Journey on Foot.* London: Hamish Hamilton.

Machado, Antônio de Alcântara. 1926. *Pathé-Baby*. São Paulo: Editorial Helios.

– 1934. "Só as grandes cidades sabem rir." *Diário da noite*, 14 August.

– 1940. *Cavaquinho e saxofone (solos)*. Rio de Janeiro: José Olympio.

– 1988. "Brás, Bexiga e Barra Funda." In *Novelas Paulistanas*, edited by Antônio de Alcântara Machado, 73–125. São Paulo: Editora Itatiaia.

Magris, Claudio, with Angelo Ara. 1982. *Trieste: Un'identità di frontiera*. Torino: Einaudi.

– 1990. *Danube: A Sentimental Journey from the Source to the Black Sea*. London: Collins Harvill.

Mahieux, Viviane. 2011. *Urban Chroniclers in Modern Latin America: The Shared Intimacy of Everyday Life*. Austin: Univ. of Texas Press.

Maître, Manuel. 1963. "Le biculturalisme gagne les salles obscures?" *La Patrie*, 19–25 September.

Mandelstam, Osip. 1973. "Conversation about Dante." In *Selected Poems*, translated by Clarence Brown and W.S. Merwin. New York: New York Review of Books.

Marchessault, Janine. 2005. *Marshall McLuhan: Cosmic Media*. London: Sage.

Marshall, Bill. 2009. *The French Atlantic: Travels in Culture and History*. Liverpool: Liverpool Univ. Press.

McAreavy, Ruth. 2009. "Transcending Cultural Differences: The Role of Language in Migrants' Integration." *Translocations: Migration and Social Change* 6 (2): 1–22.

McBride, Robert Medill. 1938. *Towns and People of Modern Poland*. New York: McBride.

McCartney, Andra, Owen Chapman, Anna Friz, and Sandra Gabriele. 2002. *Journées sonores, canale de Lachine*. http://www.andrasound.org/archive/Lachine%20Canal_ENG.pdf.

McCartney, Andra, David Paquette, David Madden, and Caitlin Loney. 2014. *Balade Montréal Equinox Soundwalk*. https://soundwalkinginteractions.wordpress.com/about.

McLuhan, Marshall. (1954) 2011. *Counterblast*. Berlin: Transmediale.

– (1962) 2011. *The Gutenberg Galaxy*. Toronto: Univ. of Toronto Press.

– 1964. *Understanding Media*. New York: McGraw-Hill.

– 1987. *Letters of Marshall McLuhan*. Edited by Matie Molinaro, Corinne McLuhan, and William Toye. Toronto: Oxford Univ. Press.

Médam, Alain. 2002. *Labyrinthes des rencontres*. Montreal. Fides.

– 2004. *Montréal Interdite*. Montreal: Liber.

Mekdjian, Sarah, Anne-Laure Amilhat-Szary, Marie Moreau, Gladeema Nasruddin, Mabeye Deme, Lauriane Houbey, and Coralie Guillemin.

2014. "Figurer les entre-deux migratoires. Pratiques cartographiques expérimentales entre chercheurs, artistes et voyageurs." *Carnets de géographes* 7.
Melhuish, Martin. 1977. "Bilingual Radio Gripe Gets Reply from Trudeau." *Billboard*, 12 March.
Meltzer, Donald. 1999. *Le Claustrum: Une exploration des phénomènes claustrophobiques.* Larmor-Plage: Hublot.
Merleau-Ponty, Maurice. 1962. *Phenomenology of Perception.* Translated by Colin Smith. London: Routledge.
Mersch, Dieter. 2008. "Kritik des Medienteleologismus: McLuhan, Flusser und Hegel." In *McLuhan Neu Lesen: Kritische Analysen zu Medien und Kultur im 21. Jahrhundert*, edited by Derrick de Kerckhove, Martina Leeker, and Kerstin Schmidt, 196–209. Transcript Verlag.
Meschonnic, Henri. 1997. *De la langue française: Essai sur une clarté obscure.* Paris: Hachette.
– 2000. *Et le génie des langues?* Vincennes: Presses Universitaires de Vincennes.
Měšťan, Antonín. 2002. "Paralely a rozdíly mezi česky a německy písícími židovskými autory z Prahy." In *Česká literatura mezi Němci a Slovany*, 118–25. Praha: Academia.
Metelsky, Georgy V. 1959. *Lithuania: Land of the Niemen.* Moscow: Foreign Languages Publishing House.
Meyrink, Gustav. 1983. *Der Golem.* Leipzig and Weimar: Gustav Kiepenheuer.
– 1995. *The Golem.* Translated by Mike Mitchell. Sawtry and Riverside: Dedalus and Ariadne.
Mezzadra, Sandro, and Brett Neilson. 2013. *Border as Method.* Durham: Duke Univ. Press.
Mezzadra, Sandro, and Naoki Sakai. 2014. "Introduction." *Politics.* Special issue of *Translation* 4. http://translation.fusp.it/issues/issue-4.
Miceli, Sergio. 2003. *Nacional estrangeiro: História social e cultural do modernism artístico em São Paulo.* São Paulo: Companhia das Letras.
– 2012. *Vanguardas em retrocesso: Ensaios de história social e intelectual do modenrismo latino-americano.* São Paulo: Companhia das Letras.
Michalitschke, Anton. 1928. *Prag (Praha) und Umgebung.* Berlin: Grieben.
Michaux, Henri. 1997. *Darkness Moves.* Translated by David Ball. Berkeley: Univ. of California Press.
Miłosz, Czesław. 1981. *Native Realm: A Search for Self-Definition.* Translated by Catherine S. Leach. Berkeley: Univ. of California Press.
– 1988. *Czesław Miłosz: Collected Poems, 1931–1987.* London: Penguin.

– 1992. *Beginning with My Streets: Essays and Recollections*. Translated by Madeline G. Levine. New York: Farrar, Strauss and Giroux.
– 1994. *A Year of the Hunter*. Translated by Madeline G. Levine. New York: Farrar, Straus and Giroux.
– 1995. "City of My Youth." In *Facing the River: New Poems*, translated by Czesław Miłosz and Robert Hass, 20. Hopewell: Ecco.
– 1999. *Road-side Dog*. Translated by Robert Hass. New York: Farrar, Strauss and Giroux.
– 2004. "Werki." In *Second Space: New Poems*, translated by Czesław Miłosz and Robert Hass, 8. New York: HarperCollins.
Mitchell, William. 1995. *The City of Bits*. London: MIT Press.
Montreal Gazette. 1977. "CHOM to Go English-Only." 30 August.
Moore, Marianne. 1982. *The Complete Poems of Marianne Moore*. London: Macmillan.
Morisset, Jean, and Éric Waddell, eds. 2001. *Vision et visages de la Franco-Amérique*. Quebec: Septentrion.
Murger, Henry. 1988. *Scènes de la vie de bohème*. Paris: Gallimard. (*National Geographic Magazine* 74 (6): 777–9. June 1938.)
Muséu da língua portuguesa. 2016. "O Museu." http://www.museudalinguaportuguesa.org.br.
Nicolas-Le Strat, Pascal. 2009. "The Interstitial Multiplicity of Big Cities." In *Stadium X – A Place That Never Was: A Reader*, edited by Joanna Warsza. Laura Palmer Foundation. http://www.laura-palmer.pl/en/projects/28/stadium-x-a-place-that-never-was-a-reader.
Nicholson, Geoff. 2008. *The Lost Art of Walking*. New York: Riverhead.
Nouss, Alexis. 2005. *Plaidoyer pour un monde métis*. Paris: Textuel.
– 2009. *Paul Celan, Les lieux d'un déplacement*. Paris: Le Bord de l'eau.
– 2013. "Exiliance: condition et conscience." https://halshs.archives-ouvertes.fr/halshs-00861246.
– 2014. "Atypologie des non-lieux." In *Glossaire des mobilités culturelles*, edited by Zila Bernd and Norah Dei Cas, 257–74. Bern: Peter Lang.
Novák, Arne. 1922. "Pražský roman?" In *Krajané a sousedé: Kniha studií a podobizen*, edited by Arne Novák, 179–83. Praha: Aventinum. First published in *Venkov* 22 April 1917.
Novak, Marcus. 2010. "The Meaning of Transarchitecture." *Fen-om Network*, 5 March. http://www.fen-om.com/network/2010/03/05/the-meaning-of-trans-architecture-marcos-novak.
Nyíri, Kristóf. 1997. "Wittgenstein Videon: Kényszer – találkozás Jarman filjével." *Metropolis* 4: 104–10.
Olson, Gary A., and Lynn Worsham. 1999. "Staging the Politics of Differ-

ence: Homi Bhabha's Critical Literacy." In *Race, Rhetoric and the Postcolonial*, edited by Gary Olson and Lynn Worsham, 3–43. Albany: State Univ. of New York Press.

Olson, Jess. 2010. "A Tale of Two Photographs: Nathan Birnbaum, the Election of 1907, and the 1908 Yiddish Language Conference." In *Czernowitz at 100: The First Yiddish Language Conference in Historical Perspective*, edited by Kalman Weiser and Joshua A. Fogel, 23–44. New York: Lexington Books.

Ostler, Nicholas. 2011. *The Last Lingua Franca: The Rise and Fall of World Languages*. London: Penguin.

Pahor, Boris. 1993. *Kosovel*. Pordenone: Studio Tesi.

Paquot, Thierry. 2010. "Le Jeu de cartes de situationnistes." CFC 204. http://www.lecfc.fr/new/articles/204-article-7.pdf.

Parry, Benita. Forthcoming. "Stylistic Irrealism as Symptom, Mediation and Critique of Peripheral Modernity." In *Peripheral Modernisms*, edited by Katia Pizzi and Patricia da Silva McNeill. Oxford: Legenda.

Pawel, Ernst. 1984. *The Nightmare of Reason: A Life of Franz Kafka*. New York: Farrar, Straus and Giroux.

Pellegrini, Ernestina. 1980. "Aspetti della cultura triestina tra Otto e Novecento." *Il Ponte* 4: 354–71.

Pelletier, Sonia, ed. 2008. *ATSA: Quand l'art passe à l'action*. Montreal: Action terroriste socialement acceptable.

Perrone-Moisés, Leyla, and Emir Rodríguez Monegal. 1983. "Isidore Ducasse et la rhétorique espagnole." *Poétique* 14 (55): 351–77.

– 2001. *Lautréamont, l'identité culturelle: Double culture et bilinguisme chez Isidore Ducasse*. Paris: L'Harmattan.

Perse, Saint-John. 1959. *Anabasis*. Translated by T.S. Eliot. London: Faber and Faber.

Peyrouzet, Edouard. 1970. "Les Enfances d'Isidore Ducasse." In *Vie de Lautréamont*, edited by Edouard Peyrouzet, ch. 2. Paris: Grasset.

Pinto, E. Pimentel. 1990. *A gramatiquinha de Mário de Andrade: Texto e Contexto*. São Paulo: Duas Cidades.

Pinto, Maria Inez Machado Borges. 1999. "Flashes do Cotidiano: Modernidade Postiça e Provincialismo na Urbes da Belle Époques, São Paulo Nos Anos 20." In *História – fronteiras: XX Simpósio Nacional da ANPUH, Florianópolis-SC, julho de 1999*, vol. 2, edited by Simpósio Nacional de História, Eunice Sueli Nodari, Joana Maria Pedro, and Zilda Márcia Gricoli Iokoi, 883–97. São Paulo, Brazil: ANPUH.

– 2001. "Crônica cinematográfica do cotidiano: Alcântara Machado e os impasses do modernismo." *Varia História* 24: 190–209.

Pizzi, Katia. 2001. *A City in Search of an Author: The Cultural Identity of Trieste*. London: Sheffield Academic Press/Continuum.

– 2005. "Quale triestinità?: Voices and Echoes from Italian Trieste." In *Kosovel's Poetics*, edited by Janez Vrečko, Boris A. Novak, and Darja Pavlič. Special issue of *Primerjalna Književnost* 28: 239–49.

– 2013. "Triestine Literature between Slovenia and Italy: A Case of Missed Transculturalism?" *Primerjalna knjizevnost* 36 (1): 81–90.

PLEPUQ. n.d. "*Fable VII*." http://plepuc.org/en/artwork/fable-vii.

Pöchhacker, Franz, and Miriam Shlesinger, eds. 2007. *Healthcare Interpreting: Discourse and Interaction*. Amsterdam: John Benjamins.

Poisson, Mathias. 2010. "Graphie du déplacement." *Les Carnets du Paysage* 20: 104–15.

Polish Research Centre. 1942. *The Story of Wilno*. London: Cornwall Press.

Prokopych, Markian. 2009. *Habsburg Lemberg: Architecture, Public Space, and Politics in the Galician Capital, 1772–1914*. West Lafayette: Purdue Univ. Press.

Prus, Bolesław. 2011. *The Doll*. Translated by David Welsh. New York: New York Review of Books.

Putnam, Robert. 2000. *Bowling Alone: America's Declining Social Capital*. New York: Simon and Schuster.

Raboy, Marc. 1990. *Missed Opportunities: The Story of Canada's Broadcasting Policy*. Montreal: McGill-Queen's Univ. Press.

Ran, Leyzer. 1974. *Yerushalayim de Lita – Jerusalem of Lithuania*. New York: Laureate Press.

Rancière, Jacques. 2001. "Ten Theses on Politics." Translated by Rachel Bowlby and Davide Panagia. *Theory and Event* 5 (3). https://muse.jhu.edu/login?auth=0&type=summary&url=/journals/theory_and_event/v005/5.3ranciere.html.

– 2006. *Film Fables*. Translated by Emiliano Battista. Oxford: Berg.

– 2011. *Les Ecarts du cinéma*. Paris: La Fabrique.

Reynolds, Richard. 2008. *On Guerrilla Gardening: A Handbook for Gardening without Boundaries*. New York: Bloomsbury.

Řezníková, Lenka. 2000. "History, Generation and Nation: Czech Writers of the 1890s in Search of Identity." In *"We" and "the Others": Modern European Societies in Search of Identity*, 53–75. Praha: Karolinum.

– 2004. *Moderna a historismus: Historické reprezentace v proměnách literatury na přelomu devatenáctého a dvacátého století*. Praha: Libri.

– 2013. "Suche nach Differenzen als Interferenzprozess: Praktiken der nationalen Abgrenzung in Prag um 1900." In *Wellenschläge: Kulturelle*

Interferenzen im östlichen Mitteleuropa des langen 20. Jahrhunderts, edited by Ute Raßloff, 99–143. Stuttgart: Steiner.

Rimbaud, Arthur. 1984. *Poésies, Un saison en enfer, Illuminations*. Paris: Gallimard.

Robb, Graham. 2000. *Rimbaud*. London: Picador.

Robinson, Jeffrey C. 2006. *The Walk: Notes on a Romantic Image*. London: Dalkey Archive.

Robinson, Richard. 2007. *Narratives of the European Border: A History of Nowhere*. London: Palgrave Macmillan.

Roelstraete, Dieter. 2010. *Richard Long: A Line Made by Walking*. London: Afterall Books.

Rolland, Daniel. 2013. "Saint-Catherine Street: Toute vérité est bonne à dire." *La Metropole*, 13 August. http://www.lametropole.com/blog/daniel-rolland/saint-catherine-street.

Rolland, Jacques. 1983. "Le sujet de l'expulsion." *Exercices de la patience* 5: 167–79.

Roth, Joseph. 2002a. "Rare and Ever Rarer in This World of Empirical Facts." In *The Collected Stories of Joseph Roth*, translated by Michael Hofmann, 66–7. New York: W.W. Norton.

– 2002b. *Weights and Measures*. Translated by David Le Vay. London: Peter Owen.

– 2003. *The Radetzky March*. Translated by Michael Hofmann. New York: W.W. Norton.

Rousseau, Cécile, and Patricia Foxen. 2006. "Le mythe du réfugié menteur: Un mensonge indispensable ?" *L'Evolution Psychiatrique* 71: 505–20.

Ruhs, Martin, and Emma Quinn. 2009. "Ireland: From Rapid Immigration to Recession." Migration Policy Institute, 1 September. http://www.migrationpolicy.org/article/ireland-rapid-immigration-recession.

Rutherford, Jonathan. 1990. "The Third Space: Interview with Homi Bhabha." In *Identity: Community, Culture, Difference*, 207–22. London: Lawrence and Wishart.

Sarmiento, Domingo Faustino. 1845. *Facundo o civilización y barbarie en las pampas argentina.* Santiago: Imprenta del Progreso.

Schießler, Sebastian Willibald. 1812. *Prag und seine Umgebungen: Ein Taschenbuch für Fremde und Einheimische*. Prag: Enders.

Schirru, Giancarlo. 2011. "Antonio Gramsci studente di linguistica." *Studi Storici* 4 (52): 925–73.

Schmitz, Walter, and Ludger Udolph. 2001. *Tripolis Praga: Die Prager Moderne um 1900*. Dresden: Thelem.

Schütz, Alfred. 1944. "The Stranger." *American Journal of Sociology* 49: 499–507.
– 1945. "The Homecomer." *American Journal of Sociology* 50: 363–76.
– 1972. "Der Fremde: Ein sozialpsychologischer Versuch." *Gesammelte Aufsätze 2. Studien zur soziologischen Theorie*. Dordrecht: Martinus Nijhof.
Sennett, Richard. 2012. *Together: The Rituals, Pleasures, and Politics of Cooperation.* New Haven: Yale Univ. Press.
Shapiro, Norman R., trans. 2004. *Creole Echoes: The Francophone Poetry of Nineteenth-Century Louisiana*. Urbana: Univ. of Illinois Press.
Shchyhlevska, Natalia. 2004. *Deutschsprachige Autoren aus der Bukowina.* Frankfurt: Peter Lang.
Shell, Marc, and Werner Sollors, eds. 2001. *The Multilingual Anthology of American Literature: A Reader of Original Texts with English Translations.* New York: New York Univ. Press.
Simay, Philippe. 2008. "Une autre ville pour une autre vie: Henri Lefebvre et les situationnistes." *Métropoles* 4. http://metropoles.revues.org/2902.
Simmel, Georg. 1984. "Digression sur l'étranger." In *L'école de Chicago*, edited by Yves and Grafmeyer and Issac Joseph, 53–77. Paris: Aubier.
Simon, Bart. 2006. "Beyond Cyberspatial Flaneurie: On the Analytic Potential of Living with Digital Games." *Games and Culture* 1 (1): 62–7.
Simon, Sherry. 2006. *Translating Montreal: Episodes in the Life of a Divided City.* Montreal: McGill-Queen's Univ. Press.
– 2012. *Cities in Translation: Intersections of Language and Memory.* New York: Routledge.
Slataper, Scipio. 1912. *Il mio Carso*. Firenze: Libreria della Voce.
– 1916. *Ibsen*. Edited by Arturo Farinelli. Turin: Bocca.
Sloterdijk, Peter. 2000. *Règles pour le parc humain.* Paris: Mille et une nuits.
Soja, Edward W. 1989. *Postmodern Geographies*. London: Verso.
Solnit, Rebecca. 2000. *Wanderlust: A History of Walking*. London: Penguin.
Sorkin, Michael. 2009. *Twenty Minutes in Manhattan*. London: Reaktion.
Spector, Scott. 2000. *Prague Territories: National Conflict and Cultural Innovation in Franz Kafka's Fin de Siècle*. Berkley: Univ. of California Press.
Spivak, Gayatri Chakravorty. 2000. "Translation as Culture." *Parallax* 6 (1): 13–24.
Šrámková, Barbara. 2010. "Max Brod – ein Mittler aus alten Zeiten." In *Praha–Prag 1900–1945: Literaturstadt zweier Sprachen, vieler Mittler*, edited by Jozo Džambo, 93–106. Passau: Karl Stutz.
Starck-Adler, Astrid. 2007. "Multiculturalisme et multilinguisme à Czernowitz: L'exemple d'Itzik Manger." *Etudes germaniques* 62 (1): 121–32.

Steiner, George. 1998. *After Babel: Aspects of Language and Translation.* Oxford: Oxford Univ. Press.

Stenberg, Peter. 1991. *Journey to Oblivion: The End of the East European Yiddish and German Worlds in the Mirror of Literature.* Toronto: Univ. of Toronto Press.

Stierle, Karlheinz. 2001. *La Capitale des signes: Paris et son discours.* Translated by Marianne Rocher-Jacquin. Paris: Editions de la Maison des sciences de l'homme. First published as *Der Mythos von Paris: Zeichen und Bewußtsein der Stadt* by Carl Hanser Verlag, 1993.

Stölzl, Christoph. 1989. *Kafkas böses Böhmen: Zur Sozialgeschichte eines Prager Juden.* Frankfurt am Main: Ullstein.

Stourzh, Gerald. 1980. "Die Gleichberechtigung der Volksstämme als Verfassungsprinzip 1848–1918." In *Die Völker des Reiches.* Vol. 3.2 of *Die Habsburgermonarchie 1848–1918*, edited by Adam Wandruszka and Peter Urbanitsch, 975–1206. Vienna: Österreichische Akademie der Wissenschaften.

Stravinskienė, Vitalija. 2011. *Tarp gimtinės ir tėvynės: Lietuvos SSR gyventojų repatriacija į Lenkiją.* Vilnius: Lietuvos istorijos institutas.

Straw, Will, and Alexandra Boutros, eds. 2010. *Circulation and the City.* Montreal: McGill-Queen's Univ. Press.

Strobl, Karl Hans. 1902. *Die Vaclavbude.* Leipzig: Staackmann.

– 1913. *Das Wirtshaus "Zum König Przemysl."* Leipzig: Staackmann.

Strong, Anne Louise. 1940. *Lithuania's New Way.* London: Lawrence and Wishart.

Stuparich, Giani. 1915. *La nazione czeca.* Catania: Battiato.

Sutzkever, Abraham. 1991. "Ode to the Dove." In *A. Sutzkever: Selected Poetry and Prose*, 273–80. Translated by Barbara and Benjamin Harshav. Berkeley: Univ. of California Press.

Tachibana, Hidehiro. 1998. "Lautréamont, écrivain créole?" *Les Lecteurs de Lautréamont: Cahiers Lautréamont* 47 (8): 441–48.

Taylor-Batty, Juliette. 2013. *Multilingualism in Modernist Fiction.* Basingstoke: Palgrave Macmillan.

Taylor, Charles. 1995. *Philosophical Arguments.* Cambridge, MA: Harvard Univ. Press.

Thompson, Mark. 2008. *The White War: Life and Death on the Italian Front 1915–1919.* London: Faber and Faber.

Thomsen, Martina. 2010. "'Historisches Prag' versus 'modernes Prag': Kontroverse Pragbilder in deutschen und tschechischen Reiseführern 1918–1945." In Becher and Knechtel, *Praha–Prag 1900–1945*, 229–47.

Thum, Gregor. 2013. "Megalomania and Angst: The Nineteenth-Century Mythicization of Germany's Eastern Borderlands." In *Shatterzone of Empires, Coexistence and Violence in the German, Habsburg, Russian and Ottoman Borderlands*, edited by Omer Bartov and Eric D. Weitz, 44–59. Bloomington: Indiana Univ. Press.

Tiberghien, Gilles. 2010. "Poétique et rhétorique de la carte dans l'art contemporain." *L'Espace géographique* 39 (3): 197–210. http://www.cairn.info/revue-espace-geographique-2010-3-page-197.htm.

Toporov, Vladimir. 2000. "Vilnius, Wilno, Vilna: Miestas ir mitas." In *Baltų mitologijos ir ritualo tyrimai*, 35–98. Vilnius: Aidai.

Torres, Jorge Fernandes. 2012. "Pratiques artistiques et imaginaires sociaux." *Inter, art actuel* 111: 4–6.

Tramer, Hans. 1961. "Die Dreivölkerstadt Prag." In *Robert Weltsch zum 70: Geburtstag von seinen Freunden*, edited by Hans Tramer, and Kurt Loewenstein, 138–203. Tel-Aviv: Bitaon.

Triangle UMNR 5206. 2013. "Presentation." http://triangle.ens-lyon.fr/spip.php?article3556.

Tyrwhitt, Jaqueline. (1885–1980). Papers of Jaqueline Tyrwhitt, 1885–1980, Royal Institute of British Architects, TYJ/16-18. RIBA British Architectural Library Drawings and Archives Collection, London, UK.

Urbanitsch, Peter. 1980. "Die Deutschen in Österreich. Statistisch-deskriptiver Überblick." In Wandruzska and Urbanitsch, *Die Völker des Reiches*, 33–153.

Van der Meulen, Sjoukje. 2010. "Between Benjamin and McLuhan: Vilém Flusser's Media Theory." *New German Critique 110* 37 (2): 181–207.

Van Drunen, Hieronymus Franciscus. 2013. "'A Sanguine Bunch.' Regional Identification in Habsburg Bukovina, 1774–1919." PhD diss., Univ. of Amsterdam. http//.www.dare.uva.nl/record/452206.

Van Duin, Pieter. 2009. *Central European Crossroads: Social Democracy and National Revolution in Bratislava (Pressburg) 1867–1921*. New York: Berhahn Books.

Vanoosthuyse, Michel. 1996. "L'espace partagé. Considérations sur quelques romans pragois au tournant du siècle." In *Allemands, Juifs et Tchèques à Prague de 1890 à 1924. Actes du colloque international de Montpellier 8–10 décembre 1994 = Deutsche, Juden und Tschechen in Prag 1890–1924*, edited by Godé Maurice, Jacques Le Rider, and Françoise Mayer, 311–19. Montpellier: Université Paul-Valéry.

Van Toorn, Peter. 1983. "The Pain Called Babel." *Antigonish Review* 53: 70–9.

– 1983. *The Rosenkrantz Country and Mountain Tea*. Toronto: McClelland and Stewart.

– 2003. *Mountain Tea and Other Poems*. Montreal: Véhicule Press.

Verdery, Katherine. 1999. *The Political Lives of Dead Bodies: Reburial and Post-socialist Change*. New York: Columbia Univ. Press.

Viader Knowles, Rachelle. 2001. "Berlin Project." University of Regina. http://uregina.ca/rvk/berlin.html.

Vojtěch, Daniel. 2010. "'Frühling in Prag' oder Konflikte – Parallelen – Interaktionen. Anmerkungen zum deutsch-tschechischen Kontext zu Beginn des 20. Jahrhunderts." In Becher and Knechtel, *Praha–Prag 1900–1945*, 183–211.

Vrecko, Janez. 2011. *Kosovel. Monografija*. Lubjana: Institute of Slovenian Literature and Literary Studies/ZRC.

Wadia, Lily-Amber Laila. 2010. *Come diventare italiani in 24 ore: Diario di un'aspirante italiana*. Siena: Barbera.

Wagner, Birgit. 2012. "Cultural Translation: A Value or a Tool?" In *Narration, Media and the Staging of Differences*, edited by Federico Italiano and Michael Rössner, 51–67. Bielefeld: transcript.

Wandruzska, Adam, and Peter Urbanitsch, eds. 1980. *Die Völker des Reiches: Die Habsburgermonarchie 1848–1918*. Vol. 1–7, 2. Wien: Österreichische Akademie der Wissenschaften.

Weeks, Theodore R. 2008. "Remembering and Forgetting: Creating a Soviet Lithuanian Capital: Vilnius 1944–1949." *Journal of Baltic Studies* 39 (4): 517–33.

Weger, Tobias. 2001. "Das 'Deutsche Prag': Von der Beständigkeit eines Mythos." *Jahrbuch für deutsche und osteuropäische Volkskunde* 44: 134–56.

Wershler, Darren. 2011. "Walking in Assassin's Creed." *Experiencing Stories with/in Digital Games.* 24th edition of the Entretiens Jacques Cartier, Concordia Univ., Montreal, 1 October 2011.

Wickramasekara, Piyasiri. 2011. *Circular Migration: A Triple Win or a Dead End*. Geneva: International Labour Office.

Wieviorka, Michel. 2004. *La Violence*. Paris: Balland.

Wigley, Mark. 2001. "Network Fever." *Grey Room* 4: 82–122.

Wilks, Yorick. 2008. *Machine Translation: Its Scope and Limits*. Berlin: Springer.

Wittgenstein, Ludwig. 1984. *PhilosophischeUntersuchungen*. Studienausgabe I. Frankfurt am Main: Suhrkamp.

Wittlin, Josef. n.d. "Reminiscences of Joseph Roth." *Joseph Roth Collection*

1897–1995. The Leo Baeck Institute New York. http://www.archive.org/stream/josephroth_07_reel07#page/n216/mode/1up.

Wolf, Michaela. 2012. *Die vielsprachige Seele Kakaniens: Übersetzen und Dolmetschen in der Habsburgermonarchie 1848–1918*. Vienna: Böhlau.

Wolff, Larry. 2010. *The Idea of Galicia: History and Fantasy in Habsburg Political Culture*. Stanford: Univ. of Stanford Press.

Wylie, Lillian. 1966. "Need No B and B Commission to Understand Jazz – Nick Ayoub." *Montreal Gazette*, July 22.

Yorke, Ritchie. 1973. "CHOM-FM Gets License Renewal in Key Decision." *Billboard*, 7 April.

Young, James E. 1993. *The Texture of Memory: Holocaust Memorials and Meaning*. New Haven: Yale Univ. Press.

Zima, Peter V. 1992. *Komparatistik: Einführung in die vergleichende Literaturwissenschaft*. Tübingen: Francke.

Zimányi, Krisztina. 2005. "Impartiality or Advocacy: Perceptions of the Role of the Community Interpreter in Ireland." MA diss., Dublin City Univ.

Contributors

LAIMONAS BRIEDIS is the author of three books and many articles on the multilingual literature and polymorphous geography of Vilnius. A native of Lithuania, Briedis studied geography, history, and comparative literature in the United States and Canada, and received a doctoral degree in human geography from the University of British Columbia. He has been a lecturer and guest speaker at numerous academic institutions and international events, including TEDx. His bestselling book, *Vilnius: City of Strangers*, has been favourably reviewed in a variety of scholarly journals and international media. As an author and commentator on current affairs, Briedis appears regularly on Lithuanian radio.

MATTEO COLOMBI is a literary scholar, comparatist, and Slavicist, and works as a research fellow at the Geisteswissenschaftliches Zentrum Geschichte und Kultur Ostmitteleuropas (Leipzig centre for the history and culture of east central Europe) in Leipzig/Germany. His major research fields are Czech and Slovene literature and culture from the nineteenth and twentieth centuries in relation to non-Slavic literatures (especially German and Italian), multiethnicity in east central Europe, popular literature, and interartistic studies (literature, film, and comics). He is the editor of *Stadt – Mord – Ordnun: Topographien des Verbrechens in der Kriminalliteratur aus Ost- und Mitteleuropa* (2012). His publications in English include "Modernism and Multiethnicity? Interwar Czech Literature from Prague and Slovenian Literature from Trieste," in *Primerjalna književnost*, 2009.

MICHAEL CRONIN holds a personal chair in the Faculty of Humanities and Social Sciences at Dublin City University, Ireland. He is the author of *Translating Ireland: Translation, Languages and Identity* (1996); *Across the Lines: Travel, Language, Translation* (2000); *Translation and Globalization* (2003); *Translation and Identity* (2006); *Translation Goes to the Movies* (2009); *The Expanding World: Towards a Politics of Microspection* (2012); and *Translation in the Digital Age* (2013). A member of the Royal Irish Academy and the Academia Europeae, and an Officer in the Ordre des Palmes Académiques, he is coeditor of the Routledge series New Perspectives in Translation Studies and editor-in-chief of the translation journal *MTM*.

MICHAEL DARROCH is associate professor of media art histories and visual culture in the School of Creative Arts, University of Windsor, Canada, and director of the IN/TERMINUS Creative Research Collective. He was a 2015 visiting fellow at the School of Advanced Study, University of London, and is a 2016–2018 McLuhan Centenary fellow at the Coach House Institute, iSchool, University of Toronto. He is coeditor of *Cartographies of Place: Navigating the Urban* (2014), and is completing a manuscript on the transatlantic and interdisciplinary legacy of the Canadian communications journal *Explorations* (1953–59). His interests include the history of media and communication theories, urban culture, border studies, theatre, language, and translation.

ROCH DUVAL obtained a PhD in philosophy at the University of Montreal in 1994 with a thesis in epistemology and free-will theories, modal logic, and possible world theories. He has published essays on Pietro Verri, Immanuel Kant, Ludwig Wittgenstein, Johan Gottfried Herder, and Thomas Thorild, among others. In the fall of 2015 he obtained a second PhD in translation studies with a thesis on the theoretical relationship between Haroldo de Campos and Max Bense. He is a translator of poetry (especially from Scandinavia) and a specialist of Brazilian literature.

ANDRE FURLANI, professor and chair of the Department of English, Concordia University, is the author of *Beckett after Wittgenstein* and *Guy Davenport: Postmodern and After*. His recent publications include "The Contradictions of Samuel Beckett" in *Modernism/modernity*, "Earlier Wittgenstein, Later Beckett" in *Philosophy and Literature*, and "The Literature of Exhausted Justification" in *PMLA*. Forthcoming is "From the Talking Cure to the Walking Cure" in *Bréac* and a chapter on post-war American literature in *The Oxford History of the Classical Reception in English*.

SIMON HAREL is a 2009 Trudeau fellow and a member of the Royal Society of Canada, and a full professor at the Université de Montréal, where he directs the Mobile Self Narratives Lab. Prior to joining Université de Montréal in 2011, he was the director of the Centre for the Study of Arts, Letters and Traditions at the Université du Québec à Montréal, in whose Department of Literary Studies he taught and conducted research for over twenty years. Over the past twenty-five years, Harel has pioneered an innovative field of research at the crossroads of literary and cultural studies. He was one of the first to examine the particularities of the experience of migration in urban areas in Quebec. His book *Voleur de parcours* (1989) is recognized as one of the most noteworthy publications in Quebec cultural studies of the 1980s and 1990s. The author or editor of over thirty publications, Harel is interested in intercultural issues, the role of the stranger in society, and vulnerability in the spaces in which we live.

BILL MARSHALL is professor of comparative literary and cultural studies at the University of Stirling, Scotland. He previously held posts at the Universities of Southampton and Glasgow, and served as the director of the Institute of Modern Languages Research in the School of Advanced Study, University of London. He is the author of *Victor Serge: The Uses of Dissent* (1992), *Guy Hocquenghem: Beyond Gay Identity* (1997), *Quebec National Cinema* (2001), *André Téchiné* (2007), and *The French Atlantic: Travels in Culture and History* (2009). He is also the editor of *Musicals – Hollywood and Beyond* (2000), *Montreal-Glasgow* (2005), and a three-volume encyclopedia on *France and the Americas* (2005). His current project is on the uses of prehistory in modern and contemporary French culture.

SARAH MEKDJIAN is a geographist/lecturer in geography at the University Grenoble Alpes and PACTE laboratory in Grenoble, France. Her research deals with critical geography, counter-cartography, and research-creation projects, dealing mainly with contemporary urban life, migrations, and the right of asylum. As a member of the European EUBorderscapes project and the antiAtlas of Borders collective, she has explored participatory mapping practices in collaboration with asylum seekers and artists. Along with papers published in French and international journals, Mekdjian is coauthor of *Crossing Maps/Cartographies Traverses*, an artistic and research device displayed in several cultural institutions, such as the Center d'Histoire de la Résistance et de la Déportation (February–May 2016, Lyon, France).

ALEXIS NUSELOVICI (pen name: Nouss) is professor of comparative literature at Aix-Marseille University after an academic career in Canada and the United Kingdom. He is a member of several research groups in Europe and North America and director of a research program hosted by the Collège d'études mondiales, Paris. He chairs Tranpositions, the comparative literature research group at his university. His publications include *La Modernité* (1995), *Dire l'événement, est-ce possible?* (with J. Derrida and G. Soussana, 2001), *Métissages: De Arcimboldo à Zombi* (with F. Laplantine, 2001), *Plaidoyer pour un monde métis* (2005), *Paul Celan: Les lieux d'un déplacement* (2010), and *La condition de l'exilé* (2015).

KATIA PIZZI is senior lecturer in Italian studies at the Institute of Modern Languages Research, University of London, where she directs the Centre for the Study of Cultural Memory. Pizzi obtained degrees at the Universities of Bologna, Kent, and Cambridge. She has published extensively on the literary culture, memory, and history of cities, including the volumes *The Literary Identities of European Cities* (2011), *Trieste: italianità, triestinità e male di frontiera* (2007), and *A City in Search of an Author: The Literary Identity of Trieste* (2001). Pizzi's current research interests include cities and the Cold War, future cities, and urban Modernism.

SHERRY SIMON is a professor in the French Department at Concordia University. She has published widely in the areas of literary, intercultural, and translation studies, most recently exploring the cultural history of linguistically divided cities. Her publications include *Translating Montreal. Episodes in the Life of a Divided City* (2006) and *Cities in Translation: Intersections of Language and Memory* (2012), both of which have appeared in French translation. She has edited or coedited numerous volumes, including *Translation Effects: The Shaping of Modern Canadian* Culture (with K. Mezei and L. von Flotow, 2014). She is a fellow of the Royal Society of Canada and a member of the Académie des lettres du Québec. She has received a Killam Research

Fellowship and the Prix André-Laurendeau from l'Association francophone pour le savoir.

WILL STRAW is professor in the Department of Art History and Communications Studies at McGill University. He is the author of *Cyanide and Sin: Visualizing Crime in 50s America*, and the coeditor of *Circulation and the City: Essays on Urban Culture* (2010), *The Cambridge Companion to Pop and Rock* (2001), and more than a dozen other volumes on popular media and culture. His articles have examined the history of disco music in Quebec, film extras, urban cultural scenes, and tabloid newspapers in the United States and Canada. His current research focuses on the culture of the urban night.

MYRIAM SUCHET is Maître de conférence en littératures francophones et françaises at Sorbonne Nouvelle – Paris 3, where she directs the Centre d'études québécoises. Graduate of the École Normale Supérieure de Lyon, agrégée de lettres modernes, she completed her doctorate in comparative literature and translation studies at Université Lille 3 and Concordia University. She was a recipient of the prize for the best thesis (France-Quebec) and the Governor General's Gold Medal. She is the author of *L'Imaginaire hétérolingue: Ce que nous apprennent les textes à la croisée des langues* (2014) and *Outils pour une traduction postcoloniale. Littératures hétérolingues* (2009). She is also the author of numerous articles, including a dossier with Samia Kassab in *Fabula*, "La langue française n'existe pas."

Index